Penguin Ed

Social M

Edited by A.

Penguin Modern Sociology Readings

General Editor
Tom Burns

Social Mobility

Selected Readings

Edited by A. P. M. Coxon
and C. L. Jones

Penguin Education

Penguin Education
A Division of Penguin Books Ltd,
Harmondsworth, Middlesex, England
Penguin Books Inc, 7110 Ambassador Road,
Baltimore, Md 21207, USA
Penguin Books Australia Ltd,
Ringwood, Victoria, Australia
Penguin Books Canada Ltd,
41 Steelcase Road West,
Markham, Ontario, Canada
Penguin Books (N.Z.) Ltd,
182-190 Wairau Road,
Auckland 10, New Zealand

First published 1975
This selection copyright © A. P. M. Coxon and C. L. Jones, 1975
Introduction and notes copyright © A. P. M. Coxon and C. L. Jones, 1975
Copyright acknowledgements for items in this volume
will be found on page 370
Made and printed in Great Britain by
Richard Clay (The Chaucer Press) Ltd,
Bungay, Suffolk
Set in Monotype Times

Contents

Acknowledgements

We should like to record our thanks to researchers associated with us on the Project on Occupational Cognition. Mrs Mary McPherson and Mrs Ruth Lockhart have given generously of their own time to help in the routine, but often taxing, aspects of the editorial task. Throughout the enterprise we have been very dependent upon the efficiency and deciphering skills of our typists, Mrs May Fraser and Mrs Margaret Cowell, who have dealt in their customary cheerful and courteous way with even greater pressure of work than they are used to. We are most grateful to them. John Bibby, of the Department of Statistics at St Andrews University, and Gary Littlejohn, of the Centre for Educational Sociology at Edinburgh, have brought several relevant papers to our attention, and we have been glad of their interest and advice.

Introduction

In every society, people and groups find themselves confined within orderings of status. The basic hurdles which so confine them consist in part of agreements about acceptable inequalities. They also result from the differential distribution of abilities, differential knowledge of or valuation of opportunity structures, and the unequal distribution of resources. Those persons and groups occupying high-status positions always have an interest in keeping up their status. They sometimes have an interest in maintaining and creating barriers to the upward movement of other groups, and some sociologists would argue that they act in defence of these interests. The study of social mobility involves consideration of the strategies which individuals and groups use, and are in turn used by. It involves the sociologist finding the ways in which different perceptions of opportunity structures arise, and the life-styles implied by particular mobility patterns; it involves consideration of the relationship between institutional, demographic and local economic factors.

For many years, sociologists have in fact restricted 'social mobility' to refer to intergenerational, vertical male occupational mobility in industrial societies. Moreover, the unit of movement has almost without exception been the individual, and in most studies the population of interest has been the nation state. The frequency table obtained by cross-tabulating father's reported occupational category with the son's current occupational category is then interpreted as a two-generational 'turnover' table. This provides the basic data for assessing differential rates of mobility, and for investigating patterns of over- and under-representation of combinations of occupational categories, upon the baseline of statistical independence between generations. The number and type of job-families or categories differs widely from study to study, and since the only well-nigh universally acknowledged distinction is between manual and non-manual jobs, this dichotomy has provided the main basis for international comparison. The intergenerational turnover table presents the number of sons in class x whose fathers were in class y, but since the basic information is usually obtained from a sample of sons, the actual stage of the career to which the data refer differs from person to person. However, if a man's occupational status changes significantly, and possibly irregularly, within his working life, then it is critical to know the precise stages of the son's and the father's career to which the data refer. For this, and other reasons outlined by Duncan in Reading 8, inferences about rates of intergenerational mobility can be very hazardous when based simply on such turnover tables.

The main problem is, however, that the turnover table conceals more of sociological import than it reveals. Most importantly it represents the end-state of an 'equifinal' process (von Bertalanffy, 1971), in the sense that quite different initial conditions and social processes can give rise to an identical final state (in this case, an identical turnover table). Because of this, it is quite impossible on the evidence of the turnover table alone to decide between quite different, and even incompatible, accounts of the social processes which gave rise to the data.

The driving force behind many mobility studies has been an interest in the degree to which modern stratification systems are 'open' in the sense of allowing a high incidence of social mobility. European and American social commentators have long been explicitly concerned with 'interchange between classes', and with the degree to which elite positions in society can attract talented personnel no matter what their social origin. Three grounds may be adduced for such concern: (a) the 'meritocratic' argument that some positions in society are functionally important and that it is in the common interest that they be filled by able people; (b) the 'egalitarian' argument that all should have equal access to the material benefits of life – or at least, that none should be handicapped by social background, or by such characteristics as sex or ethnicity; and (c) the 'historical' argument that economic and demographic factors will always force a rearrangement of families over the social structure in the long run, and that such rearrangement will occur either gradually through recruitment to desirable positions, or suddenly through revolution.

When egalitarian writers defend the existence of institutionalized inequality, they do so on functionalist grounds, one of whose arguments is that the attachment of unequal rewards to different positions is a precondition for the recruitment of appropriately talented individuals to those positions. For example, Glass (1954) indicates that a primary reason for wishing to see high mobility in a community is to increase economic and social efficiency. He argues that a 'fluid' social structure is one in which there is more likelihood that positions requiring high ability will be held by people who possess high ability, and also that such an 'open' society is in some way especially capable of adapting itself to changing circumstances. Glass and his colleagues were writing in the context of British reforms embodied in the 1944 Education Act, and, of course, an increase in access to education is a traditional prescription for removing irrational obstacles to social ascent and descent. An increased incidence of education in a society is supposed to increase its level of individual social mobility by detaching children from their parents, by increasing the level of literacy, and so speeding up the diffusion of innovations, by being associated with the provision of new types of occupation, and by encouraging the use of universalistic and rational standards in social and economic life.

Educational achievement is often impersonally certified, so that people can be selected for a broad range of occupations in terms of these qualifications rather than taking up the trade or profession of a relative. However, educational enrichment may have other effects upon a social system. Organizations which begin to recruit university graduates into administrative positions thereby cease to promote less well educated employees from lower positions within the organization. Hence educational enrichment may decrease the incidence of intragenerational mobility.

The phrase 'equality of opportunity' is often used with respect to the relationship between educational provision and social mobility, and one does well to distinguish the senses in which it is employed. One meaning is that all children should start with equal teaching in an educational and occupational marathon in which repeated testing and selection procedures eventually result in an entirely meritocratic distribution of people over occupations and other social positions. A virtue which was claimed for this, the British system after the Second World War, was that it would reduce the inheritance of privilege. In the terminology developed by Turner (1960) the mobility of academically able children was to be 'sponsored' by the school system. This ideal of equal educational opportunity differs from the one put forward by such writers as Bowles who have argued that educational provision should be made differentially, in such a way as to bring less privileged ethnic or social class groups to the same average level of performance as members of advantaged groups (see Reading 15).

If a son's status were genuinely independent of that of his father, a working-class son would not be handicapped by his parents' lack of material resources, and the status drop when a middle-class son was separated from his family of origin would be a sharp one, since he would not be able to make use of the network of relationships and resources set up by his parents and other kin. Both middle-class and working-class sons would be educated, selected and eventually employed by institutions operating according to rational and universalistic norms, and as a consequence of all these factors the association between the adult social position of the son and that of his father would be small. This brief description is a sociological gloss upon what has been meant by 'perfect mobility', perfect not in any normative sense, but in the sense that a son's status would be statistically independent of that of his father.

One of the hallmarks of post-war research was a strong emphasis upon the desirability of studying mobility by means of nationally representative samples. Even Rogoff's (1953) classic work on mobility trends in Marion County, Indiana, is often summarized with the *caveat* that 'of course' one could not validly generalize her conclusions to the whole of the United States. In many of these studies, the 'pure' case of statistical independence between generations was taken as a point from which to measure the degree to which a man's status in a particular society at a particular historical point of time depended upon that of his father. Attention was focused upon large questions such as whether or not the class structure in particular countries (especially the United States) was becoming more rigid. This is a complex question which has been examined from the historical perspective by Thernstrom (1964). Other problems which seemed to require intergenerational studies using national samples were whether or not societies differed in social mobility patterns according to their degree of industrialization, or according to their characteristic value systems (for example, their normative emphases upon ascription or achievement of status). Such studies provided an enormous amount of comparative information on the grosser forms of mobility in societies differing markedly in polity, in degree of industrialization and in cultural homogeneity. But despite the lively debates which were sustained by this paradigm, sociologists have come to view social mobility from a somewhat different perspective over the past decade.

Perhaps the most dramatic shift of attention has been from intergenerational to intragenerational mobility. The conventional study assumes that individual careers consist of essentially stable patterns of development (consistent increases or decreases in income, status, responsibilities, control of the work situation). Depending upon the degree of openness of the society, the father's social position can be considered to have a greater or a lesser effect upon the position eventually reached by his son. Svalastoga (1959) has given a diagrammatic illustration of such a life-cycle trend in social status, which appears on the opposite page.

At birth, the status of an average middle-class male becomes associated with that of his (possibly) upwardly mobile father, and remains thus associated until the son finishes schooling and enters some occupation. He then experiences a drop in status, as he begins to attain a separate social identity. If successful in life, he gradually increases his status until his retirement from active pursuits. The basic diagram can easily be altered to represent the average status changes to be expected for different social classes of persons in the same society, or for the 'average person' in different kinds of society. But even for the white middle-class man, there are changes of fortune in a career-line. For many working-class men, and almost all women, career lines are often highly erratic, punctuated by unemployment, major and rapid shifts in salary and levels of skill and responsibility required for the job. If, as seems likely, only a minority of the population are in careers characterized by regular and progressive betterment, then it becomes crucial to know something about the career pattern of both the father and son before an intergenerational comparison can be given any coherent meaning. Reflecting this change of interest, a good deal of attention has been concentrated on charting career patterns and upon obtaining systematic information upon occupational life-histories.

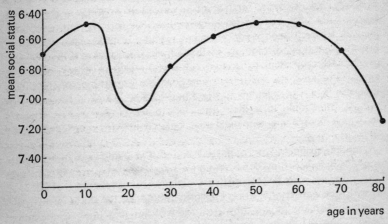

Figure 1 Average status change of a Dane from age 0 to age 80. Empirical data supplemented by extrapolation (Svalastoga, 1959, p. 308.)

The operations of the labour market, about which conventional sociological theories have had remarkably little to say, restrict very considerably the channels of occupational mobility. Some political economists have argued that the labour market operates in a differentiated way towards particular social groups, and that distinct sets of rules operate to separate the labour market into two forms. The 'primary' market offers jobs possessing 'high wages, good working conditions, employment stability and job security, equity and due process in the operation of work rules and chances for advancement' (Piore, 1971), whilst the 'secondary market' possesses precisely opposite characteristics. For our purposes it is important to note that race and sex predict very accurately a person's allocation to the particular labour market. If a person is black, or female, his or her career-structure and pattern of mobility is bound to be quite different from those located in the primary market. An alternative to the preoccupation with national sample studies would be for sociologists to concentrate upon the mechanisms and long-term processes of career mobility in particular regions and local labour markets within nation states. It is known that even within European countries there are areas with a preponderance of backward agriculture, areas of rapid industrialization, areas of declining industrial activity, areas of structural under-employment, areas with net population decline, and so forth. Few would deny that occupational mobility must have an economic base. However the tendency to aggregate these different labour markets into neatly packaged statistical nation states has continued unabated, except for a small number of studies carried out in various urban areas in the United States. This work has far-reaching implications for the future development of research and theory on social mobility. It undermines one of the basic assumptions of mobility table analysis which is that different parts of the table represent aspects of the social world in which essentially similar processes go on. It also questions the importance of the often-used distinction between manual and non-manual jobs, and demands that sociologists should turn their attention to the labour market contexts in which people are employed and become upwardly or downwardly mobile.

Another surprising omission from conventional studies of occupational mobility has been any consideration of the characteristic duality of men and jobs, which is essential for a sociological understanding of the process. In this conceptualization the basic notions are the chain formed by a given *individual's* moves through a sequence of jobs (and/or unemployment), and the chain formed by the moves of a *job-vacancy* within an organization. In the first case, the occupational life-history forms the primary source of data, whereas in the second it is the set of intra-organizational (or occupational) 'biographies'. The methodological problems involved in the representation, storage and analysis of such data are considerable (Sørensen, 1970), and – with the notable exception of the Znaniecki's use of life-history data in *The Polish Peasant* – totally infeasible before the advent of the computer. While the conventional turn-over analysis of mobility simply took two ends of each occupational life-history strand as a basis for analysis, interest now focuses on discerning patterns of similarity between entire occupational trajectories (Carr-Hill and Macdonald, 1973). Such data make it possible to examine the effect of sociological variables on different *patterns* of occupational development and upon the range and type of alternative choice-paths open at each change of job, rather than simply investigating the causes and conditions of 'upward' and 'downward' mobility. An additional bonus is that different patterns of job-stability, underemployment and racial and sexual inequalities, indicative of different segments of the labour market, each with their distinct rules and mechanisms, can be analysed in a fairly straightforward manner from occupational-history data, and this therefore allows other relevant propositions of dual labour market theory to be tested.

A further characteristic of recent approaches has been a considerably diminished reliance on the notion of prestige as a unidimensional quantitative yardstick providing the unit for measuring mobility. The concept has a certain utility as a means of modelling the causal patterning of status-related variables, but it does not deserve the central importance customarily given to it. Even if the metric of social mobility can be equated with aggregated judgements of general standing of occupations it has imposed severe limitations on the way in which social mobility is conceived. In particular, it has generally meant that the purposive facets of social mobility (the goals, aspirations, strategies, intentions of the actor) have been excluded, the interactive aspects of mobility (the network of social and associational interactions which the subjects are involved in) have been filtered out and, by requiring a highly consensual 'prestige' dimension, it excludes the question of whether the occupational structure is differentially perceived and evaluated.

What is particularly excluded from such an account is the network of relations which the individual has by virtue of his social identity, and which define the occupational position itself. Yet it is precisely these 'networks of contact' which the middle-class child uses as a resource in establishing his initial occupational status, and which go a long way to explaining high rates of occupational inheritance among professional groups. Moreover, the differences which undoubtedly exist in the facility with which people manipulate social networks are not only evident at the outset of a career. Network connections are also central in obtaining information about the labour market and job opportunities, and as Granovetter describes (Reading 20), they assume especial importance in almost all professional career moves. The move away from the idea that social mobility involves change within a consensually-defined occupational prestige-structure also means abandoning the idea that 'subjective status' and 'subjective mobility' are derivative distortions of some external social reality. Of course, occupations as job-descriptions have more or less 'objective' characteristics, and there is a sense in which the shift from job x to job y has meaning independent of a person's experience or interpretation of it. Nonetheless, a person's conception of the occupational structure is formed in a context of social interaction – as Elizabeth Bott (1971) has graphically described. This will necessarily be a restricted, partial view of the occupational structure, but it will be every bit as 'objective' as a prestige-scale. We may expect, however, that a person's occupational history, viewed as a series of exposures to relatively well-defined, sharp-focused parts of the occupational structure, is likely to be far more significant in explaining different images of society – among other things – than occupational groups membership *per se*.

The pressing need at present is not technical sophistication, but the construction of relatively simple operational theories and models of the *sociological* processes believed to underlie social mobility. Indeed, theories which can be implemented as simulation models – a specification of operational we take as minimal – scarcely exist. The tenor of these remarks suggests that a radically different approach to social mobility already exists. This is not the case. It is our opinion, however, that the outlines of such an approach can be discerned, and it is a major purpose of this collection of Readings to explore its main dimensions.

References

BERTALANFFY, L. VON (1971), *General System Theory, Foundations, Development, Applications*, Braziller.

BOTT, E. (1971), *Family and Social Network*, (2nd edn), Tavistock.

CARR-HILL, R. I., and MACDONALD, K. I. (1973), 'Problems in the analysis of life histories', *Sociol. Rev.*, Mg. 19, pp. 57–95.

GLASS, D. V. (ed.) (1954), *Social Mobility in Britain*, Routledge & Kegan Paul.

PIORE, M. J. (1971), 'The dual labor market: theory and implications', in D. M. Gordon (ed.), *Problems in Political Economy: An Urban Perspective*, D. C. Heath.

ROGOFF, N. (1953), *Recent Trends in Occupational Mobility*, Free Press.

SØRENSON, A. B. (1970), *The Occupational Mobility Process: An Analysis of Occupational Careers*, Report 125, Centre for Social Organization of Schools, Johns Hopkins University Press.

SVALASTOGA, K. (1959), *Prestige, Class and Mobility*, Heinemann.

THERNSTROM, S. (1964), *Poverty and Progress: Social Mobility in a Nineteenth Century City*, Harvard University Press.

TURNER, R. H. (1960), 'Sponsored and contest mobility and the school system', *Amer. Soc. Rev.*, vol. 25, no. 6, pp. 855–67.

Part One
Conceptual Orientation

From the student of Samuel Smiles, to the devotee of Burke's *Peerage*, everyone has their own idea about what it is for a person or a group to better themselves, to go down in the world – or simply to tread water. The sociologist claims that his approach to the study of social mobility provides a better-than-common-sense framework for understanding this aspect of society, and indeed for understanding the ideologies that different groups of people hold about it. The first major statement came with Sorokin's *Social and Cultural Mobility* (1959). In the early pages of this admirable piece of discursive scholarship, Sorokin introduced an influential metaphor for the study of stratification and mobility – a many-dimensional *social space*:

... the social space is a universe of many dimensions; and the more differentiated is the population, the more numerous are the dimensions. In order to locate an individual in the universe of the population of the United States, which is more differentiated than that of the natives of Australia, a more complex system of social coordinates must be used to indicate the more numerous groups with which one is connected. For the sake of a simplification of the task it is possible, however, to reduce the plurality of the dimensions into two principal classes, provided that each is to be subdivided into several subclasses. *These two principal classes may be styled the vertical and horizontal dimensions of the social universe* (p. 7).

Not many lines later, he proposed to restrict his analysis of social mobility to the shifting of the population along vertical dimensions of economic, political and occupational stratification, within social structures of different heights, profiles and degrees of differentiation. A further metaphor introduced by Sorokin likens the social stratification system to a social building or a social pyramid, so that the taller this building, the greater the degree of inequality. Clearly a theorist's conception of the nature and significance of mobility will be closely related to his definition of social stratification.

In order to give an adequate representation to the cumulative work carried out in the name of social mobility, we have confined our coverage almost entirely to work on the mobility of individuals, and individual men at that. However, as Miller points out in the first Reading, one might choose to focus one's attention on the mobility of *social strata* rather than on the mobility of individuals. The particular example that Miller gives – of a relative and absolute change in the position of the working class – is at present treated in sociology under the heading of the '*embourgoisement* debate', and we have not thought it useful to regard that topic as falling within our ambit. Nor have we thought it worthwhile to give space to accounts of the rise and fall in Sorokin's social space of whole professions and occupational specialities, of religious sects and other socially-organized belief systems, or of particular families and descent groups over a period of generations (but see Chapter 14 in Barber (1957) for a summary of historical analyses of family mobility).

For good or ill, the field of social mobility has come to be defined in terms of the movements of individuals along a single vertical dimension of overall social status, on which a man's status is almost always assessed in terms of the occupation he pursues. On this point, the first three Readings adopt very different points of view. The influential work of Blau and Duncan (of which more in later sections) depends upon the validity of Duncan's socioeconomic index of occupational status (often abbreviated as SEI), the rationale of which is described in the second Reading. Very briefly, the socioeconomic index for an occupation is a single score between 0 and 96, which may be described as a weighted average of (a) the proportion of men in the occupation with incomes above a certain figure, and (b) the proportion of men in the occupation with more than a certain amount of education, the relative weights being determined by (c) the proportion of people who said that the occupation had 'good' or 'excellent' general standing in the community, in a door-to-door survey carried out in the USA in 1947. The Blau and Duncan approach to the measurement of occupational status has considerable technical advantages when the sociologist comes to analyse data on individual mobility, but many of the points which Miller makes render it difficult to defend against determined criticism. Furthermore, it should constantly be borne in mind that the sociologist's tendency to scale occupational categories along an overall dimension of prestige or desirability so that the extent of 'up' or 'down' movement can be measured has profound theoretical implications. As Mayer has recently argued:

A generalized one-dimensional concept of social mobility presupposes either common value-orientations in the population to which it is to be applied or a stratification system which is organized according to one specific dimension of social inequality and has such a great impact that people have no other choice than to define their life goals and concerns in terms of this structure (1972, p. 92).

Even so, Duncan's 'continuous score' approach to measuring status was an advance on the previous sociological habit of regarding the transfer between manual and non-manual work as a crucially important index of mobility in different countries and at different periods. Miller mentions some pertinent objections to this use of the manual versus non-manual dichotomy, and others have been raised by the American social historian Stephan Thernstrom.

But in whatever way one cares to conceive the stratification system, it is a prerequisite to any sociological understanding of mobility that one should be able to move beyond naïve psychologism of the kind that gives epistemological priority to such individual factors as 'inept people being downwardly mobile', or 'people with achievement motivation getting on'. The thinking displayed by Kahl in the third Reading is a classic example. He used census material on the occupational distributions in 1920 and 1950 together with estimates of fertility differentials in the various occupational groups and some data on the relationship between father's occupation and son's occupation in a sample of sons taken in 1947, and from these he ingeniously derived estimates for the relative contributions of different components of mobility to total mobility. In a later Reading, Duncan describes Kahl's effort as an 'honorable failure', but the criticisms he brings to bear still leave this formulation as a milestone in our cumulative understanding of mobility.

References

BARBER, B. (1957), *Social Stratification: a Comparative Analysis of Structure and Process*, Harcourt, Brace & World.
MAYER, K. U. (1972), 'Dimensions of mobility space: some subjective aspects of career mobility', *Social Science Information*, vol. 11, part 5 (October), pp. 87–115.
SOROKIN, P. A. (1959), *Social and Cultural Mobility*, Collier-Macmillan; first published 1926.

1 S. M. Miller

The Concept and Measurement of Mobility

Excerpt from S. M. Miller, 'The concept and measurement of mobility', *Transactions of the Third World Congress of Sociology*, vol. 3, 1956, pp. 144–54, International Sociological Association, London.

Introduction

The recent rise in interest in mobility has not been characterized by much theoretical discussion of the concept.[1] As excellent a survey as that of Ely Chinoy (1955) has little reference to the concepts involved. If we go back to the pioneering work of Pitirim Sorokin (1928), we find almost no discussion of the concept of mobility except that it involves movement towards or away from elite positions.

Since research on mobility has expanded so rapidly, it may be well to reflect on its character, even though a full review may not be possible at this time. In the following remarks, the emphasis will be on the multi-dimensional character of mobility and on the multi-dimensional character of each of its indicators.

The mobility with which we are concerned is but one type of a wide range of behaviour. A more pronounced and widespread mobility is geographic, in which the individual may move from rural to urban or vice versa, from one part of a city to another, from one part of a country to another and from country to country. Such movement is not only sociologically important but has many implications for (social) mobility, especially when the movement is rural to urban.

In addition to geographic mobility, there are the various types of mobilities discussed in labour market analysis: movement from one job to another job in the same firm, movement to the same or a different position in another firm, movement to another industry or labour market in the same or different position. Many of these movements would constitute mobility in our sense, although most would not since the majority of occupational moves do not constitute a change in one's economic or social position.

1. The present paper has been influenced by the approach taken in the unpublished manuscript of Lipset and Zetterberg (1954). The document is, in many ways, the most advanced presentation of which the author is aware.

The concept

The clarification of a concept depends on more knowledge, but we can use as a working definition the following: the mobility with which we are concerned involves a *significant* movement in an individual's or stratum's economic, social and political position.

The concept which is best for us depends upon the problem with which we are concerned. Here, it would seem, is one of the sources of the difficulties with our concept of mobility; we have assumed that all who talk about mobility are concerned essentially with the same problems, while in actuality, there have been a variety of different concerns in studying the mobility trends. The following is an incomplete listing of the interests in mobility:

1 A concern with a description of a society – how much fluidity of movement does it have? Such information provides a basis for comparing one society with another or a society with itself at previous and later points in time.

2 A concern with the opportunities open to individuals to utilize their talents. In a sense, this is the problem listed in 1, but from the point of view of the individuals in the society.

3 An exclusive concern with movement into the elite positions in society. Other movement in society is ignored.

4 An exclusive concern with the movement of the working classes of the society. Movement of other groups is residual.

5 The effects of mobility upon class attitudes and class consciousness, particularly in the working class.

6 The effects of personal attitudes and attributes on an individual's or group's possibilities of moving, or the effects of the educational system upon an individual's or group's possibilities of moving.

7 The effects of mobility upon the mobile individual.

Despite the diversity of interests, mobility has been studied in a limited and traditional way. Namely, that mobility involves a major change up or down in an individual's occupational position. Chief issues involved are (a) how well does occupational mobility reflect all aspects of mobility and (b) what characterizes a positive or a negative change in occupational position? A number of other issues are also important, and we shall deal with them in a fairly systematic review of the steps involved in measurement of mobility. At each step, some issues are raised.

The measurement of whose mobility?

Mobility is measured as that of a family or that of an individual. The former is *intergenerational* mobility, where an individual's position is compared with that of his father and possibly that of his grandfather (Glass, 1954). One issue involved is at which points to compare the older and younger generations. Rogoff (1953) compares them at the same age: while this procedure has merit, in many cases it may be desirable to compare generations at equivalent points in career, which may not be the same as age equivalence because of changes in educational requirements.

In *intragenerational* mobility, an individual is compared with himself at another point of his career (Jaffe and Carleton, 1954). Has he moved into a higher, or lower position or has he not materially changed his position? Which points should be compared: the first job or the first *regular* job after completing education with the end of the career or the height of the career?

Frequently neglected is the *stability* of the occupational change. If workers can start an independent business but have little chance of surviving in it and therefore drop back into the working class, no effective mobility is involved. Therefore, the stability of an occupational advance must be studied.[2]

The individual career history is to be used discriminately, since individual mobility does not, of course, connote family mobility. If an individual has risen, we do not know anything about the movement of his children. Yet many of the problems of stratification, and therefore of mobility, revolve about the family as a transmitter of status.[3] If we want to turn to an analysis of mobility *trends* in society, intragenerational studies are to be interpreted carefully.

A neglected element in measurements of mobility is the possibility of *stratum mobility*, that while an individual may not be mobile, his stratum might be (Miller, 1955). Thus, some have begun to argue that the position of working-class people is improving in the United States, in both absolute and relative terms. Without leaving his stratum, the working-class son of a working-class father may show great movement, relative to his father and relative to other classes, in obtaining material goods and comfort (see Potter, 1953). While the author sees difficulties in this thesis, it is one which will, undoubtedly, be offered increasingly and will lead to more study of some of the frequently neglected *objective* characteristics of occupational position.

---

2. The issue of the stability of mobility has applicability beyond the sphere of intragenerational mobility.
3. Davis (1953) has again reminded us of this sociological orientation.

Attributes of mobility

Mobility can be measured in terms of frequency, stability and height. Some aspects of frequency are discussed below; stability has been briefly discussed above; height remains to be analysed.

Height refers to the degree of change involved in a mobility move, as compared to frequency which lumps all movements defined as mobility into one category for the purpose of calculating rates. Generally, we are interested in the size of the mobility change: has a mobile person changed his position to a small or to a great degree? While gross rates of mobility for a society as a whole or for particular segments are important, it would be well to compute rates for selected movements, e.g. from lower class into upper class. In this way, we can obtain height–frequency rates which are extremely useful.

Types of measurement and tertiary employment

Mobility data are of two kinds: data about individuals, or data about a population or aggregates (Chinoy, 1955, p. 181). The first type refers to data describing an individual's movement relative to himself or to his father, while the second type refers, for example, to occupational distributions and demographic shifts of groupings treated as a whole.

From data about aggregates, one cannot make statements about conditions of individuals (Robinson, 1950). This condition is particularly so where the categories of the aggregate data are of a crude quality. Frequently in national studies of mobility, the Colin Clark typology of primary, secondary and tertiary employment is used (Clark, 1951). If a larger percentage of individuals are now in tertiary employment than before, mobility is believed to have increased. This conclusion is based on the premise that a tertiary position is an improvement economically and socially. Yet if the category of tertiary employment is studied, it is seen to include a wide range of jobs – from a sales clerk in a department store to a fireman on a railroad train – some of which might well be improvements in occupational status but some of which probably are not.[4]

Another difficulty is that tertiary employment is the characteristic employment of women in highly industrialized societies. Yet, most of our interest in mobility is with the male, as the main transmitter of position.

4. Recently, a number of studies has appeared which are critical of the primary-secondary-tertiary categories. Most of the points raised in these criticisms apply to cross-national use of the categories; in the present paper the criticisms are made specific to the use of categories within an economy rather than among economies. The section below on 'The measurement of occupational change' introduces additional questions about the Clark approach. The critical elements have been raised in Bauer and Yamey (1951), and have been extended by Minkes (1955), Rottenberg (1953) and Gordon (1954, p. 30).

Therefore, it might be well to use occupational distribution data which referred only to males.

Ignored as well is the nature of changes within each category. For example, in the United States, relative and absolute employment in agriculture is declining, as correctly shown by the Clark system. What it does not reveal is that within the agricultural category, there may be downward mobility as a result of 'a steady decline in the possibility of moving up the so-called agricultural ladder, whose steps went from hired hand to tenant to farm owner . . .' (Chinoy, 1955, p. 184). In the Clarkian analysis, a smaller percentage in agriculture connotes mobility, but of the smaller percentage in agriculture, many may be downwardly mobile. Many who moved out of agriculture into other fields are not assured of an improvement in their economic or social circumstances, particularly if they had been farm operators.

The Clarkian approach is useful for it gives us easily accessible data (at least with a national census system) for the entire population. But it is doubtful if we can use his categories; a more microscopic examination of each occupation, viewed over time, is necessary before we lump occupations together into broad exclusive categories, indicative of a definite upward or downward mobility trend.

What is being measured?

Mobility is generally regarded not only in economic terms but in social and political as well. Studies of mobility, however, tend to concentrate on movements in occupational positions. *This emphasis neglects other dimensions of mobility: movements in economic and/or political power; movements in social position in the community*. While occupational change correlates to an extent with changes in income, social position and political power, it is not a reliable indicator of such change.[5]

A great need in mobility research is, then, to study the *variety* of dimensions rather than to restrict it to the occupational dimension (see Lipset and Zetterberg, 1954).[6] In many ways the most interesting aspects of mobility are the connections among the various systems of the community: does, for example, an improvement in occupational position inevitably lead to a change in one's relations to others in the community? Many of the dynamic aspects of the effects of mobility upon behaviour depend upon the character of such interrelationships. The frequent observation

5. Some of the difficulties involved in using occupations are discussed in the following section.
6. The typically ignored dimensions of mobility that are listed above or by Lipset and Zetterberg are incomplete and will probably vary depending on the orientation of the research problem and the resources of the researcher.

that a group whose condition is improving rapidly is the one most pressing for deep social change may be due, in part, to the unevenness of its progress.

The measurement of occupational change[7]

The difficulties in employing occupational change as an indicator of mobility illustrate the kinds of issues which are involved in using any indicator of mobility. The fact that occupational mobility predominates in sociological research on mobility is another reason for more closely examining it.

At first blush, change in occupational position seems to be a statement about objective aspects of class position.[8] Yet higher or lower are defined in terms of the prestige ratings of the occupations. Sometimes the prestige ratings are based on a particular study of a sample's ratings of occupations, as, for example, in the well-known and widely-used United States study by Hatt and North for The National Opinion Research Centre (reprinted in Bendix and Lipset, 1953, pp. 411–26). At other times it may be what is commonly regarded to be the usual way that individuals in a particular society have of rating occupations. Whatever basis is used to obtain a prestige rating, it may be that the rating is not an adequate reflector, at a particular moment of time, of changes in the objective circumstances of a job, e.g., income, skill, power over others, stability of income. We are expecting subjective statements about occupations to be accurate statements about the non-subjective dimensions of jobs – their pay, their skill requirements, etc.

How well do the community's prestige ratings reflect the objective differences among occupations? We can see the problem more clearly if we examine the crucial white-collar fields. Movement into white-collar work from factory work has been commonly regarded as mobility. In the United States, at least, the economic differentiation between factory and white-collar workers has lessened. In 1890, white-collar workers received twice as much pay as factory workers; today factory workers receive a little more pay than do white-collar workers – a radical swing (Burns, 1954). Once white-collar workers had special days off as well as paid vacations while factory workers had neither. In many cases today factory workers, through their union contracts, are better off than non-union white-collar workers. On point after point, the advantages which once marked off white-collar from factory work are diminished or overturned. Most

7. A fuller analysis of the source of the problems discussed in this section will be found in Miller (1955).
8. For the terminology 'objective' and 'subjective' see the concise review by Mayer (1953).

striking perhaps is the realization that, in not a few ways, the factory worker with a strong union and a shop steward system has more independence from the employer than the white-collar worker.

Even in the area of skill, it is not clear that the white-collar job is more demanding than the factory job. With increasing mechanization and routinization (and the pressure of automation), the office employee in the United States frequently is a machine tender like the factory worker.

In the area of income, skill and discretion, the favoured position of the white-collar worker has been reduced. Objectively, many white-collar jobs are no longer of a much higher level than factory work in terms of the attributes which distinguish jobs – mainly income and skill. Yet many investigators, despite their troubled feelings about the present day status of white-collar work (Lipset and Bendix, 1952, p. 495), use movement of factory workers or their offspring into white-collar work as an automatic marker of mobility. Largely, this procedure is followed because it is felt that white-collar work still is accorded higher *prestige* (subjective evaluation) than is factory work. There is some evidence that this higher prestige for white-collar work no longer exists (Kahl, 1953, p. 191). If the Hatt–North study were redone today, it is quite likely that the demarcations in prestige between white-collar and factory positions might be narrowed.

The use of prestige scales must be more carefully examined, for it is unclear what they show. When a person is asked to rate occupations, does he indicate how he personally rates them or how he thinks they are generally rated? Is he reporting his view of what the community thinks rather than his own personal perspective?[9] Also, are there significant differences among members of various classes and occupations in rating occupations?

Prestige rating of occupations is more complex than usually regarded and cannot be easily substituted for the study of the objective dimensions of occupations – skill, income, discretion, etc. Frequently, even what are regarded as objective differences among types of manual work, as defined by the US Census and other agencies, have to be considered with care. Is a skilled worker of today on the same level of skill as his father of 1900? Do we not now have a looser definition of 'skilled worker'? Today, the category of semi-skilled worker includes all belt-line operators, some of whom may be trained for the job in thirty minutes. Are they at the same level of skill as a semi-skilled worker of earlier periods? For the purpose of the census, perhaps yes; for the purpose of the study of mobility, they

9. Notice the wording of the Hatt–North question: '. . . please pick out the statement that best gives your own personal opinion of the general standing that such a job has . . .'.

may not be; the census classification may not have the same orientation as the mobility study.

These questions do not lead to the destructive conclusion that nothing can be done, but to a requirement that great care be taken (a) in separating objective and subjective elements and using each where they are proper, and (b) in reviewing traditional classifications and categories to see if they are appropriate for the mobility research problem.

Other indicators of mobility have to be viewed in the same careful lights, if we are to develop a full scale analysis of mobility trends in which one can have confidence. Mobility cannot be viewed in a unidimensional way, nor can its indicators be treated as having but one dimension.

Models for research

Data on mobility as such do not lend themselves to statements that 'mobility is high or low . . .'. To make such statements requires criteria to which one can relate mobility data. The construction of such criteria involves conceptual and mathematical operations.

The Goldhamer–Rogoff approach (Rogoff, 1953) looks at mobility in terms of the opportunities for it offered by the occupational structure. The raw rate of mobility is adjusted for the rate of mobility attributable to changes in the occupational structure. The residual is the mobility which is not due to the exigencies of occupational change and is thus a better indicator, it is believed, of the fluidity of a society. It might be asked whether raw rates of mobility might also be adjusted for differential class rates of fertility at particular times; the mobility of the lower classes may be due to a situation where the upper groups are not reproducing themselves. Adjusting for both occupational distribution changes and for fertility may be a better statement of fluidity in the Goldhamer–Rogoff approach.

Alternative to this approach has been the more commonly thought of question: how much mobility would one expect of a class group if its sons had access to positions equal to that of the sons of upper groups in societies (Glass, 1954, pp. 194 ff.)? Some important comments have been made in regard to the most effective ways of organizing and analysing data derived from this approach.[10]

Some kind of model is important. The best way of developing such a model depends upon the purposes of the model. For certain kinds of cross-national comparison, the Goldhamer–Rogoff approach is preferable. For a concern with problems of class identification, it would not seem to be as

10. See the articles and remarks by S. J. Prais, A. Gabor, W. Z. Billewicz, J. Durbin and W. Scott, *Population Studies*, vol. 9, 1955.

useful. Here again, we should be careful not to employ conceptual organizations for one type of problem in analysing problems of quite a different character.

Limitations on mobility analysis

Fields of research that have grown rapidly may easily become a fad, in that studies are made without regard to their usefulness or appropriateness for a given purpose but because the investigator is uncritically following a trend. Mobility research, because of its great potential contribution, might prove to have such a diverting lure. It is important, therefore, to recognize some of its limitations.

Much of the interest in mobility centres about the subjective aspects of stratification. Implicitly, many researchers are inquiring: in this particular society is mobility at a level which will retard or speed-up class consciousness and social change? Since mobility research has been primarily 'objective' in the sense that it is descriptive of the circumstances and conditions of individuals' lives, it can say little about the subjective, attitudinal response to these circumstances and conditions. We have to be very wary in moving from the data about objective conditions to statements about attitudes. Lipset and Zetterberg (1954) are on the right track, I believe, when they cite the need for not only collecting data on rates of mobility but for also studying some of the subjective reactions to situations.

If I am correct in interpreting much of the interest in mobility research as springing from an interest in trends in class consciousness, then a number of other warnings must be offered. Rates of mobility are but one pressure in the pushes and pulls which affect class consciousness. To centre only on this pressure may be misleading, for under particular circumstances other pressures may be more important. In many ways as important, if not frequently a more important element in affecting class consciousness, is the general level of economic conditions and the particular conditions of life of certain sections of the population. If, for example, working-class or peasant groups live at a chronically poor level, their class consciousness may be growing whatever mobility trends may be. Similarly, if economic conditions improve, rapid changes in class consciousness in *either* direction may take place.

These examples point to another difficulty with mobility analysis. It is essentially a long-view approach which is certainly crucial to the understanding of the dynamics of subjective class awareness. But it is only one of the long-term historical forces and experiences that is important. Nor should the short-term, more immediate forces – of war, depression, oppression – be ignored, in studying class consciousness.

Even if mobility were the major determinant of class consciousness, it would be difficult to appraise its effects. For example, if a society were divided 50 per cent into lower-class groups and 50 per cent into upper-class groups and if there were high mobility in that every individual has an equal chance of being in either class section, then 50 per cent of the sons of lower-class fathers would move into upper-class positions and 50 per cent would remain in the lower class. The upper class would have a similar breakdown, and the lower class would, therefore, be made up of 50 per cent of sons of lower-class fathers and 50 per cent of sons of upper-class fathers. In this highly mobile situation would there be any chance of class consciousness in the lower strata? The answer is likely to be yes, because 50 per cent of the lower-class groups would have a lower-class family background (assumed to be conducive to class consciousness), and 50 per cent of the lower-class group would have fallen in the class structure (also assumed to be conducive to revolutionary class activity). Thus, with high rates of mobility, class consciousness would not necessarily decline. (And what would happen if the lower class suffered economic calamities?)

Mobility is to be considered consequently, as only one of the elements in stratification, both in terms of the objective aspects of class position and in terms of the subjective attitudinal reactions to class position. [. . .]

References

BAUER, P. T., and YAMEY, B. S. (1951), 'Economic progress and occupational distribution', *Econ. J.*, vol. 61, pp. 741–55.

BENDIX, R., and LIPSET. S. M. (1953), *Class, Status and Power*, Free Press.

BURNS, R. K. (1954), 'The comparative economic position of manual and white-collar employees', *J. Bus.*, vol. 27, pp. 257–67.

CHINOY, E. (1955), 'Social mobility trends in the United States', *Amer. sociol. Rev.*, vol. 20, pp. 180–86.

CLARK, C. (1951), *The Conditions of Economic Progress*, Macmillan.

DAVIS, K. (1953), 'Reply', *Amer. sociol. Rev.*, vol. 18, pp. 378–94.

GLASS, D. V. (ed.) (1954), *Social Mobility in Britain*, Routledge & Kegan Paul.

GORDON, M. S. (1954), *Employment Expansion and Population Growth: The Californian Experience, 1900–1950*, University of California Press.

JAFFE, A. J., and CARLETON, R. O. (1954), *Occupational Mobility in the United States 1930–1960*, King's Crown Press.

KAHL, J. A. (1953), 'Educational and occupational aspirations of "common man" boys', *Harvard educ. Rev.*, vol. 23, p. 191.

LIPSET, S. M., and BENDIX, R. (1952) ,'Social mobility and occupational career patterns', *Amer. J. Sociol.*, vol. 57, pp. 366–74 and 494–504.

LIPSET, S. M., and ZETTERBERG, H. L. (1954), 'A proposal for comparative study of social mobility, its causes and consequences', unpublished, Bureau of Applied Social Research, Columbia University.

MAYER, K. (1953), 'The theory of social classes', *Harvard educ. Rev.*, vol. 23, pp. 149–67.

MILLER, S. M. (1955), 'The concept of mobility', *Social Problems*, vol. 3, pp. 65–73.

MINKES, A. L. (1955), 'Statistical evidence and the concept of tertiary industry', *Econ. Devel. cult. Change*, vol. 3, pp. 366–73.

POTTER, D. (1953), *People of Plenty*, University of Chicago Press.
ROBINSON, W. (1950), 'Ecological correlations and the behavior of individuals', *Amer. sociol. Rev.*, vol. 15, pp. 351–7.
ROGOFF, N. (1953), *Recent Trends in Occupational Mobility*, Free Press.
ROTTENBERG, S. (1953), 'Note on economic progress and occupational distributions', *Rev. Econ. Stat.*, vol. 35, pp. 168–70.
SOROKIN, P. (1928), *Social Mobility*, Harper & Row.

2 P. M. Blau and O. D. Duncan

Measuring the Status of Occupations

Excerpt from P. M. Blau and O. D. Duncan, *The American Occupational Structure*, Wiley, 1967, pp. 117–28.

Measuring the status of occupations

In this research we have followed a well-established sociological tradition: the concern with the 'vertical' aspect of occupational mobility. This preoccupation is so commonplace one sometimes forgets that it involves a rather drastic abstraction. Although the matter has not been adequately studied, there surely are characteristics of occupations affecting the interchange between them quite apart from their relative position in a hierarchy of prestige or socioeconomic status. The OCG[1] tables show, for example, that a man whose first job is laborer in a manufacturing industry is more likely to move to a craft occupation in manufacturing than to an operative job in a non-manufacturing industry, though the former move involves a greater 'social distance' on a prestige or status scale. The occupation structure intersects with other structures, such as industry, and is differentiated by a variety of factors, such as region, locality and ethnic group. Hence there are 'channels' of mobility – or factors governing access to occupational roles – that complicate the patterns of movement as compared to what can be expected on the simple metaphor of a social elevator going up or down.

If the focus on vertical mobility, therefore, involves a simplification of the actual process by which individuals find their way into occupational roles, it is nonetheless a justifiable simplification. To study one aspect of a complex phenomenon is not to deny that other aspects exist. The sociologist has an ulterior aim in directing his attention to the status hierarchy of occupations. He assumes not only that performance of an occupational role confers occupational status, but also that the latter interacts with other status attributes that in their overall configuration amount to a system of social stratification. A rather special saliency, moreover, is assumed to characterize occupational status, by comparison with other status attributes. [. . .]

In certain earlier studies of occupational mobility the research workers

1. OCG is an abbreviation for the Blau and Duncan project on Occupational Changes in a Generation [Eds.].

faced the preliminary task of establishing an occupational scale before they could undertake the main task of measuring movement along that scale (Glass, 1954; Svalastoga, 1959). We were in a more fortunate position in the OCG study, since some substantial work on occupational status had been completed before we commenced the survey.

Two approaches have dominated the investigations of occupational hierarchy carried out by students of social stratification. One is the effort to develop a socioeconomic classification scheme for occupations. Perhaps the most influential work here was that of the census statistician Alba M. Edwards (1943). His 'social-economic grouping' of occupations has been widely used in studies of occupational stratification and mobility. With certain modifications it led to the 'major occupation groups' used by the Bureau of the Census since 1940. These groups (or condensations or expansions of them) appear in various sections of the present study. To suggest that his grouping supplied a 'scale', Edwards contented himself with showing differences in average or typical levels of education and income of the workers included in the several categories: 'Education is a very large factor in the social status of workers, and wage or salary income is a very large factor in their economic status' (Edwards, 1943, p. 180).

A more recent development is the derivation of scores for *detailed* census occupation titles representing a composite index of education and income levels of workers in each such occupation. Priority for this specific technique probably belongs to social scientists in Canada (Charles, 1948; Blishen, 1958), with a similar approach being taken in this country by both a private research worker (Bogue, 1963, chap. 14 and Appendix 13) and, lately, in official publications of the US Bureau of the Census (1963, 1964).

The second approach to occupational stratification is to secure, from samples more or less representative of the general public, ratings of the 'general standing' or 'prestige' of selected occupations. Such ratings have been shown to be remarkably close to invariant with respect to (a) the composition and size of the sample of raters; (b) the specific instructions or form of the rating scale; (c) the interpretation given by respondents to the notion of 'general standing'; and (d) the passage of time (Reiss *et al.*, 1961; Hodge, Siegel and Rossi, 1964). The high order of reliability and stability evidenced by prestige ratings would commend their use in problems requiring social-distance scaling of the occupations pursued by a general sample of the working force, but for one fact: ratings have hitherto been available only for relatively small numbers of occupation titles. Many research workers have resorted to ingenious schemes for splicing *ad hoc* judgements into the series of rated occupations, but no general solution to the problem has been widely accepted.

Work currently in progress at the National Opinion Research Center promises to overcome this difficulty by supplying prestige ratings for a comprehensive list of occupations. In the absence of such ratings at the time of the OCG survey we fell back on the idea of a socioeconomic index of occupational status. The particular index we used, however, was one designed to give near-optimal reproduction of a set of prestige ratings. A full account of the construction of this index is given elsewhere (Duncan, 1961), and only a few general points need to be made before presenting some illustrations of the scale values assigned to occupations.

In the derivation of the socioeconomic index of occupational status, prestige ratings obtained from a sizable sample of the US population in 1947 were taken as the criterion. These were available for forty-five occupations whose titles closely matched those in the census detailed list. Data in the 1950 Census of Population were converted to two summary measures: the percentage of male workers with four years of high school or a higher level of educational attainment, and the percentage with incomes of $3500 or more in 1949 (both variables being age-standardized). The multiple regression of the percentage of 'excellent' or 'good' prestige ratings on the education and income measures was calculated. The multiple correlation, with the forty-five occupations as units of observation, came out as 0·91, implying that five-sixths of the variation in aggregate prestige ratings was taken into account by the combination of the two socioeconomic variables. Using the regression weights obtained in this calculation, all census occupations were assigned scores on the basis of their education and income distributions. Such scores may be interpreted either as estimates of (unknown) prestige ratings or simply as values on a scale of occupational socioeconomic status ('occupational status' for short). The scale is represented by two-digit numbers ranging from 0 to 96. It closely resembles the scales of Blishen, Bogue and the US Bureau of the Census mentioned earlier, although there are various differences in detail among the four sets of scores.

One of the most serious issues in using any index of occupational status in the study of mobility has to do with the problem of temporal stability. For the oldest cohorts in the OCG study, we were asking about a father's occupation and a first job that may have been pursued as long ago as before the First World War. We know that the occupational structure – in the sense of the relative numbers working in the several occupations – has undergone pronounced change since that time. Many new occupations have risen to prominence, whereas old ones have diminished to virtual insignificance. Granted that the OCG respondents could be accurately graded by occupational status as of 1962 and the preceding few years, can we assume that the status scale is valid for much more remote periods?

Fortunately, we now have a detailed study of temporal stability in occupational prestige ratings. The results are astonishing to most sociologists who have given the matter only casual thought. A set of ratings obtained as long ago as 1925 is correlated to the extent of 0·93 with the latest set available, obtained in 1963. The analysts conclude, 'There have been no substantial changes in occupational prestige in the United States since 1925' (Hodge, Siegel and Rossi, 1964, p. 296). Less complete evidence is available for the socioeconomic components of our index, but information available in the Censuses of 1940, 1950 and 1960 points to a comparably high order of temporal stability (Reiss et al., 1961, p. 152),[2] despite major changes in the value of the dollar and the generally rising levels of educational attainment.

Like previous investigators (Glass, 1954, p. 178), we have assumed, *faute de mieux*, that the scale of occupational status remained fixed over the half-century spanned by our current and retrospective data. Unlike such investigators, we have been able to point to some bodies of evidence supporting the approximate validity of this assumption. As compared with the unreliability in the basic reports on occupation itself, the error induced by historical variation in relative status of the occupations is likely to be minor.

Two-digit status scores are available for 446 detailed occupation titles. Of these, 270 are specific occupation categories; the remainder are subgroupings, based on industry or class of worker, of thirteen general occupation categories. The reader may consult the source publication for the scores of particular occupations of interest (Duncan, 1961, Table B-1, pp. 263–75). Here we shall only illustrate the variation of the scores by citing illustrative occupations, not always those of the greatest numerical importance (see Table 1). In most of the OCG tabulations scores were grouped into five-point intervals, and the interval midpoints were used in computing summary statistics.

Table 1 makes it clear that occupations of very different character may have similar status scores. In particular, there is considerable overlap of scores of occupations in distinct major occupation groups. Indeed, only five points separate the lowest occupation in the 'professional, technical and kindred workers' group from the highest among 'laborers, except farm and mine'. Nevertheless, the major occupation group classification accounts for three-fourths of the variation in scores among detailed occupations. The status scores offer a useful refinement of the coarser classification but not a radically different pattern of grading.

Table 1 probably does not illustrate adequately the variation by industry subclass of such occupation categories as 'operatives, not elsewhere

2. Work in progress by Hodge and Treiman further supports this point.

Table 1 Occupations illustrating various scores on the index of occupational status[a]

Score interval	Title of occupation (*frequency per 10 000 males in 1960 experienced civilian labor force in parentheses*)
90–96	architects (7); dentists (18); chemical engineers (9); lawyers and judges (45); physicians and surgeons (47)
85–89	aeronautical engineers (11); industrial engineers (21); salaried managers, banking and finance (30); self-employed proprietors, banking and finance (5)
80–84	college presidents, professors and instructors (31); editors and reporters (14); electrical engineers (40); pharmacists (19); officials, federal public administration and postal service (13); salaried managers, business services (11)
75–79	accountants and auditors (87); chemists (17); veterinarians (3); salaried managers, manufacturing (133); self-employed proprietors, insurance and real estate (9)
70–74	designers (12); teachers (105); store buyers and department heads (40); credit men (8); salaried managers, wholesale trade (41); self-employed proprietors, motor vehicles and accessories retailing (12); stock and bond salesmen (6)
65–69	artists and art teachers (15); draftsmen (45); salaried managers, motor vehicles and accessories retailing (18); self-employed proprietors, apparel and accessories retail stores (8); agents, n.e.c. (29); advertising agents and salesmen (7); salesmen, manufacturing (93); foremen, transportation equipment manufacturing (18)
60–64	librarians (3); sports instructors and officials (12); postmasters (5); salaried managers, construction (31); self-employed proprietors, manufacturing (35); stenographers, typists, and secretaries (18); ticket, station and express agents (12); real estate agents and brokers (33); salesmen, wholesale trade (106); foremen, machinery manufacturing (28); photo-engravers and lithographers (5)
55–59	funeral directors and embalmers (8); railroad conductors (10); self-employed proprietors, wholesale trade (28); electrotypers and stereotypers (2); foremen, communications, utilities and sanitary services (12); locomotive engineers (13)
50–54	clergymen (43); musicians and music teachers (19); officials and administrators, local public administration (15); salaried managers, food and dairy products stores (21); self-employed proprietors, construction (50); book-keepers (33); mail carriers (43); foremen, metal industries (28); toolmakers, and die-makers and setters (41)

[a] n.e.c. means 'not elsewhere classified'

Table 1 – *continued*

45–49	surveyors (10); salaried managers, automobile repair services and garages (4); office machine operators (18); linemen and servicemen, telephone, telegraph and power (60); locomotive firemen (9); airplane mechanics and repairmen (26); stationary engineers (60)
40–44	self-employed proprietors, transportation (8); self-employed proprietors, personal services (19); cashiers (23); clerical and kindred workers, n.e.c. (269); electricians (77); construction foremen (22); motion picture projectionists (4); photographic process workers (5); railroad switchmen (13); policemen and detectives, government (51)
35–39	salaried and self-employed managers and proprietors, eating and drinking places (43); salesmen and sales clerks, retail trade (274); bookbinders (3); radio and television repairmen (23); firemen, fire protection (30); policemen and detectives, private (3)
30–34	building managers and superintendents (7); self-employed proprietors, gasoline service stations (32); boilermakers (6); machinists (111); millwrights (15); plumbers and pipe fitters (72); structural metal workers (14); tinsmiths, coppersmiths and sheet metal workers (31); deliverymen and routemen (93); operatives, printing, publishing and allied industries (13); sheriffs and bailiffs (5)
25–29	messengers and office boys (11); newsboys (41); brickmasons, stonemasons and tile setters (45); mechanics and repairmen, n.e.c. (266); plasterers (12); operatives, drugs and medicine manufacturing (2); ushers, recreation and amusement (2); laborers, petroleum refining (3)
20–24	telegraph messengers (1); shipping and receiving clerks (59); bakers (21); cabinetmakers (15); excavating, grading and road machine operators (49); railroad and car shop mechanics and repairmen (9); tailors (7); upholsterers (12); bus drivers (36); filers, grinders and polishers, metal (33); welders and flame-cutters (81)
15–19	blacksmiths (5); carpenters (202); automobile mechanics and repairmen (153); painters (118); attendants, auto service and parking (81); laundry and dry cleaning operatives (25); truck and tractor drivers (362); stationary firemen (20); operatives, metal industries (103); operatives, wholesale and retail trade (35); barbers (38); bartenders (36); cooks, except private household (47)
10–14	farmers (owners and tenants) (521); shoemakers and repairers, except factory (8); dyers (4); taxicab drivers and chauffeurs (36); attendants, hospital and other institutions (24); elevator operators (11); fishermen and oystermen (9); gardeners, except farm, and groundskeepers (46); longshoremen and stevedores (13); laborers, machinery manufacturing (10)

continued overleaf

Table 1 – *continued*

5–9	hucksters and peddlers (5); sawyers (20); weavers, textile (8); operatives, footwear, except rubber, manufacturing (16); janitors and sextons (118); farm laborers, wage workers (241); laborers, blast furnaces, steel works and rolling mills (26); construction laborers (163)
0–4	coal mine operatives and laborers (31); operatives, yarn, thread and fabric mills (30); porters (33); laborers, saw mills, planing mills and millwork (21)

Sources: Reiss *et al.* (1961), Table B-1; US Bureau of the Census (1962), Table 201

classified' and 'laborers, not elsewhere classified'. Such variation is fairly substantial. It must be understood, however, that particularly at these levels of the census classification scheme the occupation–industry categories represent groups of jobs with quite heterogeneous specifications, although the groups are thought to be somewhat homogeneous as to the degree of skill and experience required for their performance. No one has yet faced the question of what a study of occupational mobility would look like if all the 20 000 or more detailed titles in the *Dictionary of Occupational Titles* were coded without prior grouping.

The use of occupational status scores carries a theoretical implication. We are assuming, in effect, that the occupation structure is more or less continuously graded in regard to status rather than being a set of discrete status classes. The justification of such an assumption is not difficult. One needs only to look at any tabulation of social and economic characteristics of persons engaged in each specific occupation (whatever the level of refinement in the system of occupational nomenclature). We discover that the occupations overlap – to a greater or lesser degree, to be sure – in their distributions of income, educational attainment, consumer expenditures, measured intelligence, political orientations and residential locations (to mention but a few items). [. . .]

If we choose to think of occupational status as exhibiting continuous variation, the appropriate analytical model is one that treats status as a quantitative variable. This point of view has far-reaching implications for the conceptualization of the process of mobility as well as for the analysis and manipulation of data purporting to describe the process. The repertory of statistical techniques on which we shall draw in this study, therefore, differs somewhat from the set that is conventional in mobility studies, although the techniques are quite standard in other contexts.

When deciding to work with the status index in the OCG study we were aware of one apparent source of spurious results, pointed out (in private communications) by friendly critics of an earlier regression analysis of social mobility (Duncan and Hodge, 1963). This has to do with the fact that educational attainment is a component of the index used to measure occupational achievement, whereas education appears as an independent variable in the regression equation used to predict occupational achievement. Is not a high correlation between occupation and education built into the status index, and is not the regression analysis producing findings based on circular reasoning? The criticism is germane, and the critics' point must somehow be met.

We recall that the status index is based on the empirical regression formula

$$\hat{X}_1 = 0.59\, X_2 + 0.55\, X_3 - 6.0,$$

where X_1 is the percentage of 'excellent' or 'good' ratings received by an occupation in the prestige survey, X_2 the proportion of men in the occupation with 1949 incomes of \$3500 or more, and X_3 the proportion of men in the occupation with four years of high school or higher education attainment. The coefficient of determination for the forty-five occupations is $R^2_{1(23)} = 0.83$. Using these weights for X_2 and X_3 it was possible to assign a status score (or estimated prestige score) to each occupation for which census data were available.

In the regression analysis of factors affecting individual occupational achievement, each occupation (respondent's and father's) was first coded in terms of the census detailed code, and then recoded to the two-digit status score. Thenceforth the score was treated as a number measuring the individual's occupational socioeconomic status. Note that the occupational status scores were *derived* from *aggregate* data on all males in each occupation category, but *applied* as scores characterizing *individuals*.

The first response to the critics, then, might be that the status score, interpreted as an estimate of occupational prestige, should legitimately reflect the fact that one determinant of an occupation's prestige is, in fact, the educational level of its incumbents. But because not all persons in an occupation have the same educational attainment, the formula for the status score does not by any means produce a perfect correlation between the estimated prestige of the *individual's* occupation and his educational attainment. On the other hand, in the light of our rather full knowledge of occupational prestige (Reiss *et al.*, 1961; Hodge, Siegel and Rossi, 1964, p. 296), no acceptable estimate of occupational prestige could fail to show *some* appreciable correlation between an individual's education and the prestige of the occupation in which he is engaged. It could be argued, in other words, that the apparent circularity of the procedure that was followed is simply a realistic reflection of the fact that high-prestige occupations do recruit men with superior education whereas low-prestige occupations recruit men with inferior schooling, by and large.

Another approach was taken, however, to ascertain what difference it would make in the results of a mobility study if an alternative index of occupational status were used – one not explicitly including an educational component. Instead of educational level the alternative index uses a dummy variable, Z, that refers to whether an occupation is white-collar ($Z = 1$) or manual ($Z = 0$). Prestige rating (X_1) was estimated from two variables: income level of the occupation as defined above (X_2); and the nonmanual–manual dichotomy (Z), for the same criterion group of forty-five occupations. The following empirical formula was obtained:

$$\hat{X}_1 = 0{\cdot}79\, X_2 + 19{\cdot}8\, Z + 3{\cdot}9 \qquad (R^2_{1(2Z)} = 0{\cdot}76).$$

Note that the formula attributes a 'bonus' of about twenty points for being in the white-collar group. In effect, we have two distinct formulas:

$$\hat{X}_1 = 0{\cdot}79\, X_2 + 23{\cdot}7 \quad \text{for white-collar occupations,}$$

$$\hat{X}_1 = 0{\cdot}79\, X_2 + 3{\cdot}9 \quad \text{for manual occupations.}$$

For any close student of occupational characteristics it will be no surprise to learn that the correlation between the original and the alternative formula, over the forty-five occupations, is as high as 0·96. Yet the alternative formula does not include education as a predictor. Hence if occupational status were scored according to the alternative formula and the scores were employed in a regression analysis of occupational mobility no possible suspicion of circularity could be attached to a correlation between the occupational statuses of individuals and their educational attainment.

How much difference would it have made in the findings, had the alternative procedure been employed? To answer this question a portion of the data used by Duncan and Hodge (1963) were recoded, using the alternative scoring of occupational status.

The original results, in slightly altered form, are shown alongside the revised results in Table 2. (The letter symbols here have different meanings from the preceding discussion of index construction.) The reader should evaluate the comparison for himself. It appears that no important substantive conclusions in the original report would require change if the alternative results were accepted. In the revised results the estimated direct effect of father's occupation (X) on respondent's occupation in 1950 (Y_2) falls below twice its standard error, whereas the original results clearly warranted rejection of the null hypothesis of no net effect for X. The revised results therefore support, even more strongly than the initial ones, the original conclusion that the major influence of father's occupa-

Table 2 Regression analysis: respondent's occupation on education and father's occupation, with occupational status scored by alternative formulas, for 381 white males with nonfarm background, thirty-five to forty-four years old, in the Chicago Labor Mobility Sample, 1951

Published results[a]				Revised results			

Correlation matrix

	U	Y_1	Y_2	U	Y_1	Y_2
X	0·4285	0·3470	0·3145	0·4200	0·2972	0·2835
U	—	0·4270	0·5335	—	0·3749	0·5155
Y_1	—	—	0·5517	—	—	0·5113

Regression coefficients in standard form[b]

Dep. Var.	Coefficient of				Coefficient of			
	X	U	Y_1	R^2	X	U	Y_1	R^2
Y_2	0·105	0·488	—	0·29	0·082	0·481	—	0·27
Y_1	0·201	0·341	—	0·22	0·170	0·304	—	0·16
Y_2	0·027	0·355	0·391	0·41	0·019	0·370	0·367	0·38

Path decomposition[c] of effect of X

	Total	Direct	Indirect	Total	Direct	Indirect
for Y_2	0·314	0·105	0·209	0·284	0·082	0·202
for Y_1	0·347	0·201	0·146	0·297	0·170	0·127

[a] Duncan and Hodge (1963)

[b] Standard error for each coefficient is approximately 0·05

[c] Slight variation from published figures is due to omission of squared term for education

Variables are defined as follows:
Y_2: Respondent's occupational status, 1950
Y_1: Respondent's occupational status, 1940
U: Respondent's educational attainment
X: Father's occupational status

tion on respondent's occupation is exerted indirectly, via its influence on respondent's education. Indeed, the revised results imply that its only significant influence is the indirect one via education. The revision certainly does not point to a lesser role of education in the process of occupational mobility than had been estimated previously. In view of the general similarity of the two sets of results we proceed on the assumption that a comparable alteration of the occupational status index used in the OCG analysis would also leave the main results intact. [. . .]

References

BLISHEN, B. R. (1958), 'The construction and use of an occupational class scale', *Canad. J. Econ. polit. Sci.*, vol. 24, pp. 519–31.

BOGUE, D. J. (1963), *Skid Row in American Cities*, Community and Family Study Center, University of Chicago Press.

CHARLES, E. (1948), *The Changing Size of the Family in Canada*, Census Monograph no. 1, Eighth Census of Canada, 1941, King's Printer and Controller of Stationery, Ottawa.

DUNCAN, O. D. (1961), 'A socioeconomic index for all occupations', in A. J. Reiss Jr *et. al.*, *Occupations and Social Status*, Free Press.

DUNCAN, O. D., and HODGE, R. W. (1963), 'Education and occupational mobility', *Amer. J. Sociol.*, vol. 68, pp. 629–44.

EDWARDS, A. M. (1943), *Comparative Occupational Statistics for the United States, 1870 to 1940*, Government Printing Office, Washington.

GLASS, D. V. (ed.) (1954), *Social Mobility in Britain*, Free Press.

HODGE, R. W., SIEGEL, P. M., and ROSSI, P. H. (1964), 'Occupational prestige in the United States, 1925–63', *Amer. J. Sociol.*, vol. 70, pp. 286–302.

REISS, A. J., Jr, *et al.* (1961), *Occupations and Social Status*, Free Press.

SVALASTOGA, K. (1959), *Prestige, Class and Mobility*, Gyldendal, Copenhagen.

US BUREAU OF THE CENSUS (1962), *1960 Census of Population, Final Report*, PC(1)-1D, Government Printing Office, Washington.

US BUREAU OF THE CENSUS (1963), *Methodology and Scores of Socioeconomic Status*, Working Paper no. 15, Government Printing Office, Washington.

US BUREAU OF THE CENSUS (1964), 'Socioeconomic characteristics of the population: 1960', *Current Population Reports*, Series P-23, no. 12, 31 July, Government Printing Office, Washington.

3 J. A. Kahl

Some Components of Occupational Mobility[1]

Excerpts from J. A. Kahl, *The American Class Structure*, Holt, Rinehart & Winston, 1957, pp. 252–68.

Problems of measurement

Ideally, to measure the amount of succession from one generation to the next, the research man should use a composite index of several stratification variables to indicate the class positions of a representative sample of American men and of their fathers, and compute the correlation between the two distributions.[2] If every son had the same position as his father, the correlation would be perfect and would be so indicated by a coefficient of unity. If a son's position were not related to that of his father, the coefficient would be zero. The actual coefficient would of course lie somewhere between zero and unity.

There are many difficulties that prevent the calculation of a correlation coefficient to measure the amount of succession that occurs. Correlation demands a numerical scale with many intermediate scores. The closest approximation to such a scale would be provided by a composite index of class position similar to the index of status characteristics of Warner. But the relative values of the items in such an index do not remain stable from one generation to the next. For example, a high-school education would be worth much more in 1920 than in 1950, but we do not know how much more because nobody studied Jonesville in 1920. Furthermore, it would be impossible to get adequate information about the older generation on many useful items that might be included in the index; for instance, how can one find out how a man's father identified himself or who his friends were? In most cases, the father of the respondent will be dead or living in another town and the son will be unable to answer detailed questions about him.

The most practical procedure is to use a single measurement (rather than a complex index), and one that is simple and can be supplied by the son concerning both himself and his father. Furthermore, it should have

1. Kahl's discussion is framed in terms of mobility in the United States in the present century [Eds.].
2. We simplify by dealing only with men. Married women have the same class positions as their husbands. Unmarried women will here be ignored.

relatively stable meaning from one generation to the next (and preferably, one country to another). Almost all researchers have used occupation, and they have grouped occupations into broad categories such as those of the social–economic levels of the US Bureau of the Census. [. . .]

These broad categories tend to balance many of the fine-grain changes in prestige and income that have occurred for some occupations in recent decades, and thus can be used for intergenerational comparisons. However, it should never be forgotten that the classification is a crude one and involves many shades of meaning. For instance, in the category of proprietors, managers and officials, the scheme puts all sorts of men together ranging from the president of the General Motors Corporation to the man who runs a peanut stand. The occupational classification treats these two gentlemen as equals, which they may be before God and the law, but not in the stratification system.[3]

The census figures themselves give some information regarding mobility even though they give none about the relative positions of specific fathers and specific sons. For instance, the data indicate that there were more than twice as many professional men in 1950 as in 1920. Insofar as professional men did not average two sons each, it is clear that many sons of men from lower levels had the opportunity to climb into the professional ranks. And by using a sample questionnaire for sons concerning themselves and their fathers, and combining that information with data from the census, it is possible to approximate the correlation model by constructing a table showing the proportion of men at each level who have been mobile.

If one starts with the conception of a completely closed society and then seeks to learn what factors might open it to some mobility, one discovers four causes of movement:

1 Individual mobility. Some people slip down and make room for others to move up.

2 Immigration mobility. Immigrants will cause mobility if they do not enter the system at all levels in proportion to the men already there. In the decades close to the turn of the last century millions of immigrants came to the United States and most of them went to work as semiskilled or unskilled workers in the new factories in Northern cities. Because they took these low-level jobs, they made it possible for the sons of many American fathers to climb into the white-collar ranks.

3 Reproductive mobility. The men at the upper levels of the system tend to have smaller families than those at the lower levels, thus making room at the top.

3. It should be noted that the size of the categories influences calculations of mobility. The smaller the size and the larger the number of categories, the more the mobility.

4 Technological mobility. Technological change is constantly altering the shape of the occupational distribution by creating new jobs at the upper levels. As the industrial system becomes more complex, a higher proportion of men work as technicians and administrators and a lower proportion as unskilled laborers. This upgrading of the work force creates mobility as many sons of unskilled laborers become technicians and administrators.[4]

A man who has advanced in the world as compared to his father has no idea which of the four factors made it possible for him to get ahead, and he probably would not care if he were told. But a student who looks at the system as a whole, to measure the amount of mobility and ask about trends through time, must examine each of the four factors separately. It is important to find out whether our society has been getting more or less rigid, and to predict the probable situation in the next generation. The only way we can study trends is to isolate each of the causes of mobility and then examine the historical forces impinging upon it. Let us consider the factors in reverse order from their listing above.

Technological mobility

[. . .] From 1870 to 1950 the US labor force expanded from almost thirteen million to over sixty-two million. The proportion of women increased from 15 to 30 per cent. And the distribution of jobs changed radically. Farm jobs declined from over one-half to less than one-eighth of the total, whereas urban professional, business and clerical jobs increased from one-eighth to almost one-half, and urban semiskilled jobs doubled from one-tenth to one-fifth of the available positions. During these eight decades, the life span of many a man, the country changed from a rural to a highly industrialized nation.

It has often been said that in the nineteenth century the great undeveloped farmlands of the West kept American society open, for if a man did not like his job he could pack up and move to the frontier. The farm frontier no longer exists, but instead there is a technological frontier that continually opens up new types of positions at higher levels of skill.

Let us attempt to measure the number of new openings that have been created by technical change in the space of but one generation, from 1920 to 1950. It will simplify matters to consider only men, and to take a snapshot of the situation in 1920 and compare it to that of 1950 rather than measure the process that went on all the time. By this procedure it is assumed that all the men in the labor force in 1920 have been replaced by their sons by 1950. If succession were complete and mobility did not

4. The absolute size of our society has been increasing rapidly. Immigration, differential reproduction, and technological change have distributed this increase to sons disproportionately to *their* fathers.

exist, then all sons would have jobs at the same level as those of their fathers. We shall measure the degree to which succession is not complete, or the degree of mobility, by measuring the proportion of sons who have jobs different from their fathers *solely as a result of technological redistribution of the labor force.*

Table 1 Male occupational distributions, actual and expected, 1920 and 1950

First estimate: occupational change only			
Social–economic group	*1* *Actual* *1920*	*2* *Expected* *1950*	*3* *Actual* *1950*	*4* *Mobility*
professional persons	1 062 000	1 349 000	3 025 000	+1 676 000
proprietors, managers and officials:				
farmers	6 122 000	7 775 000	4 205 000	−3 570 000
others	2 635 000	3 347 000	4 391 000	+1 044 000
clerks, salespeople and kindred	3 491 000	4 434 000	5 345 000	+ 911 000
skilled workers and foremen	5 469 000	6 946 000	7 917 000	+ 971 000
semiskilled workers	4 371 000	5 551 000	9 153 000	+3 602 000
unskilled workers:				
farm laborers	3 162 000	4 016 000	2 048 000	−1 968 000
others	6 494 000	8 248 000	5 582 000	−2 666 000
total	32 806 000	41 666 000	41 666 000	±8 204 000

Sources: for 1920, Edwards (1943, p. 187). For 1950, US Bureau of the Census (1953, Part I, US Summary, Table 53).
I have eliminated 899 000 men who did not report their occupations, and have divided the 'Service workers, except private household' by placing one-fourth in the semiskilled category and three-fourths in the unskilled category

The basic figures are shown in Table 1. The first column of the table gives the approximate distribution of the male labor force in 1920 as revealed by the census of that year. By 1950 the number of men had increased from 32 806 000 to 41 666 000, a growth of 27·01 per cent. If every category had increased at the same rate, it would have been possible for every son to have the same type of job as his father. But this was not the case. For instance, the professionals almost tripled, whereas the farmers declined by about one-third. The distribution that would have occurred if every category increased by 27·01 per cent is shown in column 2, 'Expected 1950'. The actual distribution revealed by the census of 1950 is shown in column 3, 'Actual 1950'. The difference between column 3 and column 2 is the amount of mobility that occurred, as shown in column 4, 'Mobility'. This last column indicates that 1 676 000 men had to enter professional ranks even if the sons of all professionals followed in their fathers' offices. Similarly, there had to be a million new urban proprietors and managers, almost a million new clerks and salespeople, almost a million new skilled workers and foremen, and over three million new semiskilled workers. Where did they come from? Obviously, they were sons of farmers who moved to the city, and sons of unskilled workers who climbed up the hierarchy. The total of all the new workers was 8 204 000, which represented 19·7 per cent of the labor force in 1950. Thus at least 19·7 per cent of the men working in that year had changed jobs relative to their fathers as a result of technological change.

The above estimate is a minimum one, for it assumes that the sons of men whose occupations were contracting moved directly into the expanding levels. Actually, there was much more movement, for a good proportion of the change was step-by-step. For instance, it was not too likely that a farmer's son became a professional person; rather, a skilled worker's son may have taken the professional position, the son of a semiskilled worker thus had the chance to take over the skilled job, and a farm boy moved to the city and entered the factory at the semiskilled level. Thus, one new job at the top may have meant three mobile sons. But we cannot measure step-by-step mobility from census tables; we have to get the actual father–son comparisons from a sample of currently working men. That will be done below.

There can be little argument that the 4 634 000 urban and rural men who climbed above the unskilled level had achieved an advance in the class system. Most of them moved into the semiskilled ranks, taking over the new jobs there as well as the slots vacated by hundreds of thousands of sons of semiskilled workers who donned white collars. However, the 3 570 000 sons of farm owners may not all have advanced over their fathers by their move to the city. Many entered business and the professions and did improve their stratification position. But many became semiskilled and skilled workers; they lost the independence of the farm but usually gained in income. If we assume that all proprietors are above all workers, they slipped down; if we compare their standards of living with those of their parents, they climbed up. Here is one of the cases that is more complicated than the simple occupational hierarchy can measure.

Reproductive mobility

The discussion so far has been based on two unstated assumptions, namely, that all levels reproduced themselves at equal rates, and that there was no immigration. Let us drop the first assumption while keeping the second.

There are no adequate figures on the average number of sons of men in the various occupational levels. However, it is possible to make an estimate by using a set of net reproduction rates calculated for the year 1928 and assuming that these rates held throughout the thirty-year period from 1920 to 1950.[5] In fact, the rates were changing in those years, so the estimate is a crude one and is offered as an indication of the general effects of differential reproduction rather than as a precise measurement of those effects.

Table 2 Male occupational distributions, actual and expected, 1920 and 1950

Second estimate: occupational change and differential reproduction					
Social–economic group	1 Actual 1920	2 Repro- duction rate	3 Expected 1950	4 Actual 1950	5 Mobility
professional persons	1 062 000	0·87	924 000	3 025 000	+ 2 101 000
proprietors, managers and officials:					
farmers	6 122 000	1·52	9 306 000	4 205 000	− 5 101 000
others	2 635 000	0·98	2 582 000	4 391 000	+ 1 809 000
clerks, salespeople and kindred	3 491 000	0·98	3 421 000	5 345 000	+ 1 924 000
skilled workers and foremen	5 469 000	1·22	6 672 000	7 917 000	+ 1 245 000
semiskilled workers	4 371 000	1·18	5 158 000	9 153 000	+ 3 995 000
unskilled workers:					
farm laborers	3 162 000	1·52	4 806 000	2 048 000	− 2 758 000
others	6 494 000	1·35	8 767 000	5 582 000	− 3 185 000
total	32 806 000	1·27	41 636 000	41 666 000	+11 074 000

Sources: Table 1 plus Lorimer and Osborn (1934, p. 74)

Column 2 of Table 2 shows the estimated reproduction rates for each occupational category. Although the average number of sons for all men was 1·27, the average for professional men was only 0·87 whereas the average for farmers was 1·52. Obviously, many sons of farmers had the opportunity to become professionals because of differential reproduction.

Table 2 adds the force of reproductive mobility to that of technological

5. The net reproduction rates are from Lorimer and Osborn (1934, p. 74) – all rates were increased 15 per cent in order to make the total expected equal to the total labor force in 1950. For a similar type of reasoning, but based on weaker evidence, see McGuire (1950).

mobility as shown in Table 1. The expected number of sons in 1950 in each category (column 3) is found by applying the estimated reproduction rates (column 2) to the number of fathers at each level as shown by the census of 1920 (column 1). These expectations are compared to the realities of the 1950 census (column 4) and the differences indicate the mobility that occurred (column 5).

This new calculation, which includes both technological and reproductive mobility, indicates that 11 074 000 men were mobile in the last generation, or 26·5 per cent of the labor force in 1950. Subtracting from the total the mobility caused by technological change, we arrive at the mobility caused by differential reproduction: 2 870 000 men, or 6·8 per cent of the current labor force.

Once again, this estimate is a minimum one, for it does not include step-by-step movement.

Immigration mobility

From 1920 to 1950 about two million men came to the United States and remained here (immigrant aliens minus emigrant aliens). Published figures on their occupations are not fully adequate for our purposes, but once again a rough estimate can be made. Assuming that the occupational distribution for men is the same as that for men and women combined, and assuming that these men took jobs in the United States at the same level as the occupations they declared as their usual ones, then the immigrants entered the occupational hierarchy as follows:

	%
professional persons	7·6
proprietors, managers, officials, clerks and salesmen	7·1
skilled and semiskilled workers	30·3
unskilled workers	37·6
farmers and farm laborers	12·4
miscellaneous	4·8
total	99·8

Sources: *Statistical Abstract of the United States* (1940, Table 101; 1955, Table 109). The many men who did not report occupations are omitted from the percentage distribution

Comparing these percentages to those for all men in 1950 as shown below in Table 6, we see that immigrants entered professional ranks in the same proportion as did the native-born; thus the immigrants did not affect mobility at that level. Roughly speaking, the same is true for farmers and skilled and semiskilled workers. However, the immigrants were notably under-represented in the ranks of businessmen and clerks and over-represented in the ranks of unskilled workers. There were 23·9 per cent of all men in business and clerical positions in 1950; if immigrants had entered proportionately, 478 000 would have been businessmen and clerks instead of 142 000. This deficit of 336 000 was filled by native-born men. A similar calculation shows that about 464 000 more immigrants than would be expected according to proportionate entry took unskilled positions. Consequently, about 1 per cent of the native-born men were upgraded by immigration. (This procedure, of course, ignores the question of the mobility of the immigrants with respect to their fathers.)

In other words, in the generation preceding 1950 the effect of immigration on the mobility of the native-born was almost nil. But in earlier generations the effect was much greater for two reasons: the number of immigrants was much larger, and their skills were less developed. For instance, Elbridge Sibley computed the number of native-born men crossing from the blue-collar to the white-collar ranks in the generation preceding 1930. He estimated that on the average 415 000 men were upgraded each year: 150 000 from technological change, 160 000 from differential reproduction and 105 000 from immigration (Sibley, 1942). His figures are not directly comparable to those computed here, but the relative proportions from the different causes of mobility give some indication of the decreasing importance of immigration (as well as differential reproduction) in more recent years.

Total and individual mobility

There is another way to study the rates of mobility besides analysing occupational data from the census, namely, a direct questioning of adult men regarding their occupations as compared to those of their fathers. This procedure measures total mobility from all causes. There have been several studies of this type, but only two of these used a sample representative of the entire country, and we shall examine one of them.[6]

In 1947 the National Opinion Research Center (NORC) did a national study of occupations. Included in their questionnaire was an item about

6. The other national sample is Centers (1948). There is a large sample from six cities using the current 'major occupation' classification of the census reported in Miller (1955, pp. 31–2). These two studies show substantially the same pattern as the NORC research (see note to Table 3). For local studies in California, see Davidson and Anderson (1937) and Bendix, Lipset and Malm (1954). For Minneapolis, see Hochbaum *et al.* (1955). For Indianapolis, see Rogoff (1953). Studies of this type are somewhat limited by the fact that men shift occupations during their careers. See Lipset and Bendix (1952); see also Form and Miller (1949).

Table 3 Occupations of sons and their fathers (NORC sample of 1334 men in 1947)

Occupations of sons	N	Percentage of their fathers who were:								Total
		Profes-sionals	Prop-rietors	Clerks	Skilled	Semi-skilled	Farm	Un-skilled	Don't know	
professional persons	164	23	24	10	13	5	17	7	1	100
proprietors, managers and officials, nonfarm	219	4	31	9	18	8	25	5	—	100
clerks, salespeople and kindred	294	9	23	15	21	10	16	6	—	100
skilled workers and foremen	175	3	7	4	30	14	29	12	1	100
semiskilled workers	224	2	11	6	19	19	32	10	1	100
farmers and farm laborers	189	2	2	2	3	4	84	3	—	100
unskilled workers, nonfarm	69	3	12	—	9	17	32	20	7	100

Source: NORC (1953, pp. 424–5)

I have omitted sons who were service workers, and reclassified the relatively few fathers who were service workers into the category of unskilled workers the occupation of the respondent's father. The father–son comparisons for 1334 men are shown in Table 3. Unfortunately, a sample of this size is not large enough for the number of breakdowns in the table, but, as always, we must use whatever data we have, with the usual reservations as to their adequacy.

Table 4 Total mobility, 1920 to 1950 (calculated from Tables 1 and 3)

Social–economic group	1 Actual 1950	2 NORC per cent mobile[a]	3 Number mobile
professional persons	3 025 000	77	2 329 000
proprietors, managers and officials, nonfarm	4 391 000	69	3 030 000
clerks, salespeople and kindred	5 345 000	85	4 543 000
skilled workers and foremen	7 917 000	70	5 542 000
semiskilled workers	9 153 000	81	7 414 000
farmer and farm laborers	6 253 000	16	1 000 000
unskilled workers, nonfarm	5 582 000	73	4 075 000
total	41 666 000		27 933 000

[a] Those who answered 'don't know' are here classed as unskilled

Let us apply the NORC percentages to the census data of 1950. Table 4 shows the percentage of men who told the NORC they were *not* in the same occupation as their fathers (column 2). This percentage is applied to the number of men in each category in 1950 (column 1) to provide the number of men who were mobile (column 3).

The resulting figures indicate that 27 933 000 men were mobile relative to their fathers, or 67 per cent of the labor force in 1950. This calculation includes individual mobility, technological mobility, reproductive mobility and step-by-step mobility, and we can call it *total mobility*. (The figure does not include the effects of immigration on the native-born, for both immigrants and their fathers are represented in the totals; however, it was shown above that immigration mobility was not significant in the last generation.) Subtraction of technological and reproductive mobility from the total indicates that 16 859 000 men, or 40·5 per cent of the labor force, were mobile because of individual mobility plus the step-by-step movements which multiply the effects of the other causes of mobility.

It is now possible to summarize the calculations to this point. Analysis of the available data (inadequate though they are) suggests that about

67 per cent of the men in the labor force in 1950 were mobile with respect to their fathers. This total can be broken into component factors as follows:

	% of labor force
technological mobility	19·7
reproductive mobility	6·8
individual and step-by-step mobility	40·5
total mobility	67·0

Unfortunately, this method of analysis does not permit a separate computation of the step-by-step movements. However, study of the NORC data in Table 3 indicates that mobility tends to be from adjacent groups. For instance, the professional men who were mobile came predominantly from the adjacent group of proprietors, and clerks and salesmen who were mobile came from the adjacent groups of proprietors and skilled workers more often than from levels further distant in the hierarchy. This suggests that step-by-step movements were very important, that the expansion of such levels as the professional one opened positions that were usually filled by men from intermediate levels, who in turn were replaced by men moving from farm to city or climbing out of the unskilled level. It seems fair to hazard a guess: at least half of the 40·5 per cent of individual and step-by-step mobility was a result of the step-by-step movements. If so, then individual mobility was about as important as technological mobility, and reproductive mobility was about one-third as important as either of them.[7]

Upward and downward mobility

Let us take a more detailed look at the NORC data to discern the relative rates of upward and downward movement. Assuming that each step in Table 3 represents a step in a hierarchy, and ignoring the number of steps moved by a man, the percentage of sons at each level who have moved either up or down can be calculated. The results are shown in Table 5.

These figures contain a simple pattern: between one-half and three-quarters of the men who are now professionals, proprietors, managers, clerks and skilled workers have climbed above their fathers. Compared to those who have climbed, relatively few have fallen. Four per cent of proprietors and managers, 14 per cent of skilled workers, and 32 per cent of clerks and salesmen have fallen. (Actually, the figure for clerks and

7. Note that an opening created by technological change or differential reproduction results in one mobile son (assuming no multiplication through step-by-step movements), but an opening created by individual mobility results in two mobile sons – the one who slipped down, and the one who climbed up.

salesmen exaggerates the amount of downward movement, for most of their fathers were petty proprietors, and the sons often have as much income and prestige as their fathers.)

Table 5 Upward and downward mobility (calculated from Table 3)[a]

Social–economic group, 1950	Percentage who have:[b]			
	Moved up	Moved down	Remained	Total
professional persons	77	—	23	100
proprietors, managers and officials, nonfarm	65	4	31	100
clerks, salespeople and kindred	53	32	15	100
skilled workers and foremen	56	14	30	100
semiskilled workers	43	38	19	100
farmers and farm laborers	3	13	84	100
unskilled workers, nonfarm	—	73	27	100

[a] Note that it is possible to calculate percentages in the opposite direction with meaning: for example, one could compute the percentage of sons of clerical fathers who subsequently moved up or down. Computation can be made from fathers to sons, or from sons to fathers. There is a difficulty, however, when using fathers as the base for percentages: the sample is based on sons and is therefore more representative of the generation of sons than of the generation of fathers
[b] Those who answered 'don't know' are here classed as unskilled

The semiskilled group is a catchall, with movement into it almost equally from above and below. The unskilled group is recruited primarily from farm owners and laborers, and secondarily from unskilled and semiskilled workers – this represents as much succession as downward mobility. *Thus, the upper levels have had many new recruits from below; the semiskilled level has had recruits from above and below; the bottom level has recruited from itself.*

It is possible to generalize even further: sons of upper-level fathers tend to remain there, but technological change and differential reproduction have made room for so many new men at upper levels that more than half of the current members are newcomers. At the same time the unskilled level has acquired most of its members from the bottom of the hierarchy. (It should be remembered that because the upper levels are smaller than the lower ones, a large proportion of newcomers at the top means that only a small proportion of men from the bottom have moved out.)

A man subjectively evaluates the fluidity of the system by comparing his own career to that of his immediate colleagues and his father. Consequently, we should expect that at the upper levels there would be a feeling of openness, for so many have climbed. At the bottom we should expect more of a sense of a closed system, for so many have remained. And the men at the semiskilled level should be confused, for there has been much movement in both directions.

International comparisons

How does mobility in the United States compare with that in other countries? Unfortunately, studies abroad have not used exactly the same occupational groupings, and so comparisons have to be gross and tentative. But there have been a number of studies in recent years, and they have recently been analysed by Lipset and Rogoff:

To sum up, our evidence suggests that in the United States, France and Germany, somewhere between a fifth and a quarter of those with fathers in white-collar occupations become manual workers, whereas about one-third of those whose fathers are manual workers rise to a non-manual position, and that this has been the state of affairs since before the First World War (1954, p. 565).

It seems, then, that the often-stated theory that American society is more open than others is not fully supported by the evidence. At least for urban workers, other industrialized countries appear to show about as much movement across the line from manual to nonmanual positions as does the United States. However, in the last generation there has been more rapid urbanization in the United States than in France and Germany; thus we do have more men who have changed from manual work on the farm to nonmanual work in the city.

Trends through time

Having analysed mobility into its component factors, it is now possible to look at them one at a time to see whether rates of mobility are changing, whether American society is getting more or less open.

1 Technological mobility. Let us look at the male occupational distributions as given in the censuses from 1910 to 1950. The information is in Table 6. It shows that the proportionate increase in professionals was most marked in the decades 1920–1930 and 1940–1950. The same was true for urban proprietors, managers and officials. Thus, the two top categories in the occupational hierarchy expanded most during boom periods in the business cycle.

The increase in clerks and salesmen was greatest in the twenties, slowed down in the thirties, and reversed itself in the forties.

There is no clear overall trend underlying changes in these white-collar positions. The professional group expanded most during the forties, the business group almost equally in the twenties and the forties; the clerks and salesmen seem to have stopped growing.

Looking at the other side of the coin, there is no clear indication that the rate of decline of unskilled workers and farmers is changing.

Table 6 Percentages of male occupational distributions, 1910 to 1950 (based on the US census)

Social–economic group	1910	1920	1930	1940	1950
professional persons	3·1	3·2	4·0	4·7	7·1
proprietors, managers and officials:					
farmers	19·9	18·7	15·2	13·0	9·9
others	7·9	8·0	9·0	9·1	10·3
clerks, salespeople and kindred	9·2	10·6	12·8	13·4	12·6
skilled workers and foremen	14·5	16·7	16·4	15·2	18·6
semiskilled workers	11·2	13·3	14·4	18·6	21·5
unskilled workers:					
farm laborers	14·0	9·6	9·5	8·5	4·8
others	20·2	19·8	18·8	17·6	13·1
not reported [a]					2·1
total	100·0	99·9	99·9	100·1	100·0
number	29 483 000	32 806 000	37 916 000	39 446 000	42 565 000

[a] Tables 1, 2 and 4 above omit the unreported
Sources as for Table 1, p. 46

Consequently, we must conclude that there is no reason to expect the rate of technological redistribution of the labor force to change markedly in the immediate future. Eventually the decline in the farm group will stop, for an equilibrium will be reached between the men on the farm and those in the city whom they feed. But as automation in production becomes common there may be further spurts in the growth of the technicians and the skilled workers at the expense of the unskilled and semiskilled. Technological mobility will remain a potent social force in the next generation.

2 Reproductive mobility. Here the picture is different, for differential reproduction is disappearing.

The United States Bureau of the Census has published detailed fertility information for samples of women taken from the censuses of 1910 and 1940. In each instance the data are given by five-year age groups cross-classified with the occupations of the husbands. Thus it is possible to calculate the trend in differential reproduction for women who have completed their families for five-year age groups stretching from those born in 1836 to those born in 1896.

The data have been analysed by Dennis H. Wrong of the University of Toronto.[8] He sums up his conclusions concerning native-born white women as follows:

The trend in occupational fertility differentials between 1910 and 1940 was similar in many respects to the trend in the period before 1910. All groups continued to decline in fertility, the inverse association between fertility and socioeconomic status persisted, and the percentage divergence of the fertility rates of the two agricultural classes from the average for all classes increased. All classes declined more rapidly than in the previous period ... One significant change, however, is that, although the three low fertility nonmanual classes led the decline in the first period, the four classes of nonagricultural manual workers declined more rapidly than two of the nonmanual classes in the later period. ... In an absolute sense the size of the fertility differentials between the high, the intermediate, and the low fertility groups of classes diminished between 1910 and 1940 (Wrong, 1956).

Wrong's summation can be simply illustrated. Let us compare the total number of children born to 1000 wives of professional men to the number born to 1000 wives of semiskilled workers. If we take women born between 1836 and 1840, who were child-bearing wives *before* the widespread use of contraceptives and the consequent decline in family size, we note that the wives of professionals had 4714 children, and the wives of operatives 4837 children – no substantial difference between the two groups.[9] But a generation later the difference was marked: considering women born in the period 1861–1865, the professional group had only 3335 children whereas the operative group had 4556. Although both groups declined in fertility, the former group declined much more rapidly.

If we jump to the next generation, we see that for women born in 1891 to 1895 (those who were just past child-bearing age at the time of the 1940 census), the differences between the two groups had narrowed: wives of the professional men had 2253 children, the wives of operatives, 2983.

The trend since the Second World War is still a matter of debate, but it

8. Dr Wrong very kindly sent me an advanced draft of Chapter 5 which gives a detailed analysis of the American figures and makes pointed comparisons to the British trends. The relevant government publication is US Bureau of the Census (1943–7); see also Kiser (1952) and Westoff (1954).
9. There may have been a small under-reporting of working-class children due to the somewhat higher rate of mortality among their mothers compared to professional mothers.

is probably true that the differences have narrowed still further. In recent years we have had a marked upswing in the birth rate, but the increase has been greatest among those groups who previously had the smallest families.

In general, it appears that as a country industrializes, the upper-level urban families are the first to desire smaller families, and the first to learn about effective methods of birth control. After a short period of time, both the desire and the technique are passed down to the lower levels of society, though the latter probably do not restrict their families quite so much as the upper levels. It now appears that the future pattern to be expected in the United States will be one that has three broad fertility types: urban white-collar workers, urban blue-collar workers, and farmers, with each group having slightly larger families than the preceding one (the gap between city and farm being bigger than that between white-collar and blue-collar). *Within* each group, rich couples are likely to have slightly larger families than poor ones. Thus, the simple inverse correlation of social class level and size of family will no longer exist.

Consequently, the substantial mobility that occurred in the recent past as a result of differential fertility is not to be expected in the future. There may remain a small residue of differential fertility between the white-collar and blue-collar groups as a whole, but the effects of this on mobility will be relatively small. And within the white-collar group (and possibly the blue-collar as well) it appears that differential fertility in the future will produce downward mobility.

3 Immigration mobility. Here the pattern is perfectly clear: the vast inflow of unskilled immigrants, averaging about a million a year, was stopped about 1925. Even if we continue to admit one or two hundred thousand immigrants a year, the larger size of the native population will absorb them practically without notice. Furthermore, the new immigrants are people of higher skills, and they do not all enter the occupational system at the bottom.

The recent population movement of consequence in the United States has been the migration of rural negroes to both southern and northern cities. They entered industry at the unskilled and semiskilled levels, and suffered racial discrimination which slowed their ascent into the skilled and white-collar jobs. Consequently, many white workers were pushed up a notch in the hierarchy. But this type of internal migration cannot continue indefinitely as the pool of available rural negroes will dry up. The migration of negroes in the past forty years has softened the effects of the constriction of the European inflow, but it cannot last much longer.

4 Individual mobility. Individual mobility, it will be remembered, cannot be measured from census data alone; a sampling inquiry is necessary. The procedures of public-opinion research are new, thus we have no historical comparisons available. But there is one ingenious research that contributes to our knowledge of trends in individual mobility.

Natalie Rogoff collected a sample of some 10 000 men in Indianapolis who applied for marriage licenses in 1940, and another sample of equal size for the year 1910. In each instance the men stated their occupations and those of their fathers. The resulting mobility tables automatically held constant the effects of differential fertility, for the number of fathers and the number of sons were identical. Rogoff further held constant the effects of technological change by partialing out the mobility that flowed from that cause. The final measurement was therefore one of individual mobility alone. The two samples made it possible for her to study trends through time (Rogoff, 1953).

She found that overall rates of individual movement were about the same in 1910 as in 1940. Mobility was about 20 per cent less than would be expected under completely open or random placement. Although the overall rates had not changed, some changes were noticed regarding movement across the line separating blue-collar from white-collar positions. In both periods this barrier was the hardest to cross. There was much more movement within each category (especially the white-collar group) than across from one category to the other. Rogoff found that upward movement across the line did not change from 1910 to 1940, but downward movement decreased – that is, it was easier for the sons of the men at the top to stay there despite the fact that upward mobility among the sons of those at the bottom remained constant. Unfortunately, Indianapolis is not representative of the nation as a whole, but we will have to accept Rogoff's conclusions as the best available national estimate.[10]

10. Rogoff's method was to measure actual succession and mobility against what would be expected under the principle of random placement, holding differential reproduction and technological change constant. Mobility tables constructed on this principle lead to different conclusions from tables constructed from gross father–son comparisons that do not take into account differences in the sizes of the various groups. For instance, the NORC data in Table 3 show that 23 per cent of professionals had professional fathers, whereas 30 per cent of skilled workers had skilled fathers. But when we realize that in 1920 only 3·2 per cent of fathers were professional, compared to 16·7 per cent of skilled workers, then it becomes clear that there is relatively much more inheritance among the professional than among the skilled workers. In fact, Rogoff found succession to be greatest at the top (professionals and semiprofessionals) and at the bottom (unskilled workers), and much less at intermediate levels. The same conclusion was reached in a recent extensive study in England by D. V. Glass and associates (1954). Incidentally, they made an attempt, with admittedly scanty data, to compare several countries. They found that individual succession appears to be about the same in England and the US, and slightly higher in Italy and France. (See technical comments on this study in several articles in *Population Studies*, vol. 9, 1955.)

5 *Summary*. The available evidence suggests that technological mobility has remained relatively constant during the past generation, as has individual mobility. Reproductive mobility and immigration mobility have been steadily declining and will be unimportant in the next generation (both were most important in the generation preceding 1920). But insofar as technological and individual mobility are by far the most important factors, the overall rates of mobility have not declined greatly in the last generation and probably will not do so in the next generation. American society is not becoming markedly more rigid.

References

BENDIX, R., LIPSET, S. M., and MALM, T. (1954), 'Social origins and occupational career patterns', *Indust. lab. Relat. Rev.*, vol. 7, pp. 246–61.

CENTERS, R. (1948), 'Occupational mobility of urban occupational strata', *Amer. sociol. Rev.*, vol. 13, pp. 197–203.

DAVIDSON, P. E., and ANDERSON, H. D. (1937), *Occupational Mobility in an American Community*, Stanford University Press.

EDWARDS, A. M. (1943), *US Census of Population, 1940: Comparative Occupational Statistics, 1870–1940*, Government Printing Office, Washington.

FORM, W. H., and MILLER, D. C. (1949), 'Occupational career pattern as a sociological instrument', *Amer. J. Sociol.*, vol. 54, pp. 317–29.

GLASS, D. V. (ed.) (1954), *Social Mobility in Britain*, Routledge & Kegan Paul.

HOCHBAUM, G., *et al.* (1955), 'Socioeconomic variables in a large city', *Amer. J. Sociol.*, vol. 61, pp. 31–8.

KISER, C. V. (1952), 'Fertility trends and differentials in the United States', *J. Amer. stat. Assn*, vol. 47, pp. 25–48.

LIPSET, S. M., and Bendix, R. (1952), 'Social mobility and occupational career patterns', *Amer. J. Sociol.*, vol. 57, pp. 366–74, 494–504.

LIPSET, S. M., and ROGOFF, N. (1954), 'Class and opportunity in Europe and in the United States', *Commentary*, December.

LORIMER, F., and OSBORN, F. (1934), *Dynamics of Population*, Macmillan Co.

McGUIRE, C. (1950), 'Social stratification and mobility patterns', *Amer. sociol. Rev.*, vol. 15, pp. 195–204.

MILLER, H. P. (1955), *Income of the American People*, Wiley.

NATIONAL OPINION RESEARCH CENTER (1953), 'Jobs and occupations: a popular evaluation', in R. Bendix and S. M. Lipset (eds), *Class, Status and Power*, Free Press; originally published in *Opinion News*, vol. 9, September 1947.

ROGOFF, N. (1953), *Recent Trends in Occupational Mobility*, Free Press.

SIBLEY, E. (1942), 'Some demographic clues to stratification', *Amer. sociol. Rev.*, vol. 7, pp. 322–30.

US BUREAU OF THE CENSUS (1943–7), *US Census of Population, 1940: Differential Fertility in 1940 and 1910*, Government Printing Office, Washington.

US BUREAU OF THE CENSUS (1953), *US Census of Population, 1950*, vol. 2, *Characteristics of the Population*, Government Printing Office, Washington.

WESTOFF, C. F. (1954), 'Differential fertility in the United States', *Amer. sociol. Rev.*, vol. 19, pp. 549–61.

WRONG, D. H. (1956), 'Trends in class fertility differentials in Western nations', Ph.D. thesis, Columbia University.

Part Two
Analysing Intergenerational Occupational Mobility

After the Second World War, the International Sociological Association undertook a policy of encouraging comparative research on intergenerational social mobility. Measures of the frequency of mobility were to be defined in some way and were then to be established for different countries, and related to their degree of industrialization, type of educational system, incidence of military service and so forth. The Readings of this section indicate both the achievements and the shortcomings of this comparative approach, and they readily fall into two sections. The first part consists of classic studies which analysed rates of intergenerational mobility, at different time periods, and in different nations, basically by means of the father–son turnover table. The Glass study provided the first British national estimate of occupational change between two generations. The notions of 'perfect mobility' and indices of association and dissociation, which featured centrally in later cross-national comparisons, were also introduced in this study. In a now classic review, Miller set out to compare similarities and differences in intergenerational mobility across different nations – a valiant but hazardous task in view of the wide range of differences of classification and design. An early and influential study by Rogoff (1953) had derived data on intergenerational mobility from marriage records in Indianapolis for 1910 and 1940. Tully, Jackson and Curtis summarize Rogoff's work and update it from their later study, making the Indianapolis studies unique as a three-point analysis of intergenerational change.

Despite the proliferation of national studies of occupational mobility, evidence regarding consistent transgenerational relationships has been contradictory. In large part this has been due to serious methodological shortcomings in the design and analysis of such studies. This is the main focus in the second half of the section. Yasuda shows that the index of association, used almost universally to compare mobility distribution, depends upon the occupational distribution holding in the fathers' and sons' generations, and he goes on to distinguish 'forced' from 'pure' mobility as a basis for measuring turnover. Duncan's incisive and radical critique of the assumptions and methods of conventional mobility analysis is one of the most important contributions to this area in the last ten years, and it should be read in its full form by any serious student of the subject.

After these primarily methodological Readings, both of extreme importance, and showing the need for some fundamental rethinking of mobility research, Mayer and Müller consider broader theoretical problems. Having offered a critique of sociological assumptions made in the body of research summarized by Miller, they suggest a tripartite framework to guide future thinking on the topic in terms of a macrosociological concern with the connection between social mobility and social change, an intermediate-level interest in building life-cycle models for the determinants of occupational status, and a microsociological focus upon the movements of individual actors in particular local social structures, and the actors' consciousness of these movements.

Reference

ROGOFF, N. (1953), *Recent Trends in Occupational Mobility*, Free Press.

4 D. V. Glass and J. R. Hall

Social Mobility in Great Britain: A Study of Intergeneration
Changes in Status

Excerpts from D. V. Glass and J. R. Hall, 'Social mobility in Great Britain: a study
of intergeneration changes in status', in D. V. Glass (ed.), *Social Mobility in Britain*,
Routledge & Kegan Paul, 1954, pp. 177–201.

Introduction

[. . .] We are concerned with occupational achievement, and with the relationship between fathers and sons with reference to that kind of achievement. Obviously, there are other aspects of social mobility which are entirely excluded from such an analysis. We also exclude any criterion of the social status of an individual other than his occupation. Some of the reasons for concentrating upon this single factor have already been given – the belief, supported by other material contained in this volume, that in Great Britain occupation is probably the most important single criterion of status; and also the desire to measure the behaviour of other variables against this particular variable. [. . .]

[. . .] In allocating an individual to a specific category in the social status hierarchy, the modified sevenfold classification is used. This means, in effect, that in comparing father and son we apply a single status scale, based upon attitudes expressed in 1949. Though this may be regarded as a valid approach – in the same sense as it is valid to examine changes in the cost of living in terms of the expenditure patterns prevailing in the most recent year of the series of years considered – it is clearly a restrictive one. But this restriction can only be fully overcome by taking samples of attitudes at regular intervals in the future. A further restriction involved here is that the status scale relates to men's occupations, and that the present study is indeed confined to men. This limitation has been imposed because a prestige scale for women's occupations would not be directly comparable. [. . .]

A third point which should be mentioned here is that in the present study, social mobility is examined on a rather foreshortened time-scale. Ideally, it would be desirable to measure social mobility by examining the changes in status of an individual throughout his particular generation. The study would take as the starting-point the birth year, when the individual's status was equated with that of his father, and trace the changes in achieved status throughout the active life of the individual. Applying this method to successive cohorts would yield a series of comparable status profiles, showing both the nature of intrageneration movement and its end result in the final social status distribution of the cohorts. With such an analysis, the change between the beginning and end of a generation would also be a measure of intergeneration movement in status. The sample inquiry did not, however, provide information on the occupation of the father at the time of birth of the subject; indeed, unless both subject and father were alive, it is doubtful whether a request for such information would yield reliable results. Instead, the last main occupation of the subject's father was ascertained. Hence the analysis is in general confined to a comparison of the last main status of the father with the status of the son as ascertained in 1949. Some use has been made of status profiles of the subject but the profiles derived from our investigation begin at the first occupations taken up by the subjects and not at their birth. The analysis thus tends to be static rather than dynamic, though it still yields much information on the fluidity or rigidity of the social structure.

Another type of foreshortening of the time-scale also arises, and one which only time itself can overcome. In order to have valid information on changes in status between parental and filial generations, it is necessary to know (or to be reasonably certain) that the sons are old enough to have achieved their last main status. This means, however, confining the analysis to persons aged fifty years or more in 1949, since an examination of the profiles shows that, at least until that age, there is still some movement between the various status categories. And because there is no previous comparable inquiry, the true span of comparison, if based on material so circumscribed, would be very narrow. It would also mean excluding those cohorts of individuals who had their education when the national system of secondary schools was expanding fairly rapidly, and when the ladder from the secondary schools to the universities was being built. To some extent the first point is dealt with by analysing separately the data for subjects whose eldest sons were at least twenty years old in 1949. Thus it is possible to survey three generations instead of two – grandfathers, fathers and sons – and to push back the initial point of the analysis further into the nineteenth century. On the second point, however, there is no satisfactory solution. One possible approach is to use the status profiles to see if there are measurable differences between cohorts at, say, age thirty. This is equivalent to fertility analysis which compares the total family size attained by, say, ten years' marriage duration for successive cohorts and thereby tries to gauge if completed fertility (the total family size achieved by the end of the reproductive period) is changing. In the study of fertility, however, the demographer is greatly helped by the fact that the length of the child-bearing period has not been increasing. On the contrary, the effective period of childbearing has been contracting systematically, so that it is now safer to infer completed fertility from fertility at ten years' duration of marriage than would have been the case for the marriages of fifty years ago. For social mobility, however, the reverse is likely to apply, the increase in the expectation of life being accompanied by some increase in the length of working life. Hence it may now be more speculative to infer a man's last main status from his achieved status at, say, the age of thirty years than would have been true at the beginning of the century. This also applies to the second possible method, that of attempting to project from measured status at one particular age or from a series of ages. For this is only another way of putting the first method. In sum, therefore, the results given for the more recent cohorts – generations born after the First World War – must be treated with caution. It must remain for later investigators, repeating this kind of inquiry in fifteen or twenty years' time, to establish how far the ultimate chances of mobility have been influenced by educational and other developments during the inter-war period, while the net results of the 1944 Education Act will not be fully ascertainable for another forty or fifty years.

The problems discussed so far do not exhaust the list of questions which need to be considered in measuring social mobility. [. . .]

[. . .] The question of the concept of 'perfect mobility', basic to the statistical analysis applied, is considered later in the text of the present chapter, in the section dealing with some of the new measurements of changes in social status. For the moment, however, enough of the background has been given to make it possible to proceed to the first stages of analysis of the material obtained from the sample inquiry.

Changes in status between two generations

The main analysis is based upon those of the male subjects covered by the sample inquiry who were resident in England and Wales, the subjects being classified by decades of birth in order to throw into relief changes over time. The numbers of subjects and their distribution by period of birth are shown in Table 1. Information on occupation was lacking for relatively few individuals, so that the subsequent tables are based on 94·5 per cent of the men interviewed.

The inquiry also covered Scotland, but the material for that country is less comprehensive. Because of the different educational system of Scotland, a separate and more extensive list of questions would have been needed to produce results which could meaningfully be compared with those for England and Wales. But in a compromise questionnaire serving the needs of three different investigations, this was not practicable. [. . .]

The general statistics for England and Wales are shown in Table 2, which compares the social status of the subjects interviewed with that of their

Table 1 Male subjects classified by year of birth

Date of birth	Number of subjects in sample	Father's or subject's occupation not known	Number of subjects included in study
1889 or earlier	713	34	679
1890–99	556	16	540
1900–09	777	26	751
1910–19	802	30	772
1920–29	794	39	755
1930 or later	58	1	all excluded
total	3700	146	3497

fathers. The type of analysis applied in the first stage is similar to that used by Professor Ginsberg in his pioneer study (1929), though somewhat more precise methods of measurement are involved here. The data in Table 2 are

Table 2 Distribution of the male sample according to subjects' and subjects' fathers' status category

fathers' status category	subjects' present status category							
	1	2	3	4	5	6	7	total
1	**38·8** / 48·5	14·6 / 11·9	20·2 / 7·9	6·2 / 1·7	14·0 / 1·3	4·7 / 1·0	1·5 / 0·5	100·0 (129)
2	10·7 / 15·5	**26·7** / 25·2	22·7 / 10·3	12·0 / 3·9	20·6 / 2·2	5·3 / 1·4·	2·0 / 0·7	100·0 (150)
3	3·5 / 11·7	10·1 / 22·0	**18·8** / 19·7	19·1 / 14·4	35·7 / 8·6	6·7 / 3·9	6·1 / 5·0	100·0 (345)
4	2·1 / 10·7	3·9 / 12·6	11·2 / 17·6	**21·2** / 24·0	43·0 / 15·6	12·4 / 10·8	6·2 / 7·5	100·0 (518)
5	0·9 / 13 6	2·4 / 22 6	7·5 / 34 5	12·3 / 40 3	**47·3** / 50·0	17·1 / 43 5	12·5 / 44·6	100·0 (1510)
6	0·0 / 0·0	1·3 / 3·8	4·1 / 5·8	8·8 / 8·7	39·1 / 12·5	**31·2** / 24·1	15·5 / 16·7	100·0 (458)
7	0·0 / 0·0	0·8 / 1·9	3·6 / 4·2	8·3 / 7·0	36·4 / 9·8	23·5 / 15·3	**27·4** / 25·0	100·0 (387)
total	100·0 (103)	100·0 (159)	100·0 (330)	100·0 (459)	100·0 (1429)	100·0 (593)	100·0 (424)	(3497)

given in two forms. The percentages in the horizontal rows (in the top right-hand corner of each cell) show the extent to which sons have the same status as their fathers. The series of cells in the first row, for example, shows that among the sons whose fathers were in status category 1, 38·8 per cent are themselves in category 1, 14·6 per cent in category 2, etc. Of the sons whose fathers were in category 7, none has himself achieved category 1, while 27·4 per cent are still in category 7. By looking along the diagonal in the Table (distinguished by bold type), the extent to which status has remained constant as between fathers and sons will be seen. This appears most marked for category 5 and least for category 3 – that is, 47·3 per cent of the men whose fathers were in category 5, are themselves in category 5, while only 18·8 per cent of the men whose fathers were in category 3 are themselves in category 3. Referring to the description of the categories, given below for reference, self-recruitment appears to be highest among the skilled manual and routine nonmanual workers. The kind of association between parental and filial status is also visible: the higher the status of the fathers, the smaller the proportions of sons in category 5 or lower categories.

Status categories	
Number	Description
1	professional and high administrative
2	managerial and executive
3	inspectional, supervisory and other nonmanual (higher grade)
4	inspectional, supervisory and other nonmanual (lower grade)
5	skilled manual and routine grades of nonmanual
6	semiskilled manual
7	unskilled manual

The information provided by the vertical columns (in the bottom left-hand corner of each cell) relates to the parental status of men found in given categories in 1949. Thus, of the men found to be in category 1, 48·5 per cent had fathers who were of the same status. This, too, is an indication of self-recruitment, and it will again be seen, by looking along the diagonal, that the maintenance of parental status appears most evident in category 5 and least in category 3. At the same time, there are considerable changes in status between the successive generations. The horizontal rows indicate, for example, that for men whose fathers were in category 1, over 60 per cent were found in lower categories, while for men whose fathers were in category 7, over 70 per cent were found in higher status categories than their fathers. The meaning of such changes will be discussed later.

The material from which Table 2 was compiled is used again, in a somewhat different way, in Tables 3, 4 and 5. The first Table shows the proportions of subjects who were of the same status as their fathers, or who had achieved a different status, and the chi-square test shows that the differences, noted in connection with Table 2, are significant. That is also true of the differences between subjects who achieved a higher, as compared with those who were found in a lower, status than that of their fathers where parental status is not maintained. The tendency to rise appears more

Table 3 Male subjects whose status category is the same as, or different from, that of their fathers

Subjects' fathers' status category	Subjects' status category			% col. 1 to col. 3
	Same (1)	Different (2)	Total (3)	
1	50	79	129	38·8
2	40	110	150	26·7
3	65	280	345	18·8
4	110	408	518	21·2
5	714	796	1510	47·3
6	143	315	458	31·2
7	106	281	387	27·4
total	1228	2269	3497	35·1

marked among men whose fathers were in the lower status categories (leaving aside categories 1 and 7 from which movement in one direction only is possible); but the distance traversed when changes in status occur is not very great. An attempt is made in Table 5 to express this quantitatively, by assuming that the distance between any two adjacent categories is equal to

Table 4 Male subjects whose status category is higher or lower than that of their fathers

Subjects' fathers' status category	Subjects' status category			% col. 1 to col. 3
	Higher (1)	Lower (2)	Total (3)	
1	—	—	—	
2	16	94	110	14·5
3	47	233	280	16·8
4	89	319	408	21·8
5	349	447	796	43·8
6	244	71	315	77·5
7	—	—	—	
total	745	1164	1909	39·0

one unit. This assumption is an extremely dubious one and to validate any assumption would need a new inquiry into the prestige hierarchy of occupations. Here, however, we are concerned only to see if the number of categories involved in the shift in status is large, and whether there are significant differences in this respect between the various groups of subjects.

An analysis of variance shows that the differences are significant – that the higher the parental status, the further the fall below it, which is hardly surprising since there is then a greater number of categories through which the fall can proceed. But at the same time the shifts upward or downward tend to be of a short-distance variety; where men have a status different from their fathers, they still tend to cluster round the parental category. In brief, therefore, summarizing the discussion, we may say that there is an evident

Table 5 Mean distance between fathers and sons in the hierarchical scale (distance measured in terms of number of categories)

Father's status category	Son's position relative to father	
	Higher Mean and S.E.	Lower Mean and S.E.
1	—	2·46±0·16 (85)
2	1·00±0·00 (16)	2·10±0·13 (94)
3	1·26±0·06 (47)	2·00±0·06 (233)
4	1·47±0·08 (89)	1·40±0·03 (319)
5	1·65±0·05 (304)	1·42±0·03 (447)
6	1·40±0·05 (246)	1·00±0·00 (71)
7	1·90±0·06 (281)	—
	1·62±0·03 (983)	1·62±0·02 (1249)

association between the status of fathers and sons, seemingly especially marked where the fathers were skilled manual workers or were in the professional or administrative category; that the degree of association differs significantly as between the various categories; and that where there are changes in status between fathers and sons, the sons still tend to be fairly close to their fathers' level. [. . .]

The concept of 'perfect' mobility[1]

So far the term 'social mobility' has been used to indicate changes in status between fathers and sons, irrespective of the cause of these changes. And though some indication has been given of differences in the extent to which men with parental backgrounds of specific status have themselves achieved particular status levels, no attempt has been made to measure these differences on any scale or, with reference to such a scale, to estimate if

1. It is suggested that the term 'mobility' be used for full intragenaration movement, and that for the parental–filial relationship in status the term 'association' be used. In dealing with the general concept, however it will not cause confusion to refer to 'perfect' mobility as if it applied either to mobility so defined or to 'association'.

some groups have 'too high' or 'too low' a chance of reaching the top status categories. In terms of everyday reality, there is justification for the relatively simple approach adopted in the preceding discussion. For the man in the street what matters is whether he is 'getting on in the world' as compared with his father. It is less important to him whether his higher status is due to a general increase in the proportion of 'white-collar' jobs in the community, or to a redistribution of personnel between the various status categories, a redistribution which may occur at the same time as, or independently of, changes in the overall occupational structure of the community. He does not himself necessarily experience, as a matter of personal sensation, the differences between these two methods of social mobility. And indeed he may well feel a greater sense of upward mobility with a change in the total occupational structure and a relatively low chance (as compared with an individual whose father had a higher status) of achieving high status, than if with a stationary occupational structure dominated by low prestige jobs, he has a chance of rising equal to that of any other person in his generation, whatever the status of his father. This may be illustrated by a hypothetical case. Suppose there are 100 sons, of whom 20 are the sons of nonmanual and 80 the sons of manual workers. Suppose also that in the sons' generation the job availabilities also provide 20 nonmanual and 80 manual jobs. Then even if every nonmanual job goes to the sons of manual workers, only 20 out of the 80 sons of manual workers can achieve nonmanual status. Let us assume now, however, that there is a total structural change, such that in the sons' generation there are 50 non-manual and 50 manual jobs. Then even if only 30 out of the 50 non-manual jobs go to the sons of manual workers (that is, conversely, even if every son of a nonmanual worker achieves nonmanual status), the ratio of nonmanual jobs to the sons of manual workers will be 30:80, higher than in the first case. Hence when, because a society is an expanding one, there are increased status opportunities for all, differences in opportunity between individuals of different status origins may scarcely be felt or considered.

For the social scientist, however, the *means* of achieving high status are as important as the end product. The question of *relative* mobility, of the different opportunities of gaining high status available to individuals of different social origin, is part of the problem of the recruitment of elites. And the knowledge that, to take an example, there are now more sons of manual workers in the medical profession than there were a generation ago is not a sufficient answer to the question of recruitment. It needs to be supplemented by reference to the changing numbers of medical prac-titioners in the community as a whole. Alternatively, the index of mobility should take as its basis the number of medical practitioners in the sons' generation as constituting the total opportunities then available for the practice of that particular profession.

Of course, both approaches may be followed. The sample survey results may be used to provide some indication of the changes over time in the total distribution of status opportunities, using the single standard based upon the 1949 inquiry into the prestige of occupations. The results are shown in Tables 6 and 7, the first giving the distribution of status for subjects by their decades of birth, and the second the distribution of status for fathers of subjects by decades of birth of the subjects themselves. Leaving aside the pre-1890 cohort, which covers an undefined period of years, the data still suggest a slight decline in the opportunities for high status over time, a decline which appears in the data for subjects' fathers as well as for the subjects themselves. This is not in conflict with the known fact that certain specific types of white-collar occupations have greatly expanded over the past fifty years. It would mean, however, that other occupations of comparable status have contracted to an even greater extent.[2] But since the development suggested by the statistics in Tables 6 and 7 may seem somewhat unexpected, it is worth seeing how far the trends they appear to reflect are confirmed by the results of the successive censuses of England and Wales.

Table 6 Subjects classified according to their own social status (percentage distribution)

Date of birth of subjects	Subjects' social status							
	1	2	3	4	5	6	7	All
before 1890	4·3	3·4	8·5	13·1	36·8	15·9	18·0	100·0
1890–99	2·8	5·9	12·6	14·3	34·8	16·3	13·3	100·0
1900–09	2·8	6·8	10·8	15·8	37·0	16·6	10·3	100·1
1910–19	2·9	4·3	9·8	15·2	41·2	16·1	10·6	100·1
1920–29	2·1	2·6	6·2	7·7	52·3	19·6	9·4	99·9

It should at once be emphasized that the percentages in Table 6 have a different validity from those in Table 7. The percentages in the former Table would agree with the census results, assuming the classification of occupations to be identical, provided that the sample survey was designed correctly and carried out effectively. But the percentages in Table 7 are bound to be biased in one sense. Since they are derived from information supplied by living sons or daughters, the percentages will not include those individuals of the previous generation who had no children, or whose

2. And also that the expanded opportunities in certain 'white-collar' occupations have been taken over by women.

children did not survive. And, conversely, the larger the number of children born and surviving to a man of the parental generation, the greater the probability of that man being included in the population on which Table 7 is based. Mortality is correlated negatively with social status, but so is fertility, so that the two factors will tend to counteract one another. It is unlikely, however, that they will completely cancel each other. Having

Table 7 Subjects classified according to the social status of their fathers (percentage distribution)

Date of birth of subjects	Fathers' social status							
	1	2	3	4	5	6	7	All
before 1890	5·2	4·9	11·5	15·3	41·7	14·3	7·2	100·1
1890–99	3·7	5·0	11·9	14·6	40·6	13·0	11·3	100·1
1900–09	3·5	3·7	9·1	16·6	45·3	10·8	11·1	100·1
1910–19	3·1	4·1	10·2	13·9	44·9	12·2	11·5	99·9
1920–29	3·2	4·0	7·4	13·6	42·5	15·4	13·9	100·0

regard to the historical development of social status differences in fertility, it is more probable that, relatively, the bias towards the representation of 'manual' fathers will be greater in the more recent than in the earlier cohorts of Table 7. It is because of this kind of bias that the analysis of mobility in the present symposium proceeds generally from son to father – which is a valid approach – and not from father to son. [. . .]

For the remainder of this chapter, mobility will be treated in terms of the alternative approach which we must now discuss.

Table 8

Status of fathers	Number of sons in each status category					
	Category 1		Category 2		Totals	
category 1	J	20	K	10	b_1	30
category 2	L	30	M	40	b_2	70
totals	c_1	50	c_2	50	d	100

Consider the hypothetical example given in Table 8 of the relation between parental and filial social status. Of the 100 sons observed in the present generation (c_1, c_2), 50 are in category 1 and 50 in category 2 (it is assumed that category 1 is of higher status than category 2), while of the fathers (b_1, b_2) of these sons 30 were in category 1 and 70 in category 2. There has thus been a considerable change in the distribution of status opportunities between the generations. Now, consider the generations of sons and assume that there is no association between the status of father and son – that each son has the same chance as any other son of arriving in category 1. Such a situation we describe as representing 'random' or 'perfect' mobility, meaning that there is no link between parental and filial status. In Table 8, 30 per cent of the sons had fathers in category 1, and in conditions of 'perfect' mobility these sons should in their generation take 30 per cent of the jobs available in each status category. In formal terms this is equal to $(b_1 \times c_1)/d$, or $(30 \times 50)/100$, for category 1 jobs, and $(b_1 \times c_2)/d$, or $(30 \times 50)/100$, for category 2 jobs, the answer in both cases being 15. These, then, are the expected values and may be used as reference points or standards with which to compare the actual values in the Table. In the Table, the actual number of sons (J) of category 1 background who themselves arrive in category 1 is 20, and the ratio of 20/15, or 1·3, may be called the 'index of association'. The ratio of the actual to the expected number of sons who, having category 1 fathers, arrived in category 2 jobs (K), is 10/15, or 0·67, and may be termed the 'index of dissociation'. When the expected values equal the actual values, both indices will be 1·0. The higher the degree of self-recruitment, or of maintenance of parental status, the higher will be the index of association and the lower the index of dissociation, though the upper and lower limits of both indices in practice depend upon the actual numbers in the cohorts, marginal totals and cells covered by a table. The index of association may also, of course, give a result of less than 1·0 – though this is rarely likely to be seen in practice – indicative of less self-recruitment than would be expected on a random basis. This would mean that there is reverse association between parental and filial status, and in Western society this would be very unusual. It would occur if there were, between two generations, an overturning of the processes of selection of elites – if, to take a hypothetical case, the sons of doctors were prohibited by law or custom from taking up a career in medicine!

Four points should be emphasized in connection with the use of these indices. First, the general approach itself is not original to the present study. The problem of random association was considered by a number of Italian statisticians, including Benini, Livio Livi (1950) and Chessa, while the method of taking into account generation changes in the total occupational structure of the community was put forward by Goldhamer and applied extensively by Rogoff (1951).[3] In the present study, however, the method has been developed systematically. Measures of association have been applied to intrageneration as well as intergeneration change, while

3. It may perhaps be noted, though it is not of great interest, that the method was developed here independently of Rogoff's work.

measures of dissociation have been split so as to indicate separately movement upward and movement downward in status. Tests of significance have also been devised, and these are an essential in using in an objective way the indices of association and of dissociation. For it is necessary, for example, to ascertain first that a given index of association differs significantly from 1·0 before it can be taken to show a higher or lower degree of status inertia than would be expected on a basis of equal probabilities. And if two indices differ significantly from 1·0 it is still necessary to ascertain that they differ significantly from each other before one can be said to indicate a closer or looser association than the other. Even so, the data available to us do not make it possible to say, within specified limits of confidence, that one index, differing significantly from another, is precisely n times another in size. The most we can say is that the ratio of the indices will give an approximate indication of relative size.[4]

The second point is that the assumption of 'perfect' mobility, or of the existence of equal probabilities of movement for persons of all social origins, does not assume any value system, any claim of social justice, or any basis in fact. It is, indeed, most unlikely that 'perfect' mobility would be attainable in our society or in any other, for there will probably always be some premium (if only in the sense of encouragement or stimulus) on a given parental background. Hence the fact that an index differs significantly from 1·0 means no more than that the given index has a particular statistical value.[5] The sole purpose of the concept of 'perfect' mobility is to provide a common standard which makes it possible to see the *relative* chances of status change of different generations and of men of different status backgrounds. What is important, therefore, is the *difference* between the indices for those generations or groups of men.

Thirdly, in saying that the indices of association and dissociation abstract from changes in the total availability of occupations of various levels of prestige, it should be noted that this also means abstracting from the influence of demographic factors. A constant distribution of available opportunities for the whole adult male population over two generations may, if there is differential fertility, be equivalent to an increase in the available opportunities for part of that population. This may be illustrated by another hypothetical example. Let us assume a stationary total population and distribution of status opportunities, with 300 category 1 and 700 category 2 jobs in each generation. If the categories are taken to represent 'nonmanual' and 'manual' groups of occupations, the assumed distribu-

4. On the grounds that the best estimate of the ratio is the ratio of the best estimates of the two indices.
5. That is, the difference between actual and expected frequencies is greater than can be accounted for by sampling fluctuations.

tion is not far from the real position in England and Wales.[6] Let us also assume that looking at the picture from the parental generation, each father in category 1 is replaced by 0·84 adult sons, and each father in category 2 by 1·069 adult sons, the ratio of 'manual' to 'nonmanual' replacement being 1·27. Again the assumed *ratio* is not very unreal (leaving aside the question of marriage), for the results of the Family Census showed a corresponding ratio of about 1·4 for the average number of live births per marriage of completed fertility (Royal Commission on Population, 1949, p. 29), and there would be some reduction in that figure if allowance were made for differential mortality. Given these assumptions regarding differential replacement, the 300 category 1 fathers would be replaced by 252 adult sons and the 700 category 2 fathers by 748 adult sons, making a total of 1000 males in the filial generation. If we now look at the filial generation and calculate the status distributions of the sons on the assumption of 'perfect' mobility, we shall have the position given in Table 9.

Table 9

| Status of fathers | Number of sons in each status category | | | | | |
	Category 1		Category 2		Totals	
category 1	J	76	K	176	b_1	252
category 2	L	224	M	524	b_2	748
totals	c_1	300	c_2	700	d	1000

Knowing c_1 and c_2, and also b_1 and b_2, we can fill in the cells of the Table. On the assumption of 'perfect' mobility, L, equal to $(b_2 \times c_1)/d$ must be approximately 224, whence the Table may be completed as shown. But given 300 category 1 jobs and only 252 adult sons of category 1 fathers, 48 of the men in L – of the 224 sons who arrive in category 1 although their fathers were in category 2 – must move there as a result of differential replacement, even if every son of a category 1 father maintained his parental status. In consequence, if the total distribution of status opportunities over generations is independent of differential fertility, then the greater the differential the greater the likelihood that, in the filial generation, manual workers' sons will obtain nonmanual jobs. Yet, looking simply at the Table as presented above, and without taking into account the explanation given – equivalent, therefore, to looking at status change only from the viewpoint of the filial generation – one would infer that there had been an increase in

6. See Tables 10 and 11. The 'manual' group in those tables actually includes a number of nonmanual occupations, so that a 30/70 division would not be unrealistic.

the proportion of jobs of higher status instead of, as is the case, a difference in the net replacement rates of the two categories of fathers.

Finally, it should be stressed that differences between indices of association or dissociation, assuming those differences to be statistically significant, are not self-explanatory. They do not say why a differential exists. And clearly the explanation may be very complex, compounded of differences in 'innate' intelligence, in cultural background, in parental stimulus and personal aspirations as well as in more purely economic circumstances. [. . .]

The application of indices of association and dissociation

Taking the whole group of males covered by the sample inquiry, and disregarding date of birth, the indices of association and dissociation are respectively 1·440 and 0·858, both being significantly different from unity. As has been explained, however, these facts are not of interest in themselves. The pertinent question is that of the differences between the indices for the sons of different status background, and these are shown in Tables 10 and 11. In the first Table the various indices are shown separately for each status category, the degree of dissociation being looked at from two points of view, from the parental generation and from the filial generation,

Table 10 Indices of association and dissociation

Status category	Indices of association	Indices of dissociation						
		Fathers' status	Subjects' status	Based on fathers' status		Based on subjects' status	
				Higher	Lower	Higher	Lower
I	II	III	IV	V	VI	VII	VIII
1	13·158	0·631	0·534	—	—	—	—
2	5·865	0·768	0·782	3·621	0·677	3·329	0·683
3	1·997	0·896	0·891	1·818	0·813	1·627	0·756
4	1·618	0·907	0·893	1·015	0·880	1·123	0·831
5	1·157	0·891	0·881	1·161	0·950	0·846	0·927
6	1·841	0·828	0·873	0·228	1·279	0·798	1·387
7	2·259	0·826	0·843	—	—	—	—

and also in terms of whether the sons achieved a higher or lower status than their fathers. The indices of association and dissociation are all significantly different from unity, and the extent to which the separate indices of association looked at from the filial generation differ from each other is shown by the significance matrix in Table 11. In reading this latter Table, both the columns and the rows need to be looked at. Thus in the case of category 5, the index of association is seen to be 1·157. Looking along the row, to the left, it will be seen that this index is very significantly different from the indices for categories 1 to 4, while looking downwards along the column it will be noticed that the index is also very significantly different from the indices for categories 6 and 7. Using the matrix in this way, the highest degree of differentiation among the indices is found for categories 1, 2 and 5, which differ very significantly from each other and from the indices for all other categories.

Table 11 Significant differences between indices of association for total male sample

Fathers' status category	Subjects' status category						
	1	2	3	4	5	6	7
1	13·158						
2	**	5·865					
3	**	**	1·997				
4	**	**	ns	1·618			
5	**	**	**	**	1·157		
6	**	**	ns	ns	**	1·841	
7	**	**	ns	*	**	ns	2·259

** significant at 1 per cent level
* significant at 5 per cent level
ns not significant

Summarizing the meaning of the matrix, we may say that the highest intensity of association between parental and filial status is found among subjects in categories 1 and 2, and the lowest among subjects in category 5. Subjects in other categories show an intermediate position, with category 7 showing the next highest intensity after categories 1 and 2, though being of about the same order as categories 3 and 6. Knowing the occupational contents of the various categories, category 7 would seem to have something of a residual character, while in categories 1 and 2 the intensity of association would appear to be more of an exclusivist variety. The indices of dissociation, also given in Table 10, have not been tested for significant differences, but show the kind of gradation which would, in the circumstances, be expected. This is also the case of the specific indices of dissociation given in columns V to VIII of the Table. They show that subjects with a higher status background are particularly likely to achieve a status higher than their fathers, with the converse applying to subjects of lower status background.

In all, then, the relative chances of alterations in status between fathers and sons, as measured in Table 10, are rather different from those suggested by the crude figures in Table 2. In the latter Table, the highest degree of self-recruitment appeared to be shown among skilled manual and routine non-manual workers. But this appearance was largely a product of the dominant weight of category 5 in both the parental and filial generations. That is, we should necessarily find a large proportion of the sons of skilled manual and routine nonmanual workers to be themselves in the same category as their fathers because in both generations that category contains a very large proportion of all occupied males. When we apply the concept of 'perfect' mobility, we look at the situation from a different point of view and ask: how far is the actual level of self-recruitment in the category greater than would obtain if there were no direct correlation between parental and filial status – if the only determinants were the proportion of all subjects who are the sons of skilled manual workers, and the proportion of all jobs now available which come within the skilled manual category? In answer to this kind of question the indices of association show the smallest excess of actual over expected, and hence the highest relative mobility, for the skilled manual and routine nonmanual workers. If, in such terms, we were to draw a profile over the whole status hierarchy, we should find that the category of skilled manual and routine nonmanual workers constitutes a kind of valley, with the really important peaks rising on the upper status side, culminating in the professional and high administrative occupations, which show the highest ratios of actual to expected self-recruitment.

References

GINSBERG, M. (1929), 'Interchange between social classes', *Econ. J.*, vol. 29, pp. 554–65.
LIVI, L. (1950), 'Sur la mesure de la mobilité sociale', *Population*, Jan.–March.
ROGOFF, N. (1951), 'Recent trends in urban occupational mobility', in P. K. Hall and A. J. Reiss Jr (eds.), *Reader in Urban Sociology*, Free Press.
ROYAL COMMISSION ON POPULATION (1949), *Report*, HMSO.

5 S. M. Miller

Comparative Social Mobility

Excerpts from S. M. Miller, 'Comparative social mobility', *Current Sociology*, vol. 9, 1960, pp. 1–89.

Comparative analysis: some decisions
The advantages of a cross-national approach

A cross-national, comparative approach to social mobility can contribute effectively to our understanding of society. A study of mobility in a particular nation, by itself, cannot reveal whether a rate of mobility is high or low. Benchmarks are necessary. It is, of course, possible to develop models of mobility – such as those suggested by Glass *et al.* (1954), and Lipset and Zetterberg (1954) – but these are not abstractions drawn from experience. With comparative data, it becomes possible to assert that the highest rate of mobility that has been attained in a given type of economic and social order is of a particular level, which may be deemed as one of the benchmarks of mobility. It may be used, then, in viewing rates of mobility in a society of similar or different characteristics.

More important, perhaps, is the possibility that comparative mobility analysis can lead to an isolation of the significant variables affecting mobility. The comparative method *approximates* an experimental method. Does a particular form and level of economic activity produce higher mobility than another? Are there significant differences in rates of mobility in nations of similar economic development so that non-economic factors must be introduced to explain them? The possibility then emerges after the variables are isolated of developing a general theory of mobility.

A comparative approach can also be important in analysing the consequences of mobility. Where rates of mobility are similar, do similar attitudinal complexes emerge or do additional cultural factors intrude? Lipset and Bendix (1959), for example, have suggested the substitutability of religious faith for class consciousness among 'the depressed and the failures'.

Finally, comparative studies clarify the kind of data which are most useful for analysis and turn us back to the initial issue in the study of mobility, the collection of quality data. [. . .]

Basic data

This monograph does not represent primary research. It is an effort to utilize available primary studies for the eighteen nations where data are available.

The unit of the comparisons is basically though not exclusively the nation. [. . .] For four nations, data are reported on a city (in the case of Belgium, two towns); following the suggestion of the sub-committee on Social Stratification and Mobility of the International Sociological Association, I have included these data because of the possibility that they may be representative to some degree of the national facts. In a fifth nation, we have also deviated from the practice of a national representative sample: for the Soviet Union the only available mobility information for the nation as a whole is the *émigré* study of the Russian Research Center of Harvard University. National samples and a Hungarian census are employed in the other thirteen nations.

To remind the reader of the special character of the data in these five nations, a reference is usually made in parentheses, following the name of the country, to the city, e.g. Australia (Melbourne), or to the unusual source, i.e. USSR (*émigrés*). In two nations, the United States and France, two studies are used, and they are marked as I and II as are the two town studies of Belgium. How much confidence we can have in these more than twenty reports on eighteen nations is unclear; unfortunately, the fact that they are used evidences more their availability than their validity. Comments on the studies will be found at the end of this section.

Only two-step intergenerational (father–son) mobility is studied. The outflow from a stratum is the concern; in a separate publication I intend dealing with inflow mobility and some of its correlations.

The procedure of organization has been to utilize standard outflow tables, indicating percentages of a set of strata who have moved to a specified set of strata. The language of strata and stratum may be confusing here. A stratum or occupational category or group (e.g. professional and technical; unskilled workers) are combined for purposes of comparison, as discussed later, with other similar categories into strata (manual; nonmanual; elite).

The time of the studies vary, although all are post-Second World War studies with the exception of the report on the USSR. This report is as of 1940; the other reports range from 1946 to the middle 50s. Thus, there is no exact comparability in time.

Time and age

The attempt has been made to gain some similarity in the ages of sons studied in different nations by using data on a cross-section of all sons. This decision was made because only in a few studies were age-graded data available. Consequently, conformity was maximized by taking the broadest grouping of sons. In some cases, this is not possible; for example, in the Inkeles–Bauer (1959) treatment of their data on Soviet *émigrés*, they have used only those between the ages twenty-one and forty.

The age for which father's occupation was ascertained was unspecified in some investigations, and the respondent was asked for father's occupation without any further elaboration; in others his last occupation was asked for; in one, it was asked at the age of sixty. Thus, we do not have precise comparability in the father's occupation, if intragenerational mobility has been important in the father's generation in the middle and late years of individuals' careers. I would not credit much distortion to this element.

The factor of son's age is more important, and it would be well to develop age-specific intergenerational mobility data (which would also be useful for trend analysis). The lack of comparability here may be important if the age profiles of societies differ.

Types of comparisons

Despite all the difficulties with the manual/nonmanual classification, it was decided to concentrate on comparisons of this sort. The lively interest in mobility still largely centers on crossing from manual to nonmanual work even if the line between them is wavy and changing. Downward movement of the nonmanuals as well as upward movement of the manual received special attention. [. . .]

The nonmanual category refers to all white-collar, professional and business occupations regardless of level; the middle-class strata designation applies to those in the nonmanual strata who are not in the elite occupations. Skilled workers have been placed in the working class except that, where possible, self-employed skilled workers have been placed in the nonmanual and middle-class categories. [. . .]

Although I personally dislike the term 'elite', it has been employed in the monograph because of its popularity to refer to the occupations of highest standing – usually the higher business and independent professional occupations. Frequently it is possible to note the occupational grouping with the highest standing, and the grouping with somewhat less standing but of distinctly higher standing than other occupational groupings. The first is referred to as Elite I, the second as Elite II. Special attention is paid to these groupings because of the general concern with movement into and out of top-level occupations. [. . .]

Some limitations

Even a slight familiarity with studies of mobility in more than one nation reveals the difficulties in attempting to make comparisons. The pitfalls are many – who is studied (males or males and females); alignment and realignment of occupational categories to permit comparison; the ranking of occupations. The difficulties of a single study are compounded when it is compared with another research endeavor. [. . .]

Limited by the availability of information, bound by a particular orientation to the organization of data, the monograph can at best offer only a rough indication of the nature of mobility in a number of industrial nations taken as a whole. Hopefully, its conclusions will be soon superseded as more studies are pursued on a national basis but with an international orientation in mind.

We are prisoners in many if not most cases of the coding and categorizing of the original researchers and can only recall the particular practices followed in assessing whether a difference among nations is a basic one or an artefact of the investigational procedures. [. . .]

Their fathers' sons – 1

[. . .] As will be revealed in the following analysis, rates of mobility differ markedly when varied modes of analysis are employed. In constructing rates of mobility, it should not be ignored that different types of rates shed light more on one aspect or another – processes, causes, consequences – of mobility. A summary index, for example, which corrects for variations in occupational distribution between fathers and sons may be helpful in clarifying causes of mobility and in refining the rate, but may be less useful in analysing political consequences of mobility. The rationale here has been to select indicators from the perspective of their political consequences for particular strata, particularly the manual and working classes.

No one rate can be said to express *the* rate of mobility of a nation. Rather, it is perhaps most accurate to say – 'Nation A has a higher rate of mobility *of this type* than does Nation B; Nation B has a higher rate *of this type*.'

A Manual to nonmanual

In many studies, urban workers are included with farm workers and cannot be separated out. This mixed category we have termed 'manual' to distinguish it from the 'working classes', which exclude farm workers and purport to represent those nonagricultural employees who work with their 'hands'. In Table 1 data are reported of the upward mobility of sons of fathers in the 'manual' and in the 'working-class' category.

Table 1 Nonmanual sons of manual and working-class fathers

	1 Manual into nonmanual (%)	2 Working classes into nonmanual (%)
I National data		
Denmark	24·1	[a]
Finland	11	[a]
France I	30·1	34·9
France II	29·6	32·9
Great Britain	24·8	[a]
Hungary	14·5	21·8
Italy	8·5	[a]
Japan	23·7	[a]
Netherlands	19·6	[a]
Norway	23·2	25·8
Puerto Rico	14·3	18·7
Sweden	25·5	29·3
USA I	28·8	[a]
USA II	28·7	[a]
West Germany	20·0	21·2
II Urban data		
Australia (Melbourne)	24·1	[a]
Belgium I (St-Martens-Latem)	5·7	6·4
Belgium II (Mont-Saint-Guibert)	30·9	[a]
Brazil (Sao Paulo)	29·4	[a]
India (Poona)	27·3	[a]
III Special data		
USSR (*émigrés*)	[a]	34·9

[a] Unavailable

Upward mobility for these two groups is defined as crossing into non-manual work, which includes all white-collar work, whether as employees, independent practitioners, and the self-employed in business.[1] Independent farmers are not included so that some upward movement of the manuals is excluded since movement into independent farming status is upward mobility for all who originate in farm-laboring families, and for some whose fathers were working men. As pointed out earlier, the mobility within the manual strata (e.g. from unskilled to skilled or semiskilled) is ignored; obscured as well is the lack of consistency in rates within the classification –

1. In some nations, artisans who are self-employed are classified as workers and were not reclassifiable because of coding procedures.

skilled, for example, having higher upward rates than farm workers or unskilled.

Column 1 shows that in France about 30 per cent of the sons of manual fathers ended up in nonmanual occupations. Among the nations, this is the highest rate, while the lowest rate for nations is Italy's 8·5 per cent. The range, then, is considerable. Almost as many nations have rates under 20 per cent as have rates over 20 per cent, although if we include the city data, there is an increase in the number of nations in the over 20 per cent group. Italy, Finland, Hungary, Puerto Rico and Belgium I lag behind all the others in having rates below 15 per cent. Thus, about one quarter of the nations are distinctly low.

The United States does not have the highest rate, which is that of France (and Belgium II); the differences among the high-rate nations – France, USA, Belgium II, Brazil (Sao Paulo), India (Poona) – are minor, so that we have a group of nations with a decidedly higher rate than the rest.[2]

B Working classes into nonmanual

Column 2 of Table 1 presents the data on working-class mobility into nonmanual occupations for the smaller number of nations where data are available for the more traditional occupations of skilled, semiskilled and unskilled nonagricultural labor.

The comparison between columns 1 and 2 is instructive: in all cases, working-class mobility is greater than manual. The greatest difference is found in Hungary (7·3 per cent). Only in West Germany and Belgium I is the difference of the magnitude of 1 per cent; in the other nations, 3 per cent or 4 per cent is more typical. These findings are not surprising since it is well known that it is more difficult to enter white-collar work from a rural background than from urban origins. The order of differences suggests that if we add 3–4 per cent to figures for manual mobility into nonmanual work, we shall not be far off the actual working-class upward mobility.

The range of variation in column 2 is less than that in column 1; this might be due to the unavailability of working-class figures for the nations with the lowest rate of manual into nonmanual movement. (Of the four countries, excluding Belgium I, with the lowest rates of upward manual movement, two of them, Hungary and Puerto Rico, show, however, large jumps when working-class upward mobility is studied.)

France and the USSR (*émigrés*) show the highest rate of working-class up-mobility, followed closely by Sweden. The other five nations string out

2. I had attempted to calculate a manual rate for the USSR (*émigrés*) by including peasants with those in working-class occupations. On this unsatisfactory basis, which has been dropped, the USSR (*émigrés*) manual rate would have been 28·4 per cent.

after the top three with only Belgium I (6·4 per cent) and Hungary (18·7 per cent) below the 20 per cent mark.

What can be concluded about overall upward mobility from manual and working-class occupations?

1 The United States does not have the highest upward mobility rate out of manual/working-class occupations. France, the Soviet Union and the United States are rather similar.

2 There is a fair clustering of nations – nine of the eighteen nations (Belgium counted only once despite the two discrepant reports) range between 24 per cent and 31 per cent in the manual analysis and four of eight between 24 per cent and 35 per cent in the working-class tabulation.

3 Several nations have distinctly lower rates of mobility than other nations for which data are available. These are Finland, Italy, Hungary (for the manual category only), Puerto Rico (for the manual category only) and Belgium I.

4 Whether industrial nations can be considered to have a similar rate of movement of manual/working class into nonmanual depends upon the criterion employed and whether one wishes to emphasize similarity or diversity. The Soviet Union and French working-class figures are almost twice that of Puerto Rico, but the latter is not highly industrialized. If we exclude Puerto Rico, Hungary and Belgium I from the working-class comparisons, we have a range from 21·2 (West Germany) to the 35 per cent of USSR and France I. The manual range, excluding Italy, Finland, Belgium I, Puerto Rico and Hungary, is from 19·6 per cent (Netherlands, probably too high a figure for this nation) to 30+ per cent (France I, Belgium II).

Are these ranges narrow or great? Since the studies are not strictly comparable in many ways, some variations would occur because of this situation alone. The exclusion of the nations mentioned may be defended on the basis that they have low industrialization (although Italy at least was not less industrialized than some of the nations included). Consequently, on the basis of the overall rate of mobility of manual and, to a lesser extent, working-class sons into all nonmanual occupations, I do not feel that the conclusion of Lipset and Zetterberg about the similarity of overall upward rates is misleading, although the exclusion of several nations must be noted. But if all national data are utilized, then the similarity is much less striking. It is important to note that manual sons→nonmanual occupations is only one way of studying mobility, and we shall have to study a number of other possibilities before we can reach any judgement as to the similarity of mobility rates *in general* in different nations. If one emphasizes variations within the array, as I would prefer, then the following clusters seem to exist: the high nations of France, USA, USSR; Scandinavian nations (excluding Finland), Great Britain and Japan; West Germany and the Netherlands; the low nations (Italy, Finland, Hungary and Puerto Rico).

5 Because of their deviance, the very low nations (Italy, Finland, Hungary and Puerto Rico) and the very high (France and the USSR) would be especially useful to study further in terms of historical and cultural factors. The big gap between working-class and manual rates in Hungary deserves separate study.

C Nonmanual to manual

We assume for purposes of Table 2 that movement into manual work is downward mobility for all who originate in nonmanual occupations. This assumption is especially dubious at the crossing over from lower-level nonmanual to skilled manual work. In this emphasis on the so-called 'heads/hands' movement, we are ignoring downward movement *within* the nonmanual occupation. While we take up some of this movement when we discuss movement from the elites into the middle classes, we shall not be analysing movement within the varied categories grouped together as nonmanual.

The willingness to discuss movement of nonmanuals into manual and working-class occupations arises from the great concern with the presumably political implications of this movement. The economic differentials involved in such movement may indeed be slim and often may involve an income gain, but even those most aware of these discrepancies have an interest in this kind of movement.

The most startling element in Table 2 is the fact that in three nations more than 40 per cent of sons of nonmanual families end up in manual occupations. While the Netherlands figure may result in part from the difficulties of the coding of the categories, this is unlikely to be so for Puerto Rico and Great Britain. Certainly, the differential economic and social effects of manual/nonmanual may differ widely from nation to nation, but earlier estimates have not prepared us for such a drastic change in social fortunes. The relation of the drop from nonmanual into manual occupations to concern with social status is a question that immediately arises: is it true that the easier the drop, the more the concern with status and social distance.[3]

Almost equally striking is the range between the USSR's 15 per cent and the highs of Great Britain, Netherlands and Puerto Rico. (The two Belgian

3. This hypothesis is not incompatible with Svalastoga and Carlsson's suggestion (1961, p. 43) that low mobility rates and extreme social distance go together if the low mobility rates refer to manual into nonmanual movement.

Table 2 Manual/working-class sons of nonmanual fathers

	1 Nonmanual into manual (%)	2 Nonmanual into working-classes (%)
I National data		
Denmark	36·8	a
Finland	24·0	a
France I	20·5	18·2
France II	26·9	25·9
Great Britain	42·1	a
Hungary	27·5	25·8
Italy	34·4	a
Japan	29·7	a
Netherlands	43·2	a
Norway	28·6	27·9
Puerto Rico	42·7	35·6
Sweden	27·7	25·7
USA I	19·7	18·6
USA II	22·6	a
West Germany	29·0	28·2
II Urban data		
Australia (Melbourne)	37·1	a
Belgium I (St-Martens-Latem)	8·9	7·1
Belgium II (Mont-Saint-Guibert)	3·4	a
Brazil (Sao Paulo)	18·5	a
India (Poona)	26·9	a
III Special data		
USSR (*émigrés*)	15·0	12·8

[a] Unavailable

studies, which differed markedly on upward mobility, show great similarity in downward mobility.) There is no particular clustering: the three categories of under 25 per cent, between 25 and 35 per cent, and over 35 per cent have fairly equal number of nations. While twelve nations are under 30 per cent and six above, three of the former hover about the 30 per cent mark.

D Nonmanual into working classes

Only in the case of Puerto Rico does restriction to nonagricultural 'hands' employment make a sizeable difference (7·1 per cent). In the other nations, the restriction in analysing downward movement involves 2·3 per cent or less. Nonmanual downward movement is largely into industrial occupations rather than farm labor.

The Soviet Union has the extremely low rate of one of eight sons of nonmanual origin terminating in working-class occupations. The USA and France (an average of the two figures) hover about the figure of one of five nonmanual sons, while for Norway and Sweden, one of four nonmanual sons have working-class occupations.

While we do not show the data here, a substantial part of the nonmanual into working-class and manual employment is into the skilled labor category. And the overwhelming rate of all nonmanual movements into manual is from the lower end of the nonmanual category (e.g. clerks). Nonetheless, the size of 'downward' movement raises a number of questions: among others are the purposes and practices of educational systems, the forces producing fluidity in society, and the character of reactions to downward mobility in societies where it is frequent and where it is infrequent.

E A typology of manual/nonmanual movement

Bringing together rates of movement of manual into nonmanual, and nonmanual into manual movement in Table 3 permits some very interesting comparisons. (Use of data on movement into and out of the working classes would not have a pronounced effect on the comparisons. The manual category is used so that all the nations can be included in the analysis. The USSR (émigrés) figure for upward mobility is, however, for the working classes.)

In only five of seventeen nations (omitting Belgium where the two studies are inconsistent), does up-mobility exceed down-mobility. These five nations (France, USA, Brazil (Sao Paulo), India (Poona) and USSR (émigrés)) are all characterized by relatively high up-mobility, but in not all nations with high up-mobility does this latter rate exceed the downward movement of nonmanuals into manual strata. *Downward movement is a more compelling fact about mobility than upward!* In Italy, Puerto Rico, Netherlands, Finland and, to a lesser extent, Hungary and Great Britain, the downward rate is considerably in excess of the upward. (The Dutch rate is probably high because of the coding problems of the data.)

Perhaps the most interesting aspect of manual movement into nonmanual occupations and nonmanual movement into manual occupations is their complexity. Some nations are high on one, low or middle on another; others have a different pattern. A fourfold table makes possible the

Table 3 Nonmanual into manual and manual into nonmanual

	1 Nonmanual into manual (%)	2 Manual into nonmanual (%)
I National data		
Denmark	+36·8	+24·1
Finland	−24·0	−11·0
France I	−20·5	+30·1
France II	+26·9	+29·6
Great Britain	+42·1	+24·8
Hungary	+27·5	−14·5
Italy	+34·4	−8·5
Japan	+29·7	−23·7
Netherlands	+43·2	−19·6
Norway	+28·6	−23·2
Puerto Rico	+42·7	−14·3
Sweden	+27·7	+25·5
USA I	−19·7	+28·8
USA II	−22·6	+28·7
West Germany	+29·0	−20·0
II Urban data		
Australia (Melbourne)	+37·1	+24·1
Belgium I (St-Martens-Latem)	−8·9	−5·7
Belgium II (Mont-Saint-Guibert)	−3·4	+30·9
Brazil (Sao Paulo)	−18·5	+29·4
India (Poona)	+26·9	+27·3
III Special data		
USSR (*émigrés*)	−15·0	+34·9[a]

[a] This figure is for the working classes

setting up of types or patterns of movement. If we dichotomize movement as high (over 24 per cent) or low (24 per cent or less), we have these four types of pattern:

Table 4 Patterns of up and down mobility

Nonmanual into manual	*Manual into nonmanual*	
	(*High*) +	(*Low*) −
(high) +	++ (A)	+−(B)
(low)−	−+(C)	−−(D)

Cell A represents a nation with high upward and downward mobility; Cell C, one with low rates of movement of nonmanuals into manual occupations and high rates of manual movement into nonmanual activity. (The plus or minus in Table 3 indicates whether the rate is high or low.)

Below are grouped all the nations under the patterns which typify them:

A High downward nonmanual, high upward manual ($+ +$)
Denmark
France II
Great Britain
Sweden
Australia (Melbourne)
India (Poona)

B High downward nonmanual, low upward manual ($+ -$)
Hungary
Italy
Japan
Netherlands
Norway
Puerto Rico
West Germany

C Low downward nonmanual, high upward manual ($- +$)
France I
USA I and II
Belgium II (Mont-Saint-Guibert)
Brazil (Sao Paulo)
USSR (*émigrés*)

D Low downward nonmanual, low upward manual ($- -$)
Finland
Belgium I (St-Martens-Latem)

With different cutting-off points, there would be a shifting in the nations found under each pattern; Britain and Denmark, for example, just fall into pattern A: Japan in pattern B. Whatever cutting-off points are used, the four logical types[4] would exist and would likely have empirical counterparts, as occurs with the patterns that our cutting-off points produce.

Is each pattern related to economic variables like gross national product, gross national product *per capita*, rate of growth in gross national product,

4. Employing a greater variety of classifications than 'high' or 'low' is, of course, possible and would produce additional logical, although not necessarily empirical, types.

or are social variables and historical experiences important in producing the pattern? I have begun to try to answer this question (Miller, 1960) by following a suggestion of Arnold S. Feldman to relate a variety of economic data, prepared by Simon Kuznets, to the patterns. This is only one approach to the fascinating issue of the *causes* of differences in mobility rates, a relatively unexplored problem.

The four patterns of mobility outlined here strongly suggest that rather than omnibus statements on gross similarities or differences in some overall rate of mobility, we need to develop explanations of *each* of these four different patterns in terms of their causes, processes and consequences.

To sum up, asymmetry exists among the mobility indicators: high rates of up-mobility may be associated with low or high rates of down-mobility. High rates of down-mobility may be associated with high or low rates of up-mobility. To describe the rate of upward mobility in a nation does not

Table 5 Inequality of opportunity

	1 Nonmanual into nonmanual (stability) (%)	2 Manual into nonmanual (%)	3 Index of inequality 1/2 (%)
Australia (Melbourne)	62·9	24·1	261
Belgium I (St-Martens-Latem)	91·1	5·7	1598
Belgium II (Mont-Saint-Guibert)	96·6	30·9	313
Brazil (Sao Paulo)	81·5	29·4	277
Denmark	63·2	24·1	262
Finland	76·0	11·0	691
France I	79·5	30·1	264
France II	73·1	29·6	247
Great Britain	57·9	24·8	234
Hungary	72·5	14·5	500
India (Poona)	73·1	27·3	268
Italy	63·5	8·5	747
Japan	70·3	23·7	297
Netherlands	56·8	19·6	290
Norway	71·4	23·2	308
Puerto Rico	57·3	14·3	401
Sweden	72·3	25·5	284
USA I	80·3	28·8	279
USA II	77·4	28·7	270
USSR (émigrés)	85·0	34·9	244
West Germany	71·0	20·0	355

automatically give us an estimate of down-mobility. *The varied connections of upward and downward mobility form the most important new element in the present report.*

F Inequality of opportunity

In Table 5 the ability of nonmanual sons to stay in the nonmanual levels is compared with the ability of manual sons to move into these levels. The figures of column 3 are an index of inequality since they reflect the relative advantage of nonmanual sons over manual sons in having nonmanual positions.

The Belgium I (St-Martens-Latem) index (far different from Belgium II) is the highest by a tremendous margin; the Italian and Finnish figures are next highest in showing the advantage of middle-class offspring. The Hungarian index of 500 per cent is the only other one that is higher than 401 per cent (Puerto Rico). The other nations are mainly between 230 and 355 per cent, demonstrating a considerable degree of cluster.

In no nation is the advantage of middle-class sons less than two to one (Great Britain: 234 per cent). The most common advantage is between two and a half to one and three to one. The closeness of Denmark, France, Great Britain, Sweden, USA and USSR (*émigrés*) is particularly striking. [. . .]

Their fathers' sons–II
Movement from Elites I and II

Table 6 presents data on movement out of Elite I and II combined; nations are grouped into four categories on the basis of size of Elite I and II. Column 1, reporting percentages of sons who are stable, shows considerable overlap among the four groupings. In group A, with the smallest Elites I and II, we find a considerable range. Elite sons in India (Poona) are very stable, while this is much less true in Denmark where more than two-thirds move out. Among group B nations, France II evidences high stability while Italy, as we would expect from the previous tables, has a high rate of exit from the elites. In group D, the Soviet Union (*émigrés*) Elite I and II sons have a better chance of retaining their positions than do their counterparts in the USA. Overall, in five of the fourteen nations (averaging France I and II) sons are more likely to drop out of the two upper tiers of society than to stay in them.

The mobile elite sons are more likely to move into the middle classes than into manual or agricultural pursuits. Denmark has much more outflow to the middle classes than does West Germany and India (Poona) in group A; indeed, it has the highest rate of movement from the elites into the middle classes. Only in India (Poona), Puerto Rico and the Netherlands is move-

Table 6 Movement from Elite I and II

	1 No move-ment out of elites (%)	2 Into middle classes (%)	3 Into work-ing classes (%)	4 Into manual (%)	5 Into inde-pendent farmers (%)	6 Into farm worker (%)	7 Manual into Elite I and II (%)
A under 4·6%							
Belgium I (St-Martens-Latem)	58·8	41·2	0·0	0·0	a	0·0	0·0
Denmark	31·6	57·9	a	10·5	a	a	1·1
India (Poona)	83·9	4·4	a	11·7	a	a	1·4
West Germany	56·4	27·1	14·1	14·1	2·4	0·0	1·5
B 6·5–8·5%							
France I	48·7	31·2	8·5	9·0	11·1	0·5	3·5
France II	73·5	11·6	10·7	11·6	3·3	0·8	1·6
Great Britain	44·8	37·3	a	17·9	a	a	2·2
Italy	26·0	37·5	a	36·5	a	a	1·5
Sweden	55·3	32·2	9·2	9·2	3·3	0·0	3·5
C 10–15%							
Japan	38·5	34·6	a	26·9	a	a	7·0
Netherlands	53·2	22·5	a	24·3	a	a	6·6
Puerto Rico	35·3	16·2	34·5	42·2	6·3	7·7	8·6
D over 15%							
Brazil (Sao Paulo)	71·2	27·1	a	1·7	a	a	5·3
USA I	52·6	28·1	14·0	15·8	3·5	1·8	7·8
USSR (*émigrés*)	65·8	17·1	13·2	17·1	a	4·0	14·5[b]

[a] Unavailable
[b] This figure is for the working classes

ment into the manual strata greater than movement into the middle classes. In USSR (*émigrés*) and in Italy the percentages into manual and middle classes are about the same.[5] Only in Puerto Rico (and in France I) is movement into independent farming of any consequence.

Despite the fact that elite out-mobility to the middle classes usually exceeds that to the manual strata, the latter rates are quite high. Italy and Puerto Rico, with high outflow rates, have the highest (and rather astonishing) rates of movement into the manual strata (long-range downward mobility). In the case of Puerto Rico more than four out of ten elite sons

5. France I and II figures are largely ignored because of the variations between them for movement out of the elites.

terminate in the manual level, and in Italy more than one out of three. India (Poona), with its low rate of outflow, has the bulk of it into the manual strata. The USA and USSR (*émigrés*) have very similar movement into the manual strata – about one-sixth of the sons find themselves in the manual category. The bulk of the USA I out-movement is to the middle class while the less mobile USSR (*émigrés*) elite moves equally to the middle classes and to the manual. Only in Brazil (Sao Paulo) is long-distance mobility unlikely for elite sons. No other nation has less than 9 per cent movement into the manual level. In four nations more than 24 per cent of elite sons make this move.

The initial thrust of the data is to confirm the notion of 'the circulation of the elite'. Certainly, elite sons have no firm perch in the upper tiers of society, supporting the conjecture of 'shirtsleeves to shirtsleeves in three generations'. But the slippage of elite sons does not mean necessarily that sons of other strata are moving into the elite in any great numbers, for the changing size of the elites and demographic differentials may be important here. An outflow table by itself is not sufficient, and column 7 has been appended to provide an estimate of flow to the elites from the manual strata.

A simple comparison of columns 1 and 7 shows that the chances of an elite son's staying in the upper levels are much greater than those of a manual son's rising to the elite level. Only in Puerto Rico is the opportunity of elite sons only four times greater than it is for a manual son. In all other nations, the opportunity is considerably greater – in India (Poona), for every manual son who moves into elite position, seventy elite sons are able to maintain themselves in elite occupations. In West Germany almost forty elite sons terminate in the elites for every manual son.

The larger elites have smaller ratios of comparative movement into the elites of elite sons and of manual sons, but they are still high. Especially interesting are the USA I and the USSR (*émigrés*) figures. Elite sons have an almost sevenfold advantage over manual sons in USA I, while USSR (*émigrés*) elite sons have a four-and-a-half advantage over manual sons. The relative fluidity of the USSR in these figures is probably overstated, for the *émigré* manual figure is actually for the working classes and does not include agricultural workers as does the USA I figure.

Comparing 100 per cent minus column 1, to obtain total outflow from the elite, with column 7, manual movement to the elites, gives a partial estimate of the variation between inflow and outflow. In some nations, it is high in both respects, in others, low, and in still others, mixed.

To systematize the data, movement out of the elites has been categorized as high if column 1 is under 50 per cent; if column 7 is over 3·5 per cent manual movement to elites is termed high. In Table 7, the nations are organized into a fourfold table showing the various patterns of up-and-down-mobility to and from the elites.

All four possible cells have empirical counterparts so that we have actual cases of high out-movement from the elites and low in-movement to the elites (cell 2) and low out-movement and high in-movement (cell 3). The nations with the larger elites are likely to be in the latter cell. Cell 1 comes

Table 7 Patterns of elite mobility

Elite I and II to all destinations	Manual into Elite I and II	
	(High)+	(Low)—
(high)+	++(A)	+—(B)
	Japan	Denmark
	Puerto Rico	Great Britain
		Italy
(low)—	—+(C)	——(D)
	Netherlands	West Germany
	USA I	Sweden
	USSR (*émigrés*)	India (Poona)
	Brazil (Saõ Paulo)	Belgium I (St-Martens-Latem)
		France I and II

closest to the notion of 'the circulation of elites', since there is high exit and access to elites, probably indicating rapid economic change. Only two nations (Japan and Puerto Rico) are found here. Cell 2 is unusual – high out-movement but little in-movement, perhaps indicating changes in the nature of elites and/or stagnation. Cell 3, low outflow and high inflow, is also intriguing, particularly since it includes USA I and USSR (*émigrés*), and it would be interesting to compare rates of economic growth of cell 1 nations with cell 3 countries. Cell 4, low inflow and outflow, indicates the existence of marked barriers in West Germany, Sweden, Belgium I (St-Martens-Latem), France (an average of I and II) and India (Poona). The asymmetrical nature of mobility is again supported; the intriguing question is, of course, what produces these patterns. [. . .]

Indices of association

All of the preceding comparisons have been of the crudest kind; in particular, they have been marked by lack of attention to changes in the occupational distributions (or opportunities) between the fathers' and sons' generation. The index of association as developed by Glass and his associates is one way of allowing for these occupational changes. A figure of 1 indicates perfect mobility, that the sons are proportionally represented

Table 8 Indices of association

	1 Elite I and II	2 Middle classes	3 Non- manual	4 Working classes	5 Manual
Australia (Melbourne)	a	a	1·377	a	1·389
Belgium I (St-Martens- Latem)	17·893	3·278	3·187	1·318	1·606
Belgium II (Mont-Saint- Guibert)	a		1·527	a	1·381
Brazil (Sao Paulo)	4·179	1·613	1·548	a	1·487
Denmark	9·559	1·485	1·512	a	1·304
Finland	a	a	3·855	a	1·595
France I	5·714	1·821	1·783	2·317	2·335
France II	8·378	1·811	1·878	1·791	1·611
Great Britain	5·981	1·442	1·562	a	1·195
Hungary	a	a	4·101	1·566	1·537
India (Poona)	10·663	1·672	1·586	a	1·284
Italy	3·931	2·725	2·293	a	1·281
Japan	3·277	2·179	1·944	a	1·195
Netherlands	4·805	1·985	1·839	a	1·160
Norway	a	a	2·029	1·518	1·567
Puerto Rico I	2·561	3·100	2·340	1·506	1·157
Puerto Rico II	2·427	2·541	2·154	1·338	1·072
Sweden	8·122	1·846	2·203	1·287	1·197
USA I	3·295	1·645	1·535	a	1·462
USA II	a	a	1·585	a	1·280
USSR (émigrés)	2·155	1·672	1·488	a	1·544
West Germany	11·087	1·963	1·978	1·413	1·389

[a] Unavailable

in the fathers' occupation; a figure less than 1 indicates less than proportional representation, while the usual results, those above 1, show that sons are over-represented in their fathers' occupational level.

As we would expect, sons are more likely to be over-represented in the Elite I and II strata than in any other strata.[6] In no nation is the index less than 1; the lowest figures are for USSR (émigrés) and Puerto Rico. The

6. Two figures are presented for Puerto Rico because in this nation respondents were asked the occupations of siblings as well as their father. For each father, the distribution of occupations of all his sons is given. Each row of fathers has two totals: the number of fathers and the greater number of sons. Arnold Feldman, in an unpublished note, has remarked on the ambiguity of the Rogoff analysis which does not note these two possibilities. Since both sets of information are available, indices of association have been computed using (1) total number of sons for each occupational grouping of fathers and (2) total number of fathers in the grouping. The differences are not great.

USSR (*émigrés*) index is at first surprising because of the limited outflow from the elite that earlier tables showed, but allowing for changing size of the elites, as the index of association does, indicates that elite sons are not especially prone to stay in the elites. The highest indices are found in Belgium I, Denmark, India (Poona) and West Germany, all of which have small elites.

The middle classes have a much smaller range between the 3·278 of Belgium I and the 1·442 of Great Britain. A number of other nations are low (e.g., USA I, India (Poona), Brazil (Sao Paulo), USSR (*émigrés*)). Interesting is the big drop between the elite and the middle classes for those nations having a high index of association for the former (e.g. West Germany, Belgium I, Denmark, India (Poona) and Sweden). The middle classes have much less occupational inheritance, allowing for structural changes, than the elites, indicating the much greater stability of elite sons than middle-class sons.

The nonmanual indices show a much smaller range than the elite figures but larger than any other category. The lowest indices are the 1·377 of Australia (Melbourne) and the 1·488 of the USSR (*émigrés*); the highest are found in Hungary, 4·101, and in Finland, 3·855. Most of the indices are under 2. The differences between the indices of association for USSR (*émigrés*) and the USA are smaller for the nonmanual strata (and the middle classes) than they are for the elites.

The working-class index of association shows an exceedingly small range: the low are 1·287 in Sweden and 1·318 in Belgium I; the highest figures are for France I and II, 2·317 and 1·791 respectively. Next highest is 1·566 in Hungary. The indices for this category show less variation than any other with the unsurprising exception of the manual.

The manual strata indices vary from 1·072 in Puerto Rico I, 1·157 in Puerto Rico II and 1·160 in Australia (Melbourne) to the high of 2·335 in France I, 1·611 in France II, and 1·606 in Belgium I. Five of the indices are less than 1·200. The manual strata have very low inheritance when we allow for changing economic opportunities. The relation between manual and working-class indices is unclear: in four nations the manual indices are lower than those for the working class, while in two the manual indices are higher. (France I and II are inconsistent.)

In order to make clearer any pattern that may exist among the indices of a nation, each column has been divided into high and low values.[7] Then,

7. For elites, those under 4·8 have been termed low, those above, high; for middle classes, the dividing line has been 1·7; for nonmanual, 1·9 and for manual, 1·3. Where two figures for a nation occur, they have been averaged; in the main, convergence of the two estimates has been considerable so that averaging has not changed in many situations what the rating would be if either of the two estimates had been used.

each nation has been rated to see what degree of consistency exists in the level of its indices of association. Five categories have been used: all high; very high (only one low); all low; very low (only one high) and indeterminate (all others). Table 9 summarizes the results of this classification.

Table 9 Consistency of indices of association

A All high	C All low	E Indeterminate
Belgium I	Brazil (Sao Paulo)	Australia (Melbourne)
Hungary		Belgium II
Norway	D Very low	Denmark
West Germany	Great Britain	Italy
	India (Poona)	Japan
B Very high	USA	Netherlands
Finland	USSR (émigrés)	Puerto Rico
France		Sweden

Almost as many nations have no definite pattern (E) as have a discernible one (A, B, C, D); the number of high nations (A, B) is almost as great as the number of low nations (C, D). The similarity of patterns of the USA and USSR (émigrés) is again evidenced in D.

Interpretations and conclusions

National profiles

The data presented above have been complex and variegated; the only attempts at synthesis have been the two sets of typologies (relating rates of manual movement into nonmanual levels with nonmanual movement into manual and exit from the elites with entrance into the elites). A further attempt at synthesis has been made in Table 10 which brings into one table some of the more important indices which have been employed in the study. By looking across the rows, we obtain a brief profile of each nation.

The Table shows, for example, that Great Britain has high up-mobility of the manual, high down-mobility of the nonmanual, low long-range up-mobility of the manual, low long-range up-mobility of the nonmanual, high movement out of the elites, high down-mobility of the middle classes (relative to the up-mobility of the same strata), high long-run down-mobility of elites and low indices of association for the various strata. It is possible from such information to develop new indices of total movement, of consistency of direction of movement and of distance of mobility by combining two or more columns.

What is particularly noteworthy is the close parallel of findings for USA, USSR (émigrés) and Brazil (Sao Paulo). The only divergence among them is in regard to column 7, elite I and II into manual (the low of the

Table 10 National profiles

	1 Manual into non-manual	2 Non-manual into manual	3 Manual into Elite I and II	4 Middle classes into Elite I and II	5 Total movement out of Elite I and II	6 Middle classes downward to upward movement	7 Elite I and II into manual	8 Index of association
Australia (Melbourne)	H	H	a	a	a	a	a	I
Belgium I (St-Martens-Latem)	L	L	L	L	L	L	L	H
Belgium II (Mont-Saint-Guibert)	H	L	a	a	a	a	a	l
Brazil (Sao Paulo)	H	L	H	H	L	I	L	L
Denmark	H	H	L	L	H	H	L	I
Finland	L	H	a	a	a	a	a	H
France I (Bresard)	H	L	L	L	H	L	L	H
France II (Desabie)	H	H	L	L	L	H	L	H
Great Britain	H	H	L	L	H	H	H	L
Hungary	L	H	a	a	a	a	a	H
India (Poona)	H	H	L	L	L	H	L	L
Italy	L	H	L	L	H	H	H	I
Japan	L	H	H	H	H	L	H	I
Netherlands	L	H	H	L	L	H	H	I
Norway	L	H	a	a	a	a	a	H
Puerto Rico	L	H	H	H	H	L	H	I
Sweden	H	H	L	H	L	L	L	I
USA I (Centers)	H	L	H	H	L	I	L	L
USA II (SRC)	H	L	a	a	a	a	a	L
USSR (émigrés)	H	L	H	H	L	L	H	L
West Germany	L	H	L	L	L	H	L	H

Columns 1 and 2 under 24: L; over 24: H. Column 3 under 3·6: L; over 3·6: H. Column 4 under 15·1: L; over 15·1: H. Column 5 under 50% outflow: L; over 50% outflow: H. Column 6 under 25%: L; over 25%: H. Column 7 under 15·8%: L; over 15·8%: H. H = high; L = low; I = inconsistent.

USA is very close to the breaking point). This summary strengthens the earlier references to the similarities of movement in the USA and USSR (*émigrés*). It is an interesting pattern of high upward short- and long-distance manual mobility; high upward mobility of the middle classes and relatively low downward movement; low downward motion of the non-manual and the elites; low occupational inheritance with variation among the three in extent of long-range downward mobility of the elites. It is thus a general pattern of upward mobility with limited downward mobility.

Great Britain and India (Poona) have a somewhat similar pattern: high rates of movement, but with downward and limited upward movement much more pronounced than in the previous type.

S. M. Miller 99

Less clear as a group are Italy, Japan, the Netherlands and Puerto Rico. The dominant tendency seems to be downward mobility, although in Japan and Puerto Rico access to the elites is relatively high.

It is important to reassert the earlier warnings about the mixed quality of the data. Presenting materials in tabular form tends to harden them; the fact that numbers can be used obscures the weak procedures leading to the production of these numbers. I am acutely aware of the coercive manipulations of data which have necessarily occurred in this report and hope that all the comparisons here, as in other international analyses, will be viewed as suggestive of trends, rather than adequate descriptions of nations. Inevitably, we must build on shaky foundations, but awareness of the infirmities is important to the construction of a healthy structure.

These profiles, the culmination of the data of this report, must be taken as no more than suggestive of possibilities.

Implications of the data

Asymmetry. The point of departure of the monograph has been strongly supported by the data. Mobility is not a symmetrical phenomenon – perhaps better put, at least our knowledge at this time does not reveal its symmetry. A nation can be high in one measure of mobility and low in another. The patterns just suggested should not be assumed to have a definitive character. The profiles and typologies of this report are only limited ways of organizing the data.

The connections between mobility of one kind and mobility of another kind are unclear. We must, therefore, in making comparisons, specify the measure on which the comparison is based. *The* measure of mobility does not exist, only many measures tapping different dimensions of mobility which do not, as yet at least, form a smooth pyramid.

The clear results. The most striking result of the comparisons is that on both the simple comparison of working classes into nonmanual and manual into elite strata, the Soviet Union (*émigrés*) has the highest rates. (France I has a similar working class into nonmanual rate.) These rates are probably high, but even if reduced would probably still show the Soviet Union at the top of these comparisons. On the other hand, the Soviet Union had a rather low rate of downward movement out of the nonmanual categories generally, and out of the elite strata specifically. Thus, the upward manual movement is not due to the decline of the middle classes and the elite, but to the expansion of these strata.

The United States has a high rate of manual movement into nonmanual occupations, but not one that is distinctively higher than that of France or USSR (*émigrés*). On the other hand, it is distinctively higher in the manual movement into the elite strata than all nations other than the Soviet Union (*émigrés*). [. . .]

The measure of mobility

In interpreting results, it is not only important to be aware of the different measures of mobility and the varying quality of the data, but also of the basic definition of mobility which is involved. The sociological study of mobility has been largely restricted to investigation of occupational mobility and to the prestige dimension of occupational mobility. Therefore, our comparisons of national rates of mobility are about this one slice of mobility. As Arnold Rose (n.d.) has indicated, if we were to study other aspects, such as political power of great masses of the citizenry or the degree of egalitarianism and social distance which prevails, then other results might be produced. Rose feels, for example, that nations which have already achieved high industrialization, e.g. the United States, are inevitably going to have lower rates of occupational mobility than nations at a lower stage of industrialization which necessarily have to upgrade many in order to fit them into the new technological demands of the economic structure. One way of meeting this problem would be to subtract the mobility due to changing occupational opportunities from the overall rates of mobility; where this has not been done, it is important to recognize that measures of mobility such as those reported in the present monograph, except for the index of association, are refractions to a considerable extent, although certainly not exclusively, of the occupational structure, a product of a stage of industrialization.

Annotated bibliography [8]

The following bibliography does not attempt an exhaustive reporting of the vast literature on social mobility. It lists references of the text, other works that have influenced the author but not specifically cited, and a number of articles, monographs and books not generally known that may be of use to students of mobility. Extensive bibliographies can be found in:

S. M. LIPSET, and R. BENDIX, *Social Mobility in Industrial Society*, University of California, 1959.

R. W. MACK, L. FREEMAN, and S. YELLIN, *Social Mobility: Thirty Years of Research and Theory*, Syracuse University Press, 1957 (American periodical literature).

8. We have reprinted Miller's annotated bibliography in full, and without attempting to bring it up to date. It represents a landmark which sums up the state of the field at the end of the 1950s. Comparison with the suggested Further Reading at the end of this volume will give some idea of how interests have shifted over the last decade [Eds.].

Transactions of the Second and Third World Congresses of Sociology, International Sociological Association, 1954 and 1956, contain many important articles and references.

Centro Latin-Americano de Pesquisas en Ciencas Socialis, Rio de Janeiro, has issued a variety of bibliographies on Latin America.

Department of Sociology, University of Buenos Aires, has issued a variety of bibliographies.

H. PFAUTZ, 'The current literature on social stratification: critique and bibliography', *Amer. J. Sociol.*, vol. 58, 1953.

Sociological abstracts

ANDERSON, D. H., and DAVIDSON, P. E. (1937), *Occupational Mobility in an American Community*, Stanford University Press.

ARONSON, S. (1961) *Status and Kinship in the Higher Civil Service: the Administration of John Adams, Thomas Jefferson and Andrew Jackson*, Ph.D. thesis, Columbia University, 1961. (To be published by Harvard University Press.) A detailed study showing that Jackson's officials were similar to Jefferson's in social origins and status, despite the belief in the 'democratization' of the Jacksonian period. Particularly useful in demonstrating how sociological methods and perspectives can illuminate historical analysis.

ASTROM, S. E. (1953), 'Literature on social mobility and social stratification in Finland: some bibliographic notes', *Transactions of the Westermarck Society*, vol. 2.

BAGU, S., *et al.* (1960), *Trahagot e investigaciones del instituto de sociologica'*, Universidad de Buenos Aires, Departamento de Sociologica, Publication interna no. 11, 1st revision. Bibliography of studies of social stratification in Argentina during the period 1880–1959. The Department of Sociology, under the leadership of Professor Gino Germani, has an extensive list of publications on the topic of stratification and mobility.

BARBER, B. (1957), *Social Stratification: a Comparative Analysis of Structure and Process*, Harcourt, Brace & World. A broad and very useful integration of a variety of materials on stratification and mobility. Particularly strong on historical materials.

BARBER, E. G. (1955), *The Bourgeoisie in 18th Century France*, Princeton University Press.

BAUER, R. A. (1953), 'The psychology of the Soviet middle elite: two case histories', in C. H. Kluckhorn, H. Murray, and D. Schneider (eds.), *Personality*, Knopf, pp. 633–49.

BAUER, R. A., INKELES, A., and KLUCKHORN, C. (1956), *How the Soviet System Works: Cultural, Psychological and Social Themes*, Harvard University Press, Harvard University Research Center, Russian Research Center Studies, no. 24.

BAUM, S., and YPSILANTIS, J. N. (1960), 'Social mobility in Hungary: a society in, transition', unpublished. See also YPSILANTIS and BAUM (1960).

BEALS, R. L. (1953), 'Social stratification in Latin America', *Amer. J. Sociol.* vol. 58 pp. 327–39. An important discussion of trends for all of Latin America. A broad, analytical, synthesizing survey; no data are presented. Discussion of whether a two- or three-class system best describes various nations. Emphasis is on (a) the social elite groups and access to these positions; (b) the existence, composition and outlook of a middle-class group. The orientation is primarily towards cultural and participational aspects of social class. See also WILLEMS (1953).

BENDIX, R., and BERGER, B. (1959), 'Images of society and problems of concept formation in sociology', in L. Gross, *Symposium on Sociological Theory*, Row, Peterson, pp. 92–118.

BENINI, R. (1957), *Principi di demografia*, G. Babèra, Ol., Florence.

BERGER, M. (1957), *Bureaucracy and Society in Modern Egypt*, Princeton University Press. Civil servants in several departments of the contemporary Egyptian government were interviewed. Intergenerational data on social origins are analysed.

BLAU, P. M. (1957), 'Inferring mobility trends from a single study', fourth working conference on Social Stratification and Mobility, International Sociological Association, Working Paper 13.

BLAU, P. M. (1957), 'Occupational bias and mobility', *Amer. Sociol. Rev.*, vol. 22, pp. 392–9.

BLISHEN, B. R. (1958), 'The construction and use of an occupational class scale', *Canad. J. Econ. pol. Sci.*, vol. 24, pp. 519–31. Occupations are ranked in Canada on the basis of the income and years of schooling of individuals in the occupation. Occupations are then grouped into seven classes and analysed in terms of ethnic characteristics of those in the strata.

BOLTE, K. M. (1956), 'Some aspects of social mobility in Western Germany', *Transactions of the Third World Congress of Sociology*, vol. 3, International Sociological Association, pp. 183–90.

BOLTE, K. M. (1958), 'Vom Umfang der Mobilitat in unserer Gesellschaft, *Kolner Zeitschrift fur Soziologie und Sozialpsychologie*, vol. 10, pp. 49–55.

BOLTE, K. M. (1959), *Sozialer Aufstieg und Abstieg: eine Untersuchung uber Berufsprestige and Berufsmobilitat*, Ferdinand Enke Verlag, Stuttgart. Detailed data on social mobility in the province of Schleswig-Holstein.

BOTTOMORE, T. (1954), 'Higher civil servants in France', *Transactions of the Second World Congress of Sociology*, vol. 2, International Sociological Association, pp. 143–52.

BRESARD, M. (1950), 'Mobilité sociale et dimension de la famille', *Population*, vol. 5, pp. 533–66. Presents detailed outflow and inflow mobility data for France. See also DESABIE (1956).

BRESARD, M. (1954), 'La mobilité sociale: le choix d'une échelle sociologique', *Transactions of the Second World Congress of Sociology*, vol. 2, International Sociological Association, pp. 396–402.

CARLSSON, G. (1958), *Social Mobility and Class Structure*, C. W. K. Gleerup, Lund. The standard work on intergenerational mobility in Sweden with extensive discussions of theoretical and measurement problems.

CAVALLI, L. (1959), 'La gioventu del quartiere operaio', *Le inchieste dell'ufficio studi sociali e del lavoro del commune di Genova*, no. 3, pp. 25–34.

CAVALLI, L. (1959), 'Quartiere operaio (I Metalmeccanio)', *Le inchieste dell'ufficio studi sociali e del lavoro del commune di Genova*, no. 2, pp. 11–22. Father's occupation is reported for a particular working-class population.

CENTERS, R. (1948), 'Occupational mobility of urban occupational strata', *Amer. Sociol. Rev.*, vol. 13, pp. 197–203. A major source of data for the United States on intergenerational mobility. Limited to some who are urban whites.

CENTRE INTERUNIVERSITAIRE DE SOCIOLOGIE (1959), *Etude analytique de stratification sociale: les agents des contributions directes en Belgique*, Vaillant-Carmanne, Liege. A four-university study of the social characteristics, including social origins, of the civil servants in finance.

CENTRO LATINO-AMERICANO DE INVESTIGACIONES EN CIENCIAS SOCIALES (or Centro Latino-Americano de Pesquisas en Ciencias Sociales), Rio de Janeiro. The Centre has an extensive list of publications, especially bibliographies, on stratification and mobility in Latin America.

S. M. Miller 103

CHESSA, F. (1912), *La transmission ereditaria delle professioni*, Fratelli Bocca, Torino.

CHINOY, E. (1955), 'Social mobility trends in the United States', *Amer. Sociol. Rev.*, vol. 20, pp. 180–86. A careful assessment of the American data on mobility.

CONSTAS, H. (1954), *Bureaucratic Collectivism: a Comparative Study of Pharaonic Egypt, Incan Peru and Soviet Russia*, Ph.D. thesis, New School for Social Research. Especially useful for bringing together data and observations little known to sociologists.

CONSTAS, H. (1957), 'Bureaucratic societies – old and new', Paper presented at the annual meeting of the American Sociological Society, Seattle. An attempt is made to distinguish the concept of 'bureaucratic society' as a nationalized economy ruled by a bureaucratic elite based on the institutionalization of charisma. Pharaonic Egypt, Incan Peru, classical China and the Soviet Union are offered as illustrations. Access to the elite positions is briefly discussed.

CONTI, G. (1959), *Mobilita e stratificazione social*, Taylor, Torino. A broadly-ranging review of a number of issues in the field.

COSER, L. A. (1955), 'Class and opportunity', *Commentary*, vol. 18, pp. 86–7. A critical letter on Lipset and Rogoff with particular emphasis on the lack of significance of movement from manual to nonmanual work.

COSTA PINTO, L. A. (1957), 'On economic development and social mobility', fourth working conference on Social Stratification and Mobility, International Sociological Association, Working Paper 7. Social structures are always changing, but the rate of change is not uniform in all its parts. In 'new countries' the occupational structure itself is changing as some occupations disappear and others first appear. Occupations may gain a 'halo' little related to their present-day objective characteristics; in Brazil, nonmanual occupations have such a 'halo' compared to manual, which are connected to the historical conditions of slave workers. Two rating scales of occupational prestige can coexist – the traditional and the new, the old and the changed. '. . . the old pattern still subsists but no longer prevails and the new one, though present, is not yet dominant.'

DAVIS, K. (1949). *Human Society*, Macmillan & Co.

DE JOCAS, Y., and ROCHER, G., (1957), 'Intergenerational occupational mobility in the province of Quebec', *Canad. J. Econ. pol. Sci.*, vol. 23, pp. 57–68. Standard outflow table is presented for French-Canadians in Quebec. Indices of association are computed for eight occupational categories. The distribution of occupations of French- and English-speaking fathers and sons in the Province are also analysed. Data are for 1954 and are based on official records of births and marriages.

DESABIE, J. (1956), *La mobilité sociale en France*, Bulletin d'Information no. 1, Institut National de la Statistique et des Etudes Economiques, Paris, pp. 25–63. This study has also been published in the Bulletin de la SEDELS, 11 January 1955. It contains detailed material on a variety of aspects of intergenerational mobility in France. It covers much of the same ground as the better-known BRESARD (1950) study.

DESAUNOIS, M., SALLESSE, M., and FLORQUIN, M. (1957), 'Enquête dans quelques sixième et huitième primaires des écoles adoptables de l'agglomération bruxelloise', *Revue de l'Institut de Sociologie Solvay*, vol. 30, pp. 156–77. One of several reports on the link of social class to course of study in Belgian schools.

DUMENIL, M. (1960), 'Origines sociales des cadres de l'industrie et du commerce',

Actas del Congreso International del Instituto de Clases Medias, Madrid, vol. 12, pp. 9–20. Includes data on fathers and grandfathers of French officials in industry and commerce. Other articles in the volume pertain to Spanish social structure.

EGGAR, F., HESTER, E. S., and GINZBERG, N. S. (1956), *Area Handbook on the Philippines*, vol. 1, HRAF-16, Chicago-5, Human Relations Area Files. Includes an analysis of social-class trends by Robert B. Fox.

EISENSTADT, S. N. (1951), 'The place of elites and primary groups in the absorption of new immigrants in Israel', *Amer. J. Sociol.*, vol. 57, pp. 22–31. The role of leaders in the assimilation process of different groups.

EISENSTADT, S. N. (1957), 'Some queries about the relations between social mobility and the structure of the societies in which it takes place', fourth working conference on Social Stratification and Mobility, International Sociological Association, Working Paper 2.

ENGELBORGHS-BERTELS, M., and VERDASSEN, Y. (1956), *Mont-Saint-Guibert: le rôle social de la profession*, vol. 2, Institut de Sociologie Solvay, Brussels. A detailed study of a very small community in Belgium. Detailed tables on inter- and intragenerational mobility, as well as educational data, are presented.

ERICKSON, C. (1953), 'The recruitment of British management', *Explor. Entrep. Hist.*, vol. 6, pp. 62–70. Assessment of studies of social origins of business leaders and outline of a research project.

FELDMAN, A. S. (1959), 'The interpenetration of firm and society', in G. Balandier (ed.), *Symposium*, Papers presented at International Social Science Council Round Table on Social Implications of Technical Change, Paris.

FELDMAN, A. S. (1960), 'Economic development and social mobility', *Econ. Devel. cult. Change*, vol. 8, pp. 311–21. An extensive review of Lipset and Bendix (1959), that is notable for its analysis of a variety of issues. Particularly interesting are the discussions of the heads–hands status dichotomy in different situs and the interaction of mobility rates and value patterns.

FELDMESSER, R. A. (1952), 'Social status and access to higher education: a comparison of the United States and the Soviet Union', *Harvard educ. Rev.*, vol. 27, pp. 92–106.

FELDMESSER, R. A. (1953), 'The persistence of status advantages in Soviet Russia', *Amer. J. Sociol.*, vol. 49, pp. 19–27. Data used are from the *émigré* population studied by the Russian Research Center of Harvard University.

FELDMESSER, R. A. (1955), *Aspects of Social Mobility in the Soviet Union*, Ph.D. thesis, Harvard University. A careful analysis of the implications of the Harvard *émigré* data for social mobility in the Soviet Union. A variety of breakdowns of the data utilized here that are not reported elsewhere. The author is elaborating and refining the materials (and more recent information) into a book.

FELDMESSER, R. A. (1960), 'Equality and inequality under Khrushchev', *Problems of Communism*, vol. 9, pp. 31–9.

FISHER, S. N. (1955), *Social forces in the Middle East*, Cornell University Press. General discussion of social origins occurs in several articles.

FOOTE, N. N. (1953), 'Destratification and restratification', *Amer. J. Sociol.*, vol. 58, pp. 325–6. The interplay of hierarchy and equality provides the dynamic of the American class system. An awareness of the developments emerging from these opposing intentions is necessary. Old forms of stratification erode and new forms emerge.

FRIEDRICH, C. J., and KISSINGER, H. (1956), *The Soviet Zone of Germany*, HRAF-34, Harvard-1 Human Relations Area Files. A chapter on social structure is largely concerned with social class.

FROOMKIN, J., and JAFFE, A. J. (1953), 'Occupational skill and socio-economic structure', *Amer. J. Sociol.*, vol. 59, pp. 42–8.

GINGER, R. (1954), 'Occupational mobility and American life: some historical hypotheses', *Explor. Entrep. Hist.*, vol. 6, pp. 234–44. Interesting speculations by an economic historian on the interrelationships of horizontal mobility, vertical mobility and trade union development.

GINSBERG, M. (1929), 'Interchange between social classes', *Econ. J.*, vol. 29, pp. 554–65.

GIROD, R. (1957), 'École, université, et sélection des membres des couches dirigeantes. Le cas de Genève', fourth working conference on Social Stratification and Mobility, International Sociological Association, Working Paper 4.

GIROD, R. (1957), 'Mobilité sociale en Suisse: changements de milieu d'une génération à l'autre', *Revue de l'Institut de Sociologie Solvay*, Brussels, vol. 1. Also published in *Etudes et documents du Centre de recherches sociologiques de Genève*, 1956.

GIROD, R., with HUTMACHER, W. (1957), 'Milieu social et orientation au seuil de l'enseignement du second degré, a Genève, en 1956', *Etudes et documents du Centre de recherches sociologiques de Genève*. Important materials on educational mobility and social origins of business leaders will be found in these three publications. The Centre also has a listing of all research on mobility in Switzerland.

GLASS, D. V. *et al.* (1954), *Social Mobility in Britain*, Routledge & Kegan Paul. The standard source for Britain; its procedures have become the model for many other studies.

HAJDA, J. (ed.) (1955), *A Study of Contemporary Czechoslovakia*, HRAF-15, Chicago-3, Human Relations Area Files. Chapter 6 by Hajda is on social stratification. He reports considerable mobility after 1948: many politically reliable workers were given white-collar jobs and received rapid special training; 'downward mobility characterized the politically unreliable persons, the propertied upper- and middle-class members, most members of the liberal profession, white-collar workers with lower qualifications' (pp. 138–9). 'The changing system of social relationships resulted in the decline of some standards of social evaluation and in the emergence of new ones.'

HANDLIN, O. (1942), Review of W. L. Warner *et al.*, 'The social life of a modern community', *New England Quarterly*, vol. 15, pp. 555–6.

HANDLIN, O., and HANDLIN, M. F. (1956), 'Ethnic factors in social mobility', *Explor. Entrep. Hist.*, vol. 9, pp. 1–7. A survey of the history of the USA to show the influence of ethnic background on the character of social mobility. '. . . it was through the aptitudes involved in successful entrepreneurship that the most valued places in American society were attained. And it was in regard to those aptitudes that ethnic differences had greatest significance.'

HANDLIN, O., and HANDLIN, M. F. (1957), 'Cultural aspects of social mobility' fourth working conference on Social Stratification and Mobility, International Sociological Association, Working Paper 5.

HARRISON, F. H. (1959), 'Egypt', in W. Galenson (ed.), *Labor and Economic Development*, Wiley, pp. 146–85.

HAVIGHURST, R. J. (1958), 'Education, social mobility and social change in four societies: a comparative study', *Internat. Rev. Educ.*, vol. 14, pp. 167–85. Comparison of intergenerational mobility in Australia (Melbourne), Great Britain, Brazil (Sao Paulo) and the USA (Kansas City). Special tabulations of educational and social structural data are presented.

HAVIGHURST, R. J., and NEUGARTEN, N. (1957), *Society and Education*, Allyn & Bacon. An interesting attempt to analyse American data on social mobility.

HOLLINGHEAD, A. B., and REDLICH, F. C. (1958), *Social Class and Mental Illness*, Wiley.

HOPPER, R. (1950), 'The revolutionary process: a frame of reference for the study of revolutionary movements', *Social Forces*, vol. 28, pp. 270–79.

HUTCHINSON, B. (1958), 'Structural and exchange mobility in the assimilation of immigrants to Brazil', *Population Studies*, vol. 12, pp. 111–20. A study of Sao Paulo which is broader than the title as it presents a standard intergenerational outflow table for the city as well as detailed analyses of the fate of immigrant groups. A simple measure of the influence of structural elements in mobility is presented.

INKELES, A. (1953), 'Social stratification and mobility in the Soviet Union', in R. Bendix, and S. M. Lipset (eds.), *Class, Status and Power*, Free Press, pp. 609–22.

INKELES, A., and BAUER, R. A. (1959), *The Soviet Citizen: Daily Life in a Totalitarian Society*, Harvard University Press. An extensive interpretation of Soviet life, drawing mainly though not exclusively from the Harvard study of Russian *émigrés*. Detailed analysis of stratification and mobility.

INKELES, A., and ROSSI, P. (1956), 'National comparisons of occupational prestige', *Amer. J. Sociol.*, vol. 56, pp. 329–39.

INTERNATIONAL SOCIOLOGICAL ASSOCIATION (1956), Papers presented to the Third Working Conference on Social Stratification and Mobility, Amsterdam, 16–18 December 1954, *Explor. Entrep. Hist.*, vol. 8 (Winter supplement), pp. 1–62.

ISSAWI, C. (1955), 'The entrepreneur class', in S. N. Fisher (ed.), *Social Forces in the Middle East*, Cornell University Press, pp. 116–36.

IWANSKA, A. (ed.) (1955), *Contemporary Poland: Society, Politics, Economy*, HRAF-22, Chicago-16, Human Relations Area Files. The editor has a chapter on social stratification.

JAFFE, A. J., and CARLETON, R. O. (1954), *Occupational Mobility in the United States: 1930–1960*, King's Crown Press. Useful data on intragenerational mobility.

JANOWITZ, M. (1958), 'Social stratification and mobility in West Germany', *Amer. J. Sociol.*, vol. 66, pp. 6–24. (Also published as 'Soziale Schichtung und Mobilität in Westdeutschland', *Kolner Zeitschrift fur Soziologie und Soziopsychologie*, Heft 1, 1958.) Data on intergenerational mobility and other aspects of stratification are analysed.

JAPAN SOCIOLOGICAL SOCIETY (Research Committee) (1956), *Social Mobility in Japan: an Interim Report on the 1955 Survey of Social Stratification and Social Mobility in Japan*, prepared for the Third World Congress of Sociology, May. (Abstract of this report in *Transactions of the Third World Congress of Sociology*, vol. 8, pp. 193–95. The 1958 report is a description of the tables but without the data, which can be obtained separately. The 1956 paper has considerable data, but does not have a standard outflow table, consequently I have used Nishira (1957). Also see ODAKA and NISHIRA (1959).

JAPAN SOCIOLOGICAL SOCIETY (Research Committee) (1958), *Modern Japanese Society: Its Class Structure* (English Summary).

KELSALL, R. K. (1955), *Higher Civil Servants in Britain: From 1870 to the Present Day*, Routledge & Kegan Paul. A systematic analysis with considerable mobility data.

KUIPER, G. (1957), 'Occupational stratification and mobility in the Netherlands', fourth working conference on Social Stratification and Mobility, International Sociological Association, Working Paper 15.

LANG, O. (1946), *Chinese Family and Society*, Yale University Press. 'The presence of many *déclassé* elements in a working-class group is natural in a society in a state of transition.' Data are presented for 1936 on social origins of eighty-seven Shanghai industrial workers; social origins of college and high school students are also tabulated.

LASSWELL, H. D. (1951), 'The changing Italian elite', in H. D. Lasswell and Renzo Sereno, *The Analysis of Political Behavior*, Routledge & Kegan Paul. Contains data on the social origins of the leaders of Italy in the 1930s.

LEHNER, A. (1954), 'Sur la mesure de la mobilité sociale', *Transactions of the Second World Congress of Sociology*, International Sociological Association, vol. 2, pp. 119–27.

LEVY, M. J. Jr, and SHIH, K. (1949), *The Rise of the Modern Chinese Business Class*, Institute of Pacific Relations. New York. Two essays on varied aspects of the emergence of a business class in pre-Communist China.

LIPSET, S. M., and BENDIX, R. (1959), *Social Mobility in Industrial Society*, University of California. Data from a variety of nations are analysed by Lipset and Bendix, employing a classification into manual or nonmanual occupations. On this basis, it is considered that mobility in advanced industrial economies is remarkably similar. American data on the business elite are scrutinized in order to reconcile the disparate results of several studies. Data drawn from the Oakland, California, study of the authors are analysed to bear on intragenerational and intergenerational mobility. A variety of factors influencing the rate of effects of mobility, especially in the United States, are then analysed. This work brings together a wealth of comparative materials and puts them into a cohesive framework of analysis.

LIPSET, S. M., LAZARSFELD, P. F., BARTON, A. H., and LINZ, J. (1954), 'The psychology of voting: an analysis of political behavior', in G. A. Lindzey, *Handbook of Social Psychology*, Addison-Wesley, vol. 2, pp. 1124–75.

LIPSET, S. M., and ROGOFF, N. (1954), 'Class and opportunity in Europe and the US', *Commentary*, vol. 18, pp. 562–8. Also see the critical comments by COSER (1955) and MAYER (1955).

LIPSET, S. M., and ZETTERBERG, H. L. (1954), 'A proposal for a comparative study of social mobility – its causes and consequences', Bureau of Applied Social Research, Columbia University. Most of the material has appeared in *Social Mobility in Industrial Society*, but some important discussions of the details of various studies have not been republished.

LIPSET, S. M., and ZETTERBERG, H. L. (1956a), 'A theory of social mobility', in *Transactions of the Third World Congress of Sociology*, International Sociological Association, vol. 3, pp. 155–77.

LIPSET, S. M., and ZETTERBERG, H. L. (1956b), 'Discussion on social mobility and class structure', *Transactions of the Third World Congress of Sociology*, International Sociological Association, vol. 3, pp. 74–5, 78.

LIVI, L. (1950), 'Sur la mesure de la mobilité sociale', *Population*, vol. 6, pp. 65–76. The most widely-used source of mobility data for Italy.

MACK, R. W., FREEMAN, L., and YELLIN, S. (1957), *Social Mobility: Thirty Years of Research and Theory*, Syracuse University Press. Abstracts of relevant literature from 1924 through 1953 of the following United States periodicals: *American Journal of Sociology*, *American Sociological Review* (from 1936), *Social Forces*.

MACRAE, D. G. (1958), 'Class relationships and ideology', *Sociol. Rev.*, vol. 6, pp. 261–72. '. . . the central fact remains, the status and therefore the class systems of industrial societies are founded on an identical appraisal, a uniform ideology of prestige. Secondly, this hierarchy parallels with remarkable closeness the hierarchy of income distribution.'

MAYER, K. M. (1955), 'Social mobility: America *v.* Europe', *Commentary*, vol. 19, pp. 395–6.

MILLER, S. M. (1955), 'The concept of mobility', *Social Problems*, vol. 3, pp. 65–73.

MILLER, S. M. (1956a), 'The concept and measurement of mobility', *Transactions of the Third World Congress on Sociology*, International Sociological Association, vol. 3, pp. 144–54.

MILLER, S. M. (1956b), 'Tertiary employment, white-collar work and mobility', Paper presented at the annual meeting of the Eastern Sociological Society, New York, April.

MILLER, S. M. (1960), *Report of Fifth World Conference on Social Stratification and Mobility*, Perugia, 17–18 September 1959, International Sociological Association, Louvain.

MILLER, S. M., and MISHLER, E. G. (1959), 'Social class, mental illness, and American psychiatry', *Millbank Memorial Fund Quarterly*, vol. 37, pp. 174–99.

MILLER, S. M. (1960), 'Social mobility and economic change', paper presented at the annual meeting of the Eastern Sociological Society, Boston, April.

MITRAS, J. (1960), 'Comparison of intergenerational occupational mobility patterns: an application of the formal theory of social mobility', *Population Studies*, vol. 14, pp. 163–9. Application of Markov chain analysis to several national studies of mobility.

MOORE, W. E. (1954), 'Review of N. Rogoff, *Recent Trends in Occupational Mobility*', *Public Opinion Quarterly*, vol. 18, pp. 326–7.

MORGENSTERN, O. (1950), *On the Accuracy of Economic Observations*, Princeton University Press.

MYERS, P. F., and CAMPBELL, A. A. (1954), *The Population of Yugoslavia*, US Government Printing Office, Washington, International Population Statistics Reports, Series P-90, No. 5. A compendium of information, including data on distribution of labor force by industry.

NISHIRA, S. (1957), 'Cross-national comparative study on social stratification and social mobility', *Annals of the Institute of Statistical Mathematics*, vol. 8, pp. 181–91. Contains a standard outflow table for Japanese mobility based on the 1955 study of the Research Committee of the Japan Sociological Society. Also see JAPANESE SOCIOLOGICAL SOCIETY (1956 and 1958), and ODAKA and NISHIRA (1959).

NORTH, C. C., and HATT, P. K. (1953), 'Jobs and occupations: a popular evaluation', in R. Bendix and S. M. Lipset, *Class, Status and Power*, Free Press, pp. 411–26.

ODAKA, K., and NISHIRA, S. (1959), 'Some factors related to social mobility in Japan', *Annals of the Institute of Statistical Mathematics*, vol. 10, pp. 283–8. (This is also Working Paper 10, fourth working conference on Social Stratification and Mobility, 1957). Intragenerational mobility, indices of succession, educational mobility are examined. Also see JAPANESE SOCIOLOGICAL SOCIETY (1956 and 1958), and NISHIRA (1957).

OESER, O. A., and HAMMOND, S. B. (eds.) (1954), *Social Structure and Personality in a City*, Routledge & Kegan Paul.

PAGANI, A. (1956), 'Campo di applicazione delle ricerche sulla stratificazione', *Tecnica e Organizzazione*, vol. 6.

PAGANI, A. (1957), 'Metodi di inisurazione della stratificazione sociale', *Tecnica e Organizzazione*, vol. 7.

PAGANI, A. (1957), Untitled paper, fourth world conference on Social Stratification and Mobility, International Sociological Association, Working Paper 12. Contains data on a variety of aspects of stratification and mobility in Italy. Also discussed are plans for further research.

PFAUTZ, H. (1953), 'The current literature on social stratification: critique and bibliography', *Amer. J. Sociol.*, vol. 58, pp. 391–418.

PORTER, J. (1957), 'The economic elite and the social structure in Canada', *Canad. J. Econ. pol. Sci.*, vol. 23, pp. 376–94.

PORTER, J. (1958), 'Higher public servants and the bureaucratic elite in Canada', *Canad. J. Econ. pol. Sci.*, vol. 24, pp. 483–501. Both articles provide data on the social origins of the elite occupations studied.

REDLICH, F. (1953), 'European aristocracy and economic development', *Explor. Entrep. Hist.*, vol. 6, pp. 87–91. Stress is placed on the cases where the aristocracy did have a role in economic development. Articles in the same and later issues of this periodical take up this theme in various nations. It would be worthwhile to compare movement into and out of elites in nations where the aristocracy was involved in manufacturing and commerce with nations where this did not occur.

ROBINSON, W. S. (1950), 'Ecological correlations and the behavior of individuals', *Amer. Sociol. Rev.*, vol. 15, pp. 351–7.

ROGOFF, N. (1950), 'Les recherches americaines sur la mobilité sociale', *Population*, vol. 5, pp. 669–88. Combines the NORC and Centers mobility data for the US into one matrix.

ROGOFF, N. (1952), 'Concepts and indices of social mobility', Paper for Planning Project for Advanced Training in Social Research, Columbia University, 18 November.

ROGOFF, N. (1953), *Recent Trends in Occupational Mobility*, Free Press.

ROSE, A. M. (n.d.), *Social Mobility and Social Values*, unpublished.

ROSOVSKY, H. (1954), 'The entrepreneur in Russia', *Explor. Entrep. Hist.*, vol. 6, pp. 207–33. For the period 1700 to 1850, evidence is presented to show that many serfs, while still legally serfs, carried out entrepreneurial roles.

SARIOLA, S. (1953), 'Defining social class in two Finnish communities', *Transactions of the Westermarck Society*, vol. 2.

SKINNER, G. W. (1957), *Chinese Society in Thailand: an Analytical History*, Cornell University.

SKINNER, G. W. (1958), *Leadership and Power in the Chinese Community of Thailand*, Cornell University. Fragmentary materials on mobility exist in both books. Upward mobility of Chinese in Siam was high in 1880–1910. Many anecdotes of 'rags to riches' ascent exist for this period. In the first book, a study is made of 130 leaders of the Chinese community of Bangkok. 75 per cent originated in business families; 9 per cent were members of farmer or laborer families, and 8 per cent had some intermediate urban occupation. The bulk came from rural areas. The data are gained from other respondents, and it is not clear how accurate they may be. It is also reported that 20 per cent are completely self-made men. Only 4 per cent had a year or less of schooling; 40 per cent had twelve years or more of schooling.

SMYTHE, H. H. (1959), *Some Preliminary Comments on the New Nigerian Elite*, unpublished. A general survey of the development of a post-Second World War elite in Nigeria. Regional differences are emphasized.

SMYTHE, H. H., and SMYTHE, M. M. (1960), 'Black Africa's new power elite', *South Atlantic Quarterly*, vol. 59, pp. 13–23. The Smythes have recently published a book entitled *The New Nigerian Elite*.

SOROKIN, P. A. (1958), *Social and Cultural Mobility*, Free Press.

SOVANI, N. V., and PRADHAN, K. (1955), 'Occupational mobility in Poona City between three generations', *Indian Econ. Rev.*, vol. 2(4), pp. 23–36. Detailed analysis of two- and three-generational mobility.

SVALASTOGA, K. (1958), 'The family in the mobility process', *Recherches sur la famille* Vanderhoeck and Ruprecht for UNESCO Institute of Social Sciences, University of Cologne, Gottingen, pp. 287–306.

SVALASTOGA, K. (1959), *Prestige, Class and Mobility*, Munksgaard, Copenhagen. The basic study of Denmark. Considerable attention is paid to important methodological problems of general significance.

SVALASTOGA, K., and CARLSSON, G. (1961), 'Social stratification and mobility in Scandinavia', *Sociological Inquiry*, vol. 31, pp. 23–46. Detailed review, including historical perspectives, of available data on the four nations of Scandinavia.

TOMASIC, D. (1948), *Personality and Culture in East European Politics*, George W. Stewart. A study, primarily, of Yugoslavia.

TROUTON, R. (1952), *Peasant Renaissance in Yugoslavia, 1900–1950*, Routledge & Kegan Paul.

TUMIN, M. M., and FELDMAN, A. S. (1957), 'Theory and measurement of occupational mobility', *Amer. Sociol. Rev.*, vol. 22, pp. 281–8. A discussion of the Generational Occupational Mobility Score and its application to the Puerto Rican data analysed by the authors.

TUMIN, M. M., with FELDMAN, A. S. (1961), *Social Class and Social Change in Puerto Rico*, Princeton University Press.

VAN TULDER, J. J. M. (1956), 'Occupational mobility in the Netherlands from 1919 to 1954', *Transactions of the Third World Congress of Sociology*, International Sociological Association, vol. 3, pp. 209–18.

VERSICHELEN, M. (1959), *Sociale mobiliteit; ein studie over differentiele levenskansen*, Rijksuniversiteit Te Gent, Studie-En Onderzoekcentrum voor Sociale Westenschappen, no. 1. A detailed study of a small community, St-Martens-Latem, in the vicinity of Ghent, Belgium. Age-specific data for intergenerational occupational mobility (fathers, fathers-in-law) presented. Intragenerational data also are recorded.

VON FERBER, C. (1956), 'The social background of German university and college professors since 1864', *Transactions of the Third World Congress of Sociology*, International Sociological Association, vol. 3, pp. 239–45.

WAUGH, E. (1956), 'An open letter to the Hon. Mrs Peter Rodd (Nancy Mitford) on a very serious subject', in N. Mitford (ed.), *Noblesse Oblige*, Hamish Hamilton, pp. 65–84. A satiric effort to analyse some attitudes towards the British upper classes.

WEINRYB, B. (1940), 'The occupational structure of the second generation of Jews in Palestine', *Jewish Social Studies*, vol. 2, pp. 435–80. An extensive analysis of the occupational distribution of first- and second-generation Jews in Palestine prior to the Second World War. Intergenerational mobility data are provided.

WESTOFF, C. F., BRESSLER, M., and SAGI, P. C. (1960), 'The concept of social mobility: an empirical inquiry', *Amer. Sociol. Rev.*, vol. 25, pp. 375–85. A very useful analysis of the varied dimensions of social mobility, demonstrating the limited interchangeability of the variables.

WILLEMS, E. (1953), 'Beals' social stratification in Latin America', *Amer. J. Sociol.*, vol. 59, pp. 59–60. Objections are voiced to Beals' conclusion (see OESER and HAMMOND [1954]) that strong barriers limit movement from the middle to upper class in Brazil.

YOUNG, M., and WILLMOTT, P. (1956), 'Social grading by manual workers', *Brit. J. Sociol.*, vol. 7, pp. 337–45. The Hall-Jones study was repeated with an East London working-class group. Differences were found between the overall findings for Britain; considerable variation occurred within the group.

YPSILANTIS, J. N., and BAUM, S. (1960), 'Occupational mobility of the farm population in Hungary: a peasant society at the crossroad of industrialization', Paper presented at the Rural Sociological Society, State University, Pennsylvania, 25 August. Detailed data on Hungarian mobility derived from the 1949 census. See also BAUM and YPSILANTIS (1960).

6 J. C. Tully, E. F. Jackson and R. F. Curtis

Trends in Occupational Mobility in Indianapolis

Excerpt from J. C. Tully, E. F. Jackson and R. F. Curtis, 'Trends in occupational mobility in Indianapolis', *Social Forces*, vol. 49, 1970, pp. 186–200.

The study providing a direct comparison of mobility rates over the longest time period is Rogoff's (1953) study of Indianapolis, Indiana. Since the object of our analysis will be to extend Rogoff's comparison, we shall describe her procedures in some detail.

Rogoff used as her data the occupations of grooms and their fathers as recorded on marriage license applications in Marion County, Indiana, for two time periods before the Second World War: 1905 through 1912 (referred to as the 1910 data) and 1938 through the first six months of 1941 (1940 data). Only applications of Marion County residents were included in her sample. Negroes were excluded from the 1910 data and analysed separately in the 1940 data. Cases reporting unemployment or retirement for either father or son and cases reporting the father deceased were excluded. By the nature of the data, then, never-married male residents of Marion County were excluded as were all married male residents who were married outside the county.

Rogoff's occupational code was a modification of the Intermediate List of the Bureau of the Census. It included ten major categories and over one hundred specific occupations. Some specific items were added for the 1940 period because of the creation of new occupations. Since data on age and nativity were required on the license application form, Rogoff was also able to introduce controls for these variables.

Rogoff's conclusion was that

In both time periods, all sons moved out of their class of origin at about the same rate. But the positions into which they moved varied with their occupational origins. This was especially true in 1940, indicating that the processes by which men selected and were selected for occupations were more closely related to social origins in 1940 than they had been in 1910 (1953, p. 106).

In both time periods sons were more likely to enter their father's occupation than any other single occupation. Downward mobility decreased between 1910 and 1940, but upward mobility remained about the same so that in 1940 the ratio of upward mobility to downward mobility was greater than it was in 1910.

These conclusions were reached mainly from an examination of social mobility ratios, a statistical device meant to keep changes in occupational distributions from influencing mobility comparisons. Blau and Duncan (1967, pp. 91–6), however, have criticized the use of these ratios in comparing mobility rates, showing that 'one cannot have two mobility tables with identical matrices of mobility ratios if the respective marginal distributions of the two tables differ . . .'. Hence, one could never conclude 'no change' from comparing the mobility ratios in two tables unless the marginals of the tables happened to be identical.

Duncan (1966, pp. 63ff; see also Duncan, 1968) provides a re-analysis of Rogoff's data, focusing on the linear dependence between father's and son's occupation. After assigning each of Rogoff's 114 occupational categories a two-digit socioeconomic index score, he computed the regression of son's occupational score on father's occupational score. He concluded that '. . . it would take the sociological equivalent of a micrometer to detect a difference between the 1940 and 1910 regression equations.'

Thus, the studies estimating mobility trends by comparing data collected on the same population at different times generally indicate that changes in mobility rates have been small whether the time span is relatively long (thirty years) or relatively short (ten to fifteen years). The small differences that have been observed seem to indicate an increase, rather than a decrease, in the rate of mobility.

The available studies of occupational mobility rates use a variety of analytic techniques. That the original theoretical problem has generated methods yielding several different sorts of information perhaps indicates that the question, 'Have intergenerational mobility rates changed over time?' can be constructively broken down into several more specific subquestions:

1 Have the members of the population experienced more upward mobility, stability or downward mobility than at some previous time?

This question is important in and of itself because the mobility experience of a population may have a considerable effect on their perceptions of opportunity and consequently on such dependent variables as political participation and voting choice. However, the measurement of amount of movement does not directly get at the degree of openness of permeability in the stratification system (see Duncan, 1968, pp. 696–7). This is because there are at least four factors that might be responsible for a change in the total amount of occupational movement: technological change which leads to changes in the occupational structure; differential fertility which restricts or expands the supply of sons from certain origins: net inter-

national or intranational (especially urban–rural) migration which disproportionately brings into or takes away from a nation or community persons
from certain origins; and changes in the degree of universalism in occupational allocation (cf. Matras, 1961; Blau and Duncan, 1967, pp. 429–31).

Since 'openness' in the stratification system could be taken theoretically
to refer to only this fourth factor, it is important to measure the amount of
movement due to it alone, i.e. movement that would occur if the first three
factors were not operating. This movement is presumably circulation, i.e.
in which each upward movement is balanced by one or several downward
movements. The first three factors are reflected in differences between
origin and destination marginal totals. For example, a decrease, due to
technological change, in the proportion of men in farming occupations
would make the marginal total of fathers in farming occupations larger
than the corresponding total for sons. Such differences in marginal totals
means that every son cannot become employed in the same category as his
father. Hence techniques which extract from the total observed movement
that portion in some sense due to differences between the distributions of
father's and son's occupation can help to answer a second question:

2 Are there changes over time in the amount of observed movement which
reflects 'circulation'?

In some past research this problem has been handled by computing the
minimum number of persons who would have to be shifted to make fathers'
and sons' distribution identical, and regarding the number of actual
movers in excess of this minimum as representing circulation (see Jackson
and Crockett, 1964; Jackson and Curtis, 1968, pp. 140–42). This procedure, however, is wrong, since excess movement above the minimum can
represent, in addition to circulation, moves which constitute what Blau
and Duncan (1967, pp. 25–6) term 'indirect repercussions of changes in
demand'. In other words, newly created occupational positions will
often not be filled by single direct movements from those occupations
which are constricting but rather by shorter moves from adjacent categories
which in turn may create shortages in these jobs, which in turn will be filled
by other short-range moves, etc. At present we know of no way to partition
excess movement into circulation versus such moves indirectly due to
changes in demand.

Another form of the question about changes in universalistic allocation,
and one that leads to a somewhat different analysis, is:

3 Does the occupational rank of respondents depend more on occupational
rank of origin than at some previous time?

In other words, it is important to know the extent to which movements (whether or not attributable to, say, differential fertility) end in destinations influenced by origin.

A remaining, somewhat residual question is:

4 Has the process of transition from origin to destination changed in character over time?

This question calls for a detailed examination of the matrix of father's-against-son's occupations to identify changes in patterns of supply out of, or recruitment into, specific categories (for an example, see Blau and Duncan, 1967, pp. 38 ff.). Some of the sub-questions into which this question could be divided would refer to openness of occupational allocations, but others would not.

A fruitful area for future work would be a more elegant conceptualization of these four problems. The ways in which the questions relate to one another and how answers to one of the questions puts bounds on answers to the others is far from clear. Especially this is true of questions 2 and 3, which even refer to different dependent variables: mobility on the one hand and occupational attainment on the other. It *is* clear, however, that several somewhat distinct questions are involved and as many distinct answers can be given to the general problem of change in mobility rates.

The aim of the present study is to compare 1966 and 1968 data from Indianapolis with Rogoff's earlier data from the same community, presenting analyses, where possible, to answer each of the above questions. This will allow a direct comparison of occupational mobility patterns in the same community over a longer time period than any such study to date.

Data and methods
Samples

The data for this replication come from the 1965–66 and 1967–68 Indianapolis Area Projects. The Project is a sample survey of the Indianapolis urbanized area conducted annually in January and February by the Department of Sociology at Indiana University. The 1966 and 1968 studies employed both graduate student and professional interviewers. The 1966 study is part of a comparative survey of six communities currently under analysis by Curtis and Jackson. Data from the 1968 study were made available to us by Marvin E. Olsen, the faculty director of the Project during that year.

The data for 1966 come from a systematic random sample of households listed in the Indianapolis and Suburban City Directories for 1965. The 1968 data were collected by an area probability sample with quotas (for a description of this method, see Sudman, 1966). In the 1966 study each married female respondent was asked about the occupations of her husband and his father. Therefore, data on male occupations reported by both male and married female respondents could be used. Since data on husband's–father's occupation were not collected in the 1968 study, only male respondents were used from this study.

The two studies were compared with respect to respondents' and fathers' occupational distributions. The results were sufficiently similar to allow us to combine the 1966 and 1968 samples and treat them as one sample.[1] From now on we shall refer to the combined sample as the '1967 data'.

The 1967 data differ from Rogoff's data both in the universe studied and in the mode of data collection. Rogoff used data recorded on marriage licenses for respondents who were male, residents of Marion County, neither retired nor unemployed and whose fathers were alive and neither retired nor unemployed. Since all information was recorded at the point of marriage, a strong age bias and perhaps biases of other sorts are present in her data.[2]

We wanted to match our 1967 sample survey data with Rogoff's register data as closely as possible.[3] To do this we took the following steps:

1 Since the 1967 data included no respondents who were in farming occupations, Rogoff's respondents in farming occupations were dropped from the tables used in this paper. (These causes are, however, present in certain calculations we take from Duncan's 1966 analysis.)

2 Negroes were omitted from the 1967 sample because Rogoff did not include them in her major tables. We did not try to adjust for differences in nativity.[4]

3 Our sample differs considerably from Rogoff's in age, marital status, and number of years married. To make our data more comparable to hers we

1. Within each of the origin categories, the respondents' occupational distribution for 1966 and 1968 were not significantly different (all $ps > 0.30$). Within age categories, the correlation coefficients for father's and son's occupations for the total sample were not significantly different (all $ps > 0.50$). All probabilities reported in this paper are two-tailed.
2. In Rogoff's 1910 data the age percentages were: under 24: 36·0 per cent; 24–30: 37·3 per cent; and over 30: 26·8 per cent. In 1940 these percentages were: under 24: 40·1 per cent; 24–30: 36·1 per cent; and over 30: 23·8 per cent. For the 210 1967 cases the percentages were: under 24: 18·6 per cent; 24–30: 62·4 per cent; over 30: 19·0 per cent.
3. See Carlsson (1958, pp. 85–9) for a comparison of the results of these two types of data in the study of social mobility.
4. The percentage of foreign-born sons was 10 per cent for 1910, 3 per cent for 1940, and 2 per cent for 1967. The percentage of foreign-born fathers was 25 per cent for 1910, 8 per cent for 1940, and 5 per cent for 1967.

first divided the 1967 sample into Rogoff's age categories: under 24, 24–30 and over 30.[5] Then in the over-30 group we dropped all single, divorced and widowed respondents and all respondents married over five years – the remaining cases at least roughly resemble persons over 30 applying for marriage licenses. However, single, divorced and widowed men of 30 and under were retained, on the assumption that most would probably marry in the reasonably near future. All married persons of 30 and under were also retained. Most of these marriages were in their first years: all of the under-24 group were either unmarried or had been married five years or less; 49 per cent of the 24–30 group had been married longer than five years, but only 2 per cent longer than ten years. After these modifications, we were left with 210 cases for analysis.

4 All calculations for the 1967 sample were adjusted to match Rogoff's age distribution. Contingency table cell frequencies and regression calculations were calculated separately within each age group and then reweighted by the 1940 age distribution.

Despite these attempts to ensure comparability, several discrepancies between the two bodies of data remain. First, Rogoff's data were collected from Marion County residents who *married* there; the 1967 data were collected from people *residing* in Indianapolis. The earlier samples, then, include persons who later left the city after marriage while the 1967 sample includes persons who came into the city after marriage.[6] Second, Rogoff's samples were taken at a point in the life cycle – time of marriage – that most of the people in our sample have passed by at least a few years. Finally, Rogoff's data record the occupation of the father at the time of the respondent's marriage (and omit fathers who were retired or deceased at that time), while the 1967 data refer to the father's occupation while the respondent was growing up.

We do not know the extent to which these various discrepancies might bias the comparison of rates of mobility or the extent to which they might act to cancel each other out. We believe the discrepancies are substantial enough (and the 1967 sample size small enough) to prevent us from accurately estimating small changes, but that potential discrepancies have been sufficiently controlled to allow us to pick up substantial changes which may have occurred.

5. Unfortunately, in dividing the married female respondents from the 1966 data we had to use their ages, since husband's age was not asked.
6. By comparing the length of time respondents have been married and the length of time they have lived in Indianapolis, it was concluded that 72·5 per cent of the 1967 cases probably married in Indianapolis and 21·2 per cent probably married elsewhere. For 6·3 per cent no conclusion was possible.

Measurement

The occupational rank of respondents and their fathers were measured both as an interval scale and as a scale of ranked categories.[7] To obtain the interval scale measure, the occupations were first coded into six-digit Bureau of the Census industry–occupation codes. These codes were then translated into prestige scores, namely, values on the socioeconomic index of occupations developed by Duncan (1961), using the translation program developed by McTavish (1964). These data were used to compute means and correlation coefficients.

To get a scale of ranked occupational categories to build contingency tables relating father's and respondent's occupation, we collapsed the ten categories used by Rogoff into five: professional and business (including semi-professionals), clerical and sales, skilled, semi- and unskilled (including protective service and personal service), and farmer (the farming category, of course, was used just for fathers, since there were no farmer respondents in the 1967 sample). We were forced to collapse this far in order to conserve *N*, but we wished to retain at least four categories of urban occupations in order to avoid reducing our occupational hierarchy to a dichotomy (see Duncan, 1966, pp. 83 ff. for a discussion of the weaknesses of the manual–nonmanual dichotomy). The members of the 1967 sample and their fathers were then coded into these five categories following Rogoff's (1953, Appendix B) lists of detailed occupational titles appearing in each category.

Findings

Tables 1 and 2 present preliminary materials for our investigation of changes in mobility in Indianapolis. Table 1 cross-classifies respondent's and father's occupation, using the five occupational categories collapsed from Rogoff's categories. Table 2 gives means and standard deviations of Duncan SEI scores for respondent's and father's occupation. The 1910 and 1940 calculations in Table 2 (and in Table 4) are those previously published by Duncan (1966, p. 66).

As background for our analyses of mobility, we first note several differences between the time periods in the occupational distributions of origin and destination. Table 1 shows a small rise from 1910 to 1967 in the sample proportion of sons from professional and business origins and from semi- or unskilled origins. Offsetting these is the largest and most consistent change for origins, a steady decline in the proportion of fathers reported as farmers. This decline is partly responsible for the increase in the sample mean of father's occupation from 1910 to 1967 (see Table 2),

7. For a comparison of several methods of measuring mobility, based on both interval scale and categorical data, see Miller (1964).

Table 1 Occupations of Indianapolis white males by father's occupation, for 1910, 1940 and 1967[a]

Occupation of respondent's father	Year	Occupation of respondent[b] (as percentages of row totals)				Row totals	
		Professional or business	Clerical or sales	Skilled manual	Semi- or unskilled	N (100·0 %)	Percentage of year total
professional or business	1967	54·9	16·3	7·1	21·7	50[c]	23·8
	1940	33·0	29·1	15·2	22·6	1784	18·2
	1910	33·1	26·7	20·4	19·8	1690	17·1
clerical or sales	1967	38·6	27·1	21·2	13·0	21	10·0
	1940	20·6	42·3	15·1	22·0	1090	11·1
	1910	16·1	44·2	22·3	17·4	651	6·6
skilled manual	1967	22·4	10·7	41·2	25·8	54	25·7
	1940	10·5	19·2	32·4	37·9	2713	27·7
	1910	7·6	15·3	49·0	28·1	2701	27·3
semi- or unskilled	1967	15·8	8·8	39·7	35·7	65	31·0
	1940	8·7	16·7	17·8	56·9	2633	26·9
	1910	6·3	13·1	29·2	51·4	2468	24·9
farmer	1967	26·5	2·9	23·5	47·1	20	9·5
	1940	11·8	15·8	24·1	48·2	1567	16·0
	1910	11·9	16·3	31·1	40·6	2399	24·2
all respondents	1967	30·0	12·3	28·9	28·7	210	99·9
	1940	15·4	22·4	22·1	40·1	9787	100·0
	1910	13·2	18·9	33·1	34·8	9909	100·0

[a] In this and succeeding Tables, the data for 1967 are adjusted to match the age distribution of Rogoff's 1940 data
[b] In this and succeeding Tables, married female respondents in the 1966 portion of the 1967 data are represented by the occupations of their husbands and their husbands' fathers
[c] The percentages in this row are not multiples of 2·0 per cent, as they normally would be with a base of 50, because the cell entries are not whole numbers, but age-adjusted sums of frequencies

since at each succeeding period a smaller proportion of sons came from this relatively low-ranking origin. However, the mean SEI for urban fathers also increased, from 32·0 to 38·0, reflecting a general upgrading of urban occupations.[8]

8. The probabilities associated with the differences between 1910 and 1967 in the proportion of fathers in professional and business occupations and in semi- or unskilled occupations are both <0·05. For the proportion in farming occupations, the probability is <0·001. The differences between the means of father's occupation for 1910 and 1967 are significant at the 0·001 level for both the total and the urban-origin sample.

The only consistent trend in the distribution of respondent's current occupation is an increase from 1910 to 1967 in the proportion in the professions or business. Table 2 indicates that the mean SEI of respondent's occupation increased about 11 points from 1910 to 1967. At each time point, the sons' means exceeded the fathers'.[9]

Table 2 Means and standard deviations of respondent's and father's occupation, for Indianapolis white males, for 1910, 1940 and 1967

| Sample and year | Duncan's occupational SEI score[a] | | | | |
| | Mean | | Standard deviation | | |
	Father	Respondent	Father	Respondent	N
all respondents					
1967	35·6	43·6	22·6	25·0	210
1940	31·7	34·7	21·1	21·4	9892[b]
1910	27·3	32·5	20·3	20·4	10 253[b]
respondents from urban origins					
1967	38·0	44·3	22·6	24·6	188
1940	35·1	35·7	21·5	21·7	8257
1910	32·0	33·7	21·8	20·4	7568

[a] Calculations for 1940 and 1910 are taken from Duncan (1966, p. 66)
[b] These Ns do not correspond to the Ns in Table 1 because Duncan did not omit respondents currently employed as farmers. There were 105 such respondents in 1940 and 344 in 1910. We assume that these form such a small proportion of their respective samples that their effect on the above results is negligible

Amount of mobility

Table 3 derives summary calculations from Tables 1 and 2 to analyse our first major question: has the movement experienced by Indianapolis white males changed in amount or direction from 1910 to 1967?

Looking first at the second column in the top panel of Table 3, we observe that the proportion of men experiencing a move of some kind has changed very little in the past fifty seven years in Indianapolis. Or, stated conversely, the proportion who 'inherited' (in the sense of having a job in the same rough category as the father) has stayed about the same from 1910 to 1967.

9. The difference between the proportions of respondents in the professions and business for 1910 and 1967 is significant at the 0·001 level for the total sample. The difference in means for respondents from 1910 to 1967 is significant at the 0·001 level for the total sample. For both the total sample and the urban-origin sample and for all time periods, the differences between fathers' and sons' means are significant at least at the 0·05 level.

Table 3 Occupational mobility of Indianapolis white males, for 1910, 1940 and 1967

Sample and year	Mean respondent's SEI minus mean father's SEI	Percentage mobile		N (100·0%)
		Observed	Full-equality model	
all respondents				
1967	8·0	62·6	75·3	210
1940	3·0	65·0	77·8	9787
1910	5·2	65·3	78·8	9909
respondents from urban origins				
1967	6·3	58·7	73·0	188
1940	0·6	58·3	73·9	8220
1910	1·7	54·2	72·3	7510

	Direction of occupational movement[a]					
	Sharply up-mobile	Moder-ately up-mobile	Stable	Moder-ately down-mobile	Sharply down-mobile	N (100·0%)
respondents from urban origins						
1967	14·8	21·0	41·3	13·9	9·0	188
1940	11·6	14·7	41·7	20·9	11·1	8220
1910	9·1	16·5	45·8	18·1	10·5	7510

[a] Ranking the urban occupations from high to low as professional and business, clerical and sales, skilled manual, and semi- and unskilled, a moderate move is one of one rank, a sharp move is one of two or more ranks. These measures are taken only on the urban-reared sample, since the relative rank of farmer fathers and fathers in the various urban strata is not completely clear

We now wish to examine the direction in which the movers moved. The differences between fathers' and respondents' mean SEI scores (see column 1 of the top panel) are positive at every point, meaning that the typical move is upward. The difference is larger for 1967 than for the previous periods, both for all respondents and for urban-reared respondents, suggesting an increase in the amount of upward mobility.[10]

10. The difference between the 1910 difference of means and the 1967 difference of means is significant at the 0·10 level for the total sample and at the 0·01 level for the urban-origin sample.

The bottom panel of Table 3 breaks down the observed movement in terms of direction, using the five-category scale of occupations. Here we see that 1967 respondents were somewhat less likely to be down-mobile and more likely to be up-mobile than respondents in previous years.[11] Thus a shift in the direction of mobility is evident, despite a lack of change in the total proportion of people experiencing mobility.

The second question that can be asked about changes in mobility rates is the extent to which it is induced by such factors as differential fertility. Unfortunately, our data cannot supply a figure for minimum mobility which can be used as a partial answer to this question.

Since our sample includes only a proportion of the employed male population, the marginal totals for son's occupation do not represent all of the occupational positions available to sons in the community. Differences between the fathers' and the sons' occupational distributions in this sample cannot, therefore, be used to estimate minimum or 'forced' mobility.

It may be of interest, however, to compare the observed amount of movement in each period to the amount of movement that would occur under a situation of full equality, that is, a situation in which sons from diverse origins have equal chances to attain each destination. Under this assumption, as Table 3 indicates, about 75 per cent of the men would have experienced movement at each time period. The observed amount of movement is about 75–80 per cent of that expected under full equality at each time period.[12]

Dependence

Our next major question is whether there has been any change from 1910 to 1967 in the extent to which father's occupation influences son's occupation. Table 4 gives values of measures of association between father's and respondent's occupation for 1910, 1940 and 1967. Coefficients are computed treating occupation as an interval scale (r), as a rank-order scale (Kendall's τ_c), and as a nominal scale (Cramér's V).

Duncan's (1966, pp. 63 ff.) earlier regression analysis of the 1910 and 1940 data indicated almost no differences in dependence between the two earlier periods. Slopes and correlation coefficients computed from the 1967

11. Combining the two categories of upward mobility, the difference between 1967 and 1910 is significant at the 0·01 level. Combining the two categories of downward mobility, the difference between 1967 and 1910 is significant at the 0·10 level.
12. For other comparisons of observed data with minimum mobility and full-equality models, see Carlsson (1958, pp. 103–4), Jackson and Crockett (1964), Blau and Duncan (1967, p. 104), and Ramsy (1966). For models of the relationships between mobility and aspects of the social structure, see Matras (1961, p. 1967)

data, however, indicate an increase in dependence since 1940.[13] The difference is small but not negligible – the variance in respondent's occupation explained linearly by father's occupation rises from about 15 per cent in 1940 to about 25 per cent in 1967. This finding persists in the urban-reared sample and so is not just due to the inclusion of sons of farmers.

Table 4 Dependence of respondent's occupation on father's occupation, for Indianapolis white males, for 1910, 1940 and 1967

Sample and year	Regression using Duncan's occupational SEI scores[a]			Measures of association using occupational categories		
	Intercept	Slope	Correlation coefficient	Kendall's τ_c	Cramér's V	N
all respondents						
1967	24·1	0·545	0·495	—[b]	0·263	210
1940	22·8	0·376	0·370	—	0·224	9892
1910	22·6	0·362	0·361	—	0·243	10 253
respondents from urban origins						
1967	22·7	0·569	0·522	0·280	0·259	188
1940	22·0	0·389	0·385	0·283	0·236	8257
1910	21·5	0·381	0·407	0·305	0·274	7568

[a] Regression results for 1940 and 1910 are taken from Duncan (1966, p. 66)
[b] Omitted because the relative rank of the farm-origin category and urban-origin categories is not completely clear

However, the increase in dependence is not reflected in the measures (τ_c and V) computed from categorized data. It seems likely that since the SEI scores pick up more detail in occupational rank, coefficients computed from them are more sensitive to changes in dependence than coefficients based on broad occupational categories. This suggests that future studies of change in mobility should include interval scale measures of occupational prestige as well as the usual cross-tabulations of occupational categories.

In exploring our data in an attempt to better understand the increase in linear dependence between 1940 and 1967, we came across a surprising age effect in the 1967 data. As the top panel of Table 5 shows, the linear relationship between respondent's and father's occupation is extremely high for males under 24, low for males between 24 and 30, and slightly higher for males over 30. The pattern holds, both for the total sample and for urban-reared respondents.

Although the sample size for men under 24 is very small ($N = 39$), the

13. The difference in correlations between 1940 and 1967 is significant at the 0·05 level, for both the total and the urban-origin sample.

high correlation coefficient within this group does not appear to be entirely due to sampling error. First, the difference between correlation coefficients for the under-24 and 24–30 groups seems to be an unlikely random occurrence.[14] Second, as the second and third panels of Table 5 show, the high correlation for the young age group and the low correlation for the 24–30 group appear independently in both the 1966 and 1968 subsamples, despite the differences in sampling procedures between these two studies.

Table 5 Dependence of respondent's on father's occupation, by age, for Indianapolis white males, for 1966 and 1968

Year and age	Sample and regression							
	Respondents from urban origins				All respondents			
	Inter-cept	Slope	Correla-tion coefficient	N	Inter-cept	Slope	Correla-tion coefficient	N
1967 (1966 and 1968 combined)								
under 24	12·56	0·797	0·703	37	11·68	0·812	0·720	39
24–30	29·86	0·399	0·380	117	34·04	0·331	0·311	131
over 30	28·42	0·501	0·461	34	26·88	0·527	0·471	40
1966								
under 24	10·20	0·880	0·756	15	8·72	0·904	0·784	17
24–30	31·59	0·395	0·363	75	35·63	0·327	0·301	85
over 30	31·60	0·410	0·438	22	31·65	0·409	0·426	26
1968								
under 24	15·50	0·692	0·632	22	15·50	0·692	0·632	22
24–30	26·50	0·415	0·429	42	30·69	0·348	0·346	46
over 30	17·67	0·902	0·548	12	13·45	0·989	0·595	14

We conducted further analyses to check on two possible interpretations of this result. Finding that the under-24 group was much more likely than the 24–30 group to have grown up in Indianapolis, we first thought that the difference in correlations across ages was due to migration effects. However, the above pattern of correlations appeared for both in-migrants and nonmigrants. Our second hypothesis was that the direct effect of father's occupation on son's occupation was about the same for all age groups, but

14. For the 1967 urban-origin sample the difference between the correlations for the under-24 and 24–30 groups is significant at the 0·05 level, but the difference between the correlations for the 24–30 and over-30 groups is not significant ($p > 0·60$) For the 1967 total sample, the probability associated with the difference between correlations for under 24 and 24–30 is $<0·01$ and the probability associated with the difference between the correlations for 24–30 and over 30 is $>0·30$. The regressions within each 1967 age group were found to be linear.

the total effect was different because education played a much more vital role in occupational allocation for the younger group. In both the 1966 and 1968 data, however, we found that the direct path from father's to son's occupation was much higher for the under-24 than for the 24–30 group, after education was controlled. The path from education to son's occupation was, if anything, lower for the under-24 group. Hence, neither of our interpretations of the age differences proved tenable.

The increased dependence for 1967 over 1940, therefore, seems to stem primarily from a curiously high correlation between father's and respondent's jobs in the subsample of men under 24. It is conceivable that this correlation indicates a trend toward greater occupational inheritance. However, the present data are only strong enough to support a tentative suggestion on this score. (We should also note that the effect of the under-24 cases in the overall sample is greater than their N would indicate, since they are more than double-weighted in the process of adjusting for age.)

Nature of the transition

The final question of interest is whether changes have occurred in the nature of the process by which sons from various origins move into various destinations. This is equivalent to asking whether the father-to-son transition matrices (as shown in Table 1) have changed in character over time. Because our sample size for 1967 is small we shall omit a cell-by-cell comparison of the matrices and substitute a summary procedure outlined by Duncan (1966, pp. 70–77) and used by him to compare Rogoff's 1910 and 1940 matrices.[15] We will limit our analysis, therefore, to a comparison of the 1940 and 1967 matrices.

Our basic approach will be to contrast the effects of the two matrices in 'converting' the origin distributions (or vectors) into destination vectors. We shall use the matrices in Table 1, percentaged on the row totals, for our comparison. Although it is true that the row totals cannot be taken as an indication of the occupational distribution of fathers at some earlier point in time (see Blau and Duncan, 1967, pp. 82 ff.), each row *is* a sample of men in the work force who come from a particular broad origin. Thus the row percentages validly represent conditional probabilities: given that a man from a particular (row) origin enters the labor force, they express his chances of becoming employed in each of several destination strata. It is in terms of the processes reflected by these conditional probabilities that we wish to compare the 1940 and 1967 matrices.

15. We shall not attempt here several other possible comparative procedures, for example those proposed by Goodman (1969) and Duncan's (1966. pp. 73ff.) adaptation of a method proposed by Deming. These methods require far more faith in the stability of the individual cell Ns than our sample size warrants.

Table 6 Observed and hypothetical occupational distributions of Indianapolis white males, for 1940 and 1967

Sample and occupation of respondent's father	Observed destination distributions		Hypothetical destination distributions		Observed differences	Differences due to differences in transition matrices	
	1940 origin × 1940 matrix	1967 origin × 1967 matrix	1940 origin × 1967 matrix	1967 origin × 1940 matrix		Based on 1940 origin distribution	Based on 1967 origin distribution
	(1)	(2)	(3)	(4)	$(5) = (2)-(1)$	$(6) = (3)-(1)$	$(7) = (2)-(4)$
all respondents							
professional or business	15·4	30·0	29·0	16·4	14·6	13·6	13·6
clerical or sales	22·4	12·3	11·8	22·8	−10·1	−10·6	−10·5
skilled manual	22·1	28·9	29·5	21·2	6·8	7·4	7·7
semi- or unskilled	40·1	28·7	29·7	39·6	−11·4	−10·4	−10·9
total	100·0	99·9	100·0	100·0	−0·1	0·0	−0·1
index of dissimilarity					21·4	21·0	21·3
respondents from urban origins							
professional or business	16·1	30·4	29·5	16·9	14·3	13·4	13·5
clerical or sales	23·6	13·3	13·5	23·5	−10·3	−10·1	−10·2
skilled manual	21·7	29·5	30·6	20·9	7·8	8·9	8·6
semi- or unskilled	38·6	26·8	26·4	38·7	−11·8	−12·2	−11·9
total	100·0	100·0	100·0	100·0	0·0	0·0	0·0
index of dissimilarity					22·1	22·3	22·1

We begin with the observed destination vectors for 1940 and for 1967 (see columns 1 and 2 of Table 6). They can each be considered to be the product of the origin vector for that period multiplied by the matrix of conditional probabilities for that period. The question is: are the observed differences between these destination vectors (shown in column 5) due to differences in the two transition matrices or are they due to multiplying two rather similar transition matrices by two rather different origin vectors? We can resolve this question by multiplying each of the two matrices by the same origin vector. Differences in the resulting hypothetical destination vectors will reflect differences in the transition matrices themselves.

Two reasonable candidates for this 'standard' origin vector are the origin distributions for 1940 and 1967. Column 3 of Table 6 shows the hypothetical destination vector produced by multiplying the 1940 origin vector and the 1967 matrix. We compare this vector to the one in column 1 (the product of the 1940 matrix and the 1940 vector) – the resulting differences (in column 6) reflect only differences between the two matrices. Similarly, column 7, comparing column 4 (the product of the 1940 matrix and the 1967 origin vector) with column 2, also reflects differences between the matrices.

The differences in columns 6 and 7, for both the urban-origin and the total sample, are very similar to the differences between the observed 1940 and 1967 vectors in column 5. This suggests that the differences between the observed destination vectors are mainly due to different processes in the two transition matrices, and not to differences in origin vectors. The 1967 matrix seems to produce more professional and business positions and more skilled manual positions while the 1940 matrix seems to produce more clerical, sales and semi- or unskilled positions. In other words, the 1967 relative to the 1940 transition process seems to produce an upgrading within both the non-manual and the manual categories.

Discussion

The analysis above suggests several changes in Indianapolis mobility patterns:

1 Although the proportion of white males moving out of their broad stratum of origin remained about constant from 1910 to 1967, among the movers, upward mobility became somewhat more common and downward mobility less common from 1940 to 1967.

2 The linear dependence of son's occupation on father's occupation increased moderately from 1940 to 1967; this finding seems to be mainly due to a very high correlation in 1967 for the men under twenty four years of age.

3 The process by which sons from various origins are distributed among various occupational destinations changed somewhat from 1940 to 1967. The 1967 process tended to produce more professional and business and skilled workers and fewer clerical, sales, and semi- and unskilled workers than the 1940 process.

Several comments are needed to put these findings in context. First, our analysis suggests that, at least within limits, an increase of one sort in mobility rate may occur simultaneously with a decrease of another sort. For example, our data show that an increase in upward mobility may be accompanied by a decrease in openness as indexed by a higher level of dependence of son's on father's occupation. Thus considerable upward movement *from origins* is consistent with considerable dependence, in the sense of movement *to destinations* which are highly predictable from origin.

Second, we must recognize alternative interpretations of our findings. For example, Indianapolis is not the same city in 1967 as it was in 1940 or 1910; certainly it is a larger city.[16] Rather than measuring inherent changes, perhaps we are simply charting differences in mobility processes between urban places of different sizes.

Another alternative interpretation concerns the correlation between son's and father's occupation. An increase in this correlation need not mean that ascriptive criteria are becoming more important in the assignment of occupational destinations. In particular, suppose the causal pattern of occupational assignment is (in part) as follows:

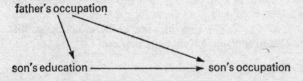

The ascriptive part of the process is mainly reflected in the arrows from father's occupation to son's education and to son's occupation. The arrow from education to occupation (assuming confounding variables are controlled) essentially reflects an achievement process, the effect on occupational allocation of abilities and background validated through performance in the school system.[17] Blau and Duncan (1967, p. 180) tentatively

16. The population of the Indianapolis SMSA was 461 000 in 1940 and 984 000 in 1965.
17. 'Performance in the school system', of course, is not limited to academic work. As Namenwirth (1969) suggests, an important aspect of the achievement process in the school system is 'adaptation to middle-class values'.

conclude from their analysis that the effect of education on occupational assignment has increased over the past several decades. They suggest, that is, that the education–occupation arrow is coming to have more weight. But the correlation between father's and son's occupation is the sum of the coefficient on the arrow directly from father's to son's occupation and the product of the coefficients on the arrows from origin to education and from education to son's occupation. Hence, this correlation could increase just because of the increase in the effect of education without any corresponding increase (or even with a decrease) in the ascriptive effect of father's occupation. In such a situation, an increase in the use of universalistic bases in occupational assignment would show up as an increase in the zero-order dependence of son's on father's occupation. Although this does not appear to be a valid explanation of our findings (see the discussion of Table 5 above) it would still seem that future attempts to gauge changes in mobility should take into account educational (and other) links in the causal process of occupational attainment.

Third, we must note that our findings are strictly limited in generality. There is no necessary reason to think that any changes observed in Indianapolis reflect changes occurring in the society as a whole (see Lane, 1968, pp. 740–41 for a discussion of this point). Nor can we automatically extrapolate our findings to other cities. And, of course, any changes in patterns of intergenerational mobility cannot be assumed to hold true for other forms of flexibility in the stratification system, including, for example, patterns of career mobility.

Finally, we must remind the reader that the 1940 and 1967 data were collected using very different methods and that the observed differences between 1940 and 1967 were only of moderate size. Given these facts, we must regard our results as only suggesting, not firmly establishing, the occurrence of changes in Indianapolis mobility patterns.

References

BLAU, P., and DUNCAN, O. D. (1967), *The American Occupational Structure*, Wiley.

CARLSSON, G. (1958), *Social Mobility and Class Structure*, Gleerup, Lund, Sweden.

DUNCAN, O. D. (1961), 'A socioeconomic index for all occupations', in A. J. Reiss Jr, *et al.*, *Occupations and Social Status*, Free Press, pp. 109–38.

DUNCAN, O. D. (1966), 'Methodological issues in the analysis of social mobility', in N. J. Smelser and S. M. Lipset (eds.), *Social Structure and Mobility in Economic Development*, Aldine, pp. 51–97.

DUNCAN, O. D. (1968), 'Social stratification and mobility: problems in the measurement of trend', in E. B. Sheldon and W. E. Moore (eds.), *Indicators of Social Change*, Russell Sage Foundation, pp. 675–719.

GOODMAN, L. A. (1969), 'How to ransack social mobility tables and other kinds of cross-classification tables', *Amer. J. Sociol.*, vol. 75, pp. 1–40.

JACKSON, E. F., and CROCKETT, H. J. Jr (1964), 'Occupational mobility in the United States: a point estimate and trend comparison', *Amer. Sociol. Rev.*, vol. 29, pp. 5–15.

JACKSON, E. F., and CURTIS, R. F. (1968), 'Conceptualization and measurement in the study of social stratification', in H. M. Blalock Jr and A. B. Blalock (eds.), *Methodology in Social Research*, McGraw-Hill, pp. 112–49.

LANE, A. (1968), 'Occupational mobility in six cities', *Amer. Sociol. Rev.*, vol. 33, pp. 740–49.

MATRAS, J. (1961), 'Differential fertility, intergenerational occupational mobility, and change in the occupational distribution: some elementary interrelationships', *Population Studies*, vol. 15, pp. 187–97.

MCTAVISH, D. G. (1964), 'A method for more reliably coding detailed occupations into Duncan's socioeconomic categories', *Amer. Sociol. Rev.*, vol. 9, pp. 402–6.

MILLER, A. D. (1964), 'Indexes of occupational status and mobility in relation to psychosomatic symptoms: a comparative study of concepts', M.A. thesis, University of North Carolina.

NAMENWIRTH, J. Z. (1969), 'Failing in New Haven: an analysis of high school graduates and dropouts', *Social Forces*, vol. 48, pp. 23–36.

RAMSY, N. (1966), 'Changes in rates and forms of mobility', in N. J. Smelser and S. M. Lipset (eds.), *Social Structure and Mobility in Economic Development*, Aldine, pp. 213–341.

ROGOFF, N. (1953), *Recent Trends in Occupational Mobility*, Free Press.

SUDMAN, S. (1966), 'Probability sampling with quotas', *Amer. Stat. Assn*, vol. 61, pp. 749–76.

7 S. Yasuda

A Methodological Inquiry into Social Mobility[1]

S. Yasuda, 'A methodological inquiry into social mobility', *American Sociological Review*, vol. 29, 1964, pp. 16–23.

Since Sorokin's pioneering work, a considerable body of information has accumulated on the subject of social mobility.[2] Concepts and measuring devices have not yet been sufficiently refined,[3] however, and present controversies among students of social mobility are partly attributable to this deficiency.[4]

The index of association, Q-coefficient, and Y-coefficient

In a discussion of the methodology of mobility measurement, devices used to measure pure mobility must be mentioned first.[5] I believe that the only

1. The Japanese original of this article was twice as voluminous, including detailed methodological discussion of both the conception and measurement of social mobility (Yasuda, 1962). In this English version the discussion will focus on problems of measurement, particularly the measurement of intergenerational mobility. The author wishes to thank Miss Patricia Golden and Dr John I. Kitsuse, who did so much to refine the English in this paper.
2. For a bibliography of cumulative achievements in the field of social mobility, see for example, Mack, Freeman and Yellin (1957).
3. Recent contributions on this point include: Carlsson (1958); Tumin and Feldman (1957); Westoff, Bressler and Sagi (1960).
4. For example, Lenski (1958a) pointed out that the controversy between Sjoberg, Peterson, and Lipset and Bendix on the one hand and Chinoy and Hertzler on the other, about the mobility trend in American society, stems mainly from failure to distinguish between intergenerational and intragenerational mobility; that is, while the rate of intergenerational mobility may have increased, the rate of intragenerational mobility has declined. Lenski might have added the distinction between pure and factual mobility. While most optimists viewing the trend of American mobility are thinking of the increase of intergenerational pure mobility, all of the sceptics are concerned with the decline of intragenerational factual mobility. (See footnote 5.)
5. *Factual mobility* is the concrete mobility of an individual. It may be caused by (1) changes in stratum composition, (2) differential change among strata in size of population (birth, death, in- and out-migration), and (3) interchange of individuals between different status categories. We cannot attribute the factual mobility of specific individuals to one of the three factors, but we can divide *total mobility*, or the total amount of factual mobility in a society. into *forced mobility* (that caused by the first two factors) and *pure mobility* (that caused by the third factor), and assess

measure used hitherto is the index of association (and dissociation), or social distance mobility, or the coefficient of association, as it is called by Glass (1954), Rogoff (1953), and Carlsson (1958), respectively. It looks very plausible indeed, taking the formula

$$N f_{ij}/n_{i.} \, n_{.j}, \qquad\qquad 1$$

when the association between the two generations is shown as in Table 1.

Table 1

Father's	Subject's status (j)				
status (i)	1	2	3	... r	Total
1	f_{11}	f_{12}	f_{13}	... f_{1r}	$n_{1.}$
2	f_{21}	f_{22}	f_{23}	... f_{2r}	$n_{2.}$
3	f_{31}	f_{32}	f_{33}	... f_{3r}	$n_{3.}$
.	.	.	.	....	.
.	.	.	.	....	.
.	.	.	.	....	.
r	f_{r1}	f_{r2}	f_{r3}	... f_{rr}	$n_{r.}$
total	$n_{.1}$	$n_{.2}$	$n_{.3}$	... $n_{.r}$	N

But when we scrutinize its range of possible values, the index turns out to be very misleading. It has a value of one in the case of perfect mobility according to Glass's terminology (that is, statistical independence), and a minimum value of zero when f_{ij} is zero. The maximum value occurs when f_{ij} is greatest. This is identical to $n_{.j}$ when $n_{i.} > n_{.j}$ (when $n_{i.} < n_{.j}$, the maximum f_{ij} equals $n_{i.}$). Hence the maximum value of the index of association A is

$$\text{Max } A = N/n_{i.} \qquad \text{when } n_{i.} > n_{.j} \qquad\qquad 2$$
$$\text{Max } A = N/n_{.j} \qquad \text{when } n_{i.} < n_{.j} \qquad\qquad 2'$$

Therefore, the index of association is not independent of the marginal distribution, being influenced by the value of $n_{i.}$ or $n_{.j}$.

This has already been pointed out and fully discussed with hypothetical data by W. Z. Billewicz (1955). As a substantive example, the index for semi-professionals in Rogoff's Indianapolis data decreased sharply from 14·61 to 6·23 because the marginal total for that occupation increased

---

their relative contributions. Pure mobility has sometimes been called individual mobility (e.g., Kahl, 1953), but this terminology is inappropriate because pure mobility is a concept at the societal level, not at the level of the individual. See Westoff, Bressler and Sagi (1960).

markedly from 1910 to 1940. Measured by the Q-coefficient to be explained below, the values are 0·913 and 0·777, which does not represent a sharp decline.

For a more striking example, the Research Committee of the Japan Sociological Society (1958) calculated values of the index for a national sample and obtained the results shown in the first column of Table 3. In Japan there are few farmers whose fathers were not farmers; hence the value of the index of association ought to be very high for the farmer group. But contrary to expectation, Table 3 shows the lowest value for farmers. This is because the farmer group had a far larger marginal than any other occupational category in the Japan of 1954, and the index of association is influenced by the size of the marginal. According to the Q-coefficient and the y'-coefficient explained below, farmers show a very high association between two generations.[6]

Now, in this situation we must adopt another index to measure pure mobility. I believe the problem is simply to measure the association between the subject's status and his father's. There are many measures of association between two qualitative attributes, but I first tried Yule's coefficient of association Q for the following reasons.

First, Q takes a maximum value of $+1$ and a minimum value of -1, and it is zero when the situation is one of perfect mobility. Secondly, among the various measures of qualitative association, Q is the only one that takes an extreme value $(+1$ or $-1)$ when only one cell of a given fourfold table is zero, as in Table 2a or 2b. Other measures of qualitative association take extreme values only when both cells on the principal or minor diagonal are zero, as in Table 2c. Since pure mobility must be considered as zero in Tables 2a and 2b also, a measure of pure mobility should give an extreme value. Therefore, traditional measures other than the Q-coefficient are not appropriate for measuring pure mobility,

The shortcomings of Q as a measure of pure mobility are as follows:

1 Because it is defined only for fourfold tables, rows and columns other than the ith row and j^{th} column in question must be combined in order to compute Q for an $m \times m$ table.

6. This criticism of the index of association is also applicable to the so-called *location quotient* some human ecologists are using, because the defining formula of the latter is the same. But while the former is defined for $m \times m$ tables where the two series of categories (statuses of two generations) are identical with each other, the location quotient is usually defined for $m \times n$ tables (where $m \neq n$). Hence in the case of regional analysis, the Q-coefficient, but not the y-coefficient explained below, can be used instead of the location quotient. For the location quotient, see, for example, Duncan, Scott and Lieberson (1960).

Table 2a

father's status	subject's status		
	j	others	total
i	f_{ij}	0	$n_i.(=f_{ij})$
others	$n._j-f_{ij}$	$N-n._j$	$N-n_i.$
total	$n._j$	$N-n._j$	N

Table 2b

father's status	subject's status		
	j	others	total
i	0	$n_i.$	$n_i.$
others	$n._j$	$N-n_i.-n._j$	$N-n_i.$
total	$n._j$	$N-n.$	N

Table 2c

father's status	subject's status		
	j	others	total
i	f_{ij}	0	$n_i.(=f_{ij})$
others	0	$N-f_{ij}$	$N-n_i.$
total	$n._j(=f_{ij})$	$N-n._j$	N

2 To obtain a Q-value for a row, column, or whole table rather than a cell, one must produce an average of the Q-values for all cells weighted by $n_i. \, n._j/N$, and that calculation is not easy to handle.

3 The formula for Q does not have a clear-cut mathematical meaning. It is formulated only as a measure to satisfy three formal conditions: that is, to give values of $+1$, -1, and zero when at least one cell on the minor diagonal is zero, at least one cell on the principal diagonal is zero, and the association is null, respectively.

Consequently, I have formulated an original measure for social mobility. As mentioned in footnote 5, the total amount of social mobility in a given society stems from two sources: forced mobility and pure mobility. Now, the factual out-mobility in the ith row in Table 1 is

$$n_i. \; -f_{ij}. \qquad\qquad\qquad 3$$

The forced out-mobility is

$$n_i. \; -\bar{n}_{i1} \qquad\qquad\qquad 4$$

where $\bar{n}_{ii}$ means the smaller of $n_{i.}$ and $n_{.i}$. Hence the pure mobility is

$$(n_{i.} - f_{ii}) - (n_{i.} - \bar{n}_{ii}) = (\bar{n}_{ii} - f_{ii}).[7] \qquad\qquad 5$$

Now pure mobility must be measured from the origin of perfect mobility. Since the pure mobility in the perfect mobility situation is

$$(n_{i.} - n_{i.}\, n_{.i}/N) - (n_{i.} - \bar{n}_{ii}) = \bar{n}_{ii} - n_{i.}\, n_{.i}/N, \qquad\qquad 6$$

a *coefficient of openness* which measures the degree of approximation to perfect mobility can be formulated as 5/6, namely

$$y_{ii} = (\bar{n}_{ii} - f_{ii})/(\bar{n}_{ii} - n_{i.}\, n_{.i}/N). \qquad\qquad 7$$

Likewise, the coefficient of openness for the sum of all strata can be defined as

$$Y = (\Sigma\, \bar{n}_{ii} - \Sigma f_{ii})/(\Sigma\, \bar{n}_{ii} - \Sigma\, n_{i.}\, n_{.i}/N). \qquad\qquad 8$$

Both y_{ii} and Y take the value of 1 when the ith cell and all the cells on the principal diagonal contain the figures expected in the perfect mobility situation and zero when there is no pure mobility.

A minor problem in the proposed formula is that the value of y can be influenced by the size of marginals when mobility is greater than perfect. This becomes apparent when we consider the other extreme value of y. Where none of the sons has the same occupation as his father, f_{ii} would be zero, and max $y_{ii} = \bar{n}_{ii}/(\bar{n}_{ii} - n_{i.}\, n_{.i}/N)$, which depends again on the size of marginal totals. But this deficiency is negligible, because f_{ii} seldom surpasses $n_{i.}\, n_{.i}/N$ in practice.[8]

Because the cells outside the principal diagonal often have values surpassing $n_{i.}\, n_{.i}/N$, we hesitate to define y_{ij} (where i $\neq$ j) by mechanically expanding the formula of the y_{ii} coefficient.

The y-coefficient shows to what degree a given society approaches the maximum mobility possible in the perfect mobility situation, strictly following the concept of pure mobility. Moreover, its calculation is very simple. Hence the y-coefficient is superior to other measures of pure mobility.

---

7. The same expression for pure mobility can be derived from the formulae for in-mobility. The factual in-mobility is $n_{.i} - f_{ii}$, the forced in-mobility is $n_{.i} - \bar{n}_{ii}$, therefore the pure mobility must be $(n_{.i} - f_{ii}) - (n_{.i} - \bar{n}_{ii}) = \bar{n}_{ii} - f_{ii}$.

8. As suggested implicitly in the preceding paragraph, a Y-coefficient of 1 does not always mean theoretically the perfectly mobile society, although the perfectly mobile society would always have a Y value of 1. But since f_{ii} seldom surpasses $n_{i.}\, n_{.i}/N$ in practice, a Y-coefficient of 1 almost always means perfect mobility.

The y-coefficient is strictly equivalent to Durbin's (1955) index I.[9] But he did not show the mathematical derivation of the new index, nor did he specify its sociological meaning. He states, 'whether I measures what the sociologist is interested in better than [the index of association] A is another matter.' In my construction of the y-coefficient, however, I have given primary consideration to its sociological meaning.

Let us now compare the Q-coefficient and the y-coefficient with the index of association. Table 3 shows those values for major occupational categories of the Japanese male population. They are calculated for the cells on the principal diagonal, and in place of the y-coefficient

$$y'_{11} = 1 - y_{11} \qquad\qquad 9$$

is used, so that larger values indicate greater distance from perfect mobility. Differences between categories are reflected most in the y-coefficient and least in the Q-coefficient. While the rank correlation between the y-coefficient and the Q-coefficient is 0·88, it is only 0·42 between the index of association and the y-coefficient, reflecting the invalidity of the index of association.

Table 4 shows the openness of various countries, as measured by the Y-coefficient.[10] Because the time point of intergenerational comparison

9. Supplementing Billewicz' criticism of the index of association, Durbin suggested a new index
$$I = (A-1)n_{11}/(N-n_{11}),$$
(where n_{11} means the larger of n_1 and $n_{.1}$), in the place of the index of association. The formula turns out to be

$$I = \left(\frac{Nf}{n\bar{n}} - 1\right)\frac{n}{N-n}$$
$$= \left(\frac{Nf}{\bar{n}} - n\right)\frac{1}{N-n}$$
$$= \left(N - n - N + \frac{Nf}{\bar{n}}\right)\frac{1}{N-n}$$
$$= 1 - \left(N - \frac{Nf}{\bar{n}}\right)\frac{1}{N-n}$$
$$= 1 - \frac{N\bar{n} - Nf}{\bar{n}(N-n)}$$
$$= 1 - \frac{\bar{n} - f}{\bar{n} - \bar{n}n/N}$$
$$= 1 - y_{11}.$$

(Here we have omitted the subscript ii for f, $\bar{n}$, and n for brevity.)

10. The original data were taken from the following sources. Because absolute figures were not given for British and German data, we calculated them from percentages and then determined Y-coefficients for those countries. Glass (1954, p. 183); Carlsson (1958, p. 93); Research Committee of the Japan Sociological Society (1958, p. 160); Janowitz (1958); Brésard (1952). The original data for the United States were taken from the 1956 Election Study, courtesy of the Survey Research Center, University of Michigan.

Table 3 Comparison of the three indexes for Japanese occupational categories

Occupation	Index of association A	Q-coefficient	Y'-coefficient
professional	6·0	0·86	0·36
managerial	3·2	0·65	0·17
clerical workers	2·2	0·52	0·15
sales workers	3·0	0·71	0·28
skilled workers	3·7	0·79	0·35
semiskilled workers	3·2	0·65	0·17
unskilled workers	4·4	0·80	0·26
farmers	1·7	0·85	0·72

varies among these countries, the sampling error of the y-coefficient is unknown, and because there are problems intrinsic to qualitative association,[11] the values in Table 4 cannot be regarded rigorously. Without these limita-

Table 4 Comparison of intergenerational pure mobility among various countries

Country	Y-coefficient
England and Wales	0·848
Sweden	0·776
United States	0·724
Japan	0·604
West Germany	0·569
France	0·535

tions, the values would reveal that England is unexpectedly open; Sweden is also more open than the United States, despite the large proportion of agricultural workers; and Japan ranks between the United States and West Germany.

The time point in intergenerational comparison

In previous studies of intergenerational mobility, it has been customary to cross-tabulate the subject's present occupational status by his father's main occupational status. But Glass (1954, p. 179), Carlsson (1958, p. 78) and Lenski (1958a) have pointed out a large pitfall in this approach. The

11. Any measure of qualitative association would be influenced by the number of categories and by the way in which the categories are delimited. See Carlsson (1958, pp. 115–16), and Goodman and Kruskal (1954).

subject's present status has not yet stabilized if he is still young, and it is lower than that of his prime of life if he is now very old. In either case the subject's present status is not comparable with his father's main status. Thus, Glass suggests that only the main occupations of persons past fifty should be studied, and Lipset and Bendix suggest that the subject's present status be compared with the father's status when he was the same age as the subject (1959, pp. 182–3).

Glass's suggestion is awkward because it omits most of the present population. The Lipset–Bendix suggestion is also awkward because it mechanically matches the two generations by age without any other considerations. An even more important objection to both is that they neglect the relation between intergenerational and intragenerational mobility. That is, their measurements of intergenerational mobility do not distinguish between that portion which is a function of the mobility advantages derived from the father's status and that which is a consequence of the son's own career mobility. The former should probably be taken as the measure of intergenerational mobility, the latter as intragenerational mobility.

Mukherjee and Hall (1954) have made an important comment on this point. They state that in previous studies of social mobility,

in most cases the problem was assumed to be solved by examining the association between the father's and subject's final status categories in a contingency table. But this is to treat the question in a static manner, and to overlook the essential dynamic character of social mobility. [And,] the analysis should ideally begin with his birth, his social status then being that of his father, and this status should be related to the successive changes in the status the individual himself achieves during his life, until he reaches stability in his final status. In this way the analysis would cover movement in time as well as in, so to speak, space (pp. 218–20).

They are correct in pointing out that the status of the father is also exposed to intragenerational change. But if they assume that a son at birth has the same status as his father and if they discard the comparison of the final statuses of the two generations, at what time-point(s) can they compare the statuses intergenerationally? It is also questionable to take birth as the origin of career.

Lenski clearly understood the complex relation between intra- and intergenerational mobility, but his technique was somewhat clumsy. He wanted to compare both generations in their forties and to eliminate the effect of the subject's intragenerational mobility. Accordingly he had to estimate the future distributions of cohorts now in their twenties and thirties and also to estimate the effect of intragenerational mobility by a rule of thumb. The error of the double estimate might be great.

I would argue that intergenerational mobility should properly be measured by the comparison of two generations' statuses at the time the career of an independent adult begins, rather than at birth or in the forties. The status of the father influences the son at that time, or cumulatively until that time, but their two statuses are not always identical. The difference in status between the two generations is not negligible, and it reflects intergenerational mobility. After the son becomes an independent adult, intragenerational mobility may occur.[12]

Rogoff's approach is very similar in respect to the time point of comparison between the two generations, though this may have been an incidental result of the type of data she employed. She compared males' occupation at marriage with fathers' occupation at the same time. There are also Japanese studies that take the father's occupation at the time the son finished his compulsory education (for example, see Honda, 1956). This again is quite similar.

It is, however, more appropriate to use the time when a young man begins his independent occupational career as a starting point, and compare the statuses of the two generations at that time. Marriage marks the onset of a kind of independent adult life, but it refers to life as a family or consumption unit. If we represent social status by occupation, the beginning of occupational career is logically more consistent than the beginning of marriage as a starting point. It is also better than the end of compulsory education for the same reason.

Incidentally, the Glass and Lipset–Bendix methods cannot analyse the trend of intergenerational mobility on the basis of one interviewing survey. Our method makes it possible to do this by studying intergenerational comparisons by cohort. This is another advantage of the method.

The following data show the mobility trend in Japan, presented according to these methodological considerations. The sample is a probability-proportionate random sample of the male population residing in Tokyo central city, regardless of original birthplace.[13] Table 5 presents Y-

12. As Lenski pointed out, the father's status may influence the son's even after the young man starts his own career. But unless both types of mobility are defined in a certain measurable way, we cannot proceed further. I think it is impossible to define intragenerational mobility as Lenski conceives it, entirely free from the effect of father's status; see Lenski (1958b).
13. The survey was conducted in October 1960 with a probability sample of 1252 adult males residing in Tokyo central city. In July 1961 a supplementary survey of the wives of the previous sample was conducted. As birth order was not included until the second survey, this information was available for only a portion of the original sample, because not all of the original sample were married and because there were non-responses in the second survey. Tokyo central city (*Tokyo-kubu* in Japanese) consists of the substantial part of the built-up area of Tokyo. Official statistics treat this area as a city, though it is not a complete political unit.

coefficients of the association between the subject's first job and his father's job at that time. While the trend is not absolutely clear because of the small size of the sample and possible specific historical conditions, it can be seen that pure mobility has increased steadily.

Table 5 *Y*-coefficient between subject's first job and father's job at that time, by cohort

Age of cohort	Y-coefficient
20–24	0·91
25–29	0·77
30–34	0·66
35–39	0·71
40–49	0·68
50–59	0·56
60+	0·64

Now, if we were to compare the subject's present job with his father's main job, as Glass and Carlsson did, what would the same data show? Table 6 shows the results of this calculation in terms of *Y*-coefficients. Since the higher the age, the more the intragenerational mobility is compounded cumulatively, the older cohorts look more open and it appears that the society is growing more rigid. This is undoubtedly illusory.

Table 6 *Y*-coefficient between subject's present job and father's main job, by cohort

Age of cohort	Y-coefficient
20–24	0·70
25–29	0·69
30–34	0·80
35–39	0·86
40–49	0·72
50–59	0·91
60+	0·90

Therefore, Glass and Carlsson's conclusion that there is no change in the trend of pure mobility in Britain and Sweden cannot be supported (Glass, 1954, pp. 185–8; Carlsson, 1958, p. 130): first, because the index of association is invalid, and second, because of the discrepancy between father's and son's stage of occupational career.

The family in generational mobility

We have hitherto regarded social mobility as a purely individual behavior, neglecting the fact that the subject and his father belong to a family unit. A more detailed scrutiny of social mobility demands recognition of some glaring problems in connection with the family.

The first is the problem of birth order. As Tumin and Feldman (1957) have already pointed out, siblings cannot be expected to be evenly mobile irrespective of birth order, even in the United States. Since in Japan the institution of primogeniture remains, birth order must inevitably be taken into account in the study of social mobility. In self-employed families, and sometimes even in employed families, the eldest son is expected to succeed his father, even though this is not necessarily fully realized in practice. It is often impossible for other sons to take the same job. This is especially true for farmers, due to the limited size of Japanese farms. Therefore, while it is not necessarily futile to analyse intergenerational mobility without reference to the difference between the eldest and other sons, this method is

Table 7 Occupational distribution of eldest sons and others, Tokyo male population

Occupation	Tokyo natives		In-migrants	
	Eldest	Others	Eldest	Others
self-employed	23·1	18·1	8·7	11·5
professional and				
managerial	8·3	6·6	19·6	6·9
clerical workers	24·8	16·4	21·7	19·4
manual workers:				
in big enterprise	16·5	13·1	14·1	14·3
in small enterprise	25·6	43·5	35·9	45·7
others	1·7	2·5	0·0	1·8
total	100·0	100·0	100·0	100·0
	(121)	(122)	(92)	(217)

decidedly less valuable. Table 7, based on data from the sample of males residing in central Tokyo, shows that irrespective of place of origin, the eldest sons have obtained better jobs than the others.[14] (This is also true for educational attainment, which is not shown here.)

14. The influence of birth order on occupational attainment is assumed to be larger in rural areas than in Tokyo. The large difference between the eldest son and the other in-migrants in the professional and managerial category (19·6 versus 6·9) in Table 7 illustrates this fact. But because eldest sons who have succeeded to their fathers' small businesses (including farms) tend to stay in their home towns, the difference in birth order does not appear in self-employed groups of in-migrants to Tokyo.

A second problem deserves closer examination. Previous studies of inter-generational mobility have always used the son as the reference point. Although they are usually termed comparisons of two generations, sons and fathers, they are more strictly a comparison between the subject and his father. Since a father may have more than one son, there is a possibility that two subjects' fathers are identical, i.e. the number of fathers is inflated. (This consideration has already been pointed out; for example, Glass, 1954, pp. 242–7.) Such inflation is not really a deficiency in research, since the comparison concerns the status of a subject *vis-à-vis* his father, with the son-subject as the reference point.

But it is equally possible to take the father as a reference point, and to compare the statuses of a subject and his sons.[15] Suppose a society consists of three families, A, B and C. Family A has an only son, who has followed his father's occupation. Family B has two sons, the elder of whom has followed in his father's footsteps. Family C has three sons, and one son other than the eldest has followed his father's occupation. Proceeding in the usual way, the mobility rate will work out to 0·50, since three out of six sons chose occupations different from their fathers'. Conversely, the occupational inheritance rate is 0·50, because three out of six sons chose the same occupation as their fathers. The picture changes, however, when the mobility pattern is viewed from the father's standpoint. In one sense, the occupational inheritance rate of this imaginary society is 100 per cent, because each of the fathers' occupations has been filled by one son. In another sense, but also from the standpoint of the father, the inheritance rate is 66·7 per cent, because two out of three of the fathers' positions have been filled by eldest sons. There is a third angle: the inheritance rate is 100 per cent for family A, 50 per cent for family B, and 33·3 per cent for family C, because in families B and C the sons have only partially succeeded their fathers occupationally. From this view, the occupational inheritance rate of the whole society would be $(1 + 0·50 + 0·33)/3 = 0·61$.

Which of these three approaches is most valid depends on the institutions of a given society and the analyst's theoretical interests. At any rate, they afford a picture different from the one obtained by the usual method.

All the viewpoints using the father as a reference require a little more information about the interviewees. The first and third require knowledge of the statuses of all the interviewees' siblings at the appropriate time point. The number of fathers should be weighted in inverse proportion to the number of siblings. The second viewpoint requires knowledge of birth-order, and only fathers of eldest sons are enumerated.

Table 8 presents an example of the second method from the father's

15. This possibility was originally suggested by Professor Susumu Kurasawa at Tokyo Gakugei University, in a personal discussion with me.

standpoint. The figures in the Table represent out-flow inheritance rates, or the percentage of fathers in a given stratum whose sons have succeeded them.[16] The figures in the left-hand column are calculated for eldest sons only. Hence that column is based on the second viewpoint. The right-hand

Table 8 Inheritance rates for Tokyo natives, calculated by two different methods

Father's occupation	Eldest son	All sons
liberal profession	16·7	6·7
self-employed	37·5	25·7
professional and		
managerial	6·3	13·2
clerical workers	71·4	53·1
manual workers:		
in big enterprise	37·5	47·8
in small enterprise	42·1	54·7
others	11·1	17·6
total	33·0	30·8

column is based on the usual approach, with the son as the reference point, so the number of fathers is inflated. In a society like Japan where primogeniture is traditional, the inheritance rate is higher from the father's standpoint than it is from the son's. This is true even in employed strata like the clerical-worker category. But Table 8 also shows that primogeniture is now followed by only one-third of Tokyo residents.

The difference between using the father and the son as reference points also holds for pure mobility analysis. In Table 3 the y'-coefficient was highest in the farmer stratum, but not equal to 1·00. This is mainly because the coefficient was calculated from the son's standpoint. If the y'-coefficient were calculated for eldest sons only, it would be closer to 1·00, and if it were calculated from the first of the three father-standpoints, it would be almost 1·00.

References

BILLEWICZ, W. Z. (1955). 'Some remarks on the measurement of social mobility', *Pop. Stud.*, vol. 9, pp. 96–100.

BRÉSARD, M. M. (1952), 'La mobilité sociale en France', *Cahiers Français d'information*, no. 196.

CARLSSON, G. (1958), *Social Mobility and Class Structure*, Gleerup, Lund, Sweden.

DUNCAN, O. D., SCOTT, W. R., and LIEBERSON, S. (1960), *Metropolis and Region*, Johns Hopkins University Press.

16. The data in Table 8 are from the Tokyo sample survey mentioned above.

GLASS, D. V. (ed.) (1954), *Social Mobility in Britain*, Routledge & Kegan Paul.

GOODMAN, L. A., and KRUSKAL, W. H. (1954), 'Measures of association for cross-classifications, I', *J. Amer. stat. Assn*, vol. 49, pp. 732–64.

HONDA, T. (1956), 'Kindai-teki Rodosha Kaikyu no Demographteki Kosatsu' (A demographic inquiry into modern working class), *Jinko Mondai Kenkyu*, no. 66.

JANOWITZ, M. (1958), 'Social stratification and mobility in West Germany', *Amer. J. Sociol.*, vol. 64, pp. 6–24.

KAHL, J. A. (1953), *The American Class Structure*, Holt, Rinehart & Winston.

LENSKI, G. E. (1958a), 'Social stratification', in J. S. Roucek, *Contemporary Sociology*, Philosophical Library, pp. 521–38.

LENSKI, G. E. (1958b), 'Trends in intergenerational occupational mobility in the United States', *Amer. sociol. Rev.*, vol. 23, pp. 514–23.

LIPSET, S. M., and BENDIX, R. (1959), *Social Mobility in Industrial Society*, University of California Press.

MACK, W., FREEMAN, L., and YELLIN, S. (1957), *Social Mobility: Thirty Years of Research and Theory*, Syracuse University Press.

MUKHERJEE, R., and HALL, J. R. (1954), 'A note on the analysis of data on social mobility', in D. V. Glass (ed.), *Social Mobility in Britain*, Routledge & Kegan Paul.

RESEARCH COMMITTEE OF THE JAPANESE SOCIOLOGICAL SOCIETY (1958), *Nippon Shakai no Kaiso-teki Kozo* (Status structure of Japanese society), Yuhikaku, Tokyo.

ROGOFF, N. (1953), *Recent Trends in Occupational Mobility*, Free Press.

TUMIN, M. M., and FELDMAN, A. S. (1957), 'Theory and measurement of occupational mobility', *Amer. sociol. Rev.*, vol. 22, pp. 281–8.

WESTOFF, C. F., BRESSLER, M., and SAGI, P. C. (1960), 'The concept of social mobility: an empirical inquiry', *Amer. sociol. Rev.*, vol. 25, pp. 375–85.

YASUDA, S. (1962), 'Shakai-Ido-Ron eno Tokeo-teki Josetsu' (A statistical introduction to social mobility study), *Shakai-Kagaku Ronshu*, Tokyo University of Education, no. 9, March.

8 O. D. Duncan

Methodological Issues in the Analysis of Social Mobility

Excerpts from O. D. Duncan, 'Methodological issues in the analysis of social mobility', in N. J. Smelser and S. M. Lipset (eds.), *Social Structure and Mobility in Economic Development*, Aldine, 1966, pp. 51-97.

Smelser and Lipset refer to the logic that economic growth should result in a pattern of high upward and low downward mobility, whilst noting that the logic is not always borne out by the data. Apparently, the logic rests on one or more assumptions that are contrary to fact. They themselves, at this juncture, call for a resort to inductive procedure: 'What is necessary is a systematic effort to relate the data of changes, classified in different ways, to the estimates of growth.'

These remarks suggest, among other things, that a sharp separation of issues in theory from problems of method is no more justified in the study of social mobility than in any other domain of inquiry. The methodologist is concerned with the grounds for accepting bodies of data as evidence for or against propositions. If he can show how verbal formulations place logically irreconcilable demands on bodies of data – those in existence, or those that might conceivably come into existence – then revision of the formulations is in order. Rather than answering the questions posed by theory, fundamental study of analytical methods is likely to make two questions grow where only one flourished before.

This paper makes two kinds of contribution. In the next section, the issue of how occupational mobility may be related to changes in occupational structure is considered in greater detail. Some positive results are obtained, but the topic is left at the point where the theorist must vouchsafe a revised formulation as a basis for further methodological and empirical explorations. The remaining sections of the paper deal with a selection of technical and methodological issues raised in the literature on intergenerational occupational mobility. The issues are ones I consider important and on which I profess to have something to say. They hardly exhaust the agenda of pressing problems. The vexing topic of what effect errors in mobility data have on conclusions, treated cursorily in the first draft of this paper, is omitted for lack of space. Other matters meriting discussion but ignored here are covered in a recent methodological paper by Yasuda (1964)[1] with most of whose points I am in general agreement, despite some reservations about specific procedures.

1. See Reading 7 [Eds.].

Occupational mobility and the transformation of occupational structures

If the reader, like the writer, finds it helpful to have the problem posed concretely rather than in purely abstract terms, he may refer to Table 1, where occupational distributions for two years are exhibited in columns *a* and *b*. The years 1960 and 1930 were selected so as to be about a generation apart. (The median age of all men who have sons born in a given year usually is around thirty or thirty-one.) The net changes in the male occupational distribution in the US during this period are matters of common knowledge – the rapid increases in proportions of white-collar, particularly professional and technical jobs; the likewise appreciable increases of occupations involving skilled or semiskilled manual work; the marked decline in proportion of laborers; and the even more pronounced decrease in percentage of farm workers, both farm operators and farm laborers. Over the period in question, moreover, the absolute size of the male labor force increased by about one-fourth.

The character of the transformation that produced these changes is not so well understood. Indeed, the information needed for a complete analysis of it is not now and may never become available. We can, nevertheless, profitably study the problem of whether certain components of the transformation could, in theory, be related to the idea of occupational mobility.

A convenient point of departure is the well-known discussion by Kahl (1957, ch. 9) which is noteworthy as an explicit formulation of the problem, superseding a mass of prior literature. Although the conclusion of the present discussion is that Kahl's effort was a failure – and for fundamental reasons, not merely because of flaws in the data available to him – it falls into the class of honorable failures which needed to be made in order to force a reexamination of the problem.

Kahl looked at US data on occupational distributions in 1920 and 1950 (which showed much the same sort of changes as those for 1930 and 1960 reproduced here). He also had available a conventional father–son mobility table derived from a 1947 survey. He then reasoned somewhat as follows. The sons in the mobility table represent a current occupational distribution, the fathers the occupations being pursued a generation ago. Equating interperiod change, 1920–50, with intergenerational net change as depicted in the marginals of the mobility table, Kahl supposed that the gross mobility revealed in the table might be decomposed into components due to 'four causes of movement': technological, reproductive, and immigration mobility, and mobility due to the fact that 'some people slip down and make room for others to move up', later referred to as 'individual mobility'. Certain additional data were used to make estimates of mobility induced by differential reproduction and immigration. Technological mobility was estimated from the dissimilarity of the two census occupational distributions for 1920 and 1950. With total mobility given in the intergenerational table and with the other three components estimated from other sources, Kahl obtains as a residual the amount of individual mobility.

Table 1 Change in occupational distribution (percentage) of the total male working force in the United States, 1930–60, and percentage distribution of men 25–64 years old in the 1962 working force by own occupation and father's occupation

| Major occupation group | Total male working force | | Male working force 25–64 years old, 1962 | | Inter-annual change | Inter-genera-tional difference |
	1960 (a)	1930 (b)	Own occupa-tion (c)	Father's occupa-tion (d)	(a)–(b)	(c)–(d)
all occupations	100·0	100·0	100·0	100·0	—	—
professional, technical and kindred workers	10·4	4·8	12·9	4·8	5·6	8·1
managers, officials and proprietors, except farm	10·8	8·8	16·2	11·8	2·0	4·4
sales workers	7·0	6·1	5·2	4·0	0·9	1·2
clerical and kindred workers	7·2	5·5	6·6	3·4	1·7	3·2
craftsmen, foremen and kindred workers	20·7	16·2	20·8	18·5	4·5	2·3
operatives and kindred workers	21·2	15·3	18·6	15·4	5·9	3·2
service workers including private household	6·5	4·8	5·5	4·8	1·7	0·7
laborers, except farm and mine	7·8	13·6	6·5	6·5	−5·8	0·0
farmers and farm managers	5·5	15·2	5·9	28·0	−9·7	−22·1
farm laborers and foremen	2·9	9·6	1·8	2·8	−6·7	−1·0

Sources: US Bureau of the Census (1958, 1962a and b)

There would be no point in criticizing Kahl's statistical procedures in detail. They are, as a matter of fact, ingenious uses of defective materials. Leaving aside the problem of data quality, the argument to be presented here is that the estimates fail because the conceptual framework for the estimates harbors fatal internal inconsistencies. The heart of the problem is Kahl's forthrightly stated assumption 'that all the men in the labor force in 1920 have been replaced by their sons by 1950'. This assumption, as will be shown, represents a confounding of the notions of occupational redistribution as it may be observed in comparing structures separated approximately by a generation of time (i.e. a span of years approximately equal to the average father–son age difference), and intergenerational mobility as it is commonly measured by comparing occupations of a generation of fathers with those of the generation of their sons.

Let us recollect how intergenerational mobility tables ordinarily are compiled. In the survey method, a sample of respondents is contacted and they are interrogated concerning their own occupations and those of their fathers. The investigator designing the survey confronts some difficult decisions. Usually he will want to know the current occupations of the respondents as well as those they may have pursued at certain times in the past. It is by no means obvious, however, how he should construe the concept of father's occupation. The latter could itself refer to a current (as of the survey date) occupational pursuit; but then a large number of fathers, deceased or retired, would have to remain unclassified. More often, the question used to elicit father's occupation is a variant of one of the following phrasings: father's last main occupation; father's longest job; father's occupation at age x (say, thirty or fifty); father's occupation when you (the respondent) were growing up. In studies using records or registers the situation is somewhat different. Information on the father's occupation typically refers to the date of the record, e.g. that of the son's birth or marriage.

Consider the predicament of a research worker in 1960 designing a survey of intergenerational occupation mobility with the aim of repeating Kahl's analysis. He might well entertain the notion of asking respondents to designate the occupations in which their fathers were engaged in the year 1930. (Actually, this form of the question on father's occupation has seldom if ever been used.) On first thought, this might seem to offer a neat solution, for the investigator could have estimated in advance that there would be about 34·9 million men in the 1960 labor force whose fathers were in the 1930 labor force (see Table 2), while the entire 1930 labor force (ages fifteen to seventy-four) included some 37·3 million males. The second thought would be less sanguine. Surely some of the fathers in the 1930 labor force had more than one son who was economically active in 1960. What about the men at work in 1930 who never had a son, or did not have one whose working life continued to 1960? This is not so easy to estimate, but an informed guess is that perhaps half of the men in the 1930 labor force did *not* have a son at work in 1960; the other half had, perhaps, on average approaching two sons apiece.

Now we are in a position to see how important it is to evaluate Kahl's assumption that 'all the men in the labor force in [1930] have been replaced by their sons by [1960]'. In point of fact, a goodly proportion of the fathers are not fully replaced within a generation. That is, of all currently (1960) working men with fathers in the 1930 labor force, nearly one-third have fathers who are still in the labor force in 1960. About half the men in the 1930 labor force were not fathers of men destined to be working in 1960 and were not, therefore, replaced by their sons. There are, on the other hand, 12·0 out of the 46·9 million members of the 1960 male labor force (ages fifteen to seventy-four) who cannot answer a question on 'father's occupation in 1930', because their fathers were still too young to be working then or had already died or ceased to work. Finally, the fathers in the intergenerational mobility table are about twice as numerous as the actual men who sired the sons, since each son reports for his father even though all his brothers do likewise.

The last problem could be handled by asking respondents to state how many brothers they have who are in the labor force. Size of fraternity then could be used as a deflation factor so as to secure an unbiased estimate of the occupation distribution of fathers in 1930. Such a procedure, however, would require some innovations in the analysis of intergenerational mobility tables.

Some of the estimates just cited, together with other figures of interest, appear in Table 2. It is a temptation to discuss at length the procedures by which these estimates were derived, since we do not automatically secure

Table 2 Male labor force 15–17 years old, 1960, by exposure to intra- and intergenerational occupational mobility, 1930–60: illustrative estimates for the US (in millions)

Father's labor force status	Members of 1960 labor force by 1930 status		Total
	Not in 1930 labor force	In 1930 labor force	
in 1930 labor force	26·1	8·8	34·9
in 1960 labor force	10·7	0·1	10·8
not in 1960 labor force	15·4[a]	8·7	24·1
not in 1930 labor force	5·5	6·5	12·0
in 1960 labor force	2·2	0·0	2·2
not in 1960 labor force	3·3	6·5	9·8
total	31·6	15·3	46·9

[a] This is the only subgroup it is strictly correct to describe as 'men in the labor force in 1930 who have been replaced by their sons by 1960'; note that the unit of enumeration, however, is the son, not the father.

data of this kind from official sources. Suffice it to say, however, that the estimates, although they involve tedious and circuitous demographic calculations, are highly approximate and are intended only to give some notion of orders of magnitude.

Looking at the matter from the point of view of men pursuing occupations in 1960, Table 2 indicates the size of the base populations exposed to various kinds of mobility over the three-decade period. As already noted, about 34·9 million, or three-fourths of the men, were exposed to the risk of intergenerational mobility. Of these, however, some 8·8 million were in the 1930 labor force along with their fathers and, therefore, were subject to intragenerational as well as intergenerational mobility, 1930–60. This leaves 26·1 million, only some 56 per cent of the 1960 labor force, who could have experienced pure intergenerational mobility. About 14 per cent (6·5/46·9 million) of the 1960 labor force was subject to pure intragenerational mobility, 1930–60; that is, the men themselves were in the 1930 labor force but their fathers were not. Finally, for nearly one-eighth of the 1960 labor force (5·5/46·9 million) neither intra- nor intergenerational mobility can be defined with reference to the dates 1930 and 1960. Cross-cutting these distinctions is the classification of men according to whether their fathers were in the 1960 labor force. Actually, there were some 13·0 million men, with fathers currently economically active, for whom cross-sectional intergenerational mobility could be defined by comparing current pursuits of sons and fathers. For only one-third of the labor force (15·4/46·9) does it make sense to regard the sons as having replaced fathers who were at work in 1930.

One way of summarizing the import of the quantities in Table 2, therefore, is to suggest that they render untenable any simple concept of replacement. When and by whom is a member of the labor force replaced? Is a father replaced when his (first) son enters the labor force? when the father leaves the labor force? when the son attains the age of his father at the son's birth? Who replaces the man who has no son? Put it this way: the transformations that occur via a *succession of cohorts* cannot, for basic demographic reasons, be equated to the product of a *procession of generations*. The writer is prepared to argue, though this is hardly the place to do so, that this brute fact is a profound key to the understanding of social continuity and social change. Indeed, a characteristically human type of society might well be impossible were the demography of the species structured differently.

At the risk of tedium, let us take another approach to demonstrating that occupational change over a period of time equivalent to a generation in length cannot be equated to a set of intergenerational changes observed in a father–son mobility table. The point can be illustrated with somewhat more adequate data than were at Kahl's disposal – a 1962 survey, 'Occupational changes in a generation' (OCG), conducted by the Bureau of the Census as an adjunct to its Current Population Survey on behalf of projects directed by Peter M. Blau and the present writer (US Bureau of the Census, 1964).

In Table 1, columns 'c' and 'd' show the distributions of OCG respondents by their own occupations and by the occupations pursued by their fathers at the time the respondents were sixteen years of age. The last two columns reveal a general resemblance between the net interannual changes in the overall occupation distribution, 1930–60, and the net intergenerational shifts shown in the OCG table. Yet these are clearly not the same set of changes, and the explanation of the discrepancies between them does not lie wholly in data error or defects in comparability between census and OCG, although such defects exist. Even supposing, for example, that many sons of farm laborers erroneously reported in OCG that their fathers were farmers, the intergenerational difference in proportion of total farm workers ($-23 \cdot 1$ per cent) is not the same as the interannual change ($-14 \cdot 4$ per cent).

This particular example is pursued further in Table 3, since a declining proportion of farm workers has been such an outstanding feature of US occupational transformation, while intergenerational mobility out of farming is conceded to be a highly significant form of mobility. If the intergenerational and interperiod comparisons here are of different orders of magnitude, then it is clear that the two are not interchangeable.

The point of Table 3 is to call attention to a set of conceptual distinctions, rather than to interpret a collection of facts. Line 1 depicts the familiar *trend* of decline in farm pursuits, known to us from *aggregate* data on the entire working force at successive points in time. In lines 2 to 8 observations are shown for selected cohorts (those making up the central age group, twenty-five to sixty-four, at each census year); the data on each line depict *intracohort* (net) *changes* in proportion in farming. Although not all age groups are shown, it is evident at once that the aggregate figure is an average (weighted) of rather widely varying proportions in the component age groups. The aggregate decrease in farming, moreover, is seen to involve two processes: the intracohort changes revealed by reading lines 3 to 7 horizontally (all but one of which changes are decreases); and the *intercohort changes* ascertained by reading the data in lines 2 to 8 along upper left to lower right diagonals (all of these changes being decreases).

In the lower half of the Table are data derived from the survey of inter- and intragenerational mobility. Respondents are classified into four groups of cohorts, approximately matching four of the cohort groups independently observed in census data. (Ideally, of course, the cohort matching

Table 3 Percentage of male working force engaged in farm work, 1900 to 1960, and percentage of 1962 male working force with farm origins and first jobs and currently in farm work, for the US

Cohort	Line number	Year						
		1900	1910	1920	1930	1940	1950	1960
Total male working force[a]	1	41·7	34·7	30·4	24·8	21·7	14·9	8·4
Male working force, selected cohorts, by date of birth								
1865–74	2	—	—	—	30·3	—	—	—
1875–84	3	—	—	—	25·0	26·0	—	—
1885–94	4	—	—	—	20·2	20·0	17·2	—
1895–1904	5	—	—	—	18·8	17·0	14·0	10·9
1905–14	6	—	—	—	—	16·9	12·6	8·7
1915–24	7	—	—	—	—	—	11·4	6·5
1925–34	8	—	—	—	—	—	—	5·5

Father's occupation by respondent's date of birth[b]	Line number	Respondents aged 16 in:			
		1913–22	1923–32	1933–42	1943–52
1897–1906	9	41·3	—	—	—
1907–16	10	—	34·6	—	—
1917–26	11	—	—	29·5	—
1927–36	12	—	—	—	22·3

Respondent's first job and 1962 occupation by date of birth	Line number	Respondents 15–24 years old in:				
		1911–30	1921–40	1931–50	1941–60	(1962)
1897–1906	13	25·5	—	—	—	11·3
1907–16	14	—	21·8	—	—	7·8
1917–26	15	—	—	16·5	—	6·3
1927–36	16	—	—	—	11·1	5·6

a Decennial Census data
b 1962 Survey: occupational changes in a generation
Sources: Line 1, US Bureau of the Census (1958, Table 2; 1963, Table 8). Lines 2–8: Jaffe and Carleton (1954, Appendix Table 1), US Bureau of the Census (1963, Table 8). Lines 9–16: Bureau of the Census (1962a)

could be made exact.) The survey data, however, do not concern the respondents' occupations at successive decennial dates. Instead, each respondent was asked to report his father's occupation as of the time the respondent was sixteen years old; and the respondent's own first full-time job, at whatever age entry into regular full-time work occurred. Both father's occupation and first job refer to experiences spread out over an interval of years.

For each of the four groups of cohorts, therefore, we have three observations – father's occupation, first job and current (1962) occupation – variation among which represents, again, intracohort change. Here, however, intracohort change is viewed in terms of the relationship between generations. Father's occupation is here regarded as the respondent's origin status, first job as the initial status in his own career. A common pattern of changes occurred in all four groups of cohorts: mobility from father's occupation to first job – compare line 9 with the first entry in line 13, etc. – resulted in a net reduction in farming; and mobility from first job to 1962 occupation – compare the two entries in line 13, etc. – again resulted in a net reduction in farming.

The capital observation in the present context is this. Neither father's occupation nor first job represents the aggregate proportion in farming at any specifiable period. This is not mere happenstance but would occur whenever an occupational structure was being transformed by a combination of inter- and intracohort changes. It is, therefore, a basic fallacy to suppose that the father–son mobility table provides in effect two samples of time. If the sons in the mobility table are, in fact, representative of the occupational structure at some recent point in time, then the distribution of sons by their fathers' occupations *cannot* represent the occupational structure at some definite prior moment in time. This has nothing to do with the fallibility of retrospective reports on father's occupation. Nor can the problem be avoided by asking for a time-specific or age-specific report on father's occupation.

The crux of the matter is that in human demography (unlike that of, say, certain insects), birth cohorts and generations are not coincident. There is, moreover, no ready translation formula for converting generational changes into intercohort or aggregate interannual changes.

Students of occupational mobility may not relish this complication of their problem. They will have to learn to live with it nonetheless. However inconvenient it may be, the fact is that the intergenerational mobility table can tell us less about how occupational structures are transformed in the course of economic development than we had hoped.

Does this mean that the conventional type of mobility study is without value? The remainder of this paper rests on the contrary assumption. Even though intergenerational mobility plays no simple and straightforward role as a mechanism in the transformation of occupational structures, we can give a straightforward rationale for analyses of the data in an intergenerational mobility table.

Instead of thinking of the classification of father's occupation as conveying information about a generation of fathers, think of it as describing the origin statuses of the sons. Particularly if the data on father's occupation apply to a time point proximate to the opening of the son's career (see Yasuda, 1964, pp. 20–21), this origin status provides a natural base line against which one can measure the son's subsequent occupational achievement. The father–son mobility table, then, becomes a table showing a cross-classification of origin by destination statuses of the cohorts included in the study. All changes – whether net shifts or gross mobility are then subject to straightforward interpretation as intracohort changes.

I do not claim that this type of analysis will answer all or even the most pressing questions that might be asked about occupational change by a student of economic development. But surely it is worth knowing how and to what extent the subsequent achieved statuses in a cohort depend on the statuses in which they started. Indeed, the recent popularity of 'the inheritance of poverty' as a diagnostic concept in public policy discussions suggests that we need to know a good deal more about this relationship.

Regarding mobility research as a species of cohort analysis clarifies at least one point on which there has been confusion. Although data in the typical mobility study are collected retrospectively (by questioning the respondent about the past), this is only a convenience in data collection. While it introduces problems of data reliability and validity, it does not commit the analyst to a backward-looking conceptual framework. The difference between retrospective and prospective designs in mobility research is probably no greater than in cohort fertility research, where we have the alternatives of collecting (retrospective) census data on children ever born and fertility history, or cumulating annually reported vital statistics. [. . .]

Comparisons over time: matrix approach

In Rogoff's original work[2] with social distance mobility ratios (somewhat misleadingly termed 'rates') the calculations are justified on the basis that structure, as represented by the relative frequencies in the several occupational classes in the two generations, must be 'partialled out' before the amount of mobility can be taken to measure the degree of 'openness' of a society. Legitimate and necessary as such abstractions are, there is also reason to be interested in methods of analysis that stick closer to the way a cohort actually is redistributed over a set of structural categories. The matrix approach (Carlsson, 1958, ch. 5) has an appeal from this point of view.

The transition matrix, or what Miller (1960, p. 7) proposes to call the 'standard outflow table', is an array of rows, each row consisting of a set

2. See the presentation of Rogoff's data in Reading 6 [Eds.].

of proportions that sum to unity. The number in the jth column of the ith row is the proportion of all sons originating in the occupation class i whose destination is class j. It is also useful to think of the distribution of all sons according to their origin classes as a single row (vector) of proportions and similarly of their destination distribution as a probability vector (Matras, 1960). Under these conventions, together with those of matrix algebra, the following notation is convenient for the discussion at hand. Let a_0 be the origin vector, A the transition matrix, and a_1 the destination vector. We then have the identity, $a_0 A = a_1$, and we may speak of the transition matrix, A, as sending the origin vector into the destination vector.

Now, if we think of the mobility experience recorded in Rogoff's data as being summarized by the two transition matrices, A (1910) and B (1940), then we may consider a comparison between A and B in terms of the structures they would produce under various assumptions. Table 4 sets forth a number of origin and destination vectors (written for convenience as columns rather than rows and in percentages rather than proportions) which are useful in making the comparison.

Note, first, that the origin vectors are in fact somewhat dissimilar. The column of differences in the bottom panel, $b_0 - a_0$, shows where the most important changes occurred over the thirty-year period. Likewise, the two destination distributions exhibit some lack of resemblance. In 1940 as compared with 1910, there was an excess of professional, semi-professional, clerical and sales, semiskilled, and protective service workers, and a deficiency of proprietor-managerial, skilled, unskilled, personal service and farm workers. The index of dissimilarity is the sum of the positive differences in the column above it. (An index of dissimilarity computed between an origin distribution and a destination distribution is identical with the percentage of net mobility. The same index also serves to compare two origin or two destination distributions, but in this case it is not interpretable as an amount of mobility.)

The third and fourth columns of differences are perhaps the most interesting. Granted that the 1910 and 1940 destination distributions differed considerably, may this not be due primarily to the fact that the respective origin distributions, as we have just seen, were not alike? The answer appears to be that the difference between the two destination distributions is *not* due so much to the origin difference, but rather to the difference between the two transition matrices, A and B. In one calculation, the 1910 origin distribution is applied to the 1940 matrix, to produce a hypothetical destination distribution, $a_0 B$, which may be compared with the actual 1910 destination distribution, $a_0 A$. In the other calculation, the same difference between matrices is seen under the condition of b_0 (1940 origin distribution) as the origin distribution. Casual inspection will reveal that either of the

Table 4 Comparison of actual and hypothetical occupation distributions (per cent) for white men marrying in Marion County, Indiana *c.* 1940 and *c.* 1910 (Rogoff data)

Major occupation group	Origin distributions		Destination distributions		Hypothetical destination distributions		Fixed point distributions	
	1910 a_o	*1940* b_o	*1910* a_oA	*1940* b_oB	a_oB	b_oA	*1910* a_∞	*1940* b_∞
professional	3·68	4·79	3·79	5·54	5·06	4·11	3·79	6·60
semi-professional	0·72	1·15	1·85	3·10	2·76	2·12	2·64	4·12
proprietors, managers and officials	12·22	12·16	7·13	6·63	6·52	7·29	6·19	6·09
clerical and sales	6·43	11·04	18·23	22·12	20·38	19·91	22·31	25·32
skilled	26·53	27·59	31·99	21·87	22·19	32·16	32·89	20·07
semiskilled	9·17	15·36	17·10	27·07	27·08	17·60	17·74	26·79
unskilled	12·25	7·28	11·95	6·91	8·56	9·95	9·29	5·48
protective service	1·56	2·44	0·96	2·32	2·46	0·91	0·79	1·94
personal service	1·26	1·66	3·65	3·38	3·58	3·53	3·45	3·18
farming	26·19	16·53	3·36	1·06	1·42	2·42	0·91	0·41
total	100·01	100·00	100·01	100·00	100·01	100·00	100·00	100·00

	Differences between distributions				
	b_o-a_o	b_oB-a_oA	a_oB-a_oA	b_oB-b_oA	b_∞-a_∞
professional	1·11	1·75	1·27	1·43	2·81
semi-professional	0·43	1·25	0·91	0·98	1·48
proprietors, managers and officials	−0·06	−0·50	−0·61	−0·66	−0·10
clerical and sales	4·61	3·89	2·15	2·21	3·01
skilled	1·06	−10·12	−9·80	−10·29	−12·82
semiskilled	6·19	9·97	9·98	9·47	9·05
unskilled	−4·97	−5·04	−3·39	−3·04	−3·81
protective service	0·88	1·36	1·50	1·41	1·15
personal service	0·40	−0·27	−0·07	−0·15	−0·27
farming	−9·66	−2·30	−1·94	−1·36	−0·50
index of dissimilarity	14·7	18·2	15·8	15·5	17·5

See text for notation used to identify columns

two comparisons of a hypothetical with an actual distribution comes out at much the same place as the comparison of the two actual destination distributions. The difference between the latter, then, inheres primarily in the matrices that produced them, not in the origins whence they came.

How big is the difference? Is an index of dissimilarity of 15–18 points a large or a small value? As in all such cases, assessment of magnitudes as important or unimportant depends on a background of typical variation in the index. In the present instance, 15 points is not a trivial magnitude, although we would expect larger index values if we compared occupation distributions separated by a longer time period, or the distribution for whites with that for nonwhites, or the distribution for men with that for women.

One final comparison is suggested by the treatment of mobility transition matrices from the viewpoint of Markov processes. I have reservations about the utility of Markov analysis for the subject of intergenerational mobility, which arise from consideration of the issues discussed in the first section of this paper. Leaving this point aside, however, one can still regard one of the statistics derived from the Markov approach as a summary of the transition matrix. This is the so-called 'fixed point' of the matrix. If there is an origin distribution, a_∞, such that $a_\infty A = a_\infty$, then a_∞ is the fixed-point vector of the transition matrix A. It is the origin distribution which is unaffected by the transition. The fixed points of the matrices A and B are shown in the last two columns of the top panel of Table 4. The last column of the lower panel reveals that the pattern and degree of differences between the two fixed points are much like those observed in the other comparisons between actual and hypothetical destination distributions.

We evidently cannot escape the conclusion that a real difference of some appreciable magnitude exists between the mobility processes represented by the 1910 and 1940 transition matrices for Indianapolis. The 1940 matrix produces more white-collar and semiskilled workers in the destination distribution, and fewer skilled and unskilled, than the 1910 matrix. If one wants to argue, as Rogoff does in her Chapter 2, that the difference between the 1910 and 1940 occupation structures was due to shifts in demand for workers of the several types of qualification, then one must regard the mobility process, as described by the transition matrix, as the *dependent variable*.

This suggestion leads to still another approach to the comparison of two mobility tables. Is it possible that differences in the 1910 and 1940 mobility patterns are due solely to shifts in the distribution of job opportunities open to young men? (The term 'opportunities' is used in place of 'demand', to acknowledge that factors on the 'supply' side, such as the educational qualifications of these men, may influence the kinds of jobs they get.) Can we, in other words, contrive a comparison between the two mobility tables putting the change in occupation structure in the role of an exo-genously determined factor, which then induces a change in mobility patterns?

The starting point of the comparison is to test the null hypothesis that all changes in the mobility table are due to proportional adjustments occasioned by changes, 1910 to 1940, in the two marginal distributions – the distribution of sons by their fathers' occupations, and the distribution of sons by their own occupations. When this hypothesis is rejected, attention will turned to the pattern of nonproportional shifts, which cannot be attributed to changing marginal distribution. [. . .]

Table 5 Deviation of frequencies in Rogoff's 1940 mobility table from those expected on the basis of proportional adjustment of the 1910 table to 1940 marginals (white men)

Father's occupation class	Son's occupation class									
	1	2	3	4	5	6	7	8	9	10
1 professional	12	6	−14	16	5	−24	1	−1	−2	
2 semi-professional	13	−15	−5	−3	17	−4	−1	−3	2	
3 proprietors, etc.	−27	−10	−10	9	24	49	−10	−9	−16	
4 clerical	11	16	8	−35	−19	30	−6	5	−4	
5 skilled	15	9	8	32	−81	7	5	4	−4	−4[a]
6 semiskilled	−6	3	13	46	−85	41	−43	13	19	
7 unskilled	7	0	1	−9	10—	59	53	−5	2	
8 protective service	2	0	−8	1	−19	14	4	8	−4	
9 personal service	6	0	3	−3	6	1	−8	0	−5	
10 farming	−33	−10	3	−54	141	−56	4	−12	14	4

[a] This combination of cells was made in computing total and interaction SS, but not in computing other SS components or in securing the a_i and b_j coefficients
Columns may not sum to zero exactly, owing to errors of rounding

In Table 5, the actual frequencies in the 1940 table are shown as positive or negative deviations from the frequencies that would have been observed in the event of strictly proportional changes. For example, fifty-nine fewer men moved from unskilled origins to semi-skilled occupations than would have appeared in the 1940 table had it shown only proportional differences from the 1910 table. The total of these deviations must, of course, add to zero. If we sum the positive deviations alone, however, we find that at least $723/9892 = 7$ per cent of the men were in classes other than those in which they would have been, in the event of proportional change, 1910–40.

In Table 6, the comparison of the hypothesis of proportional change with the 1940 actuality is given in terms of percentages of occupational inheritance for each origin class. Interestingly enough, the hypothesis produces just the right amount of inheritance over the Table as a whole; but deviations, some of them sizeable, occur for specific origin classes. In the

Table 6 Occupational inheritance (percentage of sons in same occupational class as father) in Rogoff's 1910 and 1940 mobility tables, and in hypothetical table obtained by adjusting 1910 table to 1940 marginal distributions (white men)

Father's occupation class	Observed mobility tables		1910 table adjusted to 1940 marginals
	1910	1940	
all classes	29·4	27·1	27·3
professional	21·0	28·3	25·7
semi-professional	27·0	19·3	32·5
proprietors, managers, officials	21·1	17·6	18·4
clerical and sales	43·7	42·2	45·4
skilled	48·6	32·2	35·2
semiskilled	31·6	43·2	40·5
unskilled	34·2	28·6	21·2
protective service	2·5	8·3	4·8
personal service	14·7	10·4	13·7
farmers	10·6	4·2	3·9

case of three origin classes the proportionally adjusted percentage of inheritance is farther from the 1940 observation than was the adjusted 1910 percentage. (The reader may, of course, form other kinds of comparisons to summarize the pattern of nonproportionality, making use of Table 5 and Rogoff's published tables.)

It is well to bear in mind the fact that invariance with respect to some aspects of the mobility process is compatible with variation in other aspects. The evidence from intertemporal comparisons suggests that the invariance is not to be uncovered by direct inspection of the transition matrix, even though this is precisely where Lipset and Bendix (1959) sought to discover it. This little irony of research strategy is worth some elaboration with additional empirical materials. [. . .]

Inferring consequences of mobility

Suppose a sociologist conducted a survey of a representative sample of married couples, ascertaining the number of children ever born to each couple, the occupation of the husband, and that of his father. After classifying the occupations into broad categories, he characterized the husbands whose occupations fell in a higher category than those of their fathers as having undergone upward mobility, those in a lower category as downward mobility, and those in the same category as static or stable.

Aggregating the couples in each of these three groups and similarly the numbers of births to the couples, he calculated the average number of children ever born per couple and obtained the following results:

upward	2·57
static	2·73
downward	3·01

Assuming he was confident that sampling variation could not account for these differences, the investigator would be perfectly correct in concluding that 'those who moved down are characterized by having larger families than those who moved up' (Berent, 1952, p. 250). Other students of social mobility might then examine these results and present them in a summary in which they 'stress the restriction of the size of the "family of procreation" by upwardly mobile parents: ... family size restriction is both a condition and consequence of upward mobility' (Lipset and Bendix, 1959, p. 244).

The purpose of this discussion is to suggest that the inference from the observed pattern of fertility differentials by mobility group to a conclusion about conditions and consequences is not so straightforward as it might appear. The argument hinges on the issue of how a set of data like these should be analysed. There is, however, no intention of criticizing Berent's work or, indeed, of calling into question any of his results, which he summarized quite circumspectly. On the contrary, Berent's study remains, a decade after its publication, the only worthwhile investigation of its subject. The point of view developed here is only slightly different from that of Berent, and the conclusions suggested differ from his, if at all, in respect to emphasis rather than substance. The main excuse for additional discussion of Berent's problem is that it may serve as a prototype for cases in which some quantitative characteristic or measure of behavior is the dependent variable and mobility is the independent variable. Indeed, the same example illustrates the problem of interpretation encountered whenever the independent variable is some kind of discrepancy measure – not only mobility between statuses held at two points in time, but also heterogamy, cross-pressure, status disequilibrium, or like indicators encountered in stratification research and so-called relational analysis of sociometric choices.

The gist of the argument is that one is not entitled to discuss effects of mobility (or other status discrepancy measures) until one has established that the apparent effect cannot be due merely to a simple combination of effects of the variables used to define mobility.

Berent's data are set forth in Tables 7 and 8. The first thing one might notice in Table 8 is this. Not only do mobile couples differ in their fertility from nonmobile couples of similar origin (or destination), but also non-mobile couples differ considerably among themselves according to their class position. Thus in citing at the outset a single average for static couples, we suppress a good deal of variation in occupational status within this

Table 7 Number of couples by present
social class and class of origin of
husband (Berent data)

Class of origin	Present class				
	I	II	III	IV	All
I	65	43	23	11	142
II	38	197	150	68	453
III	37	154	431	244	866
IV	5	45	162	220	432
all	145	439	766	543	1893

group. Aside from looking at the averages on the diagonal, it is perhaps not obvious just how to extract a conclusion from Table 8. Berent himself presents no less than four rearrangements of the data in this Table in an effort to convey to the reader his interpretation of their import.

Table 8 Mean number of live births per couple,
by present social class and class of origin
of husband (Berent data)

Class of origin	Present class				
	I	II	III	IV	All
I	1·74	1·79	1·96	2·00	1·81
II	2·05	2·14	2·51	2·97	2·38
III	1·87	2·01	2·67	3·69	2·81
IV	2·40	3·20	3·22	3·68	3·44
all	1·88	2·17	2·73	3·56	2·77

The suggestion put forward here is that the analyst should investigate the plausibility, for the data in question, of a simple model of additive effects. In Table 8 there are sixteen combinations of an origin class with a destination class. Now suppose that the effect of each combination, as represented by mean fertility in the corresponding cell of the Table, is regarded as a simple sum of three quantities: (1) a mean effect that applies to all couples in the sample; (2) an increment thereto for class of origin, which applies irrespective of class of destination; and (3) an increment for class of destination, which applies irrespective of class of origin.

A calculation of effects based on this additive model appears in Table 9. By comparing Tables 8 and 9 the reader may perhaps perceive that the model reproduces the data to a reasonably good approximation; that where sizeable departures from the model calculations occur, they typically

Table 9 Average number of live births per couple, by present social class and class of origin of husband, calculated from Berent data using model based on assumption of additive effects

Class of origin	Present class				
	I	II	III	IV	All
I	1·60	1·70	2·13	2·85	1·81
II	1·97	2·07	2·50	3·23	2·38
III	2·17	2·27	2·70	3·42	2·81
IV	2·59	2·70	3·12	3·85	3·44
all	1·88	2·17	2·73	3·56	2·77

pertain to a few cases only; and that there is not much pattern to the deviations. If this perception is valid, there is no need to postulate any effect for mobility *qua* mobility. The couples in the study behaved *as if* they determined their fertility by combining the fertility pattern of their class of origin with the fertility pattern of their class of destination in a simple additive or averaging process.

Consider what happens when we aggregate the calculated means in Table 9, using the frequencies in Table 7 as weights and grouping the couples according to type of mobility, as in the initial results quoted from Berent:

	Observed	Calculated
upward	2·57	2·60
static	2·73	2·76
downward	3·01	2·94

If one may ignore a discrepancy no larger than 0·07, it is obvious that *'mobility' produces no differences in fertility that cannot be fully accounted for by the additive mechanism* implied by the model. From this point of view, mobility has no consequence to be discussed, except the consequence that the mobile couple combines the fertility patterns of two classes. The restriction of fertility observed in upwardly mobile couples reflects the fact that they necessarily move to a class with a prevailing level of fertility lower than that of the class whence they originated and, in some measure, take on the pattern of their class of destination. The critic could, of course, insist that it is a matter of preference (or 'theory') whether the genuine differences between mobile and nonmobile couples are to be explained by mobility or explained away by a statistical model that posits separate effects of origin and destination classes. The critic, however, will then have to explain the variation in mean fertility on the diagonal of Table 8. The additive model accounts for this variation as well as for the difference between upwardly mobile, static and downwardly mobile couples. An interpretation using the additive model thus enjoys an advantage due to the rule of parsimony over the interpretation in terms of a mobility effect.

I have skipped over the statistical aspects of the problem, since these are treated in accessible expositions (Hill, 1959; Brownlee, 1960, pp. 515–21). Just a few notes are set down for the interested reader. The model is as follows:

$$\bar{Y}_{ij} = \bar{Y} + a_i + b_j + e_{ij},$$

where $\bar{Y}_{ij}$ is the observed mean fertility in the combination of origin class i and destination class j; $\bar{Y}$ is the grand mean (here, 2·77) for the whole sample; a_i is the effect, expressed as a deviation from the grand mean, of belonging to the ith origin class; b_j is the effect for the jth destination class; and e_{ij} is the error or interaction that appears as a deviation of the observed mean from the mean expected on the basis of the sum of the three effects. The normal equations whose solution yields the numerical values are the same in form as those introduced above in adjusting one set of frequencies in a mobility table to the marginal frequencies in another table.

According to the calculations made for this example, the respective (net) effects of the two bases of classification are as follows:

Class	Origin	Destination
I	−0·58	−0·60
II	−0·21	−0·50
III	−0·01	−0·07
IV	0·42	0·66

Thus, for couples moving from class IV to class III, the estimate appearing in Table 9 is computed as 2·77 (grand mean)+0·42 (origin effect)−0·07 (destination effect) = 3·12.

If the data are a probability sample from a well-defined universe, it is reasonable to carry out significance tests for the several effects that may be represented in the data. In the present example, standard formulas for analysis of variance for multiple classification with disproportionate sub-class numbers were used. At a conventional 0·01 level of significance, the tests showed: (1) there is non-chance variation among the sub-group means in Table 8; (2) there is non-chance variation among the means calculated from the additive model in Table 9; (3) the first source of variation, though greater than or equal to the second by algebraic necessity, is not *significantly* greater; that is, *interaction* of origin with destination is not significant (whence the willingness to discount completely any specific mobility effect); (4) the net effects for both origin class and destination class, each independently of the other, are significant.

Substantively, this last finding suggests a way to summarize the consequence of mobility for marital fertility. As far as Berent's data are concerned, one's class of origin and one's class of destination both make a difference. The consequence of mobility is membership in two classes, and one's behavior is best accounted for on the assumption that one combines the patterns of both.

Only one further comment is needed to link this discussion to the theme of comparative analysis. If studies of mobility effects are carried out in two or more countries (say), we can compare the several sets of results by inquiring whether they agree or disagree as to the relative magnitudes of the origin and destination effects, the independent significance of each, the significance or nonsignificance of interactions, and hence the need or lack of need for an interpretation invoking mobility effects. In making such comparisons, of course, we shall require some comparability as to definition of universe and study design. But detailed consistency between studies in procedures for delimiting classes is not essential, provided that we are willing to accept the procedures followed in each country as suitable for its particular situation. Thus, there is some merit to the suggestion (communicated orally by Morris Janowitz) that, in principle, it is easier to advance our knowledge of the consequences of mobility than to establish similarities or differences in respect to patterns of mobility in a comparative framework.

In summary

One who takes up the topic of this paper should always remember the observation of Frank Knight, to this effect: a man writing on methodology is in the same position as one who plays the slide trombone; unless he is very good at it, the results are more likely to interest him than his audience. No doubt the tedious exposition has served to obscure the handful of basic propositions the paper seeks to sustain:

Occupational mobility and the transformation of occupation structures. The transformation of occupational structures in the course of economic development is accomplished by a combination of elementary demographic processes, no one or combination of which is identical with, or directly translatable into, the pattern, volume or rate of occupational mobility as this may be observed in a conventional intergenerational occupational mobility table. This is not a mere methodological detail but a fundamental structural principle of social metabolism. Assumptions contrary to fact about the translatability of occupational change into occupational mobility and vice versa are most likely to produce derivations which are meaningless or, if not meaningless, simply false.

Comparisons over time. Intergenerational mobility, even if it is not easily related by a translation formula to the processes of occupational transformation, is worthy of study in its own right. Its effective study requires improvements in measurement techniques, classification procedures, and analytical models. Regression analysis, with occupational status appropriately scaled, is a straightforward and effective method of measuring the dependence of the son's achieved status upon his level of social origin. In the only published set of fully comparable data comprising two series separated by a sizeable time span (Rogoff's data for Indianapolis, 1910 and 1940), it is remarkable that the regression relationships hardly changed during a three-decade period. There were, however, some considerable modifications of the mobility *pattern*. Using either matrix analysis or an approach involving fitting constants, one gains the strong impression that these modifications occurred in consequence of the change in structure represented by alterations of the frequency distributions of origin and destination classes. The analysis of occupational inheritance is much less useful, informative, and central, from the point of view of father–son correlation or mobility patterns, than has hitherto been assumed. This statement is made in awareness of recent proposals for models of social mobility that emphasize occupational inheritance, although there is no space to review these proposals here (White, 1963; Goodman, 1965).

Comparisons between places. Interspatial comparisons of mobility patterns or rates are seriously compromised by noncomparability of study procedures. Nevertheless, to show that two mobility tables are not fully comparable is *not* to show that the two patterns of mobility are the same. Because interspatial comparisons almost always concern situations with different structures, differences in mobility patterns are to be expected. The transition matrix will reflect such differences in patterns when analysed in several alternative ways.

Occupational classification. Interspatial comparisons of factors determining (and, for that matter, consequences of) occupational mobility will be facilitated by the adoption of comparable methodology for the measurement of occupational status. It may be possible, by this strategem, to mitigate somewhat the fact that intrinsic structural differences render any equating of occupational categories dubious. Occupations can, for example, be scaled as to socioeconomic status by procedures suggested more or less independently by three or four investigators. The regression analysis of such scale values then allows comparisons of results between communities or nations that are rather more precise than can be produced by conventional methods. In carrying out the steps implied by such an approach, there is no special value in classifying occupations as white-collar versus manual. Indeed, reliance on this kind of crude distinction can conceal more than it reveals and lead to erroneous conclusions concerning the nature of relationships.

Inferring consequences of mobility. Students who have sought to infer consequences of mobility for individual behavior have approached the problem in an inverted order. Instead of classifying cases by type of mobility and showing an association between mobility type and the behavior indicator (the conventional procedure), the investigator should test the sufficiency of a model that postulates simple additive effects of the two statuses whose difference serves to define mobility. When, as happens to be the case in the illustrative material presented here, such a model is sufficient to reduce the data, there is no need nor warrant to postulate a mobility effect as such. It is enough to observe that one or both of the two statuses (origin and destination) are associated with the dependent variable.

References

BERENT, J. (1952), 'Fertility and social mobility', *Pop. Stud.*, vol. 5, pp. 244–60.
BROWNLEE, K. A. (1960), *Statistical Theory and Methodology in Science and Engineering*, Wiley.
CARLSSON, G. (1958), *Social Mobility and Class Structure*, Gleerup, Lund, Sweden.
GOODMAN, L. A. (1965), 'On the statistical analysis of mobility tables', *Amer. J. Sociol.*, vol. 70, pp. 564–85.
HILL, T. P. (1959), 'An analysis of the distribution of wages and salaries in Great Britain', *Econometrica*, vol. 27, pp. 355–81.
JAFFE, A. J., and CARLETON, R. O. (1954), *Occupational Mobility in the United States: 1930–1960*, King's Crown Press.
KAHL, J. A. (1957), *The American Class Structure*, Holt, Rinehart & Winston.
LIPSET, S. M., and BENDIX, R. (1959), *Social Mobility in Industrial Society*, University of California Press.

MATRAS, J. (1960), 'Comparison of intergenerational occupational mobility patterns: an application of the formal theory of social mobility', *Pop. Stud.*, vol. 14, pp. 163–9.

MILLER, S. M. (1960), 'Comparative social mobility', *Current Sociology*, vol. 9, pp. 1–89.

US BUREAU OF THE CENSUS (1958), *Occupational Trends in the United States, 1900 to 1950*, Working paper no. 5, Government Printing Office, Washington.

US BUREAU OF THE CENSUS (1962a), Current Population Survey of the Bureau of the Census and supplementary questionnaire, 'Occupational changes in a generation', unpublished tables, March, Government Printing Office, Washington.

US BUREAU OF THE CENSUS (1962b), Supplementary reports, *1960 Census of Population*, PC(S1)-40, Government Printing Office, Washington.

US BUREAU OF THE CENSUS (1963), 'Educational attainment', *1960 Census of Population*, Subject report PC(2)-5B, Government Printing Office, Washington.

US BUREAU OF THE CENSUS (1964), 'Life-time occupational mobility of adult males: March 1962', *Current Population Reports*, Series P-23, no. 11. Government Printing Office, Washington.

WHITE, H. C. (1963), 'Cause and effect in social mobility tables', *Behav. Sci.*, vol. 8, pp. 14–27.

YASUDA, S. (1964), 'A methodological inquiry into social mobility', *Amer. Sociol. Rev.*, vol. 29, pp. 16–23.

9 K. U. Mayer and W. Müller

Progress in Social Mobility Research?

Excerpts from K. U. Mayer and W. Müller, 'Progress in social mobility research?', *Quality and Quantity: European Journal of Methodology*, vol. 5, 1971, pp. 142–55.

Criticism of mobility studies – the main arguments

Predominantly, social mobility has been understood as vertical mobility and, in most cases, was operationalized in terms of movements between broad occupational groupings. The occupational hierarchy was usually ordered according to the prestige dimension presupposing high correlations with other factors of social rank such as education, income, deference or autonomy. Social mobility was measured as intergenerational mobility: turnover between social origin – occupational groups of fathers – and social destination – occupational groups of sons.

An essential part for providing continuity and comparability has been played by the strong emphasis on standardization by means of constructing mobility tables and their descriptive analysis by summarizing statistical measures. Pointing now to the shortcomings of this approach we wish in no way to denigrate the outstanding scholarship which has gone into building up this tradition of mobility research.

Scope of social mobility

The scope of the study of individual movements in social structure has been narrowed due to theoretical predilections and technical problems of investigation ever since Sorokin (1927, chs. 1 and 7) introduced the one-sided dichotomy between vertical and horizontal mobility.

Up and downward mobility, residential mobility and labor mobility have tended to be considered separately and even within different disciplines. Although recent studies by Wilensky (1966), Westoff, Bressler and Sagi (1960) and Blau and Duncan (1967, chs. 7 and 10), clearly show the interrelations between vertical occupational mobility in terms of prestige and various other movements, the theoretical implications of that evidence have not yet been worked out.[1]

Social mobility and social stratification

The advancement of the study of social mobility as an instrument for the study of the rigidity of class structures has suffered from the premature

1. Independently, the same point has been raised by Ruvkina (1970).

empirical treatment of vertical mobility before prior analysis of the stratification system itself. Unsolved problems of stratification theory and research have become chronic diseases of the analysis and interpretation of mobility studies and have limited the theoretical relevance of their results. These problems, e.g. the issues of classes versus strata, discontinuous strata versus continuous status-systems, objective versus subjective measurement, status of families, persons or roles, unidimensionality versus multidimensionality of status, one versus several status hierarchies, empirical determination of strata, the role of occupation in the stratification system, and the relation between local and national status systems, have largely been subject to pragmatical and *ad hoc* empirical research decisions.[2]

Critical arguments have been advanced against the prestige ranking of occupations, against the occupational classifications used and the concentration on intergenerational mobility.

Since additional membership and reference groups outside the family take an independent part in the allocation process of social positions, the exclusive interest in intergenerational mobility is increasingly less warranted and more attention should be paid to influences occurring in the course of individual careers (see Wilensky, 1966, p. 103).

Occupational prestige might be a handy guide to hierarchical classification of occupational groups, but its use as an empirical indicator of the stratification system is limited by the lack of congruence between the occupational role system and the class structure, by the lack of unanimity of a population about the prestige of occupations and by the lack of correspondence between overall prestige measures and the prestige accorded to occupational positions by those who actually or potentially occupy these positions.

Occupational classifications used by the official census do not necessarily represent meaningful strata. The actual occupations classified in one group are often too heterogeneous. The number of groups within the classification is quite arbitrary (but determines the frequency of the mobility measured).

The usual occupational classifications do not allow one to measure social distances and thereby the relative ease or difficulty with which lines are crossed.[3]

To limit the scope of studies to what can be observed and measured more precisely, i.e. the occupational system as in the Blau and Duncan (1967) study, offers a straightforward solution to these problems, but at the

2. Concerning these controversies and their bearing on mobility research see Capecchi (1967); Carlsson (1958); Dahrendorf (1959, chs. 2 and 3); Haug and Sussman (1968); Lipset and Zetterberg (1966); Svalastoga (1959); Goldthorpe (1966); Jackson and Curtis (1968).
3. A similar critical summary has been presented by J. H Goldthorpe in a lecture on mobility research given at the University of Konstanz in January 1970.

same time it is a departure from the original question – the openness or rigidity of class structure – in the direction of somewhat different goals – namely the factors of occupational success – and weakens the connection between the study of social stratification and the study of social mobility.

Social mobility and social structure

The occupational classification schemes adopted for the measurement of mobility give rise to a biased conception of compound social structure. One bias consists in the reduction of social structure to a unidimensional system of occupational status, the categories of which do not correspond to observable social entities.

The other bias results from measuring social mobility as turnover in a static classification scheme between two fixed points. The processes involved in the transition from father's to son's occupational group or from first to last job, i.e. the question of continuous or discontinuous career types, mobility channels and movements within occupational categories, have therefore received less attention than warranted.

For the most part changes of structure which could be inferred directly from changes of the marginal distributions in standard mobility tables, i.e. demographic and technological changes, have come to be regarded as 'structural' causes of social mobility. Other transformations, as for instance transformations in the distribution of political power, property or income, changes of legal requirements or the standards of social justice, have not been seriously considered – the major exception being changes in the educational system (see Goldhamer, 1968, p. 437; Bertaux, 1970).

Another consequence of occupational classification schemes as a representation of social structure seems to be the implicit bias which identifies the criterion of classification – prestige or occupational status in general – with the motivating force propelling individuals. Correspondingly the occupational inheritance from father to son appeared to be the almost only moment inhibiting mobility. By this procedure questionable assumptions about human nature or the dominant social character were incorporated but not tested (see the critique of Rose, 1964; Porter, 1968).

Mobility rates

A central concern of mobility studies has been the establishment of mobility rates, indices of the overall frequency of social mobility and its incidence in a society. They have been well summarized by Miller's trend report of 1960.

Even disregarding the difficulties in constructing and interpreting global rates (see Duncan, 1966; Capecchi, 1967; Carlsson, 1958, chs. 5 and 8; Duncan-Jones, 1970), e.g. outflow and inflow coefficients, measures based on the concept of perfect mobility or that of mathematical freedom and correlation coefficients, the utility of such summary measurements of the mobility of whole nations, cities or strata remains doubtful.

These measures could only be useful if they permitted comparisons between societies or different periods of a single society. Then they might be accepted as indicators of the relative openness, permeability or rigidity of class structures and might be related to other attributes of the structure of whole societies such as economic growth, degree of industrialization or urbanization, political stability or change.

The prevalence of non-comparable classifications, non-comparable samples, lack of correspondence between generations and cohorts, and variations in the efficiency of field procedures make it extremely difficult to meet these conditions (cf. Duncan, 1966; Wilensky, 1966).

Rates of upward and downward mobility, for instance, which are based on the presupposed barrier between manual and nonmanual occupations of the male working force, are rather crude (Dahrendorf, 1963). They falsely classify movements from skilled labour to unskilled white-collar work, they say nothing about the social distances covered by the mobile persons and they hide many important movements like those from low grade manual jobs to highly qualified crafts, from low white-collar groups to academic professions, and especially all movements out of farm occupations and between dependent occupations and entrepreneurial positions.

More subtle classificatory schemes allow more significant analysis of movements between groups, but make overall comparisons much more dangerous, since they may not be comparable between countries (Blau and Duncan, 1967, p. 435).

Although much work has gone into the assembling of data and the refinement and perfection of summary indices of social mobility, the various measures have so far yielded meagre results. No available measure has been shown to be adequate in testing the relationships between the extent of social mobility and other indicators of states and processes of social systems, e.g. national income, investment rate, population growth, degree of urbanization, level of achievement motivation, elite fluctuation, etc.[4]

Global indicators of the extent of social mobility or immobility may be interpreted as fairly accurate statements on the permeability of class structure to the extent that this class structure is represented by the categories of measurement. They serve as a rough measure of the degree

4. For attempts at international comparisons and the use of mobility rates in macrosociological analysis, see Lipset and Zetterberg (1966); Fox and Miller (1965a and b): Miller (1960); Miller and Brice (1965); Cutright (1968a). For a critique, see Bolte and Kreckel (1968); Cutright (1968b); Jones (1969); Smelser and Lipset (1966, p. 20); Svalastoga (1965).

to which equality of opportunity prevails within a given society. But such figures should not be used as an indication of the 'openness' of a society as a 'democratic' feature, since they give no insight into the quality and moral legitimacy of the processes of social selection in so far as they are informative neither about the collective standards of social justice nor about the extent of coercion which is operative in the genesis of the individual movements counted.

Mobility types

For the consequences of social mobility, some doubts have arisen as to whether the movements classified together in the usual summary measurements constitute uniform phenomena, or as to whether consequences attributed to social mobility should not be related to more refined and more empirical mobility types.[5]

Thus Gini, in his analysis of social and political consequences of mobility, for instance, differentiates between institutionalized and non-institutionalized mobility, downward partial and upward partial mobility, career and non-career mobility, objectively measured and psychologically and socially relevant mobility.

Subjective aspects of social mobility

Mobility studies have neglected almost totally what may be termed subjective aspects of individuals' movements: perceptions of structure, status satisfaction, mobility norms and values and aspirations.[6] It is not known to what extent the movements which are counted and categorized statistically correspond, if at all, to individual mobility experiences such as improvement, immobility, up and downs or skidding. Nor is it known whether the occupation or overall status of the father is the most salient subjective point of comparison.

It is hard to think of effects of social mobility on individual behavior which are not mediated through subjective experience. Thus, assumptions about the effects of social mobility do have to imply that the movements which make up a measure are neither just artefacts of measurement nor solely 'objective' constructs of the observing sociologist, but that they are experienced subjectively as social locomotion.

Mobility norms and values have played a great part in the interpretation

5. For some of the few contributions on the consequences of mobility, see Stacey (1966, 1967); Tumin (1957); Rogoff Ramsy (1965); Blau and Duncan (1967, ch. 11); Gini (1966); Simpson (1970); Thompson (1971); Lopreato and Chafetz (1970); methodological considerations of mobility consequences are discussed in Blalock (1968); Duncan (1966, pp. 90–95).
6. For a critique of that point, cf. Dahrendorf (1963, pp. 84–7); Miller (1955, pp. 71f.); Wilensky (1966, p. 131).

of data, but they were insufficiently investigated as an integral part of mobility studies. They have been studied as isolated phenomena, e.g. in Turner's *The Context of Ambition* (1964); or more often, it is merely the subjective aspects of social stratification that have been the object of research, i.e. the question of how many and which strata are being differentiated. Yet it is only speculation to assume that orientations which lead to stratified images of society would likewise influence actual mobility or immobility. And studies which are based on a static classification for the purpose of measuring mobility have also to prove that the classification chosen and the barriers presupposed therein have meaning for the individuals which are counted as moving in such classifications and between such barriers.

So far, explanations of social mobility in terms of individual motives do not stand on very firm ground. For instance, Lipset and Zetterberg's theory of universal ego-needs for recognition comes very close to committing the ecological fallacy: they try to explain the individual motives of social mobility, which is measured in prestige terms at the aggregate level, by the criterion of description, i.e. prestige orientation.[7] Such theories might be checked, at least in part, by comparing the subjective vocabulary of motives of mobile and nonmobile persons.

Approaches to mobility research

If there has been relatively small progress in mobility research and more question marks than substantial results have accumulated, this is not only because more emphasis has been placed on description than on explanation, more on mobility as an academic topic than as a political and individual problem, but also because one has attempted to resolve the riddles of mobility theory by mainly one avenue: mobility rates, i.e. the estimation of parameters of the extent of mobility for whole populations. In the following, a threefold scheme for studying social mobility is suggested.

Determinants of occupational status

The major recent study of a whole society, Blau and Duncan's *American Occupational Structure* (1967) represents both a culmination and a new point of departure of the tradition of mobility research discussed above, since it has been designed to overcome many of the shortcomings and ambiguities of that tradition: there has been a shift from descriptive mobility rates to causal analysis; the scope has been consciously narrowed to the empirically accessible occupational system; the rigid distinctions between inter- and intragenerational, vertical and horizontal mobility have

7. See Porter (1968); Rose (1964); Miller (1960. pp. 16–17); the methodological problem is discussed by Scheuch (1966) and Galtung (1967).

been loosened; many factors besides the father's occupational position have been tested and weighted, theoretical hypotheses and data analysis have come closer, and there is one goal which is never lost sight of throughout the whole study: the explanation of differential occupational success in terms of individual characteristics and structural features.

The methodological development, the reliability of the data, and the great number of tested hypotheses make the study of Blau and Duncan a model case for future mobility studies, but it also points to inherent limitations of that approach to the study of social mobility which concentrates on population parameters.

One major aspect of social theory which, since the sweeping ideas of Sorokin (1927) and Schumpeter (1953), could have been expected to be tested by mobility studies of that kind concerns relationships between the extent and intensity of mobility and other properties of societies as a whole, such as the intensity of social and political conflict, economic growth and level of intellectual activity, the degree of inequality and so on. But the mobility rate, at least as measured so far, has not been found to be a good differentiating indicator between societies or to be a trustworthy concomitant factor of linear or cyclical development. This may be due to mere methodological deficiencies of the cross-national analyses undertaken; to the fact that overall occupational inheritance is not the mobility indicator one should look for (because of its high stability over time); or to unreliable data. Only if mobility parameters would be good differentiating indicators the many national and comparable studies like Blau and Duncan's would allow better inferences about the societal significance of social mobility beyond producing highly valuable data on intra-country variations.

Studies on the macrosociological level: social mobility and social mobilization

The connection between social mobility and social change, the issues concerning the relationship between extent of social mobility on the one side, and the degree of industrialization, urbanization, participation and the spread of mass media on the other may become more clear within a research area which focuses directly on the components and conditions of modernization. Modernization implies an increasing flexibility of the variable units in a social system – individuals, sanctions, resources and positions (see Smelser and Lipset, 1966; Deutsch, 1961; Etzioni, 1968).

This research area offers theoretical concepts, e.g. K. W. Deutsch's 'social mobilization', cross-national and time-series data on many social, economic and political indicators, and adequate methods to describe and explain stability and change, causes and effects of various types of social mobility.

Moving to the macrosociological level in the study of social mobility does not remove the difficulties of assembling data. But asking about the significance of the mobility of personnel in social structure in the course of modernization instead of merely looking for societal factors explaining occupational mobility rates, one becomes more aware that various indicators of mobility could be employed and even rough but meaningful indices could serve the purpose of testing relevant hypotheses.

The meaning of social mobility – studies on the level of the individual actor

The research strategies mentioned above deal on the one hand with the measurement of gross mobility within a society explained by structural causes like the dependency of a son's status on his father's status or access to education, on the other hand with the comparative treatment of overall mobility rates as a feature of whole societies.

Since these approaches have to use highly aggregated data and have to employ simple measures, issues of social mobility as individual behavior appeared mainly at the interpretative fringe of studies.

A third level of research in which social mobility is conceived as social locomotion from the perspective of individuals should therefore be considered which more adequately could deal with such problems as:

The subjective meaning of social mobility: mobility experience, aspirations, mobility cognitions, values and norms;
The interrelations of individual movements in various role spheres;
The connection between social mobility and status inconsistency or incongruence;
The effects of social mobility on interpersonal relationships and vice versa;
The treatment of social mobility as a process, i.e. as sequences of specific positions, roles and statuses for which occupational career is but one example.[8]

Our own interest in the theory and research on social mobility concentrates on this level of the locomotion of individuals in social structure, because we believe that here assumptions implied in traditional concepts and procedures can be examined and many of the formidable difficulties of establishing and interpreting mobility rates can be avoided. If, however, social mobility is to be conceived on the level of individual actors, analytically non-committal formulas like 'movement between social positions' or 'change of status' will not suffice; one must start with a differentiated

8. The need for a perspective of mobility research focusing on individuals has been stressed by Geiger (1962) (who calls that perspective 'Anaskopie') and Miller (1955, passim; 1960, pp. 16–17).

conception of social structure and social space from the point of view of actors.

We have found it useful to conceive of the structural settings in which individuals move in the analytical terms of an extended role theory. In these terms one may start from readily observable social positions and mobility processes and then ask what abstractions are necessary for an adequate classification. People are mobile by changing social positions, but in what respects? We suggest to discriminate for our purposes between the following elements of social position: its locality, its peripheral role norms (e.g. appropriate dress or style of language), its central role norms concerning functional requirements of role performance, its inherent rewards (i.e. its social status) and its place in the class system.[9]

Accordingly we suggest that social mobility should be thought of as occurring:

1 If a person changes the locality where he occupies one or more of his social positions.

2 If a person changes in relation to the peripheral role norms, e.g. by moving from one department or factory to another or from one sports club to another, whereby the basic roles are retained, but some norms, e.g. such concerning support of unions or drinking manners, are replaced.

3 If a person is mobile in relation to the central role norms of his positions, e.g. by becoming married, by changing occupations, by changing from technical to administrative task roles, etc.

4 If a person improves or lowers his social standing, either in one status dimension of a social position, in several status dimensions of one social position, or the social ranks of all his positions.

5 If a person changes from one social class to another; (to speak of this kind of mobility presupposes of course that in the society in question either distinct social strata or social classes in the specific Marxist meaning of the term are existing).

6 An important and until now largely neglected type of social mobility results from the existence of multiple roles and statuses. To individuals, adding and giving up positions, i.e. the expansion or contraction of their position-sets, are quite significant changes, e.g. when children start school, convicted criminals lose their citizenship rights, etc. These changes are also important, because they imply possible changes in the overall status.

9 . Concerning the distinction between central and peripheral role norms, see Weinstock (1963); Dahrendorf (1953). For a revision of the concept of 'social structure' in considering individual mobility and ecological components, see Blau (1969, pp. 51, 63, 69); also Udy (1968).

From a dynamic point of view then, social mobility is institutionalized in status-sequences which are formed by typical or prevalent series of positions of different ranks, and/or role-sequences. (Looking from final positions these sequences appear as mobility channels or ways of recruitment.) These typical position-sequences together with movements in locality and changes of peripheral role norms constitute the structural basis of mobility experience.

To sociologists who are used to thinking of social mobility in narrow and strictly operational terms this conceptual approach may be disconcerting. Certainly terminologies and taxonomies should not replace problem-oriented theoretical and empirical discussion. They need not be elaborated to the last degree but they are helpful at least in so far as they serve to unify observations and point to problems and explanations which have been hidden by traditional definitions. A few advantages of this way of thinking are to be pointed out now.

Mobility studies on the individual level inspired by role theory do not have to presuppose a static classification, like a certain number of strata between which movements occur. They can start out by observing a large variety of empirically accessible movements, e.g. role changes; and it is only thereafter that the question may be raised whether a change of status was involved or not. Since the basic points of reference are not merely points of departure and destination, but ideally any point at which a mobility-step occurs, a dynamic perspective of social mobility as structured processes over time persists.[10]

Besides objective mobility special attention can be paid to attitudes toward social mobility, definitions of success, life goals and relevant values. Whereas social mobility on the macrosociological level looks like a functional answer to societal necessities and adaptations to change, the same process observed from the perspective of the individuals involved can be identified as socially determined individual experiences resulting from prior movements, evaluation of present positions and aspirations for the future.

Sorokin's crude and misleading spatial analogy of vertical and horizontal mobility as mutually exclusive categories can be modified. The elements of social position show analytical differences within the residual category of horizontal movements and relate them more usefully to status changes. They point to orientations which may operate in individual movements. Their combinations describe empirically observable movements more precisely. The assumption of the validity of prestige orientation as against other individual goals and structural constraints can be examined.

10. The use of smaller units of analysis to gain a dynamic perspective of mobility processes has already been suggested by Geiger (1962, p. 150). On the search for a diachronical conceptualization of 'structure', see Blau (1969).

The conceptual framework directs attention to connections between various movements in (1) different role spheres, (2) different status hierarchies and (3) different status dimensions. Besides changes between positions the gain or loss of position enters into the picture.

Additional explanatory theories are available: change of positions and identity formation (Strauss, 1959), status equilibration and effects of status incongruences (Hughes, 1945; Benoit-Smullyan, 1944; Lenski, 1956), role conflict and role dilemma (Gross *et al.*, 1958, ch. 5; Goode, 1960). Individual mobility does not have to be understood exclusively as strategies of maximizing social advantages, but can also be partly explained in terms of role behavior in given structural settings (i.e. institutionalized position-sets and position-sequences).

The research worker is forced to make a conscious selection from the whole range of individual movements. Thus hypotheses have to be more specific and it should be easier to relate results to theory. The terms demand a precise distinction between concepts and indicators, e.g. financial changes cannot be classified *per se* as status mobility. Boundaries between positions, roles, statuses, strata or classes are often indeterminate and therefore subject to arbitrary decisions. By starting from a detailed picture of structure and individual movements and by taking into account the perceptions and evaluations of the persons involved, these boundaries can be determined empirically.

The justification for developing such a scheme of three distinct but interrelated and complementary research strategies in the study of social mobility does not stem only from the common conviction that the traditional 'synthetic' approach has proved to be unsatisfactory in some respects; it also arises from a greater sensitivity about different data levels, methods of analysis and theoretical scope appropriate to the basic analytical units of individuals, collectivities and whole societies; this in turn leads to extra caution in drawing inferences from one level to another.[11]

References

BENOIT-SMULLYAN, E. (1944), 'Status, status types and status interrelations', *Amer. Sociol. Rev.*. vol. 9, pp. 151–61.

BERTAUX, D. (1970), 'Nouvelles perspectives de la mobilité sociale en France', Paper presented at the 7th World Congress of Sociology, Varna, Bulgaria; published in *Quality and Quantity: European J. Methodol.*, vol. 5, 1971, pp. 87–129.

BLALOCK, H. (1968), 'Review of P. Blau and O. D. Duncan, *The American Occupational Structure*, Wiley, 1967', *Amer. Sociol. Rev.*, vol. 33, pp. 296–7.

BLAU, P. (1969), 'Objectives of sociology', in R. Bierstedt (ed.), *A Design for Sociology: Scope. Objectives and Methods*, American Academy of Political and Social Science, Philadelphia.

11. On the methodological issues see Scheuch (1966) and Galtung (1967).

BLAU, P., and DUNCAN, O. D. (1967), *The American Occupational Structure*, Wiley.

BOLTE, K. M., and KRECKEL. R. (1968) 'Internationale Mobilitätsvergleiche im Bereich der Soziologie – Versuch einer kritischen Bilanz', in U. Gruber *et al.*, *Soziale Mobilität heute*, Maximilian Verlag, Herford, pp. 38–63.

CAPECCHI, V. (1967), 'Problèmes méthodologiques dans la mesure de la mobilité sociale', *Archives Européennes de Sociologie*, vol. 8, pp. 285–318.

CARLSSON, G. (1958), *Social Mobility and Class Structure*, Gleerup, Lund, Sweden.

CUTRIGHT, P. (1968a), 'Occupational inheritance: a cross-national analysis', *Amer. J. Sociol.*, vol. 73, pp. 400–416.

CUTRIGHT, P. (1968b), 'Studying cross-national mobility rates', *Acta Sociologica*, vol. 11, pp. 170–76.

DAHRENDORF, R. (1953), 'Industrielle Fertigkeiten und soziale Schichtung', *Kölner Zeitschrif i für Soziologie*, vol. 8, pp. 542–68.

DAHRENDORF, R. (1959), *Class and Class Conflict in Industrial Society*, Routledge & Kegan Paul.

DAHRENDORF, R. (1963), 'Mobility: Warum gibt es in den Vereinigten Staaten keinen Sozialismus?', *Die Angewandte Aufklärung*, Piper Verlag. München, pp. 67–87.

DEUTSCH, K. W. (1961), 'Social mobilization and political development', *Amer . pol. sci. Rev.*, vol. 55, pp. 493–514.

DUNCAN, O. D. (1966), 'Methodological issues in the analysis of social mobility', in N. J. Smelser and S. M. Lipset (eds.), *Social Structure and Mobility in Economic Development*, Routledge & Kegan Paul, pp. 51–97.

DUNCAN-JONES, P. (1970), 'Social mobility, canonical scoring and occupation classification', Paper presented at the 7th World Congress of Sociology, Varna, Bulgaria.

ETZIONI, A. (1968), 'Mobilization as a macrosociological conception', *Brit. J. Soc.*, vol. 19, pp. 243–53.

FOX, T., and MILLER, S. M. (1965a), 'Economic, political and social determinants of mobility: an international cross-sectional analysis', *Acta Sociologica*, vol. 9, pp. 76–93.

FOX, T., and MILLER, S. M. (1965b), 'Occupational stratification and mobility: intracountry variations', *Studies in Comparative International Development*, vol. 1, pp. 1–10.

GALTUNG, J. (1967), *Theory and Methods of Social Research*, Universitetsforlaget, Oslo.

GEIGER, T. (1962), 'Typologie und Mechanik der gesellschaftlichen Fluktuation', *Arbeiten zur Soziologie*, Luchterhand, Neuwied, pp. 114–51.

GINI, G. (1966), 'Social and political consequences of mobility', in N. J. Smelser and S. M. Lipset (eds.), *Social Structure and Mobility in Economic Development*, Routledge & Kegan Paul, pp. 364–94.

GOLDHAMER, H. (1968), 'Social mobility', in D. L. Sills (ed.), *The International Encyclopedia of the Social Sciences*, Macmillan.

GOLDTHORPE, J. H. (1966), 'Social stratification in industrial society', in R. Bendix and S. M. Lipset (eds.), *Class, Status and Power*, Free Press, pp. 648–59.

GOODE, W. (1960), 'A theory of role strain', *Amer. Sociol. Rev.*, vol. 25, pp. 483–96.

GROSS, N., *et al.* (1958), *Explorations in Role Analysis*, Wiley.

HAUG, M. B., and SUSSMAN, M. B. (1968), *Social Class Measurement II. The Case of the Duncan SEI*, American Sociological Association, Boston.

HUGHES, E. C. (1945), 'Dilemmas and contradictions of status', *Amer. J. Sociol.*, vol. 50, pp. 333–9.

JACKSON, E. F., and CURTIS, R. F. (1968), 'Conceptualization and measurement in the study of social stratification', in H. Blalock and A. Blalock (eds.), *Methodology in Social Research*, McGraw-Hill, pp. 112–49.

JONES, F. L. (1969), 'Social mobility and industrial society: a thesis reexamined', *Social. Quart.*, pp. 292–306.

LENSKI, G. (1956), 'Social participation, status crystallization and class consciousness', *Amer. sociol. Rev.*, vol. 21, pp. 458–64.

LIPSET, S. M., and ZETTERBERG, H. (1966), 'A theory of social mobility', in R. Bendix and S. M. Lipset (eds.), *Class, Status and Power*, Free Press.

LOPREATO, J., and CHAFETZ, J. S. (1970), 'The political orientation of skidders: a middle-range theory', *Amer. Sociol. Rev.*, vol. 35, pp. 440–76.

MILLER, S. M. (1955), 'The concept of mobility', *Social Problems*, vol. 3, pp. 65–73.

MILLER, S. M. (1960), 'Comparative social mobility: a trend report', *Current Sociology*, vol. 9, pp. 1–89.

MILLER, S. M., and BRICE, H. (1965), 'Soziale Mobilität, wirtschaftliches Wachstum und Struktur', in D. V. Glass and R. König (eds.), *Soziale Schichtung und Soziale Mobilität*, pp. 303–15.

PORTER, J. (1968), 'The future of upward mobility', *Amer. sociol. Rev.*, vol. 33, pp. 5–19.

ROGOFF RAMSY, N. (1965), 'On the flow of talent in society', *Acta Sociologica*, vol. 9, pp. 213–34.

ROSE, A. M. (1964), 'Social mobility and social values', *Archives Européennes de Sociologie*, vol. 5, pp. 324–30.

RUVKINA, R. (1970), 'To the study of relations between different kinds of mobility', Paper presented at the 7th World Congress of Sociology, Varna, Bulgaria.

SCHEUCH, E. K. (1966), 'Cross-national comparisons using aggregate data: some substantive and methodological problems', in R. W. Merritt and S. Rokkan (eds.), *Comparing Nations*, Yale University Press.

SCHUMPETER, J. A. (1953), 'Die sozialen Klassen im ethnisch homogenen Milieu', *Aufsätze zur Soziologie*, Mohr-Siebeck, Tübingen, pp. 147–213.

SIMPSON, M. E. (1970), 'Social mobility, normlessness and powerlessness in two cultural contexts', *Amer. sociol. Rev.*, vol. 35, pp. 1002–13.

SMELSER, N. J., and LIPSET, S. M. (eds.) (1966), *Social Structure and Mobility in Economic Development*, Routledge & Kegan Paul.

SOROKIN, P. A. (1927), *Social Mobility*, Harper & Row.

STACEY, B. (1966), 'Intergenerational mobility and voting', *Public Opinion Quart.*, vol. 30, pp. 133–9.

STACEY, B. (1967), 'The psychological consequences of intergenerational mobility', *Human Relations*, vol. 20, pp. 3–12.

STRAUSS, A. (1959), *Mirrors and Masks*, Free Press.

SVALASTOGA, K. (1959), *Class, Prestige and Mobility*, Gyldendal, Copenhagen.

SVALASTOGA, K. (1965), 'Gedanken zu internationalen Vergleichen sozialer Mobilität', in D. V. Glass and R. König (eds.), *Soziale Schichtung und Soziale Mobilität*, pp. 284–302.

THOMPSON, K. H. (1971), 'Upward mobility and political orientation: a reevaluation of the evidence', *Amer. sociol. Rev.*, vol. 36, pp. 223–35.

TUMIN, M. M. (1957), 'Some unapplauded consequences of social mobility in mass society', *Social Forces*, vol. 36, pp. 284–302.

TURNER, R. H. (1964), *The Context of Ambition*, Chandler.

UDY, S. H. (1968), 'Social structural analysis', *International Encyclopedia of the Social Sciences*, vol. 14, Free Press, pp. 489–95.

WEINSTOCK, A. (1963), 'Role elements: a link between acculturation and occupational status', *Brit. J. Soc.* vol. 14, pp. 144–9.

WESTOFF, C. F., BRESSLER, M., and SAGI, P. C. (1960), 'The concept of social mobility. An empirical inquiry', *Amer. sociol. Rev.*, vol. 25, pp. 375–85.

WILENSKY, H. (1966), 'Measures and effects of social mobility', in N. J. Smelser and S. M. Lipset (eds.), *Social Structure and Mobility in Economic Development*, Routledge & Kegan Paul, pp. 98–140.

Part Three
Conditions and Mechanisms of Mobility

The trend of research in social mobility is away from the analysis of empirically derived intergenerational mobility tables, which are coming to be seen as only one among several types of summarizing device. Perhaps the most significant advance in the field since the Glass study occurred with the publication of Blau and Duncan's *The American Occupational Structure* (1967) which explicitly modelled the occupational attainment process within the framework of a social mobility study. Reading 10, with the title *The Process of Stratification* gives a succinct account of the meaning of a 'path analysis' diagram and its application in a linear model of the socioeconomic life history. Blau and Duncan scaled the occupations held by a man and his father using the socio-economic index of occupational status which they described in Reading 2. Correlation coefficients could then be computed between a man's current occupational status and the occupational status of his father, and also between these and other relevant life-cycle variables, such as the amount of education received, and the status of the first job entered. The methodological advance here is that the technique of path analysis was used to decompose intercorrelations into the path coefficients of a pre-specified causal model. Blau and Duncan sound a note of caution as to the use of their approach in comparative studies of stratification systems, but perhaps it was only to be expected that the path diagram would be seized upon as a succession to the intergenerational mobility table, whose use in such comparative analysis was described in Reading 5 by Miller. Treiman (1970) has produced a very useful review article on 'Industrialization and social stratification', which uses a path model as a central organizing theme, and empirical studies which report their results along the lines of the Blau and Duncan approach are already beginning to appear in several countries. Reading 11 by Zdeněk Šafář is particularly interesting in this respect, for it deals with the occupational attainment process in a European socialist society.

The literature on organizational careers is fascinating but it has not yet been theoretically integrated with the more traditional concerns of mobility research, and rather than include a merely token contribution, we refer the interested student to Glaser's *Organizational Careers* (1968). Reading 12 by David Gordon contains his analysis of poverty and underemployment in terms of two separate approaches: the Doeringer–Piore 'dual labour market theory' and 'radical economic theory'.

Gordon addresses himself to the *absence* of upward mobility – and indeed to the absence of any career – among workers in the lower reaches of the job-market, and he considers this in historical and economic terms as a manifestation of the capitalist system in the United States. The basic argument of the labour market segmentation theorists is that it is highly misleading to assume that the same rules and processes are operative in all sections of the labour market in the same nation-state or even in the same region. Yet this is precisely what almost all traditional sociological approaches have taken for granted, and therefore if Gordon's arguments are valid, they will engender a major re-structuring of theory and method in the study of social mobility.

The idea that social mobility has consequences for the individual's personality and interpersonal relationships, or for a family's general life style and pattern of consumption is very old. Durkheim and Sorokin among many others have suggested that both upward and downward mobility disrupt the social ties which usually bind people into primary and secondary groups. At first glance, one might think that it would be easy for sociologists to produce useful empirical results in this area, by obtaining a measure of the degree of social movement and relating it to some dependent variable. However there are pitfalls. Duncan considered some of these in his discussion of mobility as an influence on fertility in Reading 8, and Lopreato and Hazelrigg mention related conceptual problems in Reading 13. One method of bypassing some of the technical difficulties in studying consequences of mobility is indicated in the case study of a factory closure reported by Aiken, Ferman and Sheppard (Reading 14), in which theoretical issues about the effects of status change upon political attitudes are grounded in a concrete report of men's reactions to redundancy.

Lastly, we devote only two Readings to the intricate topic of the relationship between formal education and social mobility. The student who intends to specialize in this topic should consult some source such as the readings edited by Hopper (1971) where useful papers by Bernstein, Bourdieu and by Hopper himself have been collected together. In Reading 15, Bowles uses historical arguments together with modern statistical data to argue that the schools have failed, and must necessarily fail, to exercise the positive discrimination in favour of underprivileged groups which is necessary for equal opportunity. Boudon takes up a related point from the now classical 'sceptical note' by Anderson (1961), and by a piece of explicit and beautifully simple model-building, shows how mobility tables generated from artificial data can be used to bring out the consequences of the sociologist's assumptions.

References

ANDERSON, C. A. (1961), 'A sceptical note on the relation of vertical mobility to education', *Amer. J. Sociol.*, vol. 66, pp. 560–70.

BLAU, P. M., and DUNCAN, O. D. (1967) *The American Occupational Structure*, Wiley.

GLASER, B. G. (ed.) (1968), *Organizational Careers: A Sourcebook for Theory*, Aldine.

HOPPER, E. (ed.) (1971), *Readings in the Theory of Educational Systems*, Hutchinson.

TREIMAN, D. J. (1970), 'Industrialization and social stratification', *Sociological Inquiry*, vol. 40, pp. 207–34.

10 P. M. Blau and O. D. Duncan

The Process of Stratification

Excerpt from P. M. Blau and O. D. Duncan, *The American Occupational Structure*, Wiley, 1967, pp. 163–77.

Stratification systems may be characterized in various ways. Surely one of the most important has to do with the processes by which individuals become located, or locate themselves, in positions in the hierarchy comprising the system. At one extreme we can imagine that the circumstances of a person's birth – including the person's sex and the perfectly predictable sequence of age levels through which he is destined to pass – suffice to assign him unequivocally to a ranked status in a hierarchical system. At the opposite extreme his prospective adult status would be wholly problematic and contingent at the time of birth. Such status would become entirely determinate only as adulthood was reached, and solely as a consequence of his own actions taken freely – that is, in the absence of any constraint deriving from the circumstances of his birth or rearing. Such a pure achievement system is, of course, hypothetical, in much the same way that motion without friction is a purely hypothetical possibility in the physical world. Whenever the stratification system of any moderately large and complex society is described, it is seen to involve both ascriptive and achievement principles.

In a liberal democratic society we think of the more basic principle as being that of achievement. Some ascriptive features of the system may be regarded as vestiges of an earlier epoch, to be extirpated as rapidly as possible. Public policy may emphasize measures designed to enhance or to equalize opportunity – hopefully, to overcome ascriptive obstacles to the full exercise of the achievement principle.

The question of how far a society may realistically aspire to go in this direction is hotly debated, not only in the ideological arena but in the academic forum as well. Our contribution, if any, to the debate will consist largely in submitting measurements and estimates of the strength of ascriptive forces and of the scope of opportunities in a large contemporary society. The problem of the relative importance of the two principles in a given system is ultimately a quantitative one. We have pushed our ingenuity to its limit in seeking to contrive relevant quantifications.

The governing conceptual scheme in the analysis is quite a common-place one. We think of the individual's life cycle as a sequence in time that can be described, however partially and crudely, by a set of classificatory or quantitative measurements taken at successive stages. Ideally we should like to have under observation a cohort of births, following the individuals who make up the cohort as they pass through life. As a practical matter we resorted to retrospective questions put to a representative sample of several adjacent cohorts so as to ascertain those facts about their life histories that we assumed were both relevant to our problem and accessible by this means of observation.

Given this scheme, the questions we are continually raising in one form or another are: how and to what degree do the circumstances of birth condition subsequent status? and, how does status attained (whether by ascription or achievement) at one stage of the life cycle affect the prospects for a subsequent stage? The questions are neither idle nor idiosyncratic ones. Current policy discussion and action come to a focus in a vaguely explicated notion of the 'inheritance of poverty'. Thus a spokesman for the Social Security Administration writes:

It would be one thing if poverty hit at random and no one group were singled out. It is another thing to realize that some seem destined to poverty almost from birth – by their color or by the economic status or occupation of their parents (Orshansky, 1963).

Another officially sanctioned concept is that of the 'dropout', the person who fails to graduate from high school. Here the emphasis is not so much on circumstances operative at birth but on the presumed effect of early achievement on subsequent opportunities. Thus the 'dropout' is seen as facing 'a lifetime of uncertain employment' (Bogan, 1965, p. 643), probable assignment to jobs of inferior status, reduced earning power and vulnerability to various forms of social pathology.

A basic model

To begin with, we examine only five variables. For expository convenience, when it is necessary to resort to symbols, we shall designate them by arbitrary letters but try to remind the reader from time to time of what the letters stand for. These variables are:

V father's educational attainment
X father's occupational status
U respondent's educational attainment
W status of respondent's first job
Y status of respondent's occupation in 1962

Each of the three occupational statuses is scaled by the index[1] ranging from 0 to 96. The two education variables are scored on the following arbitrary scale of values ('rungs' on the 'educational ladder') corresponding to specified numbers of years of formal schooling completed:

0 no school
1 elementary, one to four years
2 elementary, five to seven years
3 elementary, eight years
4 high school, one to three years
5 high school, four years
6 college, one to three years
7 college, four years
8 college, five years or more (i.e. one or more years of postgraduate study)

A basic assumption in our interpretation of regression statistics – though not in their calculation as such – has to do with the causal or temporal ordering of these variables. In terms of the father's career we should naturally assume precedence of V (education) with respect to X (occupation when his son was sixteen years old). We are not concerned with the father's career, however, but only with his statuses that comprised a configuration of background circumstances or origin conditions for the cohorts of sons who were respondents in the OCG study.[2] Hence we generally make no assumption as to the priority of V with respect to X; in effect, we assume the measurements on these variables to be contemporaneous from the son's viewpoint. The respondent's education, U, is supposed to follow in time – and thus to be susceptible to causal influence from – the two measures of father's status. Because we ascertained X as of respondent's age sixteen, it is true that some respondents may have completed school before the age to which X pertains. Such cases were doubtless a small minority and in only a minor proportion of them could the father (or other family head) have changed status radically in the two or three years before the respondent reached sixteen.

The next step in the sequence is more problematic. We assume that W (first job status) follows U (education). The assumption conforms to the wording of the questionnaire which stipulated 'the first full-time job you had after you left school'. In the years since the OCG study was designed we have been made aware of a fact that should have been considered more carefully in the design. Many students leave school more or less

1. The reader should consult Reading 2 in Part One to see how Duncan's index of occupational status was devised [Eds.].
2. OCG is an abbreviation for the Blau and Duncan project on Occupational Changes in a Generation [Eds.].

definitively, only to return, perhaps to a different school, some years later, whereupon they often finish a degree program (Eckland, 1964). [...]

In summary, then, we take the somewhat idealized assumption of temporal order to represent an order of priority in a causal or processual sequence, which may be stated diagrammatically as follows:

$(V, X) \rightarrow (U) \rightarrow (W) \rightarrow (Y).$

In proposing this sequence we do not overlook the possibility of what Carlsson calls 'delayed effects' (1958, p. 124), meaning that an early variable may affect a later one not only via intervening variables but also directly (or perhaps through variables not measured in the study).

In translating this conceptual framework into quantitative estimates the first task is to establish the pattern of associations between the variables in the sequence. This is accomplished with the correlation coefficient. Table 1 supplies the correlation matrix on which much of the subsequent analysis is based. In discussing causal interpretations of these correlations, we shall have to be clear about the distinction between two points of view. On the one hand, the simple correlation – given our assumption as to direction of causation – measures the gross magnitude of the effect of the antecedent upon the consequent variable. Thus, if $r_{YW} = 0.541$, we can say that an increment of one standard deviation in first-job status produces (whether directly or indirectly) an increment of just over half of one standard deviation in 1962 occupational status. From another point of view we are more concerned with net effects. If both first-job and 1962 status have a common antecedent cause – say, father's occupation – we may want to state what part of the effect of W on Y consists in a transmission of the prior influence of X. Or, thinking of X as the initial cause, we may focus on the extent to which its influence on Y is transmitted by way of its prior influence on W.

Table 1 Simple correlations for five status variables

Variable	Variable				
	Y	W	U	X	V
Y 1962 occupational status	—	0·541	0·596	0·405	0·322
W first-job status		—	0·538	0·417	0·332
U education			—	0·438	0·453
X father's occupational status				—	0·516
V father's education					—

We may, then, devote a few remarks to the pattern of gross effects before presenting the apparatus that yields estimates of net direct and indirect effects. Since we do not require a causal ordering of father's education with respect to his occupation, we may be content simply to note that $r_{XV} = 0.516$ is somewhat lower than the corresponding correlation, $r_{YU} = 0.596$, observed for the respondents themselves. The difference suggests a heightening of the effect of education on occupational status between the fathers' and the sons' generations. Before stressing this interpretation, however, we must remember that the measurements of V and X do not pertain to some actual cohort of men, here designated 'fathers'. Each 'father' is represented in the data in proportion to the numbers of his sons who were twenty to sixty-four years old in March 1962.

The first recorded status of the son himself is education (U). We note that r_{UV} is just slightly greater than r_{UX}. Apparently both measures on the father represent factors that may influence the son's education.

In terms of gross effects there is a clear ordering of influences on first job. Thus $r_{WU} > r_{WX} > r_{WV}$. Education is most strongly correlated with first job, followed by father's occupation, and then by father's education.

Occupational status in 1962 (Y) apparently is influenced more strongly by education than by first job; but our earlier discussion of the first-job measure suggests we should not overemphasize the difference between r_{YW} and r_{YU}. Each, however, is substantially greater than r_{YX}, which in turn is rather more impressive than r_{YV}.

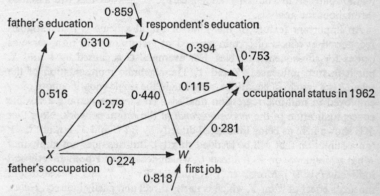

Figure 1 Path coefficients in basic model of the process of stratification

Figure 1 is a graphic representation of the system of relationships among the five variables that we propose as our basic model. The numbers entered on the diagram, with the exception of r_{XV}, are path coefficients, the estimation of which will be explained shortly. First we must become familiar with the conventions followed in constructing this kind of diagram. The link between V and X is shown as a curved line with an arrowhead at both ends. This is to distinguish it from the other lines, which are taken to be paths of influence. In the case of V and X we may suspect an influence running from the former to the latter. But if the diagram is logical for the respondent's generation, we should have to assume that for the fathers, likewise, education and occupation are correlated, not only because one affects the other but also because common causes lie behind both, which we have not measured. The bi-directional arrow merely serves to sum up all sources of correlation between V and X and to indicate that the explanation thereof is not part of the problem at hand.

The straight lines running from one measured variable to another represent *direct* (or net) influences. The symbol for the path coefficient, such as p_{YW}, carries a double subscript. The first subscript is the variable at the head of the path, or the effect; the second is the causal variable. (This resembles the convention for regression coefficients, where the first subscript refers to the 'dependent' variable, the second to the 'independent' variable.)

Finally, we see lines with no source indicated carrying arrows to each of the effect variables. These represent the residual paths, standing for all other influences on the variable in question, including causes not recognized or measured, errors of measurement, and departures of the true relationships from additivity and linearity, properties that are assumed throughout the analysis.

An important feature of this kind of causal scheme is that variables recognized as effects of certain antecedent factors may, in turn, serve as causes for subsequent variables. For example, U is caused by V and X, but it in turn influences W and Y. The algebraic representation of the scheme is a system of equations, rather than the single equation more often employed in multiple regression analysis. This feature permits a flexible conceptualization of the *modus operandi* of the causal network. Note that Y is shown here as being influenced directly by W, U and X, but not by V (an assumption that will be justified shortly). But this does not imply that V has no influence on Y. V affects U, which does affect Y both directly and indirectly (via W). Moreover, V is correlated with X, and thus shares in the gross effect of X on Y, which is partly direct and partly indirect. Hence the gross effect of V on Y, previously described in terms of the correlation r_{YV}, is here interpreted as being entirely indirect, in consequence of V's effect on intervening variables and its correlation with another cause of Y.

Path coefficients

Whether a path diagram, or the causal scheme it represents, is adequate depends on both theoretical and empirical considerations. At a minimum, before constructing the diagram we must know, or be willing to assume, a causal ordering of the observed variables. This information is external or *a priori* with respect to the data, which merely describe associations or correlations. Moreover, the causal scheme must be complete, in the sense that all causes are accounted for. Here, as in most problems involving analysis of observational data, we achieve a formal completeness of the scheme by representing unmeasured causes as a residual factor, presumed to be uncorrelated with the remaining factors lying behind the variable in question. If any factor is known or presumed to operate in some other way it must be represented in the diagram in accordance with its causal role, even though it is not measured. Sometimes it is possible to deduce interesting implications from the inclusion of such a variable and to secure useful estimates of certain paths in the absence of measurements on it, but this is not always so. A partial exception to the rule that all causes must be explicitly represented in the diagram is the unmeasured variable that can be assumed to operate strictly as an intervening variable. Its inclusion would enrich our understanding of a causal system without invalidating the causal scheme that omits it. Sociologists have only recently begun to appreciate how stringent are the logical requirements that must be met if discussion of causal processes is to go beyond mere impressionism and vague verbal formulations (Blalock, 1964). We are a long way from being able to make causal inferences with confidence, and schemes of the kind presented here had best be regarded as crude first approximations to adequate causal models.

On the empirical side, a minimum test of the adequacy of a causal diagram is whether it satisfactorily accounts for the observed correlations among the measured variables. In making such a test we employ the fundamental theorem in path analysis, which shows how to obtain the correlation between any two variables in the system, given the path coefficients and correlations entered on the diagram (Wright, 1960; Duncan, 1966). Without stating this theorem in general form we may illustrate its application here. For example,

$$r_{YX} = p_{YX} + p_{YU} r_{UX} + p_{YW} r_{WX}$$

and

$$r_{WX} = p_{WX} + p_{WU} r_{UX}.$$

We make use of each path leading to a given variable (such as Y in the first example) and the correlations of each of its causes with all other variables in the system. The latter correlations, in turn, may be analysed; for example, r_{WX}, which appeared as such in the first equation, is broken down into two parts in the second. A complete expansion along these lines is required to trace out all the indirect connections between variables thus,

$$r_{YX} = p_{YX} + p_{YU} \, p_{UX} + p_{YU} \, p_{UV} \, r_{VX} + p_{YW} \, p_{WX} + p_{YW} \, p_{WU} \, p_{UX} +$$
$$p_{YW} \, p_{WU} \, p_{UV} \, r_{VX}.$$

Now, if the path coefficients are properly estimated, and if there is no inconsistency in the diagram, the correlations calculated by a formula like the foregoing must equal the observed correlations. Let us compare the values computed from such a formula with the corresponding observed correlations:

$$r_{WV} = p_{WX} \, r_{XV} + p_{WU} \, r_{UV},$$
$$= (0 \cdot 224)(0 \cdot 516) + (0 \cdot 440)(0 \cdot 453),$$
$$= 0 \cdot 116 + 0 \cdot 199 = 0 \cdot 315,$$

which compares with the observed value of $0 \cdot 332$; and

$$r_{YV} = p_{YU} \, r_{UV} + p_{YX} \, r_{XV} + p_{YW} \, r_{WV},$$
$$= (0 \cdot 394)(0 \cdot 453) + (0 \cdot 115)(0 \cdot 516) + (0 \cdot 281)(0 \cdot 315)$$
$$= 0 \cdot 326,$$

(using here the calculated rather than the observed value of r_{WV}), which resembles the actual value, $0 \cdot 322$. Other such comparisons – for r_{YX}, for example – reveal, at most, trivial discrepancies (no larger than $0 \cdot 001$).

We arrive, by this roundabout journey, at the problem of getting numerical values for the path coefficients in the first place. This involves using equations of the foregoing type inversely. We have illustrated how to obtain correlations if the path coefficients are known, but in the typical empirical problem we know the correlations (or at least some of them) and have to estimate the paths. For a diagram of the type of Figure 1 the solution involves equations of the same form as those of linear multiple regression, except that we work with a recursive system of regression equations (Blalock, 1964, pp. 54 ff.) rather than a single regression equation.

Table 2 records the results of the regression calculations. It can be seen that some alternative combinations of independent variables were studied. It turned out that the net regressions of both W and Y on V were so small as to be negligible. Hence V could be disregarded as a direct influence on these variables without loss of information. The net regression of Y on X was likewise small but, as it appears, not entirely negligible. Curiously, this net regression is of the same order of magnitude as the proportion of occupational inheritance in this population – about 10 per cent. We might speculate that the direct effect of father's occupation on the occupational status of a mature man consists of this modest amount of strict occupational inheritance. The remainder of the effect of X on Y is indirect, inasmuch as X has previously influenced U and W, the son's education and the occupational level at which he got his start. We do not assume that the full impact of the tendency to take up the father's occupation is registered in the choice of first job.

Table 2 Partial regression coefficients in standard form (beta coefficients) and coefficients of determination, for specified combinations of variables

Dependent variable[a]	Independent variables[a]				Coefficient of determination R^2
	W	U	X	V	
U[b]	—	—	0·279	0·310	0·26
W	—	0·433	0·214	0·026	0·33
W[b]	—	0·440	0·224	—	0·33
Y	0·282	0·397	0·120	−0·014	0·43
Y[b]	0·281	0·394	0·115	—	0·43
Y	0·311	0·428	—	—	0·42

[a] V father's education, X father's occupational status, U respondent's education, W first-job status, Y 1962 occupational status

[b] Beta coefficients in these sets taken as estimates of path coefficients for Figure 1

With the formal properties of the model in mind we may turn to some general problems confronting this kind of interpretation of our results. One of the first impressions gained from Figure 1 is that the largest path coefficients in the diagram are those for residual factors, that is, variables not measured. The residual path is merely a convenient representation of the extent to which measured causes in the system fail to account for the variation in the effect variables. (The residual is obtained from the coefficient of determination; if $R^2_{Y(WUX)}$ is the squared multiple correlation of Y on the three independent variables, then the residual for Y is $\sqrt{\{1 - R^2_{Y(WUX)}\}}$. Sociologists are often disappointed in the size of the residual, assuming that this is a measure of their success in 'explaining' the phenomenon under study. They seldom reflect on what it would mean to live in a society where nearly perfect explanation of the dependent variable could be secured by studying causal variables like father's occupation or respondent's education. In such a society it would indeed be true that some are 'destined to poverty almost from birth . . . by the economic status or occupation of their parents' (Orshansky, 1963). Others, of course, would be 'destined' to affluence or to modest circumstances. By no effort of their own could they materially alter the course of destiny, nor could any stroke of fortune, good or ill, lead to an outcome not already in the cards.

Thinking of the residual as an index of the adequacy of an explanation gives rise to a serious misconception. It is thought that a high multiple correlation is presumptive evidence that an explanation is correct or nearly so, whereas a low percentage of determination means that a causal interpretation is almost certainly wrong. The fact is that the size of the residual (or, if one prefers, the proportion of variation 'explained') is *no* guide whatever to the validity of a causal interpretation. The best-known cases of 'spurious correlation' – a correlation leading to an egregiously wrong interpretation – are those in which the coefficient of determination is quite high.

The relevant question about the residual is not really its size at all, but whether the unobserved factors it stands for are properly represented as being uncorrelated with the measured antecedent variables. We shall entertain subsequently some conjectures about unmeasured variables that clearly are not uncorrelated with the causes depicted in Figure 1. It turns out that these require us to acknowledge certain possible modifications of the diagram, whereas other features of it remain more or less intact. A delicate question in this regard is that of the burden of proof. It is all too easy to make a formidable list of unmeasured variables that someone has alleged to be crucial to the process under study. But the mere existence of such variables is already acknowledged by the very presence of the residual. It would seem to be part of the task of the critic to *show*, if only hypothetically, but *specifically*, how the modification of the causal scheme to include a new variable would disrupt or alter the relationships in the original diagram. His argument to this effect could then be examined for plausibility and his evidence, if any, studied in terms of the empirical possibilities it suggests.

Our supposition is that the scheme in Figure 1 is most easily subject to modification by introducing additional measures of the same kind as those used here. If indexes relating to socioeconomic background other than *V* and *X* are inserted we will almost certainly estimate differently the direct effects of these particular variables. If occupational statuses of the respondent intervening between *W* and *Y* were known we should have to modify more or less radically the right-hand portion of the diagram. Yet we should argue that such modifications may amount to an enrichment or extension of the basic model rather than an invalidation of it. The same may be said of other variables that function as intervening causes. In theory, it should be possible to specify these in some detail, and a major part of the research worker's task is properly defined as an attempt at such specification. In the course of such work, to be sure, there is always the possibility of a discovery that would require a fundamental reformulation, making the present model obsolete. Discarding the model would be a cost gladly paid for the prize of such a discovery.

Postponing the confrontation with an altered model, the one at hand is not lacking in interest. An instructive exercise is to compare the magnitudes of gross and net relationships. Here we make use of the fact that the correlation coefficient and the path coefficient have the same dimensionality. The correlation $r_{YX} = 0.405$ (Table 1) means that a unit change (one standard deviation) in X produces a change of 0.4 unit in Y, in gross terms. The path coefficient, $p_{YX} = 0.115$ (Figure 1), tells us that about one-fourth of this gross effect is a result of the direct influence of X on Y. (We speculated above on the role of occupational inheritance in this connection.) The remainder ($0.405 - 0.115 = 0.29$) is indirect, via U and W. The sum of all indirect effects, therefore, is given by the difference between the simple correlation and the path coefficient connecting two variables. We note that the indirect effects on Y are generally substantial, relative to the direct. Even the variable temporally closest (we assume) to Y has 'indirect effects' – actually, common antecedent causes – nearly as large as the direct. Thus $r_{YW} = 0.541$ and $p_{YW} = 0.281$, so that the aggregate of 'indirect effects' is 0.26, which in this case are common determinants of Y and W that spuriously inflate the correlation between them.

To ascertain the indirect effects along a given chain of causation we must multiply the path coefficients along the chain. The procedure is to locate on the diagram the dependent variable of interest, and then trace back along the paths linking it to its immediate and remote causes. In such a tracing we may reverse direction once but only once, following the rule 'first back, then forward'. Any bidirectional correlation may be traced in either direction. If the diagram contains more than one such correlation, however, only one may be used in a given compound path. In tracing the indirect connections no variable may be intersected more than once in one compound path. Having traced all such possible compound paths, we obtain the entirety of indirect effects as their sum.

Let us consider the example of effects of education on first job, U on W. The gross or total effect is $r_{WU} = 0.538$. The direct path is $p_{WU} = 0.440$. There are two indirect connections or compound paths: from W back to X then forward to U; and from W back to X, then back to V, and then forward to U. Hence we have:

$$r_{WU} = p_{WU} + p_{WX}\, p_{UX} + p_{WX}\, r_{XV}\, p_{UV},$$

(gross)   (direct) (indirect)

or, numerically,

$$0.538 = 0.440 + (0.224)(0.279) + (0.224)(0.516)(0.310),$$
$$= 0.440 + 0.062 + 0.036,$$
$$= 0.440 + 0.098.$$

In this case all the indirect effect of U on W derives from the fact that both U and W have X (plus V) as a common cause. In other instances, when more than one common cause is involved and these causes are themselves interrelated, the complexity is too great to permit a succinct verbal summary.

A final stipulation about the scheme had best be stated, though it is implicit in all the previous discussion. The form of the model itself, but most particularly the numerical estimates accompanying it, are submitted as valid only for the population under study. No claim is made that an equally cogent account of the process of stratification in another society could be rendered in terms of this scheme. For other populations, or even for subpopulations within the United States, the magnitudes would almost certainly be different, although we have some basis for supposing them to have been fairly constant over the last few decades in this country. The technique of path analysis is not a method for discovering causal laws but a procedure for giving a quantitative interpretation to the manifestations of a known or assumed causal system as it operates in a particular population. When the same interpretative structure is appropriate for two or more populations there is something to be learned by comparing their respective path coefficients and correlation patterns. We have not yet reached the stage at which such comparative study of stratification systems is feasible.

References

BLALOCK, H. M. Jr (1964), *Causal Inferences in Nonexperimental Research*, University of North Carolina Press.
BOGAN, F. A. (1965), 'Employment of high school graduates and dropouts in 1964', *Special Labor Force Report*, no. 54, US Bureau of Labor Statistics.
CARLSSON, G. (1958), *Social Mobility and Class Structure*, Gleerup, Lund, Sweden.
DUNCAN, O. D. (1966), 'Path analysis', *Amer. J. Sociol.*, vol. 72, pp. 1–16.
ECKLAND, B. K. (1964), 'College dropouts who came back', *Harvard educ. Rev.*, vol. 34, pp. 402–20.
ORSHANSKY, M. (1963), 'Children of the poor', *Social Security Bull.*, vol. 26, pp. 1–23.
WRIGHT, S. (1960), 'Path coefficients and path regressions', *Biometrics*, vol. 16, pp. 189–202.

11 Z. Šafář

The Measurement of Mobility in the Czecho-Slovak Socialist Society

Abridged from Z. Šafář, 'Different approaches to the measurement of social differentiation and social mobility in the Czecho-Slovak socialist society', *Quality and Quantity: European Journal of Methodology*, vol. 5, 1971, pp. 179–208.

Basic approach to the social differentiation of Czecho-Slovak society

In the following we shall make an attempt at recapitulating the basic research results we consider as theoretically most relevant: we shall concentrate upon one of the central concepts of the investigation – social status.

The field research carried out towards the end of 1967 involved 13 215 respondents (male family heads); it further included data about 12 465 wives, 4546 sons, 4545 daughters and 2910 fathers of the respondents. It is fully representative of the socialized male population. The basic technique of collecting data was the standardized interview.

The starting point of the following analyses was an attempt to construct a 'synthetic' social status index. In our operationalization of status, we proceded from the assumption that it is difficult to find a single valid status index but that, in our society, the individual status is a rather complex concept including at least the following dimensions:

1 *The complexity of work* is considered in terms of the division of the respondents' occupations into six groups according to the objective complexity of the respondents' work.

2 *Participation in management.* The index consists of two components which are operatively defined as follows: the participation in management based on the socio-occupational level is deduced from the position of the individual in the institution and from the position of the institution in the society. The second component, i.e. the participation in power based on political activity performed off duty, is deduced from the membership and functions in elective organs (e.g. of the Communist Party, of the State and social organizations).

3 *The income* variable is defined by an arbitrary categorization of the respondents' net monthly income (again into six categories).

4 *Education* is defined by a categorization of the respondents' education into six groups. The educational system in Czecho-Slovakia enables us to express this in completed years of school attendance: the first category is 18 years, the second 11–17 years, the third 10–11 years, the fourth 8–9 years (+2 years of theoretical and practical special preparation), the fifth 8–9 years, the sixth less than 8 years.

5 The '*style of life*' is derived from the utilization of certain objects (car, refrigerator, etc.), from the way of spending one's leave, from leisure activities and from the housing standard and cultural activities.

As can be seen, the first three to four variables are included, in more or less substantial modifications, in the basis of the construction of most statuses known from sociological literature. Why we have selected these variables and why we are not adding (or subtracting) others is conditioned by the theoretical starting points of the research.

As Marxist sociologists, we do not agree with reducing the status indices to subjective indices, or to those involving a considerable measure of subjectivism (e.g. occupational prestige or some sort of self-rating). We further emphasize the role played by differentiation in the complexity of work and in education; this has already been studied on the occasion of investigating the intra-class differentiation in the socialist society. However, we include in the status components also the component of reward (differentiated in socialism on the basis of both the quantity and the quality of performed work), as well as the hitherto little investigated component of the style of life (involving also leisure activities) and, finally, the component of 'participation in the management of the socialist society'.

Grouping of people according to individual status characteristics
The 'synthetic' indices of social status in a socialist society could be constructed, first of all, for economically active persons, because we did not want to leave out of consideration the occupational status (complexity of work) and the participation in management based on the occupational position, although some other indices for all the respondents were used. In its most convenient form, the synthetic index of the individual's social status consists of five variables. We have proved by empirical analysis that this index helps to obtain the most homogeneous groups in relation to the other indicators of the social position.

Apart from the 'general' indices of social status, various 'reduced' indices (consisting of two or three components) were also used and some attempts to 'weigh' the components of the synthetic index were made.

As regards the content, two different kinds of indices were constructed for the respondent. One of them emphasized the individual components (e.g. income), the other emphasized the components relating to the respondent's position as the head of the family (income per head, ownership of different objects in the households, etc.). Further, we worked with the family status; this was intended to help us perceive the culmination of the process in which the individual status in the family is changing. Then the question of constructing the 'women's status' was introduced, since – in view of the incomparably more equal rights characterizing the position of the woman in socialism – we refuse to ascribe the husband's status to the wife in accordance with the practice current in the Western countries.

Finally some indices were constructed involving substantial variables, e.g. 'class-economic position' instead of complexity of work, 'voluntary economic activity' instead of complexity of work, 'voluntary political activity' instead of synthetic index of the participation in management – the last including also the occupational dimension of management. Also the simple class-economic position was tried as the simplest possible indicator of social status.

Generally speaking, the correlations in the cases where one of the indices lays less emphasis upon the 'family', 'private' and 'voluntary' characteristics, whereas the other is focused on the individual and occupational characteristics of the various status indices, are very high – ranging from 0·73 to 0·98, for the most part above 0·80; this testifies to a certain stability of these characteristics and suggests that the indices are not meaningless mathematical averages of different variables but a reflection of certain objective aspects of the vertical social differentiation of the sample under examination. The lowest correlations appear in the cases where one of the indices lays less emphasis upon the 'family', 'private' and 'voluntary' characteristics, whereas the other is focused on the individual and occupational ones. In general, the redistribution of the individual status within the family indicates a downward trend which is due to the lower occupational, educational and income statuses of the wives as well as to some specific mechanisms of the relation between the individual and the family.

As for the 'class-economic position' in its subtlest variant (see Table 1), it can, in general, play the role of an ordinal scale which approximates to the general social status. Its correlation with the most convenient social status index (S_1) is 0·74. Figure 1 shows the distribution of the status S_1 in the values of the original score.

Twenty-six categories express the score attained by adding the values of five variables composing the status S_1. The uppermost category designated as Ø 1 represents a limited number of individuals (0·1 per cent) occupying only the highest positions on the respective scales (e.g.

complex creative work, university education, income above 2500 Czecho-Slovak crowns, a high participation in management and a high style of life). The lowest category designated as Ø 6 (0·7 per cent) includes individuals occupying the lowest positions on all the scales (simplest work, incomplete elementary education without apprenticeship, income under 1250 crowns, no participation whatsoever in management, no 'positive' characteristics of the style of life during leisure and in consumption).

Table 1 Economically active respondents according to their class-economic positions and statuses S_1 in percentages

Economic position	Status 1						
	1 Highest	2	3	4	5	6 Lowest	Total
free professions (7)	—	28·6	28·6	42·9	—	—	100·0
expert employees (2347)	9·7	30·3	39·1	17·8	3·1	0·1	100·0
clerks (1034)	0·4	6·5	27·5	32·2	19·7	13·7	100·0
nonagricultural, non-manual, cooperative workers (158)	—	11·8	29·4	35·3	17·6	5·9	100·0
skilled workers (2215)	—	0·3	8·2	49·0	39·5	3·0	100·0
trained workers (2140)	—	0·1	3·2	28·3	51·5	17·3	100·0
nonagricultural, manual cooperative workers (39)	—	—	—	28·2	53·9	17·9	100·0
independent workers, nonagricultural (14)	—	7·1	7·1	—	50·1	35·7	100·0
unskilled workers (851)	—	—	0·1	4·9	35·5	59·5	100·0
agricultural workers (378)	—	—	0·8	8·2	27·8	53·2	100·0
cooperative farmers (813)	—	—	0·4	8·7	36·5	54·4	100·0
independent farmers (69)	—	—	—	1·4	17·4	81·2	100·0

Further categories, designated as Ø (see Figure 1), include individuals for whom the ranking mean on all the scales represents 2, 3, 4, 5 points. However, the formally fully consistent patterns (e.g. 3, 3, 3, 3, 3 – middle position on all the variables) are occupied by only 1·5 per cent of the sample. In all other cases, the score represents the mean value of the five components of the synthetic status.

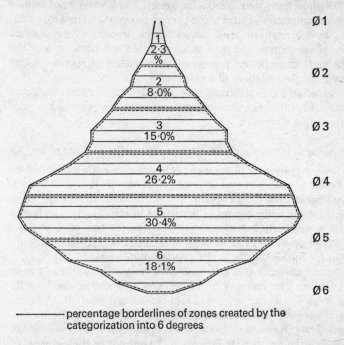

percentage borderlines of zones created by the categorization into 6 degrees

Figure 1 Distribution of status S_1 score

Of course, the construction of a status index of this kind is only a pre-liminary – and very abstract – approach to the real structure of vertical differentiation, since considerably diverse positions on the different scales are put under the same mean.

Similarly abstract, averaging and, moreover, very arbitrary is also the next step, i.e. the categorization of the scores into six zones including 2·3, 8·0, 15·0, 26·2, 30·4, and 18·1 per cent of the sample. Thus a kind of a scale of the mean social status has been devised, the main purpose of which is not to illustrate the real differentiation but to provide a uniform measure for evaluating all the other aspects of the social position in a socialist society, a measure which was itself judged and modified in the course of this evaluation, so as to reflect the reality as adequately as possible.

The procedures did not lead to very satisfactory results, as the categories constructed in this way were highly heterogenous. This is why we used the taxonomic analysis – or the clustering methods – for grouping the individuals into more homogenous categories. The impression of historically–arisen subgroups of large social clusters was created, from this point of view, by the relatively great class-economic specifity of the separate clusters, which complicated their inner structure and demonstrated the complex and contradictory process of development of socialist social relations from class relations to classless ones.

The analyses of the differentiations according to the class-economic position, status categories and clusters from the status patterns have not given very different results.

What types of people belong to the different categories of social status (S_1)

At this level of knowledge of the social differentiation in Czecho-Slovakia, we are bound to specify in greater detail and to identify the internal structure S_1 pyramid from the viewpoint of those variables that do not enter it at all, i.e. to describe in greater detail and to identify also the people belonging to the individual categories. Owing to the lack of time, however, we shall present only an example of the description of one category, and refer, for further details, to the mentioned literature.

The second category (8·0 per cent) includes nearly exclusively non-manual workers, nine-tenths of whom are experts. 'Social services' (health services, work in culture) are once again represented more than proportionately, similarly as administration and distribution ('economic workers'). The percentage of industrial occupations is great, even though not excluding the appropriate dimension. Two-thirds of the members of this category are activists, more than one-half of them are members of the Communist Party. The prevalence of Czechs is a little greater than in the first category. Nearly 40 per cent of them inhabit middle-sized towns, over one-third inhabit big cities, the rest inhabit communities having no more than 5000 inhabitants. [. . .]

Determination of the occupational status

In the work of the American authors Blau and Duncan (1967, p. 170), an attempt has been made at constructing a model of the determination of the respondents' contemporary occupational status. Here, we are not going to discuss the technical and methodological problems of applying the so-called path analysis (we refer to the cited publication where the reader will find further references), but shall focus our attention to the meritorious aspect of the matter.

The basic model has the form of the following scheme:

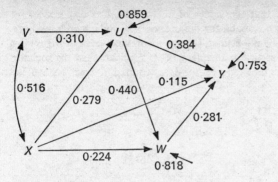

The model contains five basic variables:

Y = 1962 occupational status, W = first-job status, U = education, X = father's occupational status, V = father's education. The arrows in the scheme indicate the presupposed 'causal' connections among the separate variables. As is evident, the basis of this scheme is formed by two variables – education and the father's occupational status (at the time when his son was sixteen years old). Although we might presume the priority of the father's occupation, we are, of course, willing to accept the explanation of the authors of the model that, in view of the fact that we are studying the effect of these traits only upon the son's occupational status, both traits may be regarded as equivalent (see the bilateral arrow). As is further evident, the priority of the son's education is presupposed to be determining for the son's first job, even though the authors are aware of the fact that, for a certain number of people, this scheme might be reversed. (In the American society, the authors consider the proportion of these cases to be negligible. Due to the fact that, in Czechoslovakia, there is approximately one fourth of persons who have completed their education only after entering a job, a special scheme was reconstructed for this sample. The respective analysis is not presented here, owing to the lack of space at our disposal.)

The models allow an easy comparison between the values of the so-called path coefficients. The values of path coefficients have the advantage of substituting, in substance, a certain 'net weight' of the intensity of the respective variable's operation. Free arrows (residuals) in the variables U, W and Y indicate the 'openness' of the given system. They demonstrate that the four other variables introduced by us are *insufficient* to present a deterministic explication of a certain value, e.g. the state Y, and that also other influences, not included in the scheme, indubitably project themselves into the system.

Owing to the fact that the values of all the variables disposed of by Blau and Duncan were available for the purposes of our research, we have decided (in spite of the hitherto still vague theoretical value of the model and the uncertainty as to the adequacy of its application in the socialist society) to reconstruct the model for the data acquired in Czecho-Slovakia.

Scheme:

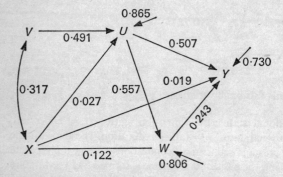

In our research, education is categorized into only six groups; the data concerning the father's occupation apply to the time when the son was entering his first job. Without doubt, the greatest problem lies in the comparability of the hierarchization of the occupational status. The methods applied in both investigations, based on different theoretical premises, differ to a considerable degree; the common trait of both the procedures is represented by the high correlation with occupational prestige gained by analogical methods, which offers the possibility to consider the data of both investigations as approximately comparable.

The comparison of our results with the American scheme reveals a number of similar, but also dissimilar, traits interpreted by us in the following way:

The openness of both systems as regards the variables introduced (see: non-essential factors) is surprisingly great. It might be interpreted by means of the premise that the variables introduced in both models determine the occupational status to an equal extent.

The test of the adequacy of the models (measured by a special test) is similar in both models.

The 'unstability' (fluidity) of the structure in Czecho-Slovakia is indicated by the difference in the coefficients r_{vx} (516:317, in Slovakia even

516:168): at present, the correlations are already becoming equalized. In our research, the further generation (i.e. the respondents and their sons) has also been subjected to study. Here, this trend is already stabilized.

At present, the determination of the respondents' occupational status by education is significantly higher in Czecho-Slovakia (compare p_{WU} and p_{YV}!).

The expressively lower path coefficients in the Czecho-Slovak model between the 'father's original occupation', and the son's education, and, finally, the respondent's occupation point to a greater openness of the Czecho-Slovak educational system as compared with the USA, and indubitably, also to a larger extent of the mobility openness of the son's career in view of the father's occupation. On the other hand, they demonstrate a higher dependence upon the sphere of 'cultural orientation' relating to the line of education. Further analysis (comparison between the Czech countries and Slovakia, and the analysis of the further generation) revealed that this phenomenon cannot be ascribed to the lack of any 'industrial immaturity' but that, as a matter of course, it is a permanent trait inherent in the socialist societies. From this point of view, it is necessary to refute the hypotheses frequently presented in the Western sociological literature concerning the 'mobility blockade' of the socialist societies.

Reference

BLAU, P. M., and DUNCAN, O. D. (1967), *The American Occupational Structure*, Wiley.

12 D. M. Gordon

Multiple Labor Markets

Excerpts from D. M. Gordon, *Theories of Poverty and Underemployment: Orthodox, Radical and Dual Labor Market Perspectives*, Lexington Books, 1972, pp. 44–79.

Dual labor market theory
Specific hypotheses

To some of those economists studying ghetto labor markets in the 1960s, it often appeared that characteristics which economists had conventionally associated with 'productivity' – like years of schooling and vocational training – had almost no influence on the employment prospects of large numbers of urban employees. In many instances, those who were rejected for jobs seemed nominally as 'qualified' as workers who were hired. The important differences among ghetto workers often seemed to center around their work preferences. Some workers frequently refused to consider jobs to which they were referred. These more particular applicants often had 'better' qualifications than those who were hired, and yet chose to remain unemployed or out of the labor force. One began to guess, in this respect, that the range of jobs available to these workers was much narrower than the range of their 'capacities' or nominal qualifications. Given that narrow range of jobs, the determinants of labor force status – whether a worker happened to be employed, unemployed, or out of the labor force – sometimes appeared to be relatively random.[1]

At least partly as a result of these perceptions, increasing attention was focused on the characteristics of jobs to which many ghetto workers seemed confined. With few exceptions, these jobs were typically menial, requiring little mental or physical dexterity. Instability of the work force

1. Many of these impressions were reinforced by data collected in the Boston ghetto labor market study, reported by Doeringer, Feldman, Gordon, Piore and Reich (1969). Data on job referrals by neighborhood manpower centers suggested, for instance, that there were no statistically significant differences between workers hired on jobs and workers rejected by employers. Nor did there seem to be significant differences between the jobs for which workers were typically hired and those for which they were rejected. Those who refused to report to interviews or refused to accept job offers were in some respects, according to the report (Doeringer *et al.*, 1969, p. 84), 'a "superior" group [with respect] to the "hires" and "rejects"'. They were slightly older, on the average, had more years of work experience, and had generally worked on better jobs in the past.

seemed not only to be accepted by employers in these job categories but often encouraged by them. The jobs paid low wages and conferred minimal status. The quality of working conditions was poor. Most important, apparently, the jobs seemed completely isolated. They were not connected to job ladders of any sort. No matter how long an employee worked at these jobs or how clearly he demonstrated his diligence or skill, there seemed to be no fixed channels through which he could rise above his original job.[2]

There seemed to many to be a critical interdependence between the characteristics of 'secondary' workers and 'secondary' jobs. The structure of jobs often seemed to the workers to prevent them from improving their wages or status on the job. In response, they often quit their jobs to earn money another way. This pattern of instability fitted into a more general pattern of life in the ghetto (and perhaps even caused it).[3] Secondary workers tended to continue their instability by habit or instinct even in those rare instances where stability might have mattered. Simultaneously, these patterns of behavior led employers increasingly to organize the structure of work and production in such a way that worker instability did not disrupt production or reduce efficiency, further prompting them to separate these jobs from the rest of the establishment. The attitudes of employees and employers seemed symbiotically to adjust to developing behavioral patterns. And once these attitudes were fixed, employee and employer expectations combined to intensify the patterns to which they were initially responding. Keyed to these behavioral trends, a separate market appeared to emerge in which both secondary workers and secondary employers were forced to operate.

These impressions gradually forged a more formal analysis of the dichotomization between the 'primary' and the 'secondary' markets. In general, as Piore (1971) argues, the two markets display distinct and identifiable features:

. . . the primary market offers jobs which possess several of the following traits: high wages, good working conditions, employment stability and job security, equity and due process in the administration of work rules, and chances for advancement. The . . . secondary market has jobs which, relative to those in the

2. For some interesting statistical evidence which seemed to help characterize the nature of these jobs at the time, see Bluestone (1968). Doeringer and Piore (1971) give a good picture of the job ladder problem, with plentiful examples.
3. Three different aspects of life in the ghetto merged with this pattern of work instability: the welfare system, the 'training economy', and the world of crime and 'hustling'. For some extended surveys of these aspects of ghetto life, with bibliographies, see Gordon (1971b, chs. 2, 4 and 5). For a useful review of the interconnections among these three sectors and the 'secondary' labor market, see Harrison (1972, ch. 5).

primary sector, are decidedly less attractive. They tend to involve low wages, poor working conditions, considerable variability in employment, harsh and often arbitrary discipline, and little opportunity to advance. The poor are confined to the secondary labor market (p. 91).

Doeringer and Piore (1971) describe three distinct kinds of employment situations in the secondary market: completely unstructured employment, classically competitive; clusters of secondary jobs with a bit of internal job structure, as in foundry work; and secondary jobs with no internal job structure which are attached to primary markets, like woodyard jobs in pulp and paper mills.

Piore (1970) makes five connected arguments which he intends to explain both the historical separation between markets and the differences in behavior between them. First, he suggests, 'the most important characteristic distinguishing jobs in the primary sector from those in the secondary sector appears to be the behavioral requirements which they impose on the work force, particularly that of employment stability.' Secondary workers are generally barred from primary jobs not because they lack certain 'work skills' but because they tend to work unreliably and intermittently.

Second, 'certain workers who possess the behavioral traits required to operate efficiently in primary jobs are trapped in secondary markets because their superficial characteristics resemble those of secondary workers.' Two kinds of discrimination seem important. There is discrimination 'pure and simple' where employers simply dislike employing workers with certain characteristics. There is also 'statistical discrimination'. In this case, employers tend not to employ members of certain groups because their superficial characteristics seem to be statistically associated with undesirable behavioral traits like unreliability. As Doeringer and Piore (1971) are careful to note, of course, many workers in the secondary market will work stably despite the extent to which their jobs encourage instability.

Third, the distinction between sectors is not so much technologically as historically determined. Many kinds of work can be technologically performed in either sector. 'Work normally performed in the primary sector is sometimes shifted to the secondary sector through subcontracting, temporary help services, recycling of new employees through probationary periods' and so on. Different jobs within the same plant can share the characteristics of either or both sectors. But once jobs come to be rooted in one sector or another, through a process of historical or institutional evolution, 'shifts in the distribution [of jobs between sectors] generally involve changes in the techniques of production and management and in the institutional structure and procedures of the enterprises in which the work is performed.' Since these changes are difficult and expensive they are infrequently made.

Fourth, 'the behavioral traits associated with the secondary sector are reinforced by the process of working in secondary jobs and living among others whose life style is accommodated to that type of employment.' Those who are channelled into the secondary sector as a result of discrimination 'tend, over time, to develop the traits predominant among secondary workers.' This grows both from work patterns on the job and from life style in the ghetto or in the family.[4]

Finally, a wide variety of historical forces have interacted to increase the likelihood of sharp separations between the two markets. (The following hypotheses draw largely from Piore (1968) and Doeringer and Piore (1971).) The increasing importance of skills acquired through on-the-job training has raised the incentive to employers to retain some (stable) employees, and has tended to create a division between those jobs and other jobs which do not require such employee retention. Trade union organization and federal social welfare legislation may have 'operated in the postwar period to sharpen the distinction between stable and unstable jobs'. The rise of federal social legislation – and particularly of minimum wages, 'the income ceiling upon the tax base of social insurance programs, the ceilings on the tax rate in the experience rating for unemployment insurance taxation, and the limited coverage of the legislation' (Piore, 1968, p. 26) has tended to encourage employment stability in those industries affected because the 'employer has an incentive to minimize the number of people on his annual payroll and avoid absenteeism, turnover, and fluctuations in demand which disperse the wage bill over a larger number of workers' (Piore, 1968, p. 26). The differential rise in union strength among different industries, and the differential industrial coverage under the National Labor Relations Act also tend to separate industries into those with stable and those with unstable work arrangements. And most important, the interactions between the process of economic growth and the changing behavioral characteristics of disadvantaged workers have accentuated these trends. Disadvantaged workers, especially those recently off the farm, have always had trouble responding to the discipline required of them in industrial organizations. That transition was traditionally abetted by the 'stick' of the sharp penalties attached to

4. For instance, 'reward and punishment in the work place are continually based upon personal relationships between worker and supervisor' in the secondary sector. In that setting, 'workers forget how to operate within the impersonal, institutional grievance procedures of the primary sector and when they do gain access to primary jobs, are frustrated by the failure of the system to respond on a personal basis and their own inability to make it respond on an institutional basis.'

unemployment and the 'carrot' of the example of successful transition by previously assimilated groups. As Piore writes:

Earlier migrants made their transition at a time when the penalties for unstable work habits were more severe. Public welfare programs have since reduced the cost of life without work and rising wage levels the threat which unemployment, especially temporary unemployment, poses to subsistence. . . . The completion, by a greater and greater portion of the total labor force of the transition to industrial work, combined with the effects of union organization and social welfare legislation, has tended to create a discontinuity along the spectrum. If workers (and jobs) of intermediate stability have not been completely eliminated, their numbers relative to those with unstable work habits may have been greatly reduced. This implies, in turn, a decline in the alternative behavioral models to which the very unstable are exposed and in the number of social groups that can serve as waystations in their transition to stable life styles. For Negroes, suburbanization combined with segregated housing patterns may have had an even stronger adverse impact upon the contacts necessary for the development of stable work habits (Piore, 1968, pp. 28, 29–30).

This analysis would also apply to women (although the dual market analysts refer to the employment problems of women only implicitly). Women are much less able than previously 'disadvantaged' workers to identify with 'advantaged' workers and to follow their model in the transition to stable work. Further, the social definition of family and sex roles continues to undercut employment stability among women. And, as the percentage of women in the labor force continues to increase, some employers seem more and more likely to move many jobs into the secondary market in response to the (expected) behavioral characteristics of secondary women employees.

In their book, Doeringer and Piore (1971) elaborate many of the institutional forces within the firm which tend to produce highly 'structured' internal labor markets, characteristic of the primary sector, and tend also to widen the gap between those markets and 'unstructured' secondary markets. They especially emphasize trends tending to increase the skill specificity of primary jobs, the importance of on-the-job training as a medium for skill acquisition, and the influence of custom (and intra-firm sociological forces) on internal labor market procedures. They argue that the historical interaction of factors which orthodox economists normally hold constant – like technology, custom, job structure, worker preferences and labor force composition – helps explain the separation of markets, and through that separation the different behavior of individuals within each market:

Employment in the secondary labor market fails to provide the kinds of job security, wages and working conditions required to stabilize the work relationship. This may occur because employers in the secondary sector cannot economically establish internal labor market conditions which are conducive to reducing turnover or because the technical aspects of the jobs are such that the reduction of turnover has little value to the employer. Second, the attitudes and demographic traits of the secondary labor force may be such that workers place little value upon job security in particular enterprises. These two explanations, while examined separately, are not independent. Unstable and undesirable jobs may encourage workers to place low value upon job security while a work force prone to turnover may make the costs of reducing turnover prohibitively high (Doeringer and Piore, 1971).

Both Bluestone (1970) and Harrison (1972) further emphasize the probable importance of the sources of the hypothesized dichotomization in a changing industrial structure. Highly-concentrated industries can afford to pay higher wages, develop more highly-structured internal labor markets, and invest more in workers' training because they can pass on their costs to consumers. Their profits are relatively untouched, according to this argument, by the expensive requisites of market structure in the primary sector.

General hypotheses

The concrete postulates of the dual labor market theory suggest some more general hypotheses about income determination and distribution in the United States. These general hypotheses are central in helping elucidate this theory's relation to the other two competing paradigms.[5]

According to the theory, a variety of social and economic forces have tended over time to produce a dichotomization of the American labor market. Given that historical separation, one must analyse the determination and distribution of income in two separate stages. At the first stage, one must explain the distribution of workers between the primary and the secondary labor markets. Given a central hypothesis that there is very little inter-sectoral mobility in the course of individual labor market careers, one should be able to approximate the present distribution of workers between markets by projecting the distribution of workers between sectors as they begin their careers. A worker's first job in the labor force, in other words, should predict the sector in which he presently works with some accuracy. (Dual market analysts would admit, it appears, that

5. This summary of general hypotheses has been inferred from the several separate discussions of the dual labor market theory. The hypotheses seem to me to arise logically from the theory's specific observations about the labor market. They are being offered here as hypotheses which might be tested empirically, not as conclusions drawn from specific empirical research. [. . .] This set of inferential hypotheses relies especially on Doeringer and Piore (1971).

white males may be able to move out of secondary jobs they hold as teen-agers.) According to nearly every version of the theory, finally, race and sex will probably serve as fairly accurate predictors of inter-sectoral allocation as workers enter the market. Both minority group workers and women are much more likely to begin their careers in the secondary sector than white males. Years of schooling may also constitute an important predictor of inter-sectoral allocation upon labor market entry. Since more and more Americans are continuing in school beyond the high school diploma, one might speculate that those who drop out of school before college are increasingly likely to appear to employers as potentially unstable employees.

At the second stage of the analysis, one must develop different behavioral models to explain the determination and distribution of income within each of the two markets, for the interaction of job and worker characteristics in each market over time has fostered different kinds of worker behavior and personality traits in the respective sectors. One should not propose – the dual market theory seems to suggest – a single set of behavioral hypotheses for both markets. The attitudes, personality traits and behavioral rules to which individuals in either sector conform will probably differ widely. Although dual market analysts have not yet developed the separate sectoral models very fully, one can begin to sketch the rough skeleton of their general hypotheses for each.

In the primary market, the dual market theory would suggest, individuals' incomes are largely determined by their respective access to different job clusters, by the relatively rigid pattern of wages attached to the job structures through which they respectively move, and by the speed with which they pass through those structures. Differential access to internal job structures is mediated primarily by relative years of formal schooling, the influence of which derives as much from the role of education as a screening device – as a way of saving money on more complicated search, screening and hiring procedures – as it does from its direct influence on worker 'productivity'. The wage patterns attached to varying job structures depend primarily on the historical influence of technological change and labor market custom – both manifested through internal 'job evaluations' more than through external price influences; the influence of external economic forces of supply and demand is much less pronounced. The speed at which workers move through the job structures depends primarily on their attitudes and on the state of economic conditions, much less on worker merit or productivity in its narrow traditional sense. Everything else equal, workers' wages will tend to increase with age as the simple effect of institutional seniority privileges, fixed through bargaining and custom.

In the secondary market, variations in total individual incomes are likely to depend more heavily on variations in hours than in wages, for variations in the former will be large and variations in the latter are likely to be extremely slight. Employers act as if all present and potential employees have more or less equal productivities – or, in more classical terms, as if secondary labor is homogeneous – and behave as if employee turnover is costless. As a result, wages will generally not reflect variations in individual characteristics but will be largely determined by the aggregate balance of supply and demand in the secondary market. Wages will also tend, consequently, to gravitate toward some homogeneous wage level, dampening wage variations among workers in that sector. Given this aggregate sectoral wage level, individual income will depend primarily on the number of hours worked, while variations in individual hourly wages will depend very little on variations in individual 'capacities' like aptitude, reasoning and vocational skill. Individual hourly wages will increase very little with steady employment at the same job; if they do increase, they increase mainly as a result of historically-determined seniority scales within secondary job clusters rather than as a result of 'productivity' increases from experience or on-the-job training. Labor supply functions are relatively indeterminate. Workers make decisions about turnover fairly capriciously, depending on their moods, their personal relations on the job and with the employer, and their inclinations toward alternative income sources. Their supply decisions depend only slightly on wage variations, primarily because those variations are usually so slight. Their supply decisions probably do depend quite directly, however, on the relationship between their family size and their total household income; those with relatively larger families and lower household incomes, *ceteris paribus*, may tend to work longer hours if they can.

Although the dual labor market theory seems sufficiently coherent to permit these concrete hypotheses about income determination and distribution, many pieces of the theory remain less certain. Several different kinds of questions are raised directly by the structure of the theory and have often been raised by its critics. Some mention of these questions seems useful, for they help clarify the boundaries of the theory and its relation to both radical and orthodox views.

First, the dual labor market theory places great emphasis on job stability as a source and an index of the division between the two markets. This difference between markets is only approximate, however, for not all workers in the primary market labor steadily at a single job and many secondary workers stay with a single job all their lives. Simple measures of job stability will not suffice to capture the distinctions between markets. The nature of the hypothesized separation seems more complicated and therefore more difficult to test. The separation arises from differences in the *potential* rewards for job stability – both objectively and as mediated by subjective evaluation. However intractable, some decent measures of this more precise formulation of the differences between sectors will be necessary in order to make very precise tests of the theory. (See Gordon, 1971a, for some further discussion of this issue.)

Second, dual market analysts have not yet reached very firm agreement about the relationship between the job and individual composition of the two sectors. In some instances, analysts suggest that the division corresponds only to differences in job characteristics and that the inter-sectoral distribution of individuals in various groups – like race and sex groups – does not provide a very accurate picture of the dual market structure. In other words, although many minority group workers, women and teens, work in secondary jobs, this view suggests that the intra-sectoral composition of workers can be fairly heterogeneous. In contrast, some others seem to equate the dual market structure with occupational segregation by demographic characteristics. According to this view, those jobs which are dominated by minority group workers – women and teens – are secondary jobs, while those jobs dominated by prime-age white males comprise the pool of primary jobs. One assumes that some balance between these two views will emerge, but the contours of that consensus have not yet grown evident.

A third and related problem concerns questions of emphasis. In some formulations of the dual labor market theory – especially some of the pieces contributed by Piore (1968, 1969, 1970) – heavy emphasis has been placed on the historical importance of changing individual attitudes as a primary source of the emergent dualism. In some other discussions – especially in Bluestone (1970) – emphasis has been placed primarily on the role of changing industrial and job structure as a primary source of the dichotomization. Once again, both suggestions seem important and one expects some resolution of the differences in emphasis to unfold.

Finally, the dual labor market theory poses a challenge which economists have not yet begun to meet. Its most important hypotheses are explicitly historical; they concern the dynamics and dialectics of changes in jobs, people and labor market operations over a period of fifty or more years. Most of these hypotheses have not arisen from historical research, however, but have been adduced from local labor market investigation and cross-sectional analysis. The dual labor market theory suggests a methodology, in other words, which its proponents have not been applying in its conception. This problem will also be confronted very soon, I suspect, as more economists turn to historical research for the answers they seek.

While the dual labor market theory is currently providing some useful perceptual tools for the study of poverty and underemployment, it may have a short half-life as an integral paradigm in economics. Many of those who helped develop the theory have begun to incorporate it into a more general radical framework, convinced that the dual market hypothesis can be generated by radical theory and that radical theory provides some important historical foundations for the specific conclusions of dual market analysis. A number of orthodox economists have also begun to incorporate the dual market perspective into their own work, developing a series of orthodox explanations for the dual market structure and some projections of its implications. [. . .]

Radical economic theory

[Editors' note. Professor Gordon concluded his discussion of dual labour market theory with the hope that it might be incorporated into a more general historical context of the kind which might be offered by a radical or Marxist methodology. The portion of the Reading which follows contains his views on radical economic theory, ending up with a series of hypotheses – which he emphasizes are as yet at a very speculative level. We have been obliged to edit this section very heavily, and in particular, we have excised an important discussion of the history of American capitalism over the last hundred years. Therefore the reader who wishes to follow up on this extract would be well advised to consult Professor Gordon's original book.]

The disciplinary matrix

Radical economists begin from six clusters of generalizations or hypotheses about capitalist economies. The radical theory of income determination and distribution cannot adequately be understood without first understanding these basic components of the disciplinary matrix defining the radical paradigm.[6]

Modes of production. Every economic mode of social organization since primitive times has been characterized by a *social division of labor*, by a division of work responsibilities among different social groups. This social division of labor is determined through, and society is therefore characterized by, the society's *mode of production*. The mode of production reflects the social relations of production in an economy. As Tucker (1969) puts it, '. . . inasmuch as the social relations of production have so far in history been successive forms of the division of labor in production, the

6. For some other general summaries and discussions of the emerging radical view, see Bronfenbrenner (1970), Sweezy (1970), Edwards, MacEwan *et al.* (1970), Gurley (1971), Gordon (1971b), various essays in the *Review of Radical Political Economics* (1971), and, most comprehensively, Edwards, Reich and Weisskopf (1972).

various historical modes of production may be described as forms of productive activity within the division of labor' (p. 14). In ancient society the mode of production was slave labor, in feudal society it was serf labor, and in capitalist society it is wage labor. Dobb (1963) further elaborates the definition: 'By mode of production Marx did not refer merely to the state of technique – to what he termed the state of productive forces – but to the way in which the means of production were owned and to the social relations between men which resulted from their connections with the process of production' (p. 7).

Classes and class conflict. The social division of labor, characterized by social relations of production, creates a division of society into economic classes. These classes inevitably clash with each other, and the course of history is determined through the growth and resolution of class conflict. Despite the absolutely central role of class in the Marxist and radical tradition, however, the concept of class has been rather inconsistently defined. In the writings of Marx and Engels in particular, as Ossowski points out (1963, p. 71), the concept has a fairly 'variable denotation'. For the purposes of this discussion, it seems important to clarify the two predominant senses in which radical theory deploys the concept of class.

First, following Marx, radicals argue that economic classes are defined *objectively* by the social relations of production. Groups of individuals sharing the same functions within the process of production constitute an *objectively-defined class*, as it were, despite themselves. (Marx called this a *Klasse an sich*.) 'In the social production which men carry on,' Marx wrote, 'they enter into definite relations that are indispensable and independent of their will' (quoted in Bottomore, 1966, p. 14). As Marx and Engels amplified this meaning of class in another context, ' . . . the class in its turn achieves an independent existence over against the individuals, so that the latter find their conditions of existence predestined, and hence have their position in life and their personal development assigned to them by their class, become subsumed under it' (1963, p. 49). The central import of this concept of objectively-defined class is that an individual's economic class constrains his activities whether or not he is aware of his membership in that economic group. In that the members of a given class share objectively-determined common circumstances and activities, they also share common economic interests (in strictly objective terms), for the economic rewards accruing to any individual within a class will depend in part on the total share captured by his class in competition with other classes. To quote Marx once more, 'Insofar as millions of families live under economic conditions of existence that separate their mode of life, their interests and their culture from those of other classes, and put them in hostile contrast to the latter, they form a class' (1963a, p. 124).

Second, radicals argue that an economic class does not fully constitute a class until its members develop *subjective* identification with the class. Marx helps evoke the importance of this concept of *subjectively-defined class* (*Klasse für sich*) in *The Poverty of Philosophy*:

Economic conditions had first transformed the mass of the people of the country into workers. The domination of capital has created for this mass a common situation, common interests. This mass is thus already a class as against capital, but not yet for itself. In the struggle . . . this mass becomes united, and constitutes itself as a class for itself. The interests it defines become class interests. But the struggle of class against class is a political struggle (1963b, p. 173).

Ossowski concludes his summary of Marx's analysis of class:

Marx, in calling a class without class consciousness a 'stratum' or a 'class in itself' . . . in contrast to a 'class for itself' . . . was expressing his conviction that a class fully deserves the name of 'class' only if members are conscious of class interests and feel class solidarity (1963, p. 139).

These two definitions of class play complementary roles in the development of radical theory. The relative emphasis with which each is applied depends in part on the historical sweep of the analysis. On the one hand, for instance, radicals may choose to concentrate on the role of class conflict in the long-run change from one mode of production to another. Since such conflicts began in primitive societies, the principal class division in society has involved the struggle between those who own the means of production and those who do not. With the very early development of social cooperation in production and with primitive technological innovation, individual men first become capable of producing more with their own labor than is necessary to sustain themselves and their families. They begin to produce a 'surplus product'. At different stages in different societies, a single ruling class, the owners of property, appropriate some of the surplus product of the producing class, providing for their own luxury, living off the surplus product of those whose labor they control. Through this appropriation, class division inevitably becomes class conflict. Mandel writes:

The producers have never accepted as normal or natural that the surplus product of their labour should be seized by the possessing classes, who thus obtain a monopoly of leisure and culture. . . . The history of mankind is nothing but a long succession of class struggles (1968, p. 175).

On the other hand, one can concentrate on various class divisions within a specific historical epoch, given a specific mode of production. At this level, depending on historical circumstances, one can conceivably identify many economic classes, 'each competing for power in a society with a multi-divisional structure' (Ossowski, 1963, p. 84). These struggles do not necessarily focus exclusively on the division of economic product, for they may involve conflict about the conditions of work or the structure of institutions. They may develop, as Ossowski puts it, as 'struggles between classes with different interests . . . antagonisms which are not confined to situations in which the appropriation of the "surplus value" is involved' (p. 84). In the objective sense, Marx would label these groups, divided from each other by their relations to the process of production, as 'strata'.

At either level of analysis, radicals emphasize that social class structure and class conflict must be viewed as dynamic processes rather than as static outcomes. As Bendix and Lipset conclude in their analysis of Marx's theory of social classes. 'This . . . makes it apparent that Marx thought of social class as a condition of group-life which was constantly generated (rather than simply given) by the organization of production' (1966, p. 9). E. P. Thompson has provided the clearest recent statement of this dynamic perspective:

By class I understand an historical phenomenon, unifying a number of disparate and seemingly unconnected events, both in the raw material of experience and in consciousness. I emphasize that it is an *historical* phenomenon. I do not see class as a 'structure', nor even as a 'category', but as something which in fact happens (and can be shown to have happened) in human relationships.
More than this, the notion of class entails the notion of historical relationship. Like any other relationship, it is a fluency which evades analysis if we attempt to stop it dead at any given moment and anatomize its structure. . . . The relationship must always be embodied in real people and in a real context. . . . We can see a *logic* in the responses of similar experiences, but we cannot predicate any *law*. Consciousness of class arises in the same way in different times and places, but never in just the same way (Thompson, 1966, pp. 9–10, emphasis in the original).

Two notes should be added to help clarify the use of the concept of class. First, Marx's notion that capitalism could be viewed increasingly as divided into two (rather than many) classes represented an analytic prediction, based on a series of historical assumptions, the fulfilment of which did not pose an ultimate test of the viability of the concept of class itself. One can use the Marxian concept of class and class consciousness to analyse a historic past which witnessed several classes, and equally to predict the rise or continued presence of many economic classes in the future. Second, it is also unnecessary to document a total and overriding class consciousness among the capitalist class to assert their existence as a class. Based on their objective role in society, and on the manifold ways in which their existence is supported by 'system-defining' institutions, capitalists constitute a class whether they have all developed full class consciousness or not. (See Edwards, MacEwan *et al.*, 1970) for some further comments on this point.)

Given these definitions of class, radicals suggest that the evolution of society – of its relations of production and its 'system-defining institutions' – can most fruitfully be analysed in terms of the dynamics of class conflict, in terms of the dialectics of struggle among classes with opposing interests. The very structure of the relations of production themselves may change over time in response to the balance of power among several different economic interests. Those structures cannot be taken as 'data' but must be analysed themselves in order to understand the behavior of individuals or of individual classes.

The drive for capital accumulation. In their analyses of the dynamic development of capitalist societies, radicals pay special attention to a central driving force – the unceasing attempt by owners of capital continuously to increase their absolute and relative share of capital by nearly any means. The forces of competition among capitalists whether among small independent shopkeepers or corporate giants, inevitably spur owners of capital to protect themselves against their competitors by producing more goods and accumulating more and more profit. Marx sometimes referred to this drive for accumulation as the 'werewolf hunger' of capitalists. As Mandel describes it, 'the capitalist mode of production thus becomes the first mode of production in the history of mankind the essential aim of which appears to be *unlimited increase in production*. . . .' (1968, p. 133, emphasis in the original). Because this dominates the priorities of the society, as Edwards, MacEwan *et al.* put it, 'human needs become subordinated to the needs of the market and to capital expansion' (1970, p. 356).

System-defining institutions. In any society, no matter what its mode of production, a basic set of system-defining institutions, rooted in the relations of production, helps define and determine the nature and content of social relations among individuals in that society. In capitalist societies, the most important and most distinctive feature of the mode of production is its organization of labor by means of the wage-contract. As Dobb writes:

Thus capitalism was not simply a system of production for the market – a system of commodity-production as Marx termed it – but a system under which labour-power had 'itself become a commodity' and was bought and sold on the market like any other object of exchange. Its historical prerequisite was the concentration of ownership of the means of production in the hands of a class, consisting of only a minor section of society, and the consequential emergence of a property-less class for whom the sale of their labour-power was their only source of live-lihood. Productive activity was furnished accordingly by the latter, not by virtue of legal compulsion, but on the basis of a wage-contract (1963, p. 7).

Recent anthropological evidence has made clear that this basic organization of work and labor originated historically with capitalist societies, that antecedent societies organized work in different ways. (See especially Polanyi, 1968.) Writing about this singular characteristic of production in capitalist societies, Marx himself said, 'Without it [there is] no capital, no bourgeoisie, no bourgois society.' (1967, p. 46).

In addition to this central institution, Edwards, MacEwan *et al.* isolate four other system-defining institutions in capitalist societies:

. . . control of the work process by those who own and control capital, including the concomitant loss of control by the worker over his activities during the hours of work; the legal relations of ownership, by which income distribution is deter-mined through payments to owners for the use of their productive factors; *homo economicus*, the system of personality traits characteristic of and functional to capitalism, including especially the system of individual gain incentives; and the ideology which abstracts and organizes 'reality' in such a way as to justify and facilitate the operation of the other institutions (1970, p. 353).

Together these institutions frame the specific historical processes through which different capitalist societies develop. They also considerably re-inforce the powers of the owners of property to fulfil their basic objectives.

The state. The state, in the radical view, operates ultimately to serve the interests of the controlling class in a class society. Since the 'capitalist' class fundamentally controls capitalist societies, the state functions in capitalist societies to serve that class.[7] It does so either directly, by pro-viding services only to members of that class, or indirectly, and probably more frequently, by helping preserve and support the system of basic institutions which support and maintain the power of that class. In general, as Sweezy summarizes the radical view, the state may fulfil those roles in three ways:

In the first place, the state comes into action in the economic sphere in order to solve the problems which are posed by the development of capitalism. In the second place, where the interests of the capitalist class are concerned, there is a strong predisposition to use the state power freely. And, finally, the state may be used to make concessions to the working class provided that the consequences of not doing so are sufficiently dangerous to the stability and functioning of the system as a whole (1968, p. 249).

7. For the most comprehensive discussion of the radical theory of the state, see Milliband (1969).

Edwards, MacEwan *et al.* clarify the essentially passive manner in which the state is able to fulfil its functions in a mature capitalist society:

If, as according to our hypothesis, the state is dominated by the capitalist class, then the operations of the state should reflect the needs of the capitalist class. In modern capitalist states, when the basic institutions have been thoroughly established, the maintenance and preservation of these institutions upon which the structure of class and privilege depends is of the greatest importance to the capitalist class. The uninhibited operation of the economic institutions will continue to bestow power, wealth and prestige upon the capitalists. They do not need the state to enhance their position, only to assure it (1970, p. 359).

Internal contradictions. The specific evolution of capitalist societies is heavily influenced by three internal contradictions, by three instances of an historical tendency which generates a contradictory historical tendency so fundamentally in conflict with that initial trend that some kind of qualitatively new historical process must develop. The nature of the ultimate resolution cannot be anticipated *a priori*, but depends on the specific dynamics of the concrete situation.

1 In the Marxist view, man achieves his fullest self-realization through work, through production, through the creative development and application of all his capacities. Increasingly in capitalist societies, man is denied this self-realization by the progressive division of labor. Owners of capital, locked in competition, seek constantly to improve efficiency and increase their control over the work process by mechanization and specialization within the process of production. Instead of providing opportunities for workers' 'all-round development', as Marx put it, the capitalist dynamic tends increasingly to transform the 'worker into a crippled monstrosity, by forcing his detail dexterity at the expense of a world of productive capabilities and instincts. . . .' (Marx, 1967a, p. 360).

As the division of labor proceeds, radicals hypothesize, man becomes increasingly alienated from his product, increasingly oppressed by the contradiction between the constraints of specialization and his desire for creative, unspecialized production. The one process – the division of labor – creates an opposing process – the increasing dissatisfaction of workers with their lives in production. As Marx put it (1967a), the divisions of labor in capitalism 'mutilate the labourer into a fragment of a man, degrade him to the level of an appendage of a machine, destroy every remnant of charm in his work and turn it into a hated toil. . . .' (1967a, p. 645). The sociologist William Foote Whyte has put the problem succinctly: 'The satisfactions of craftsmanship are gone, and we can never call them back. If these were the only satisfactions men could get out of their immediate work, their work would certainly be a barren experience' (quoted in Bell, 1960, p. 244).

This contradiction requires some kind of resolution, for the workers cannot continue their increasing dissatisfaction forever. Marx had predicted that it would result in the revolution of the proletariat. One could equally predict that capitalists will attempt increasingly and continuously to provide compensatory satisfaction for workers, especially through their lives as consumers. As Herbert Gintis (1970a) has argued, for instance, the 'dialectics of economic growth' provide the constant promise to workers that their own or their children's futures will provide them with more goods and therefore with greater happiness, making up for their present unhappiness. The resolution of the contradiction obviously depends on its specific historical manifestation, on the development of class consciousness and the relative strength of different classes.

2 Through the quest for accumulation, capitalists develop increasingly complex productive institutions. These institutions lead more and more to what Mandel calls the 'objective socialization of production'. Men no longer work individually, producing for their own needs. The division of labor, the evolution of corporate structures, and the expansion of markets under capitalism all effect an increasing interdependence among men as producers. Mandel writes: 'The work of each is indispensable to the survival of all, so that each can survive only thanks to the work of thousands and thousands of other men' (1968, p. 170).

But this objective interdependence creates a complementary and ultimately contradictory requirement. If capitalists are to retain their fundamental power, they must try to prevent objective interdependence among workers from generating subjective cooperation against capitalists; if such cooperation developed, if classes attained a *subjective definition*, then the joint power of workers might threaten the privileges of capitalists. So, in various ways, capitalist institutions encourage an individualistic ideology, based on individual gain incentives and frequently ruthless competition among individuals. Brought into objective relationships of social cooperation in production, men are induced subjectively to compete against those with whom they cooperate.

Increasingly, in short, workers cooperate and compete at the same time. Some kind of resolution becomes increasingly necessary to dissolve the heightening tensions of that contradiction. On the one hand, workers might try, as Marx predicted, cooperatively to seize the control of the means of production so that competition among classes was more or less eliminated. On the other hand, in quite different ways, one could predict that workers (or potential workers) might try to avoid the tensions by avoiding the cooperative work process all together. In an overwhelmingly competitive world, they might try to avoid the tensions of objectively co-operating in work with others against whom they must also compete. They might 'drop out', bumming for a living or seeking to work at crafts by themselves.

3 In capitalist societies, enormous increases in social wealth finally create the possibility that class conflict could cease. Society begins to produce enough so that *everyone* in society could acquire opportunities for leisure and creative activity. Mandel explains this development clearly.

It is the capitalist mode of production that, by the extraordinary advance of the productive forces which it makes possible, creates for the first time in history the economic conditions needed for the abolition of class society altogether. The social surplus product would suffice to reduce extensively the working time of all men, which would ensure an advance of culture that would enable functions of accumulation (and management) to be exercised by the whole of society (1968, p. 177).

But capitalists depend on the preservation of class privilege in order con-tinuously to maintain or increase their relative shares. Given their basic power within the context of capitalist institutions, they are able roughly to maintain their privileges and their share of surplus product. Workers become more and more conscious of the gap between their actual stan-dards of living and their potential standards of living under more egali-tarian distributions. (Sociologists have installed this notion as the concept of relative deprivation.) The basic contradiction between the size of the pie and its distribution – between the actual leisure of a few and the po-tential leisure of nearly all – intensifies, and some resolution of the contra-diction seems necessary.[8] On the one hand, workers may rebel, as Marx predicted, and eradicate the contradiction by providing everyone equal shares according to need. On the other hand, to pick another kind of potential resolution, the quality of life available for consumption through leisure may deteriorate so rapidly that leisure becomes a relatively un-attractive good of which lower classes are not quite so jealous. Through externalities like noise and pollution, the quality of life may grow so undesirable for everyone – including the 'leisure class' – that class com-petition for that undesirable good tends to diminish.

All of these general hypotheses frame the formulation of a general radical theory of income determination and distribution. According to

8. Many interpretations of the civil rights movement in the United States involved this kind of argument. The concept of 'relative deprivation' was widely applied. Blacks saw the goods on television, began to taste a few of them, and wanted their equal share. For several statements of this argument, see Clark and Parsons (1967).

orthodox theory, as noted above, wage equals marginal product in equilibrium, and the distribution of wages corresponds to the distribution of marginal products. In radical theory, there are two stages to the determination and distribution of income. First, a complex set of individual, social, economic and technological forces determines an individual worker's productivity (expressed as average productivity) on a specific job. This average productivity varies both with the worker's 'capacities' and with the characteristics of his job. Second, the relative power of employers and employees determines the share of the worker's total product paid to the worker in wages. He receives some of the product as wages and the employer receives the rest as surplus product. The worker's final wage thus depends *both* on his individual productivity *and* on the relative power of the class to which he belongs.

The radical theory thus combines the radical concept of class with orthodox notions of supply and demand. In many of the same ways as orthodox theory postulates, radical theory expects that supply and demand, reinforced to a certain extent by the forces of competition, will affect an individual's productivity; the market price of a product, for instance, obviously affects the value of an individual's marginal product in the radical model just as it does in the orthodox model. But the radical model also postulates that the class division in society and the relative distribution of power among classes will affect the distribution of individual income as well. An individual's class, ultimately, will affect *both* his productivity, through the allocation of social resources to investment in the workers of his class and through the differential access of different classes to different kinds of complementary capital, *and* his relative share of final product.

As radicals emphasize again and again, the entire process is dynamic. Employers seek to affect two different kinds of variables, since they seek constantly either to increase or at least to maintain their relative share of total product: they hope both to increase their workers' average products, *ceteris paribus*, and to decrease (or hold down) their workers' share of that product. Workers seek to increase their income – and thus either to increase their relative productivities, *ceteris paribus*, or to increase their shares. The capitalist drive for accumulation and the internal contradictions of capitalism all bring continuous changes in the institutions of a given capitalist society. At the same time, continuous changes in a society's 'superstructure' affect the distributions of productivity and of class power. At any moment, capitalists may find it in their collective long-run interest to intensify their exploitation of workers if they can, trying more rapidly to increase their share of total product. At another moment, capitalists may find it in their long-run interest to permit a slight increase in relative wages – in order to foster higher standards of living among workers and, through better nutrition and health, develop more productive workers; in order to undercut worker dissatisfaction by allowing higher consumption; or in order to intensify competition among different classes of workers by allowing the relative shares of some classes to rise. The fact that capitalists compete with each other over product market shares does not obviate the simultaneous dynamic of their collective class interest. The relative shares of all capitalists are increased, for instance, if workers compete among themselves (along racial lines, to pick one possible dimension), rather than presenting united demands of the capitalists; if the state refuses to provide legislation enabling unionization; if the state fails to provide a decent income maintenance program so that some workers are still driven by what Weber called 'whip of hunger'; or if state-supported schools instil all workers with an orientation toward monetary rewards and with some general 'productive' skills required in employment, especially if the schools are financed not by the capitalists alone but by all citizens.

Mandel captures some of the dynamic flavor of the radical model in the following passage:

In fact, it is not the absolute level of wages that matters to capital. The latter prefers, certainly, that wages should be as low as possible in its own enterprises – but it wants at the same time to see wages as high as possible paid in competing enterprises or by the employers of its customers! What matters to capital is the possibility of extracting more surplus labor, more unpaid labor, more surplus value, more profit from its workers. The growth in the productivity of labor, which makes possible the growth of relative surplus value, implies the possibility of a slow rise in real wages . . . on condition that the equivalent of these increased real wages is produced in an ever shorter period of time, i.e. that wages rise less quickly than productivity. . . .

The rise in real wages does not follow *automatically* from the rise in the productivity of labor. The latter only creates the *possibility* of such a rise, within the capitalist framework, provided profit is not threatened. For this potential increase to become actual, two interlinked conditions are needed: a favorable evolution of relations of strength in the labor market . . . and effective organization . . . of the wage workers which enables them to abolish competition among themselves and so to take advantage of these 'favourable market conditions' (1968, p. 145).

The general radical theory can be further illustrated and described, but it cannot be further specified. In the abstract, the model is indeterminate because its specification depends on the flow and circumstances of history. As Sraffa (1960) and Bhaduri (1969) have pointed out, the orthodox model achieves a certain determinacy at the macro-level by fixing the 'rate of exploitation' as a constant. The radical model argues that the 'rate of exploitation' cannot be held constant but is determined by social forces just as clearly as the rate of profit and the wage rate – that it is all one big simultaneous system.[9] Further specification and determination of the model awaits discussion of a particular historical period; it depends both on the stage of capitalism being considered and on the 'superstructure' of the society in question. [. . .]

Effects on productivity. Three closely related hypotheses about changes in the determination and distribution of productivity seem most important for understanding present labor market operations.[10]

1 It seems likely that variations in worker productivity have grown increasingly dependent on the amount of time workers spend on their specific jobs. In the first phases of nineteenth-century industrial capitalism, a generalized kind of work stability was necessary. The entire work force had to be disciplined to accept orders, report to work, and respond to wage incentives. But it did not take a worker long on any particular job to achieve the maximum productivity possible in that job. Since then, production processes have grown increasingly complex, hierarchical and interdependent. Two related effects have become important, each of them helping cause the growing importance of on-the-job training. First, the 'general skills' of many workers have become increasingly insufficient as measures of their relative 'productivity', for many skills must be adjusted to the requirements and procedures of the specific work place before they have any value. Traditionally, many physical skills could be applied in similar ways in many different settings. Gradually, this has changed as production grows more interdependent. A machine worker must learn not only how to operate his machine in general but specifically how to operate it within a given production process, for the machine's operation may be modified by its relationship to other machines in the individual establishment.[11]

Second, many of the specific skills that workers must learn on the job in order to be productive can be learned, increasingly, *only* through simple and continuous tenure on the job; the time necessary for learning them cannot be reduced by formal instruction on the job. Each individual member of an interdependent production process must learn to relate to

9. To quote Bhaduri, 'Marx left open the question of how the rate of exploitation is determined. He viewed it himself in terms of the balance of class forces. . . .' (1969, p. 538).
10. Most of the hypotheses in this section are similar to some of the observations in Doeringer and Piore (1971); indeed, the radical theory is similar to the dual labor market and internal labor market analyses of the determinants of *productivity*, but differs from them in its simultaneous emphasis on the importance of *class*.
11. Doeringer and Piore (1971) provide many illustrations of this development.

his fellow employees, as Maurice Dobb puts it: 'with a discipline that is something akin to that which coordinates the separate instruments of an orchestra' (1963, p. 359). Workers, like orchestra members, cannot be taught the common rhythm in the abstract, but must pick it up by working together. To be more productive, in other words, every worker must understand the requirements not only of his job but of the entire work process. Assembly-line workers can learn quickly how to turn a screw, but it takes time for them to learn enough about the entire process to be able to spot other defects and to identify the sources of defects. (See Rapoport, 1967, for one example.) Many white-collar workers often perform extremely menial tasks most of the time, the skills which they can learn quickly. They may answer phones, run errands or stamp forms. But their value to the firm depends increasingly on the subtlety of their knowledge of the firm's operations. If a form doesn't come across their desks on schedule, they must know where to look for it. If a secretary needs to arrange a meeting on quick notice, she must know where to find the participants. (See Crozier, 1971, for some interesting evidence.)

In general, potential job stability has probably become an increasingly important criterion to employers in filling many jobs, for workers are likely to become increasingly productive *on that job* the longer they remain on the job.[12]

2 It becomes increasingly useful, at the same time, for employers to try to organize job structures and to define the nature of job clusters in such a way that those jobs requiring employee stability are clearly separated from those which do not. The devices necessary to ensure stability often become expensive – through whatever special work adjustments and monetary incentives may prove necessary – and it becomes increasingly efficient for employers to confine those extra expenses to the narrowest range of jobs they can. They would rather avoid, in other words, being forced to spread those expenses over all their jobs. Ideally, if they have the freedom to act rationally, they will try to calculate the 'costs and benefits' of different clusters of jobs in order to try simultaneously to minimize the costs of devices necessary to ensure stability and to minimize the efficiency losses from unstable workers. Given the rise of complex production processes and the continued presence of some jobs in which stability is *not* important, it therefore seems likely that employers will seek to balkanize the labor market, defining different clusters of jobs for which they establish quite different entry requirements. The entry requirements, in turn, will

12. Lockwood (1958) and Crozier (1971) have the most interesting general discussion and evidence of these trends for white-collar work. Doeringer and Piore provide some interesting illustrations for blue-collar work. In Gordon (1972), I have emphasized the similarities between developments in the office and factory worlds.

emphasize or de-emphasize potential stability depending on the job cluster. To pick a notable example, employers have found it increasingly convenient – I would hypothesize – to separate secretarial jobs into two clusters: to create typing pools in which women do nothing besides typing, in which job stability makes almost no difference, and for which evidence of job stability is not particularly important; and to separate those jobs from more conventional secretarial jobs – like the 'personal secretary' – for which specific skills like typing are probably less important than simple job stability, and for which entry requirements tend increasingly to emphasize characteristics associated with potential stability.[13]

3 Given the increasing importance of job stability for many (relatively more 'productive') jobs, it has probably become more and more difficult for a firm to devise tests which accurately measure a worker's potential productivity. If a worker is supposed to shovel dirt, brute strength can be tested fairly easily. If an assembler must use his hands with dexterity, his skill can be tested by presenting him with round pegs and round holes. If a secretary must do nothing more than type letters, spelling and typing abilities can be tested quite precisely. But when an employee's potential contribution to the firm will depend ultimately on how long he stays with the firm, it becomes extremely difficult to test for that 'skill'. Psychological tests are probably too insensitive to differentiate potential stability among broad classes of workers. It becomes increasingly likely that employers will often rely on superficial characteristics as approximate predictors of potential stability. If it has been generally true in the past that certain demographically-identified groups have had relatively low average job stability, employers will be more and more likely to discriminate against those groups in filling jobs requiring stability. The more identifiable the demographic criterion, the easier it is to apply.[14]

Effects on class definition and class power. At the same time, five hypotheses about changes in the process of class definition and the distribution of class power seem especially important. In slightly different ways, each of these hypotheses 'predicts' that employers will find it more and more in their interest to attempt to forge a highly-stratified labor market, with at least several *objectively defined* economic classes, in order both to fill secondary jobs and to forestall the development of revolutionary class consciousness.

13. Lockwood (1958) provides a wide variety of illustrations of these developments in the office setting. He also provides some specific comments which reinforce this example of the evolution of the typing pool.
14. Doeringer and Piore (1971), and Piore (1970) provide some helpful expansion of these employer imperatives.

1 Gradually through these 100 years, the (putative) homogeneity of labor in the late nineteenth century began to dissolve. At the beginning, around 1870, much of the nonagricultural work force was moving into operative and laborer jobs in mining, manufacturing and transportation, a harbinger of Marx's expectations that an industrial labor force would fuse. Before that trend culminated in complete proletarian homogeneity, however, other industrial and occupational trends took over. Service and white-collar employment grew much more prominent, even within manufacturing. The labor force became increasingly dispersed over a wide variety of industries and occupations.[15]

This dispersion was likely to have two closely related effects. First, the nature of work itself no longer so clearly defined the working class, for a wide variety of working conditions became common within the labor force. Since some jobs offered 'better' working conditions than others – were somehow cleaner or less exhausting – and since firmly-established patterns of assimilation were beginning to make it possible for those in the less desirable jobs to identify with those in more desirable (principally white-collar) jobs, it probably became rather more likely that those in less desirable jobs would develop a consciousness about their working conditions, demanding better working conditions or threatening to quit for better work. Second, to the extent that blue-collar workers did in fact develop a certain class consciousness, unionize, and demand some of the perquisites of more attractive jobs, there was a danger that their demands would be satisfied in such a way that all workers, even those without class consciousness, would benefit at the expense of employers. It became likely that the relative share of all workers would increase, in other words, rather than the shares of those more limited numbers who demanded better conditions.

As a result, employers were likely to try to develop a stratified labor market in order to accomplish two complementary objectives. They were likely to seek, on the one hand, to minimize the extent to which those in jobs with less desirable working conditions could identify with those in more desirable jobs. If they could, they would try to segregate white-collar workers from blue-collar workers, create or permit the development of a class identity among more advantaged white-collar workers to distinguish them from blue-collar workers, and to impose some sharp barriers between the different kinds of jobs, like educational requirements. To the extent that employers could accomplish this stratification, it became

15. Indeed, in statistical terms, the evidence suggests that conditions also became much more heterogeneous even *within* occupations; many indices of dispersion and inequality suggest that intra-occupational heterogeneity – given standard occupational categories – has been increasing for some time. See Gordon (1972).

more likely that blue-collar workers would accept their poorer working conditions (relative to those of white-collar workers) because they did not have the necessary credentials and education to move on to jobs with better opportunities. And employers were likely to seek, on the other hand, to segregate sharply those blue-collar or secondary workers who could potentially identify with white-collar workers – and who might therefore develop class consciousness – from those blue-collar or secondary workers who were not likely to develop class consciousness, in order, obviously, to limit the potential costs of concessions to workers who made determined demands. Employers would seek to do this in two ways. First, they would seek to stratify jobs in order objectively to separate job clusters from each other and consequently to establish 'fire trails', as it were, to limit the potential spread of costly concessions. Second, they were likely to try to fill the worst jobs with those who were least likely to identify with advantaged workers. Gradually, as the composition of the American labor force changed, it became relatively easy for employers to reserve the most 'secondary' jobs for teens, women and minority group workers with quite confident expectations that they would not identify with more advantaged workers and develop a common consciousness about the disadvantages of their jobs.[16]

2 Trends in urbanization and migration tended to create precisely the same employer requirements. Traditionally, the disadvantaged status of many workers had been justified and reinforced by the rigidity of social distinctions by birth: in the late nineteenth century, the distinctions between native-born/English-speaking workers and foreign-born/foreign-language workers seemed sharp and effective. With the steady process of migration, increasingly complex urban social structures, and continuing infusions of disadvantaged foreign (or southern) migrants into northern industrial cities, the traditional distinctions probably began to erode. Regular patterns of assimilation were established and, at least among white immigrants, some firmly-rooted, relatively continuous avenues for upward mobility and social assimilation (either intra- or intergenerationally) became quite manifest. As with the trends described earlier, these mobility patterns raised the likelihood that less advantaged workers would identify with those ahead of them, demand better working conditions, or leave their less desirable jobs in order to train themselves. And employers were equally likely to respond by trying to stratify markets, to create subjective distinctions among groups of workers, and to channel into secondary jobs those workers who were least likely to identify with more advantaged workers.

16. For some similar perspectives on some of these issues, see Blau and Duncan (1967), and Leggett (1968).

By the mid-twentieth century, these trends had acquired a momentum of their own; employers were somewhat caught in their own dynamic. Since the frontier had closed and the waves of foreign migration had ceased, blacks in northern ghettos were tending increasingly to regard themselves as the last immigrant group; no one else was coming along to fill in behind them at the bottom. And yet, because their skin color made it relatively unlikely that they would identify with more advantaged white workers ahead of them, many blacks – especially younger males – probably began to respond to these perceptions by developing even more unstable work habits than previously disadvantaged groups; they saw little hope that they could climb above the bottom rungs by working stably and diligently to better themselves. Women, for different reasons, were also likely to continue working intermittently, given the requirements of the family, the kinds of expectations molded in them by their experiences in school, family and labor market, and the small probability that they would identify with other previously disadvantaged groups of male workers who had moved upward by developing stable habits. Teenagers, finally, were increasingly likely to expect that they would continue through school and to work as teens solely to pick up spare cash. This meant that they cared less about retaining the same job for very long and developed increasingly unstable work habits over time. And, as all three of these groups increased their share of the labor force, employers found themselves left, quite frequently, with only the most unstable elements of the work force with which to fill many different kinds of jobs. Some employers were undoubtedly forced, on many occasions, to organize an increasing proportion of their employment around the behavioral patterns of unstable employment.[17] And once these organizational adjustments were made, they reinforced, in turn, the burgeoning instability (or expectations of instability) among those three secondary groups.[18]

3 The rise of unions, obviously, also encouraged employers to seek to stratify the labor force and the relations of production in such ways as to limit the potential extent of unionization. They were encouraged to establish separate pools of secondary employment, for instance, which permitted and even encouraged such unstable patterns of behavior among their workers that they were unlikely to develop a common class consciousness toward unionizing themselves. This would also mean that other unions

17. Perhaps more frequently, employers chose to place new types of jobs or clusters of jobs in the secondary market when they first developed. This seems to have been the case with keypunch operators.
18. Leggett (1968) provides one of the most useful discussions of this theme, building his analysis around the concept of the 'uprooted'.

found it increasingly difficult to organize those pockets of workers. Employers were encouraged, as well, to emphasize the differences among different groups of workers – particularly between blue-collar and white-collar workers – in order to limit the extent to which non-unionized workers would identify with those already in unions. It probably encouraged them, in particular, to stimulate or reinforce a sense of 'professionalism' among many white-collar workers in the hopes that that emergent occupational identity would lead many workers to seek to differentiate themselves from unionized, primarily blue-collar workers. And, finally, it also encouraged them to fill the least desirable jobs with workers toward whom union members had reason to feel hostile, in order to try to limit the energy with which union members would move toward increasing their ranks.[19]

4 With technological change, there is always a danger of increasingly high unemployment (at constant levels of demand and constant levels of labor force participation). Also, new technology sometimes creates new skill requirements which general institutional education can often meet better than specific on-the-job training. Both of these trends make it convenient for employers to increase the (often arbitrary) general education requirements they impose as hiring standards for jobs of constant skills. Encouraging the labor force to stay in school through higher levels can then serve a dual purpose. It cuts down the amount of time any potential worker will spend in the labor force, therefore reduces the potential size of the pool of the unemployed, and therefore undercuts some potentially threatening developments to the system as a whole. It also imposes on the general public the costs of certain kinds of training, freeing private firms of these costs. *But*, the longer most workers remain in school, the less effective are traditional stratifications between those with no schooling and

19. It may not, of course, be coincidental that white male unionists felt a certain hostility toward blacks and women in the jobs below them, for they may have been encouraged to feel threatened by the competition of lower-wage workers – encouraged, at least, by the use of blacks as strike-breakers in the period around the First World War. See Spero and Harris (1968). For more general historical discussion of the union movement, which supports some of these observations, see Ulman (1961). This phenomenon has probably been widespread. Many mechanisms in our society, radicals suggest, serve the function of inducing workers in the lower and middle strata to tolerate their conditions because they feel superior to those below them. Wilensky (1966) refers to this as the 'consolation prize hypothesis' and Lockwood speaks of the 'deferential' mode of consciousness among workers: 'deferentials' are very conscious of status gradations in society and are adept, he writes, at discovering 'groups with an even lower status than their own' (1966, p. 253). For more general comments on these functions of inequality, see Weisskopf (1972).

those with some. It becomes necessary either to adjust relative educational distinctions upward (establishing college as a new boundary between groups of workers, for instance), or to devise new forms of distinction on the job or within labor market institutions (to replace previous distinctions created by education).[20]

5 Finally and perhaps most important, the nature of work incentives has changed radically over time, with probably fundamental implications for the ways in which employers seek to organize the 'relations of production'. Formerly, as noted above, industrial workers were frequently paid by a piece-work or wage bonus system of remuneration. Under those systems, employers hardly had to worry about the clarity and impact of incentives for employees to labor well and hard. If a worker produced more, in a given period of time, he would earn more. With the switch to bureaucratic and more complicated modes of production, an individual's contribution to output gradually became less distinguishable from that of other workers, for it became increasingly difficult to identify an individual worker's 'piece'. Wage incentives, one would therefore hypothesize, tend to become less effective as a result. Employers can no longer precisely measure the productivity of many individual workers in strictly quantitative terms, and must increasingly depend on their own relatively qualitative judgements about relative worker merit and productivity. Especially under automation, Daniel Bell writes, '. . . with continuous flow, a worker's worth can no longer be evaluated in production units' (1960, p. 270). But if employers singled out individual workers for monetary reward on the basis of those (relatively more arbitrary) qualitative judgements, workers might become much less willing to respond to those (relatively more arbitrary) incentives, and grow relatively more offended by them. Since workers have been taught to orient themselves toward monetary gain incentives, they probably tend to develop a sense of equity about how those rewards are tossed around.

One important alternative for employers, as a result, is to establish hierarchical incentives to replace monetary rewards. They can reward 'more productive' workers with higher status and better jobs rather than with more money. The advantage of these incentives is that employers can more easily justify the application of their qualitative judgements of workers as a basis for reward; they can justify their singling out of certain workers on a qualitative basis because they, the employers, are the only ones who know the requirements of higher jobs and must make their own

20. See Gintis (1970b) and Bowles (1971, 1972) for useful discussions of these trends in the functional importance of education. On earlier history, see Katz (1968).

projections about which employees would perform better on those jobs. Workers themselves are much less able to evaluate the accuracy of the employers' judgements, and are relatively less likely to be offended by them.[21]

This means, of course, that employers must create a desire among employees for higher status and better jobs. It becomes increasingly likely that employers will seek to develop in the labor force a kind of 'hierarchy fetishism' – a continual craving for more and better job titles and status, the satisfaction of which leads eventually to intensified hunger for still more and better job titles and job status. The objective is best satisfied, as David Lockwood has written, by a 'widespread consensus about the rank order of status groups in the community, so that lower strata regard their lowly position less as an injustice than as a necessary, acceptable, and even desirable part in a natural system of inequality' (1966, p. 254).

And in order to satisfy this 'hierarchy fetishism', employers probably find it increasingly useful to create constantly and perpetually differentiated job categories – if for no other reason – in order to provide new and relatively compelling fodder for the fetishistic craving. This incentive–utility of job hierarchies and the increasing division of labor may or may not converge with the dictates of efficiency criteria on strictly technological grounds. Whatever the relationship between the two kinds of criteria for job design and organization, hierarchical job structures and specialized labor attain an independent rationale, over and above efficiency rationale.[22]

And, in order to create hierarchical incentives without providing too many mobility opportunities – in order to satisfy 'hierarchy fetishism' without simultaneously establishing a continuum of relationships among workers along which they can develop common class consciousness – employers may find it useful to forge hierarchical ladders within clearly differentiated job clusters. For incentive reasons alone, that is, they may seek to 'balkanize' the labor market and to proliferate job titles within each 'balkanized' cluster.[23]

21. As unions become more powerful in manufacturing, however, this kind of incentive works less effectively because the unions begin to stabilize the criteria for promotion and define qualifications for jobs. So, for instance, employers play around with the work environment to see if they can make workers happy enough to work more efficiently – viz. the Hawthorne Experiment at Western Electric. For some general comments on these problems of motivation in blue-collar work, see Bell (1960) and Friedmann (1955).
22. The analogy with Marx's concept of 'commodity fetishism' is obviously intended, for both desires, if inculcated, serve similar purposes in resolving the tension among workers about their lives as producers.
23. Lockwood (1958) has provided some illustrative evidence of some of these imperatives.

236 Conditions and Mechanisms of Mobility

Cumulative effects. The joint effects of the first two sets of hypothesized trends seem obvious and fundamental. I have summarized those effects in five separate clusters of summary hypotheses.

1 It becomes increasingly likely that employers will seek to balkanize the labor market, creating highly stratified clusters of jobs quite distinctly separated from each other. These stratifications have independent utility by productivity and class criteria. In addition, it seems especially likely that some of the separate strata will be organized to permit and encourage highly unstable work behavior, both to limit the expenses of devices necessary to ensure worker stability and to limit the potential spread of class consciousness among the most disadvantaged (and secondary) workers.

2 It becomes equally likely that employers will seek to fill the most disadvantaged and unstable jobs with minority group workers, women and teenagers, for three separate reasons. First, as employers have had to rely increasingly on statistical discrimination, they have undoubtedly found it easiest to discriminate by race, sex and age; these characteristics can hardly be disguised by workers very easily, and – at least until very recently – society has tolerated implicit and explicit discrimination against these groups. Second, these groups have all developed quite independent expectations of (and relative resignation to) secondary and unstable work patterns. Third, these three groups are least likely to identify with more advantaged groups and to develop a class consciousness about their relatively 'oppressed' working conditions.

In short, the functional economic importance to employers of general economic discrimination by race, age and sex has probably grown increasingly important over time.[24] The creation and preservation of stratified, secondary work clusters has therefore probably developed an independent utility to employers, and their ability generally to fill those jobs with a relatively resigned secondary labor pool satisfies their needs quite precisely.

3 Whether or not it is required by technological change, it seems increasingly likely that the specialization of labor will continue. Apart from efficiency criteria, *ceteris paribus*, the specialization of labor is justified by and quite useful for the stratification of the labor force and the establishment of limits to the spread of class consciousness. As Harold Wilensky writes in this context: 'Advanced specialization has made for finer distinctions of status and a multiplication of occupational worlds' (1966, p. 27).

24. This is *not* a hypothesis that actual discrimination in fact increased, but only that – relative to other devices for satisfying some employer objectives – such discrimination became more critical as a potential recourse. Contradictory forces may also have countered such attempts.

4 Whether or not it is required by technological change, equally, the hierarchical organization of work is likely to continue. Employers probably find it more and more useful to create relatively meaningless and arbitrary status distinctions on the job and within the productive process, for at least three related reasons. Hierarchies establish a new and effective kind of incentive to replace the wage incentive under piece-work and wage bonus systems. Hierarchies also help ensure that workers will stay on the job longer, and thus develop certain kinds of productivities which cannot be acquired except through simple and continuous tenure; to promote stability, in other words, employers find it partially sufficient to create the illusion of mobility by creating trees of artificial job positions which workers can climb branch by meaningless branch. Third, the erosion of several traditional class divisions (like language and place of birth) have created the need for new stratification mechanisms. Both educational stratification and hierarchical stratification on the job serve equally to replace those traditional mechanisms.

5 The importance of job characteristics in determining relative income among workers has undoubtedly grown in importance, as a result of all these trends, for job structures have probably tended increasingly to dominate relative opportunities among workers for skill acquisition. The more that skills must be developed within specific job situations, the more the structure and distribution of those job opportunities tends to affect the distribution of skills among workers. Abstract, generalized individual abilities (like reasoning and reading abilities) become less and less important in determining or explaining variations in labor market status and income.

References

BELL, D. (1960), *End of Ideology*, Free Press.
BENDIX, R., and LIPSET, S. M. (1966), 'Karl Marx's theory of social classes', in R. Bendix and S. M. Lipset (eds.), *Class, Status and Power*, Free Press.
BHADURI, A. (1969), 'On the significance of recent controversies on capital theory: a Marxian view', *Econ. J.*, September.
BLAU, P. M., and DUNCAN, O. D. (1967), *The American Occupational Structure*, Wiley.
BLUESTONE, B. (1968), 'Low wage industries and the working poor', *Poverty and Human Resources Abstracts*, March–April.
BLUESTONE, B. (1970), 'The tripartite economy: labor markets and the working poor', *Poverty and Human Resources*, July–August.
BOTTOMORE, T. B. (1966), *Classes in Modern Society*, Vintage Books.
BOWLES, S. S. (1971), 'The weakest link: contradictions in US higher education', unpublished thesis, Harvard University, January.
BOWLES, S. S. (1972), 'Unequal education and the reproduction of the social division of labor', in R. C. Edwards, M. Reich and T. E. Weisskopf (eds.), *The Capitalist System*, Prentice-Hall.

BRONFENBRENNER, M. (1970), 'Radical economics in America: a 1970 survey', *J. econ. Lit.*, September.

CLARK, K., and PARSONS, T. (eds.) (1967), *The Negro American*, Houghton Mifflin.

CROZIER, M. (1971), *The World of the Office Worker*, University of Chicago Press.

DOBB, M. (1957), *Wages*, Cambridge University Press.

DOBB, M. (1963), *Studies in the Development of Capitalism*, International Publishers.

DOERINGER, P. B., and PIORE, M. J. (1970), 'Equal employment opportunities in Boston', *Industrial Relations*, May.

DOERINGER, P. B., and PIORE, M. J. (1971), *Internal Labor Markets and Manpower Analysis*, Heath.

DOERINGER, P. B., FELDMAN, P., GORDON, D. M., PIORE, M. J., and REICH, M. (1969), 'Urban manpower programs and low-income labor markets: a critical assessment', unpublished, Manpower Administration, US Department of Labor, January.

EDWARDS, R. C., MACEWAN, A., *et al.* (1970), 'A radical approach to economics: basis for a new curriculum', *Amer. econ. Rev.*, May.

EDWARDS, R. C., REICH, M., and WEISSKOPF, T. E. (eds.) (1972), *The Capitalist System*, Prentice-Hall.

FRIEDMANN, G. (1955), *The Anatomy of Work*, Free Press.

GINTIS, H. (1970a), 'New working class and revolutionary youth', *Rev. rad. Pol. Econ.*, Summer.

GINTIS, H. (1970b), 'Neo-classical welfare economics and individual development', Occasional Paper no. 3, Union for Radical Political Economics, Ann Arbor.

GORDON, D. M. (1971a), 'Class, productivity and the ghetto: a study of labor market stratification', Ph.D. thesis, Harvard University.

GORDON, D. M. (1971b), *Problems in Political Economy: An Urban Perspective*, Heath.

GORDON, D. M. (1972), 'From steam whistles to coffee breaks: notes on office and factory work', in I. Howe (ed.), *Blue-Collar World*, a special issue of *Dissent*, Winter.

GURLEY, J. G. (1971), 'The state of political economics', *Amer. econ. Rev.*, May.

HARRISON, B. (1972), *Education, Training and the Urban Ghetto*, Johns Hopkins University Press.

KATZ, M. B. (1968), *The Irony of Early School Reform*, Harvard University Press.

LEGGETT, J. (1968), *Class, Race and Labor*, Oxford University Press.

LOCKWOOD, D. (1958), *The Blackcoated Worker: A Study in Class Consciousness*, Allen & Unwin.

LOCKWOOD, D. (1966), 'Sources of variation in working-class images of society', *Sociol. Rev.*, November.

MANDEL, E. (1968), *Marxist Economic Theory* (trans. B. Pearce), Monthly Review Press.

MARX, K. (1963a), *The 18th Brumaire of Louis Bonaparte*, International Publishers.

MARX, K. (1963b), *The Poverty of Philosophy*, International Publishers.

MARX, K. (1967a), *Capital*, vol. 1, International Publishers.

MARX, K. (1967b), *The Class Struggles in France, 1848–1850*, Labor News.

MARX, K., and ENGELS, F. (1963), *The German Ideology*, International Publishers.

MILLIBAND, R. (1969), *The State in Capitalist Society*, Basic Books.

OSSOWSKI, S. (1963), *Class Structure in the Social Consciousness* (trans. S. Patterson), Free Press.

PIORE, M. J. (1968), 'Public and private responsibilities in on-the-job training of disadvantaged workers', MIT Economics Department Working Paper no. 23, June.

PIORE, M. J. (1969), 'On-the-job training in the dual labor market', in A. Weber et al., *Public–Private Manpower Policies*, Industrial Relations Research Association, Madison, Wisconsin.

PIORE, M. J. (1970), 'Manpower policy', in S. Beer and R. Barringer (eds.), *The State and the Poor*, Winthrop.

PIORE, M. J. (1971), 'The dual labor market: theory and implication', in D. M. Gordon (ed.), *Problems in Political Economy, an Urban Perspective*, Heath.

POLANYI, K. (1968), *Primitive, Archaic and Modern Economics* (ed. G. Dalton), Doubleday.

RAPOPORT, R. (1967), 'Life on the line', *Wall Street Journal*, 24 July.

REVIEW OF RADICAL POLITICAL ECONOMICS (1971), Special issue on radical paradigms in economics, vol. 3, no. 2.

SPERO, S., and HARRIS, A. (1968), *Black Worker*, Atheneum.

SRAFFA, P. (1960), *Production of Commodities by Means of Commodities*, Cambridge University Press.

SWEEZY, P. (1968), *The Theory of Capitalist Development*, Monthly Review Press.

SWEEZY, P. (1970), 'Toward a critique of economics', *Rev. rad. pol. Econ.*, May.

THOMPSON, E. P. (1966), *The Making of the English Working Class*, Vintage; Penguin, 1970.

TUCKER, R. C. (1969), *The Marxian Revolutionary Idea*, Norton.

ULMAN, L. (1961), 'The development of trades and labor unions', in S. Harris (ed.), *American Economic History*, McGraw-Hill.

WEISSKOPF, T. E. (1972), 'Capitalism and inequality', in R. C. Edwards, M. Reich and T. E. Weisskopf (eds.), *The Capitalist System*, Prentice-Hall.

WILENSKY, H. L. (1966), 'Class, class consciousness and American workers', in W. Haber (ed.), *Labor in a Changing America*, Basic Books.

13 J. Lopreato and L. E. Hazelrigg

The Attitudinal Consequences of Status Change

Excerpt from J. Lopreato and L. E. Hazelrigg, 'Intragenerational versus intergenerational mobility in relation to sociopolitical attitudes', *Social Forces*, vol. 49, 1970, pp. 200–210.

Recent work in social stratification has pointed to the question of whether vertical mobility, when measured *intra*generationally, has different attitudinal 'consequences' than when it is measured *inter*generationally. In the absence of systematic data, the temptation has been to predict that a person's political perspectives and evaluations are changed less by his experiences of intragenerational or 'career' mobility than by those of intergenerational mobility (Wilensky and Edwards, 1959; Wilensky, 1966, Janowitz and Curtis, 1957; Dahrendorf, 1959; Westoff, Bressler and Sagi, 1960).

Major statements on the issue

Following Durkheim's (1951, pp. 242–54; see also Sorokin, 1959, pp. 522–6; Ellis and Lane, 1967) analysis of the anomic effects of social mobility, Janowitz and Curtis (1957) suggest that the disruptions attending mobility are greatest with respect to the individual's primary-group affiliations. To the extent that other members of a person's family and circle of close friends do not experience similar transitions in status, at least two of his major sources of normative support are fragmented, and in consequence he suffers some degree of personal strain. Since adult primary-group bonds tend to be anchored in generational age-groups, intragenerational mobility should produce greater strains than status change across generational lines (see Blau, 1956, pp. 293–4). As a means of resolving such strain, the intragenerationally mobile may, in effect, partially deny judgements of mobility by rejecting critical aspects of culture in the class of destination and retaining those of his origin culture.

Wilensky and Edwards (1959), in their examination of ideological adjustments to downward mobility, report some evidence that bears upon this line of argument. They find that, among manual workers thirty years of age and older, career skidding is more closely related to ideologically conservative attitudes than is skidding between generations. For the younger workers the relationship is reversed. Thus the authors conclude (somewhat ambiguously) that career mobility is 'much more influential than intergenerational mobility in shaping the adult perspectives of all but very young workers and older educated workers.' Wilensky has recently elaborated on this conclusion by suggesting that 'where mobility rates are high and a success ideology prevails,' the referents used in the evaluation of class situations vary by age, 'and the comparison with the father may be relevant only for young men' (1966, p. 103). For older men the important comparisons of success and failure are likely to be made within the career context, not with their fathers' positions in the status hierarchy (see also Wilensky, 1960).

A third statement of the issue is given by Dahrendorf. In his treatment of the 'classless society', he observes that where 'the personnel of classes changes between generations only, there is a sufficient degree of stability to permit the formation of conflicting interest groups' (1959, pp. 219-23). Where, on the other hand, a high rate of mobility *within* generations prevails, such stability is precluded and class interests and consciousness do not coalesce. But, Dahrendorf argues, the barriers to a person's social ascent 'are sure to be . . . higher . . . for intragenerational mobility than for mobility between generations' (1959, p. 59). Thus, his theory for class conflict in industrial society is safeguarded.

Although Dahrendorf does not spell out the reasoning or implications of his position, these can be easily extracted from his contextual remarks. In industrial society, barriers to intergenerational mobility are both less frequently encountered and less insurmountable because of the institutionalization of education as a 'transmission belt' from social-origin status to entry into the labor market. To be sure, educational attainments are still in significant measure tied to social-origin status, such that children of working-class parentage have poorer chances of completing college, say, than middle-class or elite offspring. Nonetheless, while critical inequities remain, the movement toward equal opportunity has been substantial when viewed in historical perspective.[1] Aside from the differential consequences of social-origin status itself, educational attainment – either simply the number of years of schooling or, oftentimes, additional and more incisive measures of ability – has become the single greatest determinant of occupational achievement.

For intragenerational mobility, conversely, there is no comparably effective institutionalized avenue of occupational advancement. Indeed, many scholars (cf. Sjoberg, 1960, pp. 191-2; Chow, 1966, pp. 38-40; Schumpeter, 1951, p. 168) have argued that as the institutionalization of

1. On the role of education in institutionalized recruitment processes, compare Lipset and Bendix (1959, pp. 189-91); Sjoberg (1960, pp. 191, 239-44); Floud, Halsey and Martin (1956); Chow (1966); Foster (1965, pp. 255-9, 297ff.); Goldthorpe (1966); Coleman (1965); Blau and Duncan (1967).

intergenerational paths increases, the traditional modes of within-generation advancement, such as the apprenticeship or the older pattern of 'seeking lordship' (see Gibbs, 1953), lose their efficacy. Substitute modes, better adapted to the complexities and fluidity of an industrial technology, have not yet been developed; or where they are available, as in adult 'continuing education' programs, they have not yet been implemented in significant degree.

With increasing industrialization, then, mobility from one class to a higher class is more often the result of early and formal schooling, typically occurs at the time of entry into the labor force, and is less often the product of career effort. Mobility within careers is generally constrained by class boundaries, very often even by industry lines (see Blau and Duncan, 1967, p. 37) and distinctions between bureaucratic functions. Perhaps the clearest example of such education-linked constraints is provided by post-Restoration Japan, wherein the structure of occupational and educational status became rather highly crystallized (see Passin, 1965, pp. 288 ff.). Career advancement was (and still is to a large extent) specific to three more or less distinct channels, each with its own entry requirements: a labor or production channel (elementary school), a lower administrative channel ('middle school' graduates), and a higher executive channel (university graduates, especially Tokyo University). Once a person enters a given channel, mobility into a higher channel is improbable.

Where interclass mobility does occur within the course of the career, it entails an expenditure of personal effort that is substantially greater than the effort expended by the intergenerational achiever. In a sense, the latter type of mobility is somewhat less in the nature of 'achievement' (as opposed to 'ascription'), inasmuch as the individual is 'sponsored' (see Turner, 1960) by his family and by the state, even though the process may be portrayed as a 'contest' in which all participants have equal opportunities.

Moreover, the career achiever's effort must be greater also because of resistances or barriers imposed by old-established members of the class of destination. In the case of movement between social origin and career entry, the intervening educational experience serves as a kind of 'purification rite', wherein the potential recruit to a higher class is stripped of his original 'vulgar' cultural orientations and socialized anticipatorily in new ones. But because career achievers are typically older and therefore (presumably) more firmly imbued in the orientations of their origin culture, entrance to a higher class means (again, presumably) a more difficult process of resocialization. The career achiever is likelier to bring with him his vulgar background, and against this possibility the old-timers of the higher class offer resistances. It is in this sense that blocked *career* mobility may lead to a confirmation and even intensification of working-class political perspectives.

Some clarifications

Social mobility within and between generations can be conceptualized in one of two related yet analytically distinguishable ways. Figure 1 will aid us in making this distinction.

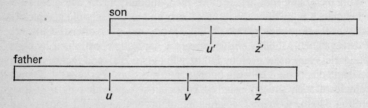

u, u' = career-entry status
v = father's status while son is in school
z, z' = current status

Figure 1 Status comparisons between father and son generations

The conceptualization typically found in the literature on mobility, including the discussions by Wilensky and Edwards (1959) and by Wilensky (1966), takes as its theoretical point of departure the notion of social comparison behavior. It emphasizes the different reference points against which a person's current status may be compared, by himself or by the sociologist-observer, *retrospectively*. From the vantage point of the person's present occupation (z' in the figure), comparison may be made to his social-origin status (v), in which case it is considered intergenerational mobility, or to some previous point in his own career history, such as first job (u'), in which case it is considered intragenerational mobility.

But mobility may also be conceptualized in terms of the different points within a person's life history at which significant alterations of status occur. The theoretical point of departure here is not social comparison behavior *per se* but rather the *chronology* of actual status changes. Defined in this fashion, 'intergenerational' mobility – perhaps better referred to as *social inheritance* (or the absence thereof) – concerns status changes that take place at the inception of a person's effective career activity. It juxtaposes social-origin status (v) and career-entry status (u'). Intragenerational mobility is concerned with the 'second leg' of a person's life history, namely, status changes within the career span, as measured by a juxtaposition of career entry (u') and current status (z'). This second conceptualization of mobility appears to be the one that Dahrendorf has in mind, since it would be meaningless to predict higher barriers to mobility within as opposed to between generations unless these types of mobility pertained to different stages in the person's life history.

Both conceptualizations are perfectly legitimate constructions, although use of the same terminology (i.e. 'intergenerational' and 'intragenerational') to describe patterns of movement in both can be confusing. The methodological distinction between the two conceptualizations must be kept in mind firmly, or the ensuing confusion can become quite serious with regard to analyses of the correlates and consequences of different mobility patterns. Quite clearly, the foregoing demonstrates that Wilensky and Edwards, on the one hand, and Dahrendorf, on the other, are referring methodologically to different phenomena, even though they seem to be in agreement in arguing that sociopolitical attitudes are somehow altered more by experiences of intergenerational mobility than by experiences of intragenerational mobility.

Depending on which conceptualization is employed, a given individual may be labeled differently with respect to his mobility history. Table 1 illustrates this, using a two-class model.[2] We have identified the two

Table 1 Conceptualizations of intragenerational and intergenerational mobility

Social origin	Career initiation	Career now	Mobility descriptions	
			Retrospective	*Chronological*
working class (wc)	wc	wc	intergenerational-stable	intergenerational-stable
			intragenerational-stable	intragenerational-stable
		mc	*intergenerational-upward*	*intergenerational-stable*
			intragenerational-upward	*intragenerational-upward*
	mc	wc	intergenerational-stable	intergenerational-upward
			intragenerational-downward	intragenerational-downward
		mc	intergenerational-upward	intergenerational-upward
			intragenerational-stable	intragenerational-stable
middle class (mc	wc	wc	intergenerational-downward	intergenerational-downward
			intragenerational-stable	intragenerational-stable
		mc	*intergenerational-stable*	*intergenerational-downward*
			intragenerational-upward	*intragenerational-upward*
	mc	wc	intergenerational-downward	intergenerational-stable
			intragenerational-downward	intragenerational-downward
		mc	intergenerational-stable	intergenerational-stable
			intragenerational-stable	intragenerational-stable

2. Although the Table is based on a two-class model, the methodological conclusions derived from it are independent of the number of classes or strata employed.

conceptualizations as the *retrospective* (defined in terms of the observer's temporal position and exemplified by the Wilensky–Edwards study) and the *chronological* (defined in terms of the subjects' biography of actual status changes and exemplified in Dahrendorf's discussion).

Of the eight combinations of actual status change represented in the table, four are not identically described by the two conceptualizations. The one factor that is common to these four, and that differentiates them from the four consistently labeled patterns of status change, is the occurrence of career mobility. This reflects the divergent methodological approaches of the two conceptualizations, as shown in Figure 1. In effect, the retrospective conceptualization cannot by itself distinguish between what is career mobility and what is status change between social origin and career entry.

As an illustration, consider the second set of mobility descriptions in Table 1 (the descriptions are italicized): a person of working-class origin whose career entry was also working-class but who is currently the occupant of a middle-class position. According to the chronological conceptualization of mobility, this person is intergenerationally stable and intragenerationally upwardly mobile. But according to the retrospective conceptualization, this same person is designated an achiever in respect to *both* types of mobility. Looking backward in time from the vantage of his current position, his present status is higher than both his social origin and his career entry, even though he changed status only once. In this sense, it may be noted, Wilensky and Edwards' (1959) 'pure' career skidders had actually experienced an increase in status from working-class origins to middle-class career entries, and *then* began skidding.[3]

A good many studies of the consequences and correlates of vertical social mobility have been based upon the conceptualization of intergenerational mobility that is here illustrated by the position of Wilensky and Edwards. As Figure 1 makes clear, utilization of this conception in *ex post facto* analyses of mobility blends experiences of status alteration that occur between social origin and career entry with experiences of career movement. Thus, it is entirely possible that some of the effects and correlative changes which previous studies have attributed to 'intergenerational' mobility are in large (if not full) measure attributable to the career or *intragenerational* component. [. . .]

3. Unless their theoretical discussion belies their method of defining the 'pure' career skidder, this is necessarily so, inasmuch as they used a two-class model.

References

BLAU, P. M. (1956), 'Social mobility and interpersonal relations', *Amer. Sociol. Rev.*, vol. 21, pp. 290–95.

BLAU, P. M., and DUNCAN, O. D. (1967), *The American Occupational Structure*, Wiley.

CHOW, YUNG-TEH (1966), *Social Mobility in China*, Atherton.

COLEMAN, J. S. (ed.) (1965), *Education and Political Development*, Princeton University Press.

DAHRENDORF, R. (1959), *Class and Class Conflict in Industrial Society*, Stanford University Press.

DURKHEIM, E. (1951), *Suicide*, Free Press.

ELLIS, R. A., and LANE, W. C. (1967), 'Social mobility and social isolation: a test of Sorokin's dissociative hypothesis', *Amer. Sociol. Rev.*, vol. 32, pp. 237–53.

FLOUD, J. E., HALSEY, A. H., and MARTIN, F. M. (1956), *Social Class and Educational Opportunity*, Heinemann.

FOSTER, P. (1965), *Education and Social Change in Ghana*, University of Chicago Press.

GIBBS, M. (1953), *Feudal Order*, Schumann.

GOLDTHORPE, J. H. (1966), 'Social stratification in industrial society', in R. Bendix and S. M. Lipset (eds.), *Class, Status, and Power*, Free Press, pp. 648–59.

JANOWITZ, M., and CURTIS, R. E. (1957), 'Sociological consequences of occupational mobility in a US metropolitan community', Working Paper 1, submitted to the fourth working conference on Social Stratification and Social Mobility, International Sociological Association, December.

LIPSET, S. M., and BENDIX, R. (1959), *Social Mobility in Industrial Society*, University of California Press.

PASSIN, H. (1965), 'Japan', in J. S. Coleman (ed.), *Education and Political Development*, Princeton University Press, pp. 272–312.

SCHUMPETER, J. A. (1951), *Imperialism and Social Classes*, Kelley.

SJOBERG, G. (1960), *The Pre-Industrial City*, Free Press.

SOROKIN, P. A. (1959), *Social and Cultural Mobility*, Free Press.

TURNER, R. H. (1960), 'Sponsored and contest mobility and the school system', *Amer. Sociol. Rev.*, vol. 25, pp. 855–67.

WESTOFF, C. F., BRESSLER, M., and SAGI, P. C. (1960), 'The concept of social mobility: an empirical inquiry', *Amer. Sociol. Rev.*, vol. 25, pp. 375–85.

WILENSKY, H. L. (1960), 'Work, careers and social integration', *Int. soc. Sci. J.*, vol. 12, pp. 543–60.

WILENSKY, H. L. (1966), 'Measures and effects of social mobility', in N. J. Smelser and S. M. Lipset (eds.), *Social Structure and Mobility in Economic Development*, Aldine.

WILENSKY, H. L., and EDWARDS, H. (1959), 'The skidder: ideological adjustments of downwardly mobile workers', *Amer. Sociol. Rev.*, vol. 24, pp. 215–31.

14 M. Aiken, L. A. Ferman and H. L. Sheppard

Adjustment to Job Displacement

Excerpts from M. Aiken, L. A. Ferman and H. L. Sheppard, *Economic Failure, Alienation and Extremism,* University of Michigan Press, 1968, pp. 152–65.

In this report, we have sought to isolate and examine the main factors which might explain the adjustment to job displacement among a group of older automobile workers, made jobless by the closing of the operations of the Packard Motor Company in Detroit in 1956. We have been particularly concerned with the factors that anchor workers to the norms, values and behavior patterns of a society in which they have encountered sudden and serious economic distress. Thus, in a broader perspective, this is an inquiry into the roots and mechanisms of social integration in a large industrial society. Throughout our study, two parallel theoretical questions have concerned us: (1) what social factors hinder or facilitate adaptation to sudden status changes and (2) what is the *relative* influence of economic experiences, as against group memberships, on the continued stability of individuals in the face of socially disruptive events? [. . .]

The analysis of data in this study showed that it was possible to chart a network of relationships between predisplacement statuses, unemployment experiences, economic deprivation and the measures of social integration. Predisplacement statuses predispose the worker to certain types of unemployment experiences, differing in such factors as length of unemployment and finding and holding a job. These experiences, in turn, determine the extent of economic deprivation. Finally, the degree of economic deprivation will influence the social integration of the worker, as evidenced by responses indicating his satisfaction with life and lack of anomia. Knowing the level of economic deprivation among the respondents permits us to predict certain aspects of their adjustment to job displacement.

The importance of economic deprivation as an influence on social integration seems quite clear. The relationship between economic deprivation and social integration remained even when we introduced predisplacement statuses and unemployment experiences as controls. It is also interesting to note that economic deprivation was highly related to stability in rates of social contact with relatives and friends, and somewhat related to stability in rates of social contact with former co-workers and neighbors. The most deprived workers were less stable in these social contacts than other workers. The significance of the latter finding is that it reinforces our general inference about the impact of economic deprivation on social integration because stability in rates of social participation may be a behavioral reflection of emotional states.

Economic deprivation, job mobility and job displacement

As noted, the measure of *economic deprivation* was a central concept in this study, relating workers' post-shutdown experiences to a wide range of attitudes and behavior. Economic deprivation affected a worker's life and the degree to which changes in his life have been for the worse and for the better. The greater the degree of economic deprivation, the greater was his belief that changes for the worse had taken place in his life.

Economic deprivation resulting from unemployment was the greatest determinant of anomia. Workers with the greatest number of economic setbacks (fewer savings, more debts, reduced expenditures on essentials) were more apt to perceive the world as unintelligible, uncontrollable and unfriendly.

Such perceptions are also engendered by losing a new job found after the shutdown – especially if the new job paid more than the regular job at the Packard company. On the other hand, workers who found a new job paying wages higher than the old one *and* who retained the job experienced little, if any, psychic or behavioral malintegration.

'Psychic withdrawal' is one product of economic deprivation; it is a social–psychological type of response, dealing with verbally stated attitudes and mental states. But economic deprivation has other social consequences on the *behavioral* side. For example, social participation with one's relatives was negatively associated with degree of economic deprivation. This participation was even more highly associated, negatively, with the experience of being an upwardly mobile two-time loser. Unemployment and length of unemployment *per se* are *necessary* conditions for psychic withdrawal (as measured by anomia and life satisfaction) and social withdrawal (as measured by reduced interaction with relatives), but they are not *sufficient* conditions. The data clearly indicate that economic deprivation and two-time job loss (especially the loss of a higher-paying job) are among these sufficient conditions. One of the practical outcomes of this process is that the worker, by reducing his contacts with relatives and friends, eliminates one of the major sources for new job leads.

Employer demand for workers is, of course, indispensable for a jobseeker's success – but this demand does not guarantee success if the worker himself reacts to his situation of joblessness in such a way as to be unable to take advantage of the 'structure of opportunities'. This statement is not meant to place 'blame' on the unemployed worker for his plight but, rather, to point to those obstacles that must be coped with by public and private programs if we wish to be more fully effective in combating the social and individual pains of unemployment.

The fact that the nature of job changes (as measured by current employment status and by stability of wage-rate changes) was the *crucial* variable in degree of political alienation is provocative: workers never reemployed and those reemployed at wage rates *similar* to the rates received at Packard – even including those workers no longer reemployed – appear to have registered *less* political alienation than workers undergoing some type of *change* after the Packard shutdown. To put this another way, if a worker experienced a *change* in wage rates on a new job obtained after the Packard shutdown – regardless of whether he kept or lost it, and regardless of the direction of that change in rates – he was more likely to have greater political alienation than if he had *remained* unemployed after the shutdown or had obtained a new job at roughly the same wage rate. This finding is also evident even if he lost the new job paying the same rate. [. . .]

The adjusted mean scores of political alienation shown in Table 1 reveal that the *lowest* averages prevailed among workers with minor rate changes (regardless of current employment status) and among workers

Table 1 Adjusted average scores of political alienation

Job change status	N	Average score
stable, reemployed but no longer working	50	2·92
never reemployed	60	2·51
stable, still reemployed	68	2·68
upward *change*, reemployed but no longer working	12	3·09
upward *change*, still reemployed	35	3·11
downward *change*, still reemployed	15	3·15
downward *change*, reemployed but no longer working [. . .]	20	3·27

The scores were statistically adjusted so as to hold constant the effects of other variables, while focusing attention on the effects of job change status. For details of the technique used (multiple classification analysis), the reader should consult the original source. [Eds.]

never re-employed; and that the *highest* scores prevailed among the remainder, i.e. workers obtaining an increase *or* decrease in post-Packard wage rates – regardless of current employment status. To be sure, the still reemployed workers in our sample who experienced *some* type of change in wage rates on the new job did not have the highest political alienation scores, but their scores were much closer to those of the two-time losers who also had, when on their new jobs, either higher *or* lower wage rates relative to the Packard rates, than they were to all the other workers (the never reemployed and the ones who obtained new jobs without any increase or decrease in wage rates).

Race and job displacement

Our study once again points up the special problems of Negro workers who become unemployed after long job stability, through no fault of their own. [. . .]

Negro ex-Packard workers fared no worse than whites as far as reemployment and length of unemployment are concerned. Nevertheless, it is significant that if they did find a new job, Negroes were more likely to have obtained employment at lower-than-Packard wage rates. The proportion of Negroes obtaining new jobs at lower wage rates was twice that among whites.

It is easy and perhaps even fashionable these days to jump to the conclusion that discrimination is the full explanation of this type of finding. But the more sophisticated type of analysis carried out in this report reveals quite clearly that 'Negro-ness' explained little, if any, of the variations between whites and Negroes in their post-shutdown labor market experiences in Detroit. Instead, age, skill level and schooling played much more significant roles in determining the job-finding success of the ex-Packard workers, including Negroes. In other words, Negroes *as such* were not discriminated against in the labor market as much as older, less skilled, less educated job-seekers were. [. . .]

In contrast to what our objective measures revealed, the subjective measures indicated that Negroes, to a much greater extent than did whites, personally felt that their jobs had changed for the worse. We must consider the possibility that a long-term, high-seniority job at a company like Packard means much more for Negroes than for whites. Such a job is not easy to obtain for Negro Americans, and if and when that type of job is lost, the trauma may be more salient for them, more salient than our measures of wage changes, and length of unemployment can reveal.

The *social* fact of being a Negro in American society, then, does carry with it more connotations than can be gleaned through our measures of economic insecurity and deprivation, even through degree of education. It is not completely accurate, therefore, to say that if Negroes had the same economic, occupational and educational status as whites – at this point in history, at least – all of their outlooks on life and society would be no different from those held by whites. Regardless of our objective measures of post-displacement experiences, the fact that a Packard worker was a

Negro not only meant that he felt that his job situation was worse but it also meant, for example, that he was higher in his feelings of anomia, political alienation, and more favorably inclined toward governmental activism in the economy.

Theoretical implications of the study

To what extent do the results of this study substantiate and/or modify prevailing theories of social integration? We will limit our discussion to the theories of the French sociologist Emile Durkheim and the work of the American sociologists Seymour Lipset and William Kornhauser. Durkheim viewed the root of social malintegration to be in the sudden and frequent status shifts that are inherent in mass industrial society. The consequence of such shifts was to destroy basic group loyalties and attachments to prevailing normative patterns. The work of Lipset and Kornhauser does not contradict the basic Durkheim thesis; rather, it tends to focus the cause of malintegration on two different kinds of sociological data. Lipset emphasizes negative economic experiences and insecurities (e.g., length of unemployment) as the straining influence, while Kornhauser views the loss of group memberships in the 'mass society' – particularly associational memberships – as being primary. Although the study was not designed specifically to test all or one of these theories, some of the findings do bear on these three theoretical perspectives.

Durkheimian theory and job displacement

The findings of this study indicate that reemployed displaced workers who experience job mobility in terms of their wages are less socially integrated than are reemployed workers who do not experience changes in wages or those who remain unemployed. Job mobility had its most deleterious effects on the upwardly mobile two-time losers. These findings are consistent with Emile Durkheim's theories concerning the social consequences of changes and fluctuations in the economic order. Job fluctuation and change as well as labor market failure are found to result not only in strong feelings of anomia and political alienation but also in a reduced pace of social life, as measured by the frequency of social interaction with relatives, friends and co-workers.

Among the ex-Packard workers, it was the individual who had to adjust to status changes more than once who had the highest anomia scores, the greatest alienation from the political institutions, and the lowest social participation. Since all of the workers had essentially undergone at least one status change – the shutdown experience itself – it would seem that it is repeated status change, inherent in reemployment, coupled with the demand for consecutive, dramatic adjustments, that is most likely to weaken individual ties to the social order. It is ironic that the workers who were not reemployed in any job were better integrated than the workers who experienced successive changes in reemployment. Prolonged unemployment was undoubtedly an unpleasant experience for these workers, but it was marked by a relative stability of expectations that was clearly not present in the case of workers who were called on to make adaptations to successive changes. Although a single status change, such as job displacement, may place strains on the individual's attachment to accepted groups and values, it is successive changes inherent in reemployment experiences that pose the greatest threat by creating a milieu of uncertainty about the worthwhileness of existing group ties and values.

Mobility and situational factors in job displacement

Durkheim's major theoretical contribution to an understanding of social integration was in his emphasis on *status change*. Neglected in his theoretical formulation was any mention of the *structure of the situation* in which the individual finds himself *after* the change. There may be dimensions of this situation that could influence social integration. What do our data suggest on this possibility?

Our data show that the situational factor (the degree of economic deprivation) was more important than the mobility factor (post-displacement job pattern) in shaping the attitudes and behavior of displaced workers. Economic deprivation was more productive of alienatory attitudes and behavior (anomia, dissatisfaction with life and withdrawal from contact with kin and friends) than mobility. *It is the absence or presence of financial strains that shapes the displaced worker's outlook on life and social participation.*

It is interesting to examine these findings in the light of Durkheim's hypothesis about the relationship between social mobility and consequent social posture of the individual. Durkheim (1951) postulated a direct relationship between the sudden and frequent status changes inherent in mobility experiences and consequent social malaise and disorientation of the individual. His followers have largely accepted this hypothesis and have given little thought to the role of situational variables in inhibiting the consequences of sudden status changes. Janowitz has raised a question about the role of primary and secondary group structures in modifying the consequences of social mobility and Kornhauser has analysed the importance of these group variables in social mobility and status change.

Our findings suggest that another dimension of the worker's situation is an important factor in the modification of the consequences of mobility; namely, the degree of economic deprivation. It is likely that the number and intensity of group memberships and social contacts are directly related

M. Aiken, L. A. Ferman and H. L. Sheppard 253

to the worker's financial resources. Many primary group activities with kin and friends demand material or social reciprocity, which is dependent on the availability of financial resources. Lack of finances may also lead to exclusion from secondary groups (e.g., the lodge, church membership, the neighborhood clubhouse). The exact nature of the interaction is not clear without further study, but our data suggest that a lack of financial resources may affect social ties in two possible ways. First, economic deprivation may produce reactions of anomia (or alienation), and these psychic states place severe limitations on social interaction. Reduced interactions may well produce more intense anomia and further weaken the individual's social ties. Second, the lack of financial resources may severely restrict access to various forms of group life, which may lead to further economic, as well as social, isolation.

It is not change in itself that triggers attitudinal and behavioral reactions, but, rather, the significance given to these changes by dimensions of the worker's immediate situation (e.g., economic deprivation). Changes in jobs, positive or negative, may be a minor influence on the worker's life if he continues to exercise some control over his social environment. This control is accomplished partially through the availability of economic resources. It may very well be that it is necessary to reexamine the Durkheim hypothesis and further specify the conditions under which the effects of mobility may be modified.

Economic insecurity, mass society and political orientation

The data in this study suggest that economic insecurity variables (e.g., the number of months unemployed and changes in wage rates) are more likely to affect political orientations than the absence or presence of group memberships in a condition of mass society. But we must be cautious in using the findings of this study to give a definitive answer to the controversy over whether economic experience or associational membership is *the* factor in the development of political orientations. The mass society theory of William Kornhauser (1959) emphasized associational memberships as insulators against extremist political orientations, and as we have indicated, these data were not available in our study. The other indicators of primary group membership apparently do not support the thesis that group memberships *per se* are effective insulators against political extremism.

The economic insecurity thesis of Seymour Lipset more nearly fits the data in this study. But even here, some caution must be taken in interpretation. The concept of economic insecurity is not a unitary variable. There are a number of indicators that could be classified under this variable (number of months unemployed, negative shifts in wage rates, current employment status, loss of economic resources). It is quite clear that political orientations may be explained to a greater or lesser extent, depending on the measure that is used to represent economic insecurity. The use of length of unemployment to represent economic insecurity, a practice quite common in unemployment research, masks other subtle relationships between economic experiences and political orientation. The data in this study clearly show that although length of unemployment and economic deprivation refer to a common concept – economic insecurity – the relationship between these measures and political orientations are sufficiently different as to require a separate analytical treatment. Our study results suggest that the use of length of unemployment as *the* indicator of economic insecurity is misleading, particularly when discussing the political consequences of economic insecurity.

Social policy

[. . .] The increase in anomia, and in political extremism, the erosion of self-confidence, have their impacts on the social order. In addition to their political implications, it is possible for the 'two-time losers' and for workers with many months of protracted unemployment to acquire attitudes and behavior patterns that then become obstacles to effective job-seeking. High anomia and extreme political alienation (which includes a loss of faith in the government), along with a withdrawal from interaction with friends and relatives, can eventually lead to a withdrawal from the job-seeking process. A concrete example of this can be seen in the finding from a recent study which revealed that the longer a worker had been unemployed, the fewer attempts he had made to seek employment in the months prior to being interviewed.[1] The crucial point is that when employment opportunities do increase, such attitudes and behavior patterns may *prevent* large numbers of workers from seeking out such opportunities.[2]

Thus vicious circles are generated. But they can be broken and it is at this point of the circle's circumference that direct 'reaching-out' actions are required on the part of private and public programs. Whether we approach such actions from the standpoint of improving their job or economic status does not matter. In fact, the two are inextricably related. What does matter is that after prolonged recessions, economic measures *per se* might not suffice as a solution to the unemployment problems of individuals.

1. See Sheppard and Belitsky (1966).
2. A recent study for the National Institute for Mental Health has indicated that among whites in Appalachia, a long-term chronically depressed area, their mental health conditions have deteriorated to a point where there is no positive response to training and job opportunities.

More specifically, certain categories of individual workers may undergo this process to a greater extent than other categories. These categories may refer to geographical areas, such as in parts of Appalachia. Negro workers are more vulnerable than whites; older workers more than younger ones. Both of the former groups typically experience more long-run unemployment. In the case of Negroes, there are national, aggregate data that suggest very strongly that such a process takes place. Among nonwhites of twenty-five to fifty-four years of age, the proportion of males not in the labor force has been steadily increasing from 1957 onward, from 45 per 1000 non-institutionalized civilians to 60 per 1000 in 1964. Among whites in the same age group, however, the proportion has remained relatively constant (between 27 and 29 per 1000).[3]

As our own study indicates, careful statistical analysis makes a strong case for the growing belief that racial discrimination or prejudice *per se* is becoming less and less an adequate explanation for the poor employment status of Negroes. Since our study, the evidence is even stronger that poor educational background and lower skill levels, rather than race, are becoming more crucial as determinants of the success of Negro job seekers.[4] We do not mean that discrimination and prejudice have been eliminated as barriers for Negro workers. But as employer discrimination becomes less and less possible (or more difficult) to exercise, the problem of Negro employment becomes one, *objectively*, of education and training. Many Negroes and many unsophisticated whites will continue, subjectively, to interpret this problem as due exclusively to racial discrimination and prejudice. They are correct only if we trace the roots of poor education and training to their origins in discrimination in access to equal educational opportunities. [. . .]

There is also reason to believe that, contrary to some popular notions, a large part of our poor were not born poor – that the process of impoverization may begin during the working years of adult workers, especially those experiencing the kind of plant-shutdown trauma described in this volume. The fact that in a two-year period alone, more than 185 000 workers were affected by 525 mass layoffs should be sufficient notice that in good times and bad, individuals are vulnerable to drastic changes in their statuses.

3. However, inter-age analysis suggests that in any given year, older whites have a high labor force 'drop-out' rate.
4. See Sheppard and Striner (1966).

References

DURKHEIM, E. (1951), *Suicide*, Free Press.

JANOWITZ, M., and MARVICK, D. (1956), *Competitive Pressure and Democratic Consent*, Bureau of Government, Ann Arbor.

KORNHAUSER, A. (1965), *Mental Health of Industrial Workers*, Wiley.

KORNHAUSER, A., SHEPPARD, H. L., and MAYER, A. J. (1956), *When Labor Votes*, University Books.

KORNHAUSER, W. (1959), *The Politics of Mass Society*, Free Press.

LIPSET, S. M., LAZARSFELD, P. F., and BARTON, A. H. (1954), 'The psychology of voting: an analysis of political behavior', in G. Lindzey and E. Aronson (eds.), *The Handbook of Social Psychology*, vol. 2, Addison-Wesley.

LIPSET, S. M. (1963), *Political Man*, Doubleday.

SHEPPARD, H. L., and BELITSKY, A. H. (1966), *The Job Hunt*, Johns Hopkins University Press.

SHEPPARD, H. L., and STRINER, A. (1966) *Civil Rights, Employment and the Social Status of American Negroes*, Upjohn Institute.

15 S. Bowles

Unequal Education and the Reproduction of the Social Division of Labor

Excerpts from S. Bowles, 'Unequal education and the reproduction of the social division of labor', in M. Carnoy (ed.), *Schooling in a Corporate Society: The Political Economy of Education in America*, McKay, 1972, pp. 36–64.

The evolution of capitalism and the rise of mass education

In colonial America, and in most pre-capitalist societies of the past, the basic productive unit was the family. For the vast majority of male adults, work was self-directed, and was performed without direct supervision. Though constrained by poverty, ill health, the low level of technological development and occasional interferences by the political authorities, a man had considerable leeway in choosing his working hours, what to produce and how to produce it. While great inequalities in wealth, political power and other aspects of status normally existed, differences in the degree of autonomy in work were relatively minor, particularly when compared with what was to come.

Transmitting the necessary productive skills to the children as they grew up proved to be a simple task, not because the work was devoid of skill, but because the quite substantial skills required were virtually unchanging from generation to generation, and because the transition to the world of work did not require that the child adapt to a wholly new set of social relationships. The child learned the concrete skills and adapted to the social relations of production through learning by doing within the family. Preparation for life in the larger community was facilitated by the child's experience with the extended family, which shaded off without distinct boundaries, through uncles and fourth cousins, into the community. Children learned early how to deal with complex relationships among adults other than their parents, and children other than their brothers and sisters.[1]

Children were not required to learn a complex set of political principles or ideologies, as political participation was limited and political authority unchallenged, at least in normal times. The only major socializing institution outside the family was the church, which sought to inculcate the

---

1. This account draws upon two important historical studies: Aries (1965) and Bailyn (1960). Also illuminating are anthropological studies of education in contemporary pre-capitalist societies. See, for example, Kenyatta (1962, pp. 95–124). See also Morgan (1966).

accepted spiritual values and attitudes. In addition, a small number of children learned craft skills outside the family, as apprentices. The role of schools tended to be narrowly vocational, restricted to preparation of children for a career in the church or the still inconsequential state bureaucracy (Aries, 1965).[2] The curriculum of the few universities reflected the aristocratic penchant for conspicuous intellectual consumption (Kearney, 1971).

The extension of capitalist production, and particularly the factory system, undermined the role of the family as the major unit of both socialization and production. Small peasant farmers were driven off the land or competed out of business. Cottage industry was destroyed. Ownership of the means of production became heavily concentrated in the hands of landlords and capitalists. Workers relinquished control over their labor in return for wages or salaries. Increasingly, production was carried on in large organizations in which a small management group directed the work activities of the entire labor force. The social relations of production – the authority structure, the prescribed types of behavior and response characteristic of the work place – became increasingly distinct from those of the family.

The divorce of the worker from control over production – from control over his own labor – is particularly important in understanding the role of schooling in capitalist societies. The resulting social division of labor – between controllers and controlled – is a crucial aspect of the class structure of capitalist societies, and will be seen to be an important barrier to the achievement of social-class equality in schooling.

Rapid economic change in the capitalist period led to frequent shifts of the occupational distribution of the labor force, and constant changes in the skill requirements for jobs. The productive skills of the father were no longer adequate for the needs of the son during his lifetime. Skill training within the family became increasingly inappropriate.

And the family itself was changing. Increased geographic mobility of labor and the necessity for children to work outside the family spelled the demise of the extended family and greatly weakened even the nuclear family (see Bailyn, 1960; Smelser, 1959). Meanwhile, the authority of the church was questioned by the spread of secular rationalist thinking and the rise of powerful competing groups.

While undermining the main institutions of socialization, the development

2. In a number of places, e.g., Scotland and Massachusetts, schools stressed literacy so as to make the Bible more widely accessible. See Cipolla (1969) and Morgan (1966, ch. 4). Morgan quotes a Massachusetts law of 1647 which provided for the establishment of reading schools because it was 'one chief project of that old deluder, Satan, to keep men from knowledge of the Scriptures'.

of the capitalist system created at the same time an environment – both social and intellectual – which would ultimately challenge the political order. Workers were thrown together in oppressive factories, and the isolation which had helped to maintain quiescence in earlier, widely dispersed peasant populations was broken down (Engels and Marx, 1951; Marx, 1935). With an increasing number of families uprooted from the land, the workers' search for a living resulted in large-scale labor migrations. Transient, even foreign, elements came to constitute a major segment of the population, and began to pose seemingly insurmountable problems of assimilation, integration and control (see, for example, Thernstrom, 1964). Inequalities of wealth became more apparent, and were less easily justified and less readily accepted. The simple legitimizing ideologies of the earlier period – the divine right of kings and the divine origin of social rank, for example – fell under the capitalist attack on the royalty and the traditional landed interests. The general broadening of the electorate – first sought by the capitalist class in the struggle against the entrenched interests of the pre-capitalist period – threatened soon to become an instrument for the growing power of the working class. Having risen to political power, the capitalist class sought a mechanism to ensure social control and political stability (Simon, 1960).

An institutional crisis was at hand. The outcome, in virtually all capitalist countries, was the rise of mass education. In the United States, the many advantages of schooling as a socialization process were quickly perceived. The early proponents of the rapid expansion of schooling argued that education could perform many of the socialization functions that earlier had been centered in the family and, to a lesser extent, in the church (Bailyn, 1960). An ideal preparation for factory work was found in the social relations of the school: specifically, in its emphasis on discipline, punctuality, acceptance of authority outside the family, and individual accountability for one's work.[3] The social relations of the school would replicate the social relations of the work place, and thus help young people adapt to the social division of labor. Schools would further lead people to accept the authority of the state and its agents – the teachers – at a young

3. A manufacturer, writing to the Massachusetts State Board of Education from Lowell in 1841 commented: 'I have never considered mere knowledge . . . as the only advantage derived from a good Common School education. . . . [Workers with more education possess] a higher and better state of morals, are more orderly and respectful in their deportment, and more ready to comply with the wholesome and necessary regulations of an establishment. . . . In times of agitation, on account of some change in regulations or wages, I have always looked to the most intelligent, best educated and the most moral for support. The ignorant and uneducated I have generally found the most turbulent and troublesome, acting under the impulse of excited passion and jealousy' (quoted in Katz, 1968, p. 8). See also Bruck (1971).

age, in part by fostering the illusion of the benevolence of the government in its relations with citizens.[4] Moreover, because schooling would ostensibly be open to all, one's position in the social division of labor could be portrayed as the result not of birth, but of one's own efforts and talents.[5] And if the children's everyday experiences with the structure of schooling were insufficient to inculcate the correct views and attitudes, the curriculum itself would be made to embody the bourgeois ideology.[6] Where precapitalist social institutions, particularly the church, remained strong or threatened the capitalist hegemony, schools sometimes served as a modernizing counter-institution.[7]

4. In 1846 the annual report of the Lowell, Massachusetts, School Committee concluded that universal education was 'the surest safety against internal commotions' (*1846 School Committee Annual Report*, pp. 17–18). It seems more than coincidental that, in England, public support for elementary education – a concept which had been widely discussed and urged for at least half a century – was legislated almost immediately after the enfranchisement of the working class by the electoral reform of 1867. See Simon (1960). Mass public education in Rhode Island came quickly on the heels of an armed insurrection and a broadening of the franchise. See Carlton (1966).

5. Describing the expansion of education in the nineteenth century, Katz concludes: '... a middle class attempt to secure advantage for their children as technological change heightened the importance of formal education assured the success and acceptance of universal elaborate graded school systems. The same result emerged from the fear of a growing, unschooled proletariat. Education substituted for deference as a source of social cement and social order in a society stratified by class rather than by rank' (Katz, 1970).

6. An American economist, writing just prior to the 'common school revival', had this to say: 'Education universally extended throughout the community will tend to disabuse the working class of people in respect of a notion that has crept into the minds of our mechanics and is gradually prevailing, that manual labor is at present very inadequately rewarded, owing to combinations of the rich against the poor; that mere mental labor is comparatively worthless; that property or wealth ought not to be accumulated or transmitted; that to take interest on money let or profit on capital employed is unjust. ... The mistaken and ignorant people who entertain these fallacies as truths will learn, when they have the opportunity of learning, that the institution of political society originated in the protection of property' (Thomas Cooper, *Elements of Political Economy*, 1828, quoted in Carlton, 1966, pp. 33–4).

Political economy was made a required subject in Massachusetts high schools in 1857, along with moral science and civic polity. Cooper's advice was widely but not universally followed elsewhere. Friedrich Engels, commenting on the tardy growth of mass education in early nineteenth-century England, remarked: 'So shortsighted, so stupidly narrow-minded is the English bourgeoisie in its egotism, that it does not even take the trouble to impress upon the workers the morality of the day, which the bourgeoisie has patched together in its own interest for its own protection' (Engels, 1968).

7. See Thernstrom (1964). Marx said this about mid-nineteenth century France: 'The modern and the traditional consciousness of the French peasant contended for mastery ... in the form of an incessant struggle between the schoolmasters and the priests' (Marx, 1935, p. 125).

The movement for public elementary and secondary education in the United States originated in the nineteenth century in states dominated by the burgeoning industrial capitalist class, most notably in Massachusetts. It spread rapidly to all parts of the country except the South.[8] In Massachusetts the extension of elementary education was in large measure a response to industrialization, and to the need for social control of the Irish and other non-Yankee workers recruited to work in the mills.[9] The fact that some working people's movements had demanded free instruction should not obscure the basically coercive nature of the extension of schooling. In many parts of the country, schools were literally imposed upon the workers (Katz, 1968, 1970).

The evolution of the economy in the nineteenth century gave rise to new socialization needs and continued to spur the growth of education. Agriculture continued to lose ground to manufacturing; simple manufacturing gave way to production involving complex interrelated processes; an increasing fraction of the labor force was employed in producing services rather than goods. Employers in the most rapidly growing sectors of the economy began to require more than obedience and punctuality in their workers; a change in motivational outlook was required. The new structure of production provided little built-in motivation. There were fewer jobs such as farming and piece-rate work in manufacturing in which material reward was tied directly to effort. As work roles became more complicated and interrelated, the evaluation of the individual worker's performance became increasingly difficult. Employers began to look for workers who had internalized the production-related values of the firm's managers.

The continued expansion of education was pressed by many who saw schooling as a means of producing these new forms of motivation and discipline. Others, frightened by the growing labor militancy after the Civil War, found new urgency in the social-control arguments popular among the proponents of education in the antebellum period.

A system of class stratification developed within this rapidly expanding educational system. Children of the social elite normally attended private schools. Because working-class children tended to leave school early, the class composition of the public high schools was distinctly more elite than the public primary schools (Katz, 1968). And as a university education ceased to be merely training for teaching or the divinity and became

8. Janice Weiss and I are currently studying the rapid expansion of southern elementary and secondary schooling which followed the demise of slavery and the establishment of capitalist economic institutions in the South.
9. Based on the preliminary results of a statistical analysis of education in nineteenth-century Massachusetts being conducted jointly with Alexander Field.

important in gaining access to the pinnacles of the business world, upper-class families used their money and influence to get their children into the best universities, often at the expense of the children of less elite families.

Around the turn of the present century, large numbers of working-class and particularly immigrant children began attending high schools. At the same time, a system of class stratification developed within secondary education.[10] The older democratic ideology of the common school – that the same curriculum should be offered to all children – gave way to the 'progressive' insistence that education should be tailored to the 'needs of the child'.[11] In the interests of providing an education relevant to the later life of the students, vocational schools and tracks were developed for the children of workingclass families. The academic curriculum was preserved for those who would later have the opportunity to make use of book learning, either in college or in white-collar employment. This and other educational reforms of the progressive education movement reflected an implicit assumption of the immutability of the class structure.

The frankness with which students were channelled into curriculum tracks, on the basis of their social-class background, raised serious doubts concerning the 'openness' of the social-class structure. The relation between social class and a child's chances of promotion or tracking assignments was disguised – though not mitigated much – by another 'progressive' reform: 'objective' educational testing. Particularly after the First World War, the capitulation of the schools to business values and concepts of efficiency led to the increased use of intelligence and scholastic achievement testing as an ostensibly unbiased means of measuring the product of schooling and classifying students (Callahan, 1962; Cohen and Lazerson, 1970; Cremin, 1961). The complementary growth of the guidance counseling profession allowed much of the channelling to proceed from the

10. Sol Cohen (1968) describes this process. Typical of the arguments then given for vocational education is the following, by the superintendent of schools in Cleveland: 'It is obvious that the educational needs of children in a district where the streets are well paved and clean, where the homes are spacious and surrounded by lawns and trees, where the language of the child's playfellows is pure, and where life in general is permeated with the spirit and ideals of America – it is obvious that the educational needs of such a child are radically different from those of the child who lives in a foreign and tenement section' (Elson and Bachman, 1910). See also Cremin (1961, ch. 2) and Cohen and Lazerson (1970).

11. The superintendent of the Boston schools summed up the change in 1908: 'Until very recently (the schools) have offered equal opportunity for all to receive *one kind* of education, but what will make them democratic is to provide opportunity for all to receive such education as will fit them *equally well* for their particular life work' (Boston, *Documents of the School Committee, 1908*, no. 7, p. 53; quoted in Cohen and Lazerson, 1970).

students' own well-counseled choices, thus adding an apparent element of voluntarism to the system.

The legacy of the progressive education movement, like the earlier reforms of the mid-nineteenth century, was a strengthened system of class stratification within schooling which continues to play an important role in the reproduction and legitimation of the social division of labor.

The class stratification of education during this period has proceeded hand in hand with the stratification of the labor force. As large bureaucratic corporations and public agencies employed an increasing fraction of all workers, a complicated segmentation of the labor force evolved, reflecting the hierarchical structure of the social relations of production. A large middle group of employees developed, comprising clerical, sales, bookkeeping and low-level supervisory workers (see Reich, 1971). People holding these occupations ordinarily had a modicum of control over their own work; in some cases they directed the work of others, while themselves under the direction of higher management. The social division of labor had become a finely articulated system of work relations dominated at the top by a small group with control over work processes and a high degree of personal autonomy in their work activities, and proceeding by finely differentiated stages down the chain of bureaucratic command to workers who labored more as extensions of the machinery than as autonomous human beings.

One's status, income and personal autonomy came to depend in great measure on one's place in the work hierarchy. And in turn, positions in the social division of labor came to be associated with educational credentials reflecting the number of years of schooling and the quality of education received. The increasing importance of schooling as a mechanism for allocating children to positions in the class structure played a major part in legitimizing the structure itself.[12] But at the same time, it undermined the simple processes which in the past had preserved the position and privilege of the upper-class families from generation to generation. In short, it undermined the processes serving to reproduce the social division of labor.

In pre-capitalist societies, direct inheritance of occupational position is common. Even in the early capitalist economy, prior to the segmentation of the labor force on the basis of differential skills and education, the class structure was reproduced generation after generation simply through the inheritance of physical capital by the offspring of the capitalist class. Now that the social division of labor is differentiated by types of competence and educational credentials as well as by ownership of capital, the problem of inheritance is not nearly so simple. The crucial complication arises

12. The role of schooling in legitimizing the class structure is spelled out in Bowles (1971).

because education and skills are embedded in human beings; unlike physical capital, these assets cannot be passed on to one's children at death. In an advanced capitalist society in which education and skills play an important role in the hierarchy of production, then, the absence of confiscatory inheritance laws is not enough to reproduce the social division of labor from generation to generation. Skills and educational credentials must somehow be passed on within the family. It is a fundamental theme of this essay that schools play an important part in reproducing and legitimizing this modern form of class structure.

Class inequalities in US schools

Unequal schooling reproduces the social division of labor. Children whose parents occupy positions at the top of the occupational hierarchy receive more years of schooling than working-class children. Both the amount and the content of their education greatly facilitates their movement into positions similar to those of their parents.

Because of the relative ease of measurement, inequalities in years of schooling are particularly evident. If we define social-class standing by the income, occupation and educational level of the parents, a child from the 90th percentile in the class distribution may expect on the average to achieve over four and a half more years of schooling than a child from the 10th percentile.[13] As can be seen in Table 1, social-class inequalities in the number of years of schooling received arise in part because a disproportionate number of children from poorer families do not complete high school.[14] Table 2 indicates that these inequalities are exacerbated by social-class inequalities in college attendance among those children who did graduate from high school: even among those who had graduated from high school, children of families earning less than $3000 per year were over six times as likely *not* to attend college as were the children of families earning over $15 000.[15]

Because schooling, especially at the college level, is heavily subsidized by the general taxpayer, those children who attend school longer have

13. The data for this calculation refer to white males who were aged twenty-five to thirty-four in 1962. See Bowles (1970a).
14. Table 1 understates the degree of social-class inequality in school attendance because a substantial portion of upper-income children not enrolled in public schools attend private schools. Private schools provide a parallel educational system for the upper class. I have not given much attention to these institutions as they are not quantitatively very significant in the total picture. Moreover, to deal extensively with them might detract attention from the task of explaining class inequalities in the ostensibly egalitarian portion of our school system.
15. For recent evidence on these points, see US Bureau of the Census (1969, nos. 183 and 185).

Table 1 Percentage of male children aged sixteen to seventeen enrolled in public school, and percentage at less than the modal grade level, by parent's education and income, 1960[a]

Parent's education	Enrolled in public school	Below modal level
Less than 8 years family income:		
less than $3000	66·1	47·4
$3000–4999	71·3	35·7
$5000–6999	75·5	28·3
$7000 and over	77·1	21·8
8–11 years family income:		
less than $3000	78·6	25·0
$3000–4999	82·9	20·9
$5000–6999	84·9	16·9
$7000 and over	86·1	13·0
12 years or more family income:		
less than $3000	89·5	13·4
$3000–4999	90·7	12·4
$5000–6999	92·1	9·7
$7000 and over	94·2	6·9

Source: US Bureau of the Census (1962, Table 5)
[a] According to Census definitions, for sixteen-year-olds, ninth grade or less and for seventeen-year-olds, tenth grade or less define as below the modal level. Father's education is indicated if father is present; otherwise mother's education is indicated

access for this reason alone to a far larger amount of public resources than those who are forced out of school or who drop out early (Hansen and Weisbrod, 1970). But social-class inequalities in public expenditure on education are far more severe than the degree of inequality in years of schooling would suggest. In the first place, per-student public expenditure in four-year colleges greatly exceeds that in elementary schools; those who stay in school longer receive an increasingly large *annual* public subsidy.[16] Second, even at the elementary level, schools attended by children of the poor tend to be less well endowed with equipment, books, teachers and other inputs into the educational process. Evidence on the relationship between the level of school inputs and the income of the neighborhoods that the schools serve is presented in Table 3 (see also Sexton, 1961). The

16. In the school year 1969–70, per-pupil expenditures of federal, state and local funds were $1490 for colleges and universities and $747 for primary and secondary schools (US Office of Education, 1969).

Table 2 College attendance in 1967 among high school graduates, by family income[a]

Family income[b]	Percentage who did not attend college
less than $3000	80·2
$3000–3999	67·7
$4000–5999	63·7
$6000–7499	58·9
$7500–9999	49·0
$10 000–14 999	38·7
$15 000 and over	13·3

Source: US Bureau of the Census (1969, no. 185, p. 6)
[a] Refers to individuals who were high school seniors in October 1965 and who subsequently graduated from high school; 53·1 per cent of all such students did not attend college
[b] Family income for twelve months preceding October 1965

data in this table indicate that both school expenditures and more direct measures of school quality vary directly with the income levels of the communities in which the school is located.

Table 3 Inequalities in elementary school resources: percentage difference in resource availability associated with a 1 per cent difference in mean neighborhood family income

Resource	Within cities 1	Between cities 2
current real education expenditure per student	n.a.	0·73[b]
average real elementary schoolteacher salary	0·20[a]	0·69[b]
teacher–student ratio	0·24[a]	n.a.
real expenditure per pupil on teacher salary	0·43[a]	n.a.
verbal ability of teacher	0·11[a]	1·20[a]

Sources: [a] Owen (1972a)
[b] Owen (1972b)

Inequalities in schooling are not simply a matter of differences in years of schooling attained or in resources devoted to each student per year of schooling. Differences in the internal structure of schools themselves and in the content of schooling reflect the differences in the social-class compositions of the student bodies. The social relations of the educational process ordinarily mirror the social relations of the work roles into which most students are likely to move. Differences in rules, expected modes of behavior, and opportunities for choice are most glaring when we compare levels of schooling. Note the wide range of choice over curriculum, life style and allocation of time afforded to college students, compared with the obedience and respect for authority expected in high school. Differentiation occurs also within each level of schooling. One needs only to compare the social relations of a junior college with those of an elite four-year college (see Binstock, 1971), or those of a working-class high school with those of a wealthy suburban high school, for verification of this point (Friedenberg, 1965).[17]

The various socialization patterns in schools attended by students of different social classes do not arise by accident. Rather, they stem from the fact that the educational objectives and expectations of both parents and teachers, and the responsiveness of students to various patterns of teaching and control, differ for students of different social classes.[18] Further, class inequalities in school socialization patterns are reinforced by the inequalities in financial resources documented above. The paucity of financial support for the education of children from working-class families not only leaves more resources to be devoted to the children of those with commanding roles in the economy; it forces upon the teachers and school administrators in the working-class schools a type of social relations which fairly closely mirrors that of the factory. Thus, financial considerations in poorly supported working-class schools militate against small intimate classes, against a multiplicity of elective courses and specialized teachers (except disciplinary personnel), and preclude the amounts of free time for the teachers and free space required for a more open, flexible educational environment. The lack of financial support all but requires that students be treated as raw materials on a production line; it places a high premium on obedience and punctuality; there are few opportunities for independent, creative work or individualized attention by teachers. The well-financed schools attended by the children of the rich can offer much greater opportunities for the development of the capacity for sustained independent work and the other characteristics required for adequate job performance in the upper levels of the occupational hierarchy.

Much of the inequality in American education exists between schools,

17. It is consistent with this pattern that the play-oriented, child-centered pedagogy of the progressive movement found little acceptance outside of private schools and public schools in wealthy communities. See Cohen and Lazerson (1970).
18. That working-class parents seem to favor more authoritarian educational methods is perhaps a reflection of their own work experiences which have demonstrated that submission to authority is an essential ingredient in one's ability to get and hold a steady, well-paying job.

but even within a given school different children receive different educations. Class stratification within schools is achieved through tracking, differential participation in extracurricular activities, and in the attitudes of teachers and guidance personnel who expect working-class children to do poorly, to terminate schooling early, and to end up in jobs similar to those of their parents (see, for example, Hollingshead, 1949; Warner and Lunt, 1941; Rosenthal and Jacobson, 1968; Schafer, Olexa and Polk, 1970).

Not surprisingly, the results of schooling differ greatly for children of different social classes. The differing educational objectives implicit in the social relations of schools attended by children of different social classes has already been mentioned. Less important but more easily measured are differences in scholastic achievement. If we measure the output of schooling by scores on nationally standardized achievement tests, children whose parents were themselves highly educated outperform children of parents with less education by a wide margin. A recent study revealed, for example, that among white high school seniors, those whose parents were in the top education decile were on the average well over three grade levels ahead of those whose parents were in the bottom decile.[19] Although a good part of this discrepancy is the result of unequal treatment in school and unequal educational resources, much of it is related to differences in the early socialization and home environment of the children.

Given the great social-class differences in scholastic achievement, class inequalities in college attendance are to be expected. Thus one might be tempted to argue that the data in Table 1 are simply a reflection of unequal scholastic achievement in high school and do not reflect any *additional* social-class inequalities peculiar to the process of college admission. This view, so comforting to the admissions personnel in our elite universities, is unsupported by the available data, some of which is presented in Table 4. Access to a college education is highly unequal, even for children of the same measured 'academic ability'.

The social-class inequalities in our school system and the role they play in the reproduction of the social division of labor are too evident to be denied. Defenders of the educational system are forced back on the assertion that things are getting better, that inequalities of the past were far worse. And, indeed, some of the inequalities of the past have undoubtedly been mitigated. Yet, new inequalities have apparently developed to take their place, for the available historical evidence lends little support to the idea that our schools are on the road to equality of educational opportunity. For example, data from a recent US Census survey reported in Table 5 indicate that graduation from college has become increasingly

19. Calculation based on data in Coleman *et al.* (1966), and methods described in Bowles (1970a).

dependent on one's class background. This is true despite the fact that the probability of high school graduation is becoming increasingly equal across social classes. On balance, the available data suggest that the number of years of schooling attained by a child depends upon the social-class standing of his father at least as much in the recent period as it did fifty years ago.[20]

Table 4 Probability of college entry for a male who has reached grade 11

| Ability quartiles[a] | Socioeconomic quartiles[a] | | | |
| | Low | | | High |
	1	2	3	4
low 1	0·06	0·12	0·13	0·26
2	0·13	0·15	0·29	0·36
3	0·25	0·34	0·45	0·65
high 4	0·48	0·70	0·73	0·87

Source: Based on a large sample of US high school students as reported in Flannagan and Cooley (1966)
[a] The socioeconomic index is a composite measure including family income, father's occupation and education, mother's education, etc. The ability scale is a composite of tests measuring general academic aptitude

The argument that our 'egalitarian' education compensates for inequalities generated elsewhere in the capitalist system is so patently fallacious that few persist in maintaining it. But the discrepancy between the ideology and the reality of the US school system is far greater than would appear from a passing glance at the above data. In the first place, if education is to compensate for the social-class immobility caused by the inheritance of wealth and privilege, education must be structured so as to yield a negative correlation between social-class background of the child and the quantity and quality of his schooling. Thus, the assertion that education compensates for inequalities in inherited wealth and privilege, is falsified not so much by the extent of the social-class inequalities in the school system as by their very existence, or, more correctly, by the absence of compensatory inequalities.

Moreover, if we turn from the problem of intergenerational immobility to the problem of inequality of income at a given moment, a similar

20. See Blau and Duncan (1967). More recent data do not contradict the evidence of no trend toward equality. A 1967 Census survey, the most recent available, shows that among high school graduates in 1965, the probability of college attendance for those whose parents had attended college has continued to rise relative to the probability of college attendance for those whose parents had attended less than eight years of school. See US Bureau of the Census (1969, no. 185).

Table 5 Among sons who had reached high school, percentage who graduated from college, by son's age and father's level of education

Son's age in 1962	Likely dates of college graduation[a]	Father's education						
		Less than 8 years	Some high school		High school graduate		Some college or more	
			Per cent graduating	Ratio to <8	Per cent graduating	Ratio to <8	Per cent graduating	Ratio to <8
25–34	1950–59	7·6	17·4	2·29	25·6	3·37	51·9	6·83
35–44	1940–49	8·6	11·9	1·38	25·3	2·94	53·9	6·27
45–54	1930–39	7·7	9·8	1·27	15·1	1·96	36·9	4·79
55–64	1920–29	8·9	9·8	1·10	19·2	2·16	29·8	3·35

Source: Based on US Census data as reported in Spady (1967)
[a] Assuming college graduation at age 22

argument applies. In a capitalist economy, the increasing importance of schooling in the economy exercises a disequalizing tendency on the distribution of income even in the absence of social-class inequalities in quality and quantity of schooling. To see why this is so, consider a simple capitalist economy in which only two factors are used in production: uneducated and undifferentiated labor, and capital, the ownership of which is unequally distributed among the population. The only source of income inequality in this society is the unequal distribution of capital. As the labor force becomes differentiated by type of skill or schooling, inequalities in labor earnings contribute to total income inequality, augmenting the inequalities inherent in the concentration of capital. This will be the case even if education and skills are distributed randomly among the population. The disequalizing tendency will of course be intensified if the owners of capital also acquire a disproportionate amount of those types of education and training which confer access to high-paying jobs.[21] A substantial negative correlation between the ownership of capital and the quality and quantity of schooling received would have been required merely to neutralize the disequalizing effect of the rise of schooling as an economic phenomenon.

21. A simple statistical model will elucidate the main relationships involved. Let y (individual or family income) be the sum of w (earnings from labor, including embodied education and skills, L) and k (earnings from capital, K), related according to the equation $y = w+k = aK^A L^B$. The coefficients A and B represent the relative importance of capital and labor as sources of income. The variance of the logarithm of income (a common measure of inequality) can then be represented by the following expression:

var log $y = A^2$var log $K + B^2$var log $L + 2AB$ covar (log L, log K).

The first term on the right represents the contribution of inequalities in capital ownership to total inequality, the second measures that part of total income inequality due to inequalities of education and skills embodied in labor, and the third represents the contribution to income inequality of social class inequalities in the supply of skills and schooling. Prior to the educational differentiation of the labor force, the variance of labor was zero. All workers were effectively equal. The variance of the logarithm of income would then be due entirely to capital inequality and would be exactly equal to A^2var log K. The rise of education as a source of income and labor differentiation will increase the variance of the logarithm of embodied labor unless all workers receive identical education and training. This is true even if the third term is zero, indicating no social class inequalities in the provision of skills and education.

To assert the conventional faith in the egalitarian influence of the rising economic importance of education, one would have to argue that the rise of education is likely to be associated with either (1) a fall in A, the relative importance of capital as a source of earnings; (2) a decrease in the size of the covariance of the logarithms of capital and labor; (3) a decrease in the inequality of capital ownerships; or (4) an increase in equality in the supply of education. While each is possible, I see no compelling reason why education should *produce* these results.

And while some research has minimized the importance of social-class biases in schooling (see, for example, Hauser, 1970), nobody has yet suggested that class and schooling were inversely related!

Class culture and class power

The pervasive and persistent inequalities in American education would seem to refute an interpretation of education that asserts its egalitarian functions. But the facts of inequality do not by themselves suggest an alternate explanation. Indeed, they pose serious problems of interpretation. If the costs of education borne by students and their families were very high, or if nepotism were rampant, or if formal segregation of pupils by social class were practiced, or if educational decisions were made by a select few whom we might call the power elite, it would not be difficult to explain the continued inequalities in US education. The problem of interpretation, however, is to reconcile the above empirical findings with the facts of our society as we perceive them: public and virtually tuition-free education at all levels, few legal instruments for the direct implementation of class segregation, a limited role for 'contacts' or nepotism in the achievement of high status or income, a commitment (at the rhetorical level at least) to equality of educational opportunity, and a system of control of education which, if not particularly democratic, extends far beyond anything resembling a power elite. The attempt to reconcile these apparently discrepant facts leads to a consideration of the social division of labor, the associated class cultures, and the exercise of class power.

I will argue that the social division of labor – based on the hierarchical structure of production – gives rise to distinct class subcultures. The values, personality traits and expectations characteristic of each subculture are transmitted from generation to generation through class differences in family socialization and complementary differences in the type and amount of schooling ordinarily attained by children of various class positions. These class differences in schooling are maintained in large measure through the capacity of the upper class to control the basic principles of school finance, pupil evaluation and educational objectives. This outline, and what follows, is put forward as an interpretation, consistent where testable with the available data, though lacking as yet in firm empirical support for some important links in the argument.

The social relations of production characteristic of advanced capitalist societies (and many socialist societies) are most clearly illustrated in the bureaucracy and hierarchy of the modern corporation.[22] Occupational

22. Max Weber referred to bureaucracy as the 'most rational offspring' of discipline, and remarked: '. . . military discipline is the ideal model for the modern capitalist factory . . .' (Weber, 1958, p. 261).

roles in the capitalist economy may be grouped according to the degree of independence and control exercised by the person holding the job. Some evidence exists that the personality attributes associated with the adequate performance of jobs in occupational categories defined in this broad way differ considerably, some apparently requiring independence and internal discipline, and others emphasizing such traits as obedience, predictability and willingness to subject oneself to external controls.[23]

These personality attributes are developed primarily at a young age, both in the family and, to a lesser extent, in secondary socializing institutions such as schools (see, for example, Bloom, 1964). Because people tend to marry within their own class (in part because spouses often meet in our class-segregated schools), both parents are likely to have a similar set of these fundamental personality traits. Thus, children of parents occupying a given position in the occupational hierarchy grow up in homes where child-rearing methods and perhaps even the physical surroundings tend to develop personality characteristics appropriate to adequate job performance in the occupational roles of the parents.[24] The children of managers and professionals are taught self-reliance within a broad set of constraints (see Winterbottom, 1953; Kohn, 1963); the children of production-line workers are taught obedience.

Although this relation between parents' class position and child's personality attributes operates primarily in the home, it is reinforced by schools and other social institutions. Thus, to take an example introduced earlier, the authoritarian social relations of working-class high schools complement the discipline-oriented early socialization patterns experienced by working-class children. The relatively greater freedom of wealthy suburban schools extends and formalizes the early independence training characteristic of upper-class families.

Schools reinforce other aspects of family socialization as well. The aspirations and expectations of students and parents concerning both the type and the amount of schooling are strongly related to social class (see, for example, Lipset and Bendix, 1959; Iwand and Stoyle, 1970). The expectations of teachers, guidance counselors and school administrators ordinarily reinforce those of the students and parents. Schools often encourage

23. For a survey of the literature see Robinson, Athanasiou and Head (1969).
24. Note, for example, the class differences in child rearing with respect to the importance of obedience. See Kohn (1964) and Dolger and Ginandes (1946). See also the study of differences in child-rearing practices in families headed by bureaucrats as opposed to entrepreneurs by Miller and Swanson (1958). Also Maccoby, Gibbs et al. (1954). While the existence of class differences in child rearing is supported by most of the available data (but see Lewis, 1965), the stability of these differences over time has been questioned by Bronfenbrenner (1963).

students to develop aspirations and expectations typical of their social class, even if the child tends to have 'deviant' aspirations.

It is true that to some extent schools introduce common elements of socialization for all students regardless of social class. Discipline, respect for property, competition and punctuality are part of the implicit curriculum of virtually all schools. Yet, given the existing institutional arrangements, the ability of a school to change a child's personality, values and expectations is severely limited. The responsiveness of children to different types of schooling seems to depend importantly upon the types of personality traits, values and expectations developed through the family. Furthermore, children spend a small amount of time in school – less than one-quarter of their waking hours over the course of a year. Thus schools are probably more effective when they attempt to complement and reinforce rather than to oppose the socialization processes of the home and neighborhood. It is not surprising, then, that social-class differences in scholastic achievement and other measures of school success are far greater than would be accounted for by differences in the measured school financial resources and other inputs (quality and quantity of teachers, etc.) alone (Bowles, 1970b).

In this interpretation class differences in the total effect of schooling are primarily the result of differences in what I have called class subculture. The educational system serves less to change the results of the primary socialization in the home than to ratify them and render them in adult form. The complementary relationship between family socialization and schools serves to reproduce patterns of class culture from generation to generation.

The operation of the labor market translates differences in class culture into income inequalities and occupational hierarchies. The personality traits, values and expectations characteristic of different class cultures play a major role in determining an individual's success in gaining a high income or prestigious occupation. The apparent contribution of schooling to occupational success and higher income seems to be explained primarily by the personality characteristics of those who have higher educational attainments.[25] Although the rewards to intellectual capacities are quite limited in the labor market (except for a small number of high-level jobs), mental abilities are important in getting ahead in school. Grades, the probability of continuing to higher levels of schooling, and a host of other school success variables are positively correlated with 'objective' measures of intellectual capacities. Partly for this reason, one's experience in school reinforces the belief that promotion and rewards are distributed fairly. The

25 This view is elaborated in Gintis (1971). For other studies stressing the noncognitive dimensions of the schooling experience, see Parsons (1959); Dreeben (1968).

close relationship between educational attainments and later occupational success thus provides a meritocratic appearance to mask the mechanisms that reproduce the class system from generation to generation.

So far, the perpetuation of inequality through the schooling system has been represented as an almost automatic, self-enforcing mechanism, operating only through the medium of class culture. An important further dimension of the interpretation is added if we note that positions of control in the productive hierarchy tend to be associated with positions of political influence. Given the disproportionate share of political power held by the upper class and their capacity to determine the accepted patterns of behavior and procedures, to define the national interest, and in general to control the ideological and institutional context in which educational decisions are made, it is not surprising to find that resources are allocated unequally among school tracks, between schools serving different classes, and between levels of schooling. The same configuration of power results in curricula, methods of instruction, and criteria of selection and promotion that confer benefits disproportionately on the children of the upper class.

It is not asserted here that the upper class controls the main decision-making bodies in education, although a good case could probably be made that this is so. The power of the upper class is hypothesized as existing in its capacity to define and maintain a set of rules of operation or decision criteria – 'rules of the game' – which, though often seemingly innocuous and sometimes even egalitarian in their ostensible intent, have the effect of maintaining the unequal system.

The operation of two prominent examples of these rules of the game will serve to illustrate the point. The first important principle is that excellence in schooling should be rewarded. Given the capacity of the upper class to define excellence in terms on which upper-class children tend to excel (e.g., scholastic achievement), adherence to this principle yields inegalitarian outcomes (e.g., unequal access to higher education) while maintaining the appearance of fair treatment.[26] Thus the principle of rewarding excellence serves to legitimize the unequal consequences of schooling by associating success with competence. At the same time, the institution of objectively administered tests of performance serves to allow a limited amount of

26. Those who would defend the 'reward excellence' principle on the grounds of efficient selection to ensure the most efficient use of educational resources might ask themselves: why should colleges admit those with the highest college entrance examination board scores? Why not the lowest, or the middle? According to conventional standards of efficiency, the rational social objective of the college is to render the greatest *increment* in individual capacities ('value added', to the economist), not to produce the most illustrious graduating class ('gross output'). Yet if incremental gain is the objective, it is far from obvious that choosing from the top is the best policy.

upward mobility among exceptional children of the lower class, thus providing further legitimation of the operations of the social system by giving some credence to the myth of widespread mobility.

The second example is the principle that elementary and secondary schooling should be financed in very large measure from local revenues. This principle is supported on the grounds that it is necessary to preserve political liberty. Given the degree of residential segregation by income level, the effect of this principle is to produce an unequal distribution of school resources among children of different classes. Towns with a large tax base can spend large sums for the education of their disproportionately upper-class children, without suffering a higher-than-average tax rate.[27] Because the main resource inequalities in schooling thus exist between, rather than within, school districts,[28] and because no effective mechanism exists for redistribution of school funds among school districts, poor families lack a viable political strategy for correcting the inequality.[29]

The above rules of the game – rewarding 'excellence' and financing schools locally – illustrate the complementarity between the political and economic power of the upper class. In each case, adherence to the rule has the effect of generating unequal consequences via a mechanism that operates largely outside the political system. As long as one adheres to the 'reward excellence' principle, the responsibility for unequal results in schooling appears to lie outside the upper class, often in some fault of the poor – such as their class culture, which is viewed as lying beyond the reach of political action or criticism. Likewise, as long as the local financing of schools is maintained, the achievement of equality of resources among children of different social classes requires the class integration of school districts, an objective for which there are no effective political instruments as long as we allow a market in residential properties and an unequal distribution of income.

Thus, the consequences of an unequal distribution of political power among classes appear to complement the results of class culture in maintaining an educational system that has been capable of transmitting status from generation to generation, and capable in addition of political survival in the formally democratic and egalitarian environment of the contemporary United States.

27. Some dimensions of this problem are discussed in S. Weiss (1970).
28. Recall that Owen, whose data appear in Table 3, found that the relationship of various measures of teacher quality to the family income level of the area served by the schools was considerably higher between cities than within cities.
29. In 1969, federal funds constituted only 7 per cent of the total financing of public elementary and secondary schooling. Moreover, current distribution formulas governing state and federal expenditures are only mildly egalitarian in their impact. See Simon and Grant (1969).

The role of the schools in reproducing and legitimizing the social division of labor has recently been challenged by popular egalitarian movements. At the same time, the educational system is showing signs of internal structural weakness (see Bowles, 1971). These two developments suggest that fundamental change in the schooling process may soon be possible. Analysis of both the potential and the limits of educational change will be facilitated by drawing together and extending the strands of our argument.

The limits of educational reform

If the above attempt to identify the roots of inequality in American education is convincing, it has done more than reconcile apparent discrepancies between the democratic forms and the unequal content of that education. For it is precisely the sources of educational inequality which we must understand in order to develop successful political strategies in the pursuit of educational equality.

I have argued that the structure of education reflects the social relations of production. For at least the past 150 years, expansion of education and changes in the forms of schooling have been responses to needs generated by the economic system. The sources of present inequality in American education were found in the mutual reinforcement of class subcultures and social-class biases in the operations of the school system itself. The analysis strongly suggests that educational inequalities are rooted in the basic institutions of our economy. Reconsideration of some of the basic mechanisms of educational inequality lends support to this proposition. First, the principle of rewarding academic excellence in educational promotion and selection serves not only to legitimize the process by which the social division of labor is reproduced. It is also a basic part of the process that socializes young people to work for external rewards and encourages them to develop motivational structures fit for the alienating work of the capitalist economy (Gintis, 1971). Selecting students from the bottom or the middle of the achievement scale for promotion to higher levels of schooling would go a long way toward equalizing education, but it would also jeopardize the schools' capacity to train productive and well-adjusted workers.[30] Second, the way in which local financing of schools operates to maintain educational inequality is also rooted in the capitalist economy, in this case in the existence of an unequal distribution of income, free markets in residential property, and the narrow limits of state power. It seems unwise to emphasize this aspect of the long-run problem of equality in education, however, for the inequalities in school resources resulting from the localization of finance may not be of crucial importance in maintaining

30. Consider what would happen to the internal discipline of schools if the students' objective were to end up at the bottom of the grade distribution!

inequalities in the effects of education. Moreover, a significant under-mining of the principle of local finance may already be underway in response to pressures from the poorer states and school districts.

Of greater importance in the perpetuation of educational inequality are differential class subcultures. These class-based differences in personality, values and expectations, I have argued, represent an adaptation to the different requirements of adequate work performance at various levels in the hierarchical social relations of production. Class subcultures, then, stem from the everyday experiences of workers in the structure of production characteristic of capitalist societies.

It should be clear by this point that educational equality cannot be achieved through changes in the school system alone. Nonetheless, attempts at educational reform may move us closer to that objective if, in their failure, they lay bare the unequal nature of our school system and destroy the illusion of unimpeded mobility through education. Successful educational reforms – reducing racial or class disparities in schooling, for example – may also serve the cause of equality of education, for it seems likely that equalizing access to schooling will challenge the system either to make good its promise of rewarding educational attainment or to find ways of coping with a mass disillusionment with the great panacea.[31]

Yet, if the record of the last 150 years of educational reforms is any guide, we should not expect radical change in education to result from the efforts of those confining their attention to the schools. The political victories of past reform movements have apparently resulted in little if any effective equalization. My interpretation of the educational consequences of class culture and class power suggests that these educational reform movements failed because they sought to eliminate educational inequalities without challenging the basic institutions of capitalism.

Efforts to equalize education through changes in government policy will at best scratch the surface of inequality. For much of the inequality in American education has its origin outside the limited sphere of state power, in the hierarchy of work relations and the associated differences in class culture. As long as jobs are defined so that some have power over many and others have power over none – as long as the social division of labor persists – educational inequality will be built into society in the United States.

31. The failure of the educational programs of the War on Poverty to raise significantly the incomes of the poor is documented in Ribich (1968). In the case of blacks, dramatic increases in the level of schooling in relation to whites have scarcely affected the incomes of blacks relative to whites. See R. Weiss (1970). It is no wonder that Booker T. Washington's plea that blacks should educate themselves before demanding equality has lost most of its once widespread support.

References

ARIES, P. (1965), *Centuries of Childhood*, Vintage Books.

BAILYN, B. (1960), *Education in the Forming of American Society*, University of North Carolina Press.

BINSTOCK, J. (1971), 'Survival in the American college industry', unpublished.

BLAU, P. M., and DUNCAN, O. D. (1967), *The American Occupational Structure*, Wiley.

BLOOM, B. (1964), *Stability and Change in Human Characteristics*, Wiley.

BOWLES, S. (1970a), 'Schooling and inequality from generation to generation', Paper presented at the Far Eastern Meetings of the Econometric Society, Tokyo.

BOWLES, S. (1970b), 'Toward an educational production function', in W. L. Hansen (ed.), *Education, Income and Human Capital*, National Bureau of Economic Research.

BOWLES, S. (1971), 'Contradictions in US higher education', unpublished.

BRONFENBRENNER, U. (1963), 'Socialization and social class through time and space', in W. W. Kallenbach and H. M. Hodges (eds.), *Education and Society*, C. E. Merrill.

BRUCK, D. I. (1971), 'The schools of Lowell, 1824–1861: A case study in the origins of modern public education in America', senior thesis, Harvard College, Department of Social Studies, April.

CALLAHAN, R. (1962), *Education and the Cult of Efficiency*, University of Chicago Press.

CARLTON, F. T. (1966), *Economic Influences upon Educational Progress in the United States, 1820–1850*, Teachers College Press.

CIPOLLA, C. (1969), *Literacy and Economic Development*, Penguin.

COHEN, D., and LAZERSON, M. (1970), 'Education and the industrial order', unpublished.

COHEN, S. (1968), 'The industrial education movement, 1906–1917', *Amer. Quart.*, vol. 20, pp. 95–110.

COLEMAN, J. S., *et al.* (1966), *Equality of Educational Opportunity*, vol. 2, US Office of Education, Washington.

CREMIN, L. (1961), *The Transformation of the School: Progressivism in American Education, 1876–1957*, Knopf.

DOLGER, L., and GINANDES, J. (1946), 'Children's attitudes towards discipline as related to socioeconomic status', *J. exp. Educ.*, vol. 15, pp. 161 5.

DREEBEN, R. (1968), *On What is Learned in School*, Addison-Wesley.

ELSON, W. H., and BACHMAN, F. P. (1910), 'Different course for elementary school', *Educ. Rev.*, vol. 39, pp. 361–3.

ENGELS, F. (1968), *The Condition of the Working Class in England*, Stanford University Press.

ENGELS, F., and MARX, K. (1951), *The Communist Manifesto*, Allen & Unwin.

FLANNAGAN, J. C., and COOLEY, W. W. (1966), *Project TALENT, One Year Follow-up Studies*, Cooperative Research Project no. 2333, School of Education, University of Pittsburgh.

FRIEDENBERG, E. Z. (1965), *Coming of Age in America*, Random House.

GINTIS, H. (1971), 'Education, technology and worker productivity', *American Economic Association Proceedings*, vol. 61, pp. 266–79.

HANSEN, W. L., and WEISBROD, B. (1970), 'The distribution of costs and direct benefits of public higher education: the case of California', *J. Human Resources*, vol. 5, pp. 361–70.

HAUSER, R. (1970), 'Educational stratification in the United States', *Sociol. Inqu.*, vol. 40, pp. 102–29.

HOLLINGSHEAD, A. B. (1949), *Elmstown's Youth*, Wiley.

IWAND, T., and STOYLE, J. (1970), 'Social rigidity: income and occupational choice in rural Pennsylvania', *Econ. bus. Bull.*, vol. 22, pp. 25–30.

KATZ, M. B. (1968), *The Irony of Early School Reform*, Harvard University Press.

KATZ, M. B. (1970), 'From voluntarism to bureaucracy in US education', unpublished.

KEARNEY, H. F. (1971), *Scholars and Gentlemen; Universities and Society in Pre-Industrial Britain*, Cornell University Press.

KENYATTA, J. (1962), *Facing Mount Kenya*, Vintage Books.

KOHN, M. (1963), 'Social class and parent–child relationships: an interpretation', *Amer. J. Sociol.*, vol. 68, pp. 471–80.

KOHN, M. (1964), 'Social class and parental values', in R. Coser (ed.), *The Family*, St Martin's Press.

LEWIS, H. (1965), 'Child-rearing among low-income families', in L. Ferman *et al.* (eds.), *Poverty in America*, University of Michigan Press.

LIPSET, S. M., and BENDIX, R. (1959), *Social Mobility in Industrial Society*, University of California Press.

MACCOBY, E. E., GIBBS, P. K., *et al.* (1954), 'Methods of child-rearing in two social classes', in W. E. Martin and C. B. Stendler (eds.), *Readings in Child Development*, Harcourt Brace & World.

MARX, K. (1935), *The 18th Brumaire of Louis Bonaparte*, International Publishers.

MILLER, D., and SWANSON, G. (1958), *The Changing American Parent*, Wiley.

MORGAN, E. S. (1966), *The Puritan Family: Religion and Domestic Relations in Seventeenth Century New England*, Harper & Row.

OWEN, J. D. (1972a), 'The distribution of educational resources in large American cities', *J. human Resources*, vol. 7, pp. 26–38.

OWEN, J. D. (1972b), 'Towards a public employment wage theory: some econometric evidence on teacher quality', *Ind. lab. Rel. Rev.*, vol. 25, pp. 213–22.

PARSONS, T. (1959), 'The school class as a social system: some of its functions in American society', *Harvard educ. Rev.*, vol. 29, pp. 297–318.

REICH, M. (1971), 'The evolution of the US labor force', in R. Edwards, M. Reich and T. Weisskopf (eds.), *The Capitalist System*, Prentice-Hall.

RIBICH, T. (1968), *Education and Poverty*, Brookings Institute, Washington.

ROBINSON, J. P., ATHANASIOU, R., and HEAD, K. (1969), 'Measures of occupational attitudes and occupational characteristics', Survey Research Center, University of Michigan.

ROSENTHAL, R., and JACOBSON, L. (1968), *Pygmalion in the Classroom*, Holt, Rinehart & Winston.

SCHAFER, W. E., OLEXA, C., and POLK, K. (1970), 'Programmed for social class: tracking in high school', *Trans-action*, vol. 7, no. 12, pp. 39–46.

SEXTON, P. C. (1961), *Education and Income*, Viking Press.

SIMON, B. (1960), *Studies in the History of Education, 1780–1870*, vol. 1, Lawrence & Wishart.

SIMON, K. A., and GRANT, W. V. (1969), *Digest of Educational Statistics, 1969*, Department of Health, Education and Welfare, Washington.

SMELSER, N. J. (1959), *Social Change in the Industrial Revolution*, University of Chicago Press.

SPADY, W. G. (1967), 'Educational mobility and access: growth and paradoxes', *Amer, J. Sociol.*, vol. 73, pp. 273–86.

THERNSTROM, S. (1964), *Poverty and Progress: Social Mobility in a 19th Century City*, Harvard University Press.

US BUREAU OF THE CENSUS (1962), *1960 Census of Population*, PC-2(5a), Government Printing Office, Washington.

US BUREAU OF THE CENSUS (1969), *Current Population Reports*, Series P-20, Government Printing Office, Washington.

US OFFICE OF EDUCATION (1969), *Digest of Educational Statistics, 1969*, Government Printing Office, Washington.

WARNER, W. L., and LUNT, P. S. (1941), *The Social Life of a Modern Community*, Yale University Press.

WEBER, M. (1958), 'The meaning of discipline', in H. H. Gerth and C. W. Mills (eds.), *From Max Weber: Essays in Sociology*, Oxford University Press.

WEISS, R. (1970), 'The effects of education on the earnings of blacks and whites', *Rev. Econ. Stat.*, vol. 52, pp. 150–59.

WEISS, S. (1970), 'Existing disparities in public school finance and proposals for reform', Research Report to the Federal Reserve Bank of Boston, no. 46, February.

WINTERBOTTOM, M. (1953), 'The sources of achievement motivation in mothers' attitudes toward independence training', in D. C. McClelland *et al.* (eds.), *The Achievement Motive*, Appleton-Century-Crofts.

16 R. Boudon

Social Mobility in Utopia

Excerpts from R. Boudon, 'Essai sur la mobilité sociale en Utopie', *Quality and Quantity*, vol. 4, 1970, pp. 213–42. Translated by Howard Davis.

Studies of social mobility are an especially good starting-point for epistemological and methodological reflection on the current state of sociology. On the one hand because such studies are very numerous (as can be seen from an inspection of the bibliographies compiled by Capecchi, 1967, and earlier by McRae, 1953–4; Pfautz, 1952; Rogoff, 1950; or Floud, 1950). On the other hand 'empirical' studies of social mobility give an impression of being repetitive rather than cumulative, (as Capecchi, 1967, and Bertaux, n.d., have observed) while the relation between these empirical studies and the theories outlined by various authors, whether those of Sorokin (1927), Parsons (1953), Davis and Moore (1945), or of others, more often than not appears to be either very unclear or non-existent.

These difficulties are seen to be particularly acute by several authors of important empirical work on social mobility. G. Carlsson (1961) underlines the methodological obstacles which make international comparisons and study of trends in social mobility especially difficult. Svalastoga (1959) describes the character of measures of social 'status'[1] as necessarily crude. [. . .]

The uncertainty of the relationship between theory and empirical research is self-evident. For instance, Svalastoga maintains a functionalist perspective, adapted from Sorokin, Parsons and Davis and Moore, whilst Carlsson rejects it. Both Svalastoga and Sorokin hold that the functioning of societies demands that optimal mobility rates be located midway between a minimum and a maximum. Carlsson, by contrast, is inclined to think that they are rather the outcome of power relations between classes. But one would search in vain in the empirical data produced by either of the two authors for confirmation of one or other of these two theories – even assuming that it is appropriate to speak of 'theory' here.

Sociologists' continuing ignorance on questions of mobility, despite the

---

1. Studies of intragenerational mobility by Roger Girod show particularly clearly the benefits to be gained from a more precise and 'theory conscious' definition of professional categories than is currently used. See for example Girod (1970).

accumulation of empirical research, has been exposed in a spectacular way in a famous article by Anderson (1961). Having re-analysed three studies which related to the United States, Sweden and Great Britain, Anderson arrived at the conclusion that, whilst these studies have some useful content, it is evident that schooling has much less influence on mobility than is generally believed. Of particular relevance is the table which he obtained from a study carried out by Centers (1949) on a sample of 416 people, and which is reproduced below. This table shows the social status of the son relative to that of the father, as a function of the level of schooling of the son compared to that of the father (Table 1).

Table 1 Distribution of son's socioeconomic status and education relative to father's, from Centers (1949) (cited by Anderson, 1961)

| Son's education relative to father's | Son's status relative to father's | | | |
	Higher	Same	Lower	Total
higher	134	96	61	291
same	23	33	24	80
lower	7	16	22	45
total	164	145	107	416

An elementary statistical analysis of this table shows that it approximates more closely to a model which assumes that the two variables are independent than to a model which assumes maximal dependence between the son's status and his education relative to his father's.[2]

We will see later that a table such as this, despite appearances to the contrary, *may not be incompatible with the hypothesis of maximal influence of schooling on mobility*. But we will postpone the examination of this point to underline the critical importance of Anderson's article: it allows us to grasp the fact that, despite the accumulation of research, we are incapable of answering a question as crucial, and yet as apparently elementary, as knowing whether schooling is or is not an important determinant of mobility in the sort of societies we live in. Why is this so?

There is no easy answer to this question, which suggests the need for inquiries which take into account aspects relevant to history, sociology, and to the philosophy of the social sciences. We have provided several approaches to this subject in two earlier publications, and we propose to systematize these in an article currently in preparation (Boudon, 1969;

2. The *independence* model is based upon the usual statistical definition of independence $(n_{ij}/N) = (n_i/N)(n_j/N)$. [. . .] Thus under this hypothesis, the estimate of element (1,1) is $115 = 291(164/416)$. Under the second hypothesis, it is equal to $164 = \min(291,164)$. (See Anderson, 1961, Appendix 1). [Eds.]

in press). We will also leave aside the general epistemological problem posed by research into social mobility in order to concentrate on one point in particular: we will attempt to show that a breakthrough in this field might occur if more care was taken, prior to the analysis of empirical data, to establish theoretical schemes in a language that makes it possible to establish a connection between theory and data. If, in other words, one is prepared to regard social mobility data not as facts which can be read straight off, but as having arisen from *processes* which develop within specific social *systems*. This implies that an effort be made to represent these *processes* as accurately as possible. Since Sorokin (1927), it has been known that individuals are successively 'filtered' through a set of *selection agencies* (family, school, etc.) in terms of certain rules, which vary from one social system to another. [. . .]

We will look at several idealized cases which correspond to social systems endowed *with two selection agencies*: the family and the school. In doing this we will try to follow through a number of efforts which have been made to lay the foundations of a formal analysis of systems of intergenerational social circulation in society, and especially those of Bertaux (1969, pp. 454–66).

The system of intergenerational circulation in Utopia

Our concern here will be to analyse the phenomena of mobility, and the relations between schooling and mobility in particular, in a country well-known to the sociologist: Utopia.

At a certain period in the history of Utopia, the social system and the educational system were governed by simple rules, which can be described in the following way:

1 The population of the country is divided into three classes: C_1, the lower; C_2, the middle; C_3, the upper.

2 In the period under consideration there is no perceptible change in the distribution of the population between these three classes.

3 Three levels of schooling can be distinguished in Utopia: S_1, lower; S_2, middle; S_3, higher.

4 In the past, Utopian society was characterized by the fact that for the most part the people were either C_1S_1 (lower class, low level of schooling), or C_2S_2 (middle class, medium level of schooling), or C_3S_3 (upper class, advanced level of schooling). It was rare to find C_1S_2 or C_2S_1 individuals, for example. This was because the level of schooling was to a large extent both a means of perpetuating social distinctions and also a sign of those distinctions. Today, this state of affairs is still far from being eradicated. On the contrary, by means of the complex mechanisms which we cannot

enlarge upon here, society does its best to keep a high level of correlation between C and S. In other words, society seeks to ensure that the majority of individuals are C_1S_1, C_2S_2, or C_3S_3 and that the number of C_1S_3, C_3S_1, C_3S_2, etc., individuals is kept to a minimum. In short, Utopia is characterized by a marked inequality of access to education in terms of social class.

5 Various factors, which we cannot dwell upon here, have led Utopia to opt for a regular increase in the rates of educational provision.

6 The industrial, technical and scientific development of the country has meant that educational achievement plays an important role in determining the class to which an individual will belong at the end of his school career. [. . .]

We shall defer the question of how far the general rules of Utopia can be considered as applicable to our society and look at their consequences for the processes of social mobility in that country.

Since empirical studies are extremely rare in Utopia, we will not try to find tables of relevant data and will proceed directly by the method of deduction.

The model which follows is obtained from a specification based on the above propositions. [. . .]

Model 1

(a) We assume first of all, in accordance with rules 1 and 2, that the distribution of the population between the three classes C_1, C_2 and C_3 does not vary during the period of investigation. For every 1000 Utopians, 400 belong to class C_1, 400 to class C_2 and 200 to class C_3.

(b) The second assumption is that the social inequalities in education are not only great, but are *as great as they possibly can be* (the meaning of this will be made clear later).

(c) On the other hand, the level of schooling will be ascribed maximum efficacy in determining post-school social status (we will see below what this means).

(d) In accordance with rule 5 we will assume that in each generation there is a growth in the total numbers in S_2 and S_3. To give these ideas some content, let us suppose that the growth rate is 10 per cent. At the outset, for every 1000 Utopians, 400 had reached the level S_1, 400 the level S_2 and 200 the level S_3.

(e) For the moment we will [. . .] assume that fertility is the same for all three classes in the period under consideration.

Together, rules 1 to 6 and (a) to (e) are enough to define a system whose evolution can be 'simulated' for any chosen period. For reasons of common sense, as well as space, we will be content with simulating just a few generations. [. . .]

The situation at the start (generation 1) is summed up in Table 2.

Table 2 Model 1: Relation between social status and level of schooling (generation 1)

	C_1	C_2	C_3	Total
S_1	400	0	0	400
S_2	0	400	0	400
S_3	0	0	200	200
total	400	400	200	1000

This table simply shows the distribution of first generation Utopians in the system of social classes and levels of schooling.

In this first generation we are clearly still at the stage of the kind of system described so well by Schelsky (1957) in which the level of schooling is the sign of social classification.

In the following generation (generation 2), the values which correspond to levels of schooling S_2 and S_3 increase by 10 per cent. For every thousand places in the educational system, there are 440 at level S_2, 220 at level S_3 and, therefore, 340 at level S_1. Then, applying the principle of maximum

Table 3 Allocation of level of schooling to the second generation according to social status of family of origin

	S_1	S_2	S_3	Total
C_1	340	60	0	400
C_2	0	380	20	400
C_3	0	0	200	200
total	340	440	220	1000

inequality in education, we arrive at Table 3. This table shows the distribution of Utopians whose social status, by family is C_1, C_2 or C_3 in the three tiers of the school system, S_1, S_2 and S_3 respectively.

In this table, C_3 individuals have been given priority of place in S_3. The remaining 20 places in S_3 have subsequently been allocated to C_2 individuals. Hence it follows that there can only be 380 who are C_2S_2, since the total number of C_2s is 400. So there are 60 remaining places in S_2 for C_1 individuals. The 340 S_1 places will be filled by C_1s.[3]

Once their education is complete, the second generation Utopians will experience a redefinition of social status. Although until then their status had been that of their family of origin, they now acquire a new status. The distribution of these new statuses follows the principle of the maximum efficacy of education, in accordance with rule (c). Thus the status C_3 will be granted first of all to individuals with a level of schooling S_3, then the excess or shortage will be distributed in the best way until the allocation is complete.

This brings us on to Table 4. Consistent with rule 2, it can be seen that the proportion of Utopians in classes C_1, C_2 and C_3 respectively is identical to that of the preceding generation.

The same principles of construction are used in this table as in the previous one: the 200 places which are available in C_3 are assigned to 200 of the 220 S_3 by virtue of the principle of the maximum efficacy of education. On the other hand, the surplus of S_3 places means that only 20 of them will be filled by C_2s. Proceeding step by step like this leads eventually to Table 4.

Table 4 Allocation of social status
in terms of level of schooling attained
(second generation)

	C_1	C_2	C_3	Total
S_1	340	0	0	340
S_2	60	380	0	440
S_3	0	20	200	220
total	400	400	200	1000

(Notice in passing that this table is the same as the previous one except that the rows and columns have been switched over. As we shall see, this identity will disappear if certain of the model's hypotheses are changed, and especially if the hypothesis of between-class differences of fertility is introduced.)[4]

Let us now examine the mobility which has occurred between generations 1 and 2. Or, in other words, which is the table of intergenerational mobility corresponding to this first experiment?

3. The reader will have noticed that the model introduces certain minor hypotheses which we deliberately avoided referring to earlier. In particular it abolishes any distinctions on the grounds of sex. It also ignores the formal problems posed by the concept of *generation*.
4. The interested reader should refer to the original paper. [Eds.]

We have seen in Table 4 that 200 individuals were attributed with social status C_3 in the second generation. These 200 individuals were drawn from the 220 individuals who reached the S_3 level of schooling in this generation. As Table 3 shows, 200 of these 220 individuals originated from families of C_3 status and 20 from families of C_2 status. As we assumed that status in the second generation was attributable exclusively in terms of attained level of schooling (principle of maximum efficacy of education), we will assume that the 20 individuals excluded from C_3 in the second generation, despite having an S_3 level of schooling, came in the proportion of 20/220 from families of C_2 status and in the proportion of 200/220 from families of C_3 status. It follows from this that, of the 200 C_3s in the second generation, 200 (20/220) $\sim$ 18 come from families of C_2 status and 200 (200/220) $\sim$ 182 from families of C_3 status. We will therefore insert 18 and 182 in the second and third rows of the third column in the table of intergenerational mobility (Table 5).

Of course, the $200 - 182 = 18$ individuals of C_3 family status and of S_3 level of schooling who could not be placed in C_3 will find themselves in C_2 (hypothesis of maximum efficacy of education). The same will be true for the $20 - 18 = 2$ individuals of familial status C_2 and S_3 level of education who could not be classed in C_3: they have the first claim to two places in C_2.

Table 5 Construction of the table of intergenerational mobility between the first and second generation

First generation	Second generation			Total
	C_1	C_2	C_3	
C_1		52		400
C_2		330	18	400
C_3		18	182	200
total	400	400	200	1000

The total number of individuals who have reached the S_2 level of schooling in the second generation is 440. But in the second generation the number of places available in C_2 is only 400 and, moreover, $18 + 2 = 20$ of these 400 places are already occupied by individuals of S_3 level of schooling who could not be classed in C_3. So 380 of the total number of places in C_2 are available for the 440 individuals of S_2 level of schooling. Of these 440 individuals, 60 come from a C_1 family background and 380 from a C_2 background. By virtue of the principle of maximum efficacy of education, we will therefore assume that the 380 places which are available in C_2 in the second generation will revert to the individuals of C_1 social origin in the proportion $60/(60+380) = 60/440$, and to individuals of C_2 social origin in the proportion $380/(60+380) = 380/440$. Hence the number of individuals of C_1 social origin who attain to C_2 status is $380 (60/440) \sim 52$. As for the individuals of C_2 social origin and S_2 level of schooling who are found in C_2, they number $380 (380/440) \sim 328$. Two more individuals should be added to this total of 328, namely those who, it will be remembered, are also of C_2 origin, have the S_3 level of schooling, but who could not be found places in C_3. To sum up, 330 people remain in C_2 from one generation to the next, while 52 people pass from C_1 to C_2.

We can now insert 52 and 330 in the first and second rows of the second column of Table 5.[5]

The completion of the table is therefore quite straightforward (Table 6).

Table 6 Intergenerational mobility between the first and second generation

First generation	Second generation			Total
	C_1	C_2	C_3	
C_1	348	52	0	400
C_2	52	330	18	400
C_3	0	18	182	200
total	400	400	200	1000

The element (1,3), i.e. the element in the first row of the third column, is of course equal to 0, since the total in the 3rd column is equal to 200. It follows that the element (1,1) is equal to $400-52 = 348$, since the element

5. Bertaux (1969) takes up certain suggestions made in particular by Lipset (Lipset and Bendix, 1959, pp. 57ff.) and Rogoff (1953) in her distinction between gross mobility and net mobility, and by Anderson (1961). and applies this kind of 'step by step' analysis to the study of forced mobility which results from the evolution of social structures (distribution of individuals among the social categories). He uses the term 'structural' mobility to refer to the mobility which is a necessary consequence of social structural change between one generation and the next. The present model shows that *structural* mobility can occur even when the social structure remains unchanged from one generation to another. Here, the entire 'observed' mobility is *structural* by definition. It should therefore be understood that the proportion of structural mobility which is claimed to exist in a society is closely dependent on the complexity of the theoretical model of circulation which is used. In our terminology, Bertaux's *structural* mobility is the mobility which we obtain in a social system characterized (1) by the maximal dominance of the upper classes, (2) by the existence of a single agency of selection (in this case the family).

(1,3) is equal to 0. Hence it follows that the element (2,2) is equal to $400 - 348 = 52$.

Lesson one

The first lesson which can be drawn from the model is that, even in a system which is characterized by a radical inequality of social classes in education, some social mobility develops of necessity, provided that the level of schooling reached has a certain efficacy with respect to social rating, and also that the structure of the educational system is less rigid than the social structure.

From this basic statement we can extract the proposition that a system with radical inequality in education does not effectively fulfil the function of reproducing social classes except in special circumstances which are not those of Utopia, since a rigid system of maximum inequality in education is associated there with the downward mobility of elites and upward mobility of less privileged classes. Moreover, these rates of mobility increase steadily, as we shall see below.

It is true that we have made the assumption here of the *maximum* efficacy of education with regard to social classification. But it is easy to show that the foregoing result remains valid *whatever* the assumed degree of efficacy of education. If this efficacy decreases, there is a corresponding decrease in rates of mobility. But they only reach zero if education has no bearing whatsoever on social classification. It is doubtful whether this is so, in Utopia or anywhere else.

It can also be shown by inspection of Table 6 that the hypotheses introduced by the model in fact lead to a system of exchange from one generation to another – between C_1 and C_2 on the one hand, C_2 and C_3 on the other. What we actually see is that 52 individuals have crossed over from $C_1 \to C_2$ and an equal number have taken the opposite path $C_2 \to C_1$. Similarly, 18 individuals have crossed over from $C_2 \to C_3$ and an equal number from $C_3 \to C_2$. A further consequence of this system of exchange is that it puts the middle classes (C_2) in a rather awkward position because their members experience downward movement three times more often than social ascent.

The process continued

It is easy to extend the above procedure to subsequent generations. We will carry it through to the fourth generation. As the working through is the same as above, we will simply set out the tables of fictitious data which derive from the model:

Table 7 Second generation:
allocation of level of schooling
according to class of origin

	S_1	S_2	S_3	Total
C_1	274	126	0	400
C_2	0	358	42	400
C_3	0	0	200	200
total	274	484	242	1000

Table 8 Allocation of new status
according to schooling

	C_1	C_2	C_3	Total
S_1	274	0	0	274
S_2	126	358	0	484
S_3	0	42	200	242
total	400	400	200	1000

Table 9 Intergenerational mobility between
the second and third generation

First generation	Third generation			Total
	C_1	C_2	C_3	
C_1	306	94	0	400
C_2	94	271	35	400
C_3	0	35	165	200
total	400	400	200	1000

Table 10 Third generation:
allocation of level of schooling
according to class of origin

	S_1	S_2	S_3	Total
C_1	202	198	0	400
C_2	0	334	66	400
C_3	0	0	200	200
total	202	532	266	1000

Table 11 Allocation of new status according to schooling

	C_1	C_2	C_3	Total
S_1	202	0	0	202
S_2	198	334	0	532
S_3	0	66	200	266
total	400	400	200	1000

Table 12 Intergenerational mobility between the third and fourth generation

Third generation	Fourth generation			Total
	C_1	C_2	C_3	
C_1	277	123	0	400
C_2	123	227	50	400
C_3	0	50	150	200
total	400	400	200	1000

There is a regular increase in mobility resulting from the regular increase in the rates of schooling. Of course, since on the one hand the only difference between Tables 7 and 10, and between them and Table 3, is in the distribution of levels of schooling, and since on the other we come to the tables of intergenerational mobility by the same principles, these tables are only distinguishable from those for the next generation by the strength of the rates of mobility. As for the mobility structure, it remains unchanged: in particular, the exchanges between C_1 and C_2 and between C_2 and C_3 are still found to occur.

However, it should be noted that as this process develops there is a steady decline in the situation of the elites (increase in the rates of downward mobility), whereas the situation of the middle classes gradually improves. Referring back to the tables of intergenerational mobility, it can be seen that for the C_2 individuals, the *ratio* between rates of downward mobility and rates of upward mobility is decreasing: $52/18 = 2 \cdot 9$, $94/35 = 2 \cdot 7$, $123/50 = 2 \cdot 5$. On the other hand, the *rates* of downward mobility continue to *increase*.

It is clear that in spite of the apparent simplicity of the rules which govern Utopia, the processes of mobility are really quite complicated.

We will have another opportunity to appreciate this complexity in having a second look at the problem posed by Anderson, using our own data as the point of departure.

Anderson's problem

The hypotheses of Model 1 state that:

1 The social inequalities in education are at a maximum;

2 The effect of education on the allocation of social status is at a maximum.

An interesting problem is posed in the form of the relationship between the son's social status relative to the father's and the son's level of schooling relative to the father's. Briefly, it is a matter of reconstructing a table analogous to the Centers–Anderson table, using our own fictitious data as a basis. The reader will recall that this table (Table 1) led Anderson to doubt the efficacy of level of schooling in the determination of social status.

Let us consider the pair formed by the third and fourth generations (Tables 8 to 12).

According to Table 8, there are 200 S_3C_3 individuals in the third generation. According to Table 10, these 200 people have 200 offspring who reach the S_3 level of schooling. Of these 200, according to Table 11, a proportion 66/266 reach the C_2 social position and a proportion 200/266 level C_3. Thus we have:

third generation   fourth generation

$$S_3C_2\left(200 \times \frac{66}{266} = 50\right)$$

$$S_3C_3(200)$$

$$S_3C_3\left(200 \times \frac{200}{266} = 150\right)$$

Let us now consider the 42 people who, according to Table 8, are S_3C_2 in the third generation. Of these 42 people, a proportion 334/400 will be S_2 and a proportion 66/400 will be S_3 (Table 10). From among the S_2s a proportion 198/532 will be C_1 and a proportion 334/532 will be C_2. From the S_3s a proportion 66/266 will be C_2, while a proportion 200/266 will be C_3.

To sum up:

third generation   fourth generation

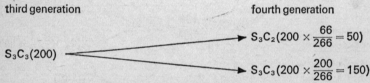

$$C_1\left(35 \times \frac{198}{532} = 13\right)$$

$$S_2\left(42 \times \frac{334}{400} = 35\right)$$

$$C_2\left(35 \times \frac{334}{532} = 22\right)$$

$$S_3C_2(42)$$

$$C_2\left(7 \times \frac{66}{266} = 2\right)$$

$$S_3\left(42 \times \frac{66}{400} = 7\right)$$

$$C_3\left(7 \times \frac{200}{266} = 5\right)$$

The same procedure can be followed quite simply for the other categories of Table 8. We find the following:

third generation   fourth generation

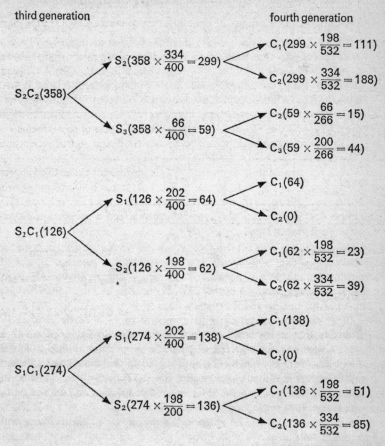

third generation

$S_2C_2(358)$
  $S_2(358 \times \dfrac{334}{400} = 299)$
    $C_1(299 \times \dfrac{198}{532} = 111)$
    $C_2(299 \times \dfrac{334}{532} = 188)$
  $S_3(358 \times \dfrac{66}{400} = 59)$
    $C_2(59 \times \dfrac{66}{266} = 15)$
    $C_3(59 \times \dfrac{200}{266} = 44)$

$S_2C_1(126)$
  $S_1(126 \times \dfrac{202}{400} = 64)$
    $C_1(64)$
    $C_2(0)$
  $S_2(126 \times \dfrac{198}{400} = 62)$
    $C_1(62 \times \dfrac{198}{532} = 23)$
    $C_2(62 \times \dfrac{334}{532} = 39)$

$S_1C_1(274)$
  $S_1(274 \times \dfrac{202}{400} = 138)$
    $C_1(138)$
    $C_2(0)$
  $S_2(274 \times \dfrac{198}{200} = 136)$
    $C_1(136 \times \dfrac{198}{532} = 51)$
    $C_2(136 \times \dfrac{334}{532} = 85)$

We are now in a position to use our fictitious data as a basis for the construction of a table which is structured in the same way as the one which Anderson drew from Centers. This table sets out the relationships between the son's social status relative to the father's, and the son's level of schooling relative to the father's (Table 13 overleaf).

This table is obviously very different from the Anderson–Centers table – but that should be no cause for surprise. The hypotheses which can be formulated with respect to Utopia clearly cannot be transposed in their pure form to the United States.

It has the advantage that it raises an important methodological, even epistemological, question. The fact is that an attempt to interpret the table at its face value suggests that *the level of schooling exerts a weak influence on social mobility*: no more than approximately one half of the Utopians who have a higher level of education than that of their father attain a higher status. On the other hand, a very large proportion of those who have a lower level of education than that of their father retain their original status.

Table 13 Relationship (by deduction from model 1) between son's social status relative to father's and son's level of schooling relative to father's

| Son's level of schooling relative to father's | Social status of son relative to father's | | | |
	Higher	Same	Lower	Total
higher	129	66	50	245
same	44	501	111	656
lower	0	86	13	99
total	173	653	174	1000

However, we know that this table is derived from a model which postulates the *maximal influence of level of education on mobility*. It will be remembered that this hypothesis is expressed in the fact that social status is granted simply by merit of the level of education and the 'places' which are available in each status category.

These observations give rise to a general problem: is it possible to effectively analyse the meaning of a mobility table – whether of the kind which Anderson has drawn from Centers or the more conventional tables of mobility – without having first constructed an analytic schema? We are well aware that in Utopia, as elsewhere, the phenomena of mobility depend on a certain number of basic interdependent variables and consequently form a *system* (temporal evolution of social structure, that is, the distribution of individuals between categories, strata or social classes; temporal evolution of the educational structure, that is, the distribution of individuals between the categories of the educational system; social class differences in fertility; influence of schooling on social mobility; social inequalities in education, etc.). Actual mobility matrices are consequent upon these complex relations which bind the different variables to each other. Are not, then, attempts to interpret them at their face value bound to be arbitrary? Even apparently quite ordinary and straightforward indices which could be formed in this context are not without their pitfalls. Applying Anderson's method for Table 13 it would be possible to create an index of the influence of education on mobility. This would involve locating the structure of Table 13 on a continuum bounded at one extreme by an independence structure and bounded at the other by a structure of maximum efficacy of education (those sons who have a higher level of education have first claim to a higher social status than their father, etc.). Table 13 would appear to approximate more closely to the first than to the second of these extremes. But that does not put us in a position to find out, even approximately, the laws by which Utopia is actually governed.

A whole set of variations can be played on the general theme which was set out in Model 1. It would be possible, for example, to investigate the effects of social class differences in fertility. The hypotheses could be further elaborated by an inquiry into the effects of social structural evolution. [. . .]

It is quite obvious that several of the axioms set out above in the form of *rules* are either caricatures or else schematic in relation to real situations: no system is as thoroughly inegalitarian as that of Utopia. On the other hand, the influence of education on mobility is never at a maximum. These remarks suggest the possibility of further variations: one could assume, for example, that the influence of education on social mobility is inversely related to the diffusion of education. Similarly, it could be assumed that there is progress towards the reduction of inequalities of opportunity in education.

It would be equally possible to weaken the privileges given in the previous model to C_3s relative to C_2s, to C_2s relative to C_1s, to S_3s relative to S_2s, to S_2s relative to S_1s. Until now we have retained the assumption that in the case of competition between S_3 and an S_2, for example, the S_3 would *always* be given preference, but we might be content to assume that this happens *more frequently*. This is certainly more realistic but it has the disadvantage of adding several extra dimensions to the parametric space connected with the model, making the logic of analysis that much more complicated.[6]

The lesson of a journey to Utopia

The major lesson which can be drawn from this sociological outing to Utopia is that one way to give meaning to 'empirical data' on mobility would involve an attempt to give formal expression to the social processes of which these data are the outcome. To date, the efforts of model builders have been more directed towards the structural analysis of the data which has been collected, especially those intergenerational mobility tables (see

6. At an even higher level of complexity, the *more frequently* could be replaced by *with greater probability*. At this stage we would be entering the realm of stochastic models. But it seems reasonable to proceed in an orderly fashion and not to tackle this kind of model until the 'deterministic' models have been adequately dealt with.

for example the studies by Svalastoga, 1959; Carlsson, 1961; or Goodman, 1965).

In our opinion such attempts at formal expression, directly applied to 'empirical data', can only be of limited significance.

Instead, as we have pointed out, it is important first of all to find a way to model the basic social processes, the remote consequences of which are the tables of intergenerational mobility. The issue here, in other words, is to take seriously the obvious sociological evidence that mobility data do not make sense except as the product of a social system and the processes which stem from the social system.

Why is this evidence so regularly ignored in studies of social mobility? There is no straightforward answer and there may well be more than one reason for the phenomenon. It could be to some extent a result of the *atomistic* perspective which accompanied the renewal of 'empirical sociology' after the Second World War. It may also have to do with the common practice of those who engage in empirical sociology in assuming that the meaning of a set of data becomes obvious on reading, provided that suitable indices have been constructed, without first taking care to formulate an explanatory theoretical schema. It is also possible that this phenomenon is a product of the fact that the 'theoretical' language of sociology has not developed at the same rate as empirical research, at least in the area we are concerned with: which explains why a reading of Sorokin's *Social Mobility* still gives the impression of modernity after nearly fifty years. This is because it represents one of those rare attempts in which the sociologist could be said to submit himself to the standards which any scientist subscribes to, being concerned to develop theoretical schemas before approaching the empirical data and being aware of the need to express these schemas in a language such that they can be related to the data.

References

ANDERSON, C. A. (1961), 'A sceptical note on education and mobility', in A. H. Halsey, J. Floud and C. A. Anderson (eds.), *Education, Economy and Society*, Free Press.

BERTAUX, D. (1969), 'Sur l'analyse des tables de mobilité sociale', *Revue française de Sociologie*, vol. 10, pp. 448–90.

BERTAUX, D. (n.d.) 'Nouvelles perspectives sur la mobilité sociale en France', unpublished, CES, Paris.

BOUDON, R. (1969), 'Analyse secondaire et sondage sociologique', *Cahiers internationaux de Sociologie*, vol. 47, pp. 15–34.

BOUDON, R. (in press), 'Notes sur la notion de théorie en sociologie', *Archives Européennes de Sociologie*.

CAPECCHI, V. (1967), 'Problèmes méthodologiques dans la mesure de mobilité sociale', *Archives Européennes de Sociologie*, vol. 8, pp. 285–318.

CARLSSON, G. (1961), *Social Mobility and Class Structure*, Gleerup, Lund, Sweden.

CENTERS, R. (1949), 'Education and occupational mobility', *Amer. Sociol. Rev.*, vol. 14, pp. 143–4.

DAVIS, K., and MOORE, W. E. (1945), 'Some principles of stratification', *Amer. Sociol. Rev.*, vol. 10, pp. 242–9.

FLOUD, J. (1950), 'Educational opportunity and social mobility', *Yearbook of Education*, Evans, pp. 117–36.

GIROD, R. (1970), 'Mobilité en cours de carrière', *Cahiers Vilfredo Pareto*, vol. 22–3, pp. 273–313.

GOODMAN, L. (1965), 'On the statistical analysis of mobility tables', *Amer. J. Sociol.*, vol. 70, pp. 564–85.

LIPSET, S. M., and BENDIX, R. (1959), *Social Mobility in Industrial Society*, University of California Press.

McRAE, D. G. (1953–4), 'Social stratification. A trend report and bibliography', *Current Sociology*, vol. 2, pp. 3–74.

PARSONS, T. (1953), 'A revised analytical approach to the theory of social stratification', in R. Bendix and S. M. Lipset (eds.), *Class, Status and Power*, Free Press, pp. 92–129.

PFAUTZ, H. W. (1952), 'The current literature on social stratification. Critique and bibliography', *Amer. J. Sociol.*, vol. 58, pp. 391–418.

ROGOFF, N. (1950), 'Les recherches americaines sur la mobilité sociale', *Population*, vol. 4, pp. 669–88.

ROGOFF, N. (1953), *Recent Trends in Occupational Mobility*, Free Press.

SCHELSKY, H. (1957), *Schule und Erziehung in der industriellen Gesellschaft*, Werkbund Verlag, Würzburg.

SOROKIN, P. (1927), *Social Mobility*, Harper & Row.

SVALASTOGA, K. (1959), *Prestige, Class and Mobility*, Gyldendal, Copenhagen.

Part Four
Recent Developments

It is widely assumed that, whether governments intend it or not, social mobility is affected by their policies. An obvious case in point here is the assumption behind many social reforms of this century that the extension of educational provision is a natural promoter of mobility and a reducer of inequality. This assumption appears to be false, or at least over-simple, for the cumulative evidence of academic research and government reports in Britain, at least, has recently been summarized as follows:

Social inequalities in access to selective secondary education have been somewhat reduced over the past 50–60 years. But the reduction has, in the first place been small. . . . In the second place, the reduction of social inequalities is not a new, post-1944 phenomenon, but the continuation of a long-term, gradual trend. And in the third place, it has been confined to entry into selective secondary education, while access to the universities has remained more or less unaffected. The general increase of grammar school places has benefited children of all social classes, but working-class children proportionately rather more than others. The general increase of university places has perhaps, if anything, benefited children of the upper and middle strata more than those from the lower stratum. Certainly, the overall expansion of educational facilities has been of greater significance than any redistribution of opportunities (Westergaard and Little, OECD 1967).

In this authoritative review, which considerations of space kept us from reprinting, Westergaard and Little pointed to the persistence of wide differences in educational provision between different local education authorities, and between the state system as a whole and the private school system. Such a focus on educational outcomes (and mobility outcomes) as a function of the allocation of money and resources has been the subject of important recent work in Britain by Byrne and Williamson (1973). The approach taken by Miller and Roby in Reading 17 takes up this theme, in explicit relationship to the ways in which sociologists think of mobility. One important trend then is likely to be in the direction already charted by Miller and by workers at such institutions as the Harvard Center for Educational Policy Research (e.g. Jencks *et al.*, 1972).

More than any other branch of sociology, the study of social mobility has attracted competent statisticians and builders of mathematical models. Of course there is always the temptation to dismiss such approaches as being arid, scientistic or lacking in sociological insight, but this is partly due to the fact that many of us come to sociology through the arts rather than through the sciences and find it difficult to read mathematical arguments sufficiently slowly and carefully to digest their terse elegance. However, the secret is simply to take it slowly, and not to go on to the next line until one has mastered the preceding few.

One of the most common ways of representing the process of occupational mobility is by means of that branch of probability theory known as Markov chains. Pullum provides an overview of this family of models in Reading 18, and shows that, whilst the simplest model is seriously inadequate, it can be modified in various ways to cope with such failings as the persistent overestimation of occupational inheritance. White's approach represents a radical change of focus (Reading 19). He argues that neither individuals nor jobs, taken separately, can provide an adequate unit for studying mobility. When a man moves out of a job, a vacancy occurs. As it is filled, it moves through the occupational system, and the 'vacancy chain' provides a framework for a quite new approach to mobility. In Reading 20 Granovetter's work on channels of mobility information stresses a related point – *weak* social network links are crucial to the individual in obtaining job information and, in turn, individual mobility has the effect of linking different social networks. Duncan's linear causal models represent a different tradition, and though we have not been able to include any of his more recent work to demonstrate developments of the basic life-cycle model outlined in Reading 10, such work is proceeding apace (Duncan, Featherman and Duncan, 1972).

References

BYRNE, D. S., and WILLIAMSON, W. (1973), 'Research, theory and policy in education: some notes on a self-sustaining system', in *Education, Economy and Politics*, Open University Course E352, Block 5, Open University Press.
DUNCAN, O. D., FEATHERMAN, D. L., and DUNCAN, B. (1972), *Socioeconomic Background and Achievement*, Seminar Press.
JENCKS, C., *et al.* (1972), *Inequality: A Reassessment of the Effect of Family and Schooling in America*, Basic Books.
WESTERGAARD, J., and LITTLE, A. (1967), 'Educational opportunity and social selection in England and Wales: trends and policy implications', in *Social Objectives in Educational Planning*, OECD.

17 S. M. Miller and P. Roby

Social Mobility and Social Policy

Excerpt from S. M. Miller and P. Roby, 'Strategies for social mobility: a policy framework', *American Sociologist*, vol. 6, 1971, pp. 18–22 (Supplement).

Since the Second World War, the discussion of social mobility has moved on three levels: from presentation of the *facts* and patterns of mobility to *explanations* of these patterns to an analysis of *policies* that might induce changes in the profiles of stratification and mobility of a society. Social mobility can no longer be considered a residual or a derivative of immutable structural trends. It is a variable that is affected by public policy, whether through acts of commission or omission.

Social policy is the impetus of the current study of mobility. Although all three levels of discussion – facts, explanations and policies – are intertwined, policy is now the dominant concern. The facts of social mobility show to what extent policy is effective; success or failure of policy should affect explanation; and, of course, explanation should guide policy. Unfortunately, such smoothness is untypical, for explanations of mobility patterns are not very secure. Policy is a guide to explanation more frequently than the reverse; as we assess and change policy, we begin to understand some of the difficulties or, hopefully, possibilities in the stratification and mobility picture. We can then generate hypotheses to explain the outcomes, which can be tested by new policies.

In the mid-fifties, led principally by Seymour Martin Lipset and his associates (1954, 1959, 1966), there was an emphasis upon structural elements in producing mobility.[1] Given a certain level of technology, certain mobility rates and patterns would emerge. The emphasis was more on the explanation of the apparent facts of contemporary mobility rates and patterns than on explicating the variables that could produce change in these rates and patterns. Today, we are beginning to question these structural and normative explanations that do not focus on variables susceptible to policy change. In both low-income nations and high-income nations, planners and politicians have to move to attain higher rates of mobility and are therefore searching for the fulcrums of change rather than for the inevitabilities of structure.

Prior to the work of Lipset on structural analysis was the work of David

1. For an analysis of other variables, see Fox and Miller (1966).

Glass (1954) who emphasized the impact of education on mobility. Indeed, in many countries schooling and off-the-job manpower-training programs have become the primary ways of attempting to effect social mobility.

In the last few years, we have had dismaying reports about the effectiveness of education as a promoter of social mobility. The Robbins report (United Kingdom Commission on Higher Education, 1963) in Great Britain has shown, to the surprise of many, that the relative proportion of working-class students in universities has not changed over several decades despite the expansion of university places. In the United States, an outpouring of literature has shown that while more education is available to all, the distribution of educational resources is still closely linked to social class factors (Campbell, 1966; Hobson, 1970; Sexton, 1961; The Southern Center for Studies in Public Policy and the NAACP Legal Defense and Educational Fund, 1969; Weisbrod and Hansen, 1969). In addition, the report of Coleman, Campbell and Hobson (1966) is interpreted to show that school-related factors are less important than family-related factors in educational outcomes.

Obviously, to expand educational programs without redistributing or equalizing educational opportunities does not drastically change social mobility rates, particularly for those at the bottom of the social structure. Perhaps there is equally little impact on social mobility rates where educational opportunities are equalized but out-of-school environmental conditions of students are not.

Promotion of social mobility: new directions

Disappointment in educational programs is leading to three levels of further policy work: educational reform, income and education, and stratum mobility.

Educational reform

This first level is in direct continuity with the educational emphasis of the past. It seeks further educational reform in several directions. In the United States, there has been pressure toward more education in very early childhood; the major program of this effort is Operation Head Start. The assumption is that if children with cultural and language limitations are given aid in these areas before they come to school, the school will have less difficulty in working with them. Results have been disappointing. The initial gains of children who have attended Head Start programs erode after they enter schools that do not continue to respond to their needs (Wolff and Stein, 1965a and b). Nevertheless, the programs have important payoffs in that they identify remedial health defects and advance general awareness of the need for preparing children for school. Efforts are being made to improve schools by insisting on accountability in schools' performance with their students and by offering incentives to good performance. Through pressure, public censure and reward for meritorious work, the hope is to induce schools to perform more adequately than they have before.

Another major educational reform aims at anti-credentialism and the expansion of continuing or recurrent education (Illich, 1970; Miller, 1968, 1970; Miller and Kroll, 1970; Miller and Reissman, 1969). The first assumption of this perspective is that the educational prerequisites for many, if not most, jobs are inappropriately high (Berg, 1970). A second assumption is that education and training, rather than under-age-thirty experiences, should be regarded as lifetime necessities or interests. The third assumption is that people can be better developed on the job than they now are and, indeed, that on-the-job training and experience may prove better than formal education for teaching many people. While the primary discussion has been in terms of high-income, high-education countries, the anti-credentialism/continuing education approach is probably even more applicable to low-income, low-education nations (Illich, 1970).

Three policy lines follow from this perspective. One is to reduce inappropriate educational requirements for jobs so that talented or developable persons with limited formal schooling can obtain good jobs. The second is to develop routes to higher-level jobs for those who have relatively little schooling. The third, connected with the second, is to build and expand a system of recurrent education, connecting formal schooling with the education and development that take place on the job. Many European countries with long experience in the apprenticeship mode are now looking to this way of developing competence, a way that does not rely exclusively (in form at least) on early or formal schooling. In the United States, manpower programs are moving in this direction, even though it is not fully recognized that these programs are in effect a third-tier, continuing-education system.

Another approach to educational reform is a program that provides cash payments to induce or allow individuals to go further in school. Many countries throughout the world provide stipends (cash subsidies) to university students. To some extent, family allowance programs serve the same function; they make it possible for individuals to stay in school without reducing family income through lost earnings from work or without adding extra expenses. In the United States, the Neighborhood Youth Corps (NYC) provides cash to high school students under the guise of helping them to secure training. Since many in-school NYC programs offer little training, in effect they mainly function as a way of augmenting a family's resources so as to make it easier for the children of the family to remain in school.

Income and education

This second new level in policy work is the 'cash (income) strategy', most sharply articulated by Lee Rainwater (1970) who argues that it will not be possible to improve the educational outcomes for children from poor families without improving the incomes of their families. In a sense, higher income is a necessary take-off stage for advancement in education. Children whose family's income has increased are more likely to do well in school even though the school has not changed. Thus, educational performance is seen as a function of family income.

There is much that is very attractive in this policy proposal. Its one drawback is that the relationship between education and income is not simple. As shown elsewhere (Miller and Roby, 1970) the education of the parents rather than family income is highly associated with the educational performance of children. Despite this limitation, it is important not only to improve schools *but to increase the income of families in order to improve children's educational prospects.*

There are, of course, political obstacles to overcome in providing cash payments to families instead of spending public funds for education. In many countries, however, expenditures on education are undergoing critical assessment. The result may be that both cash and educational programs lose, rather than that cash strategies benefit. This is an occurrence we would obviously wish to avoid.

Stratum mobility or lessened inequality

The third level toward promoting social mobility enlarges on the second one, In doing so, it more sharply connects social policy with social mobility concerns. The emphasis is openly upon stratum, group or collective mobility rather than upon individual mobility, aiming at promoting a particular type of stratum mobility rather than at increasing individual mobility. The type of stratum mobility to which we refer is that in which the economic, social, and/or political level of the bottom group in society is improved relative to groups above it. At the same time no other group - not immigrants from outside the society and not a marginal group from within - is drawn into a new bottommost position. The objective is to redistribute income and other resources to groups at the bottom of the society so that the difference between them and higher-income groups is reduced (Miller, 1968). Furthermore, lessening income differences between groups reduces the (income) significance of individual social mobility.

Unlike the second-level approach, the concern here is not with educational take-off but with drastically changing the conditions of individuals. This may be done largely but not solely by directly increasing the income of families, a strategy that involves a variety of economic policies. The most important, perhaps, is the provision of transfer payments such as social security, family allowances, unemployment insurance and the like, to lower income groups.

Direct cash payments could be accompanied by indirect benefits or services. For example, as Elizabeth Durbin (1969) has pointed out, employers frequently pay white-collar workers when they are ill. This is a form of sickness benefit that is not generally extended to blue-collar workers, who are paid on an hourly basis. Thus a government program of sickness benefits reduces some of the differentials in well-being between white-collar workers and blue-collar workers. As Gorz (1965) and Wedderburn (1970) have shown, there is a wide range of other so-called fringe benefits that accentuates the inequalities of blue-collar workers.

Another tool for lessening inequality or improving stratum mobility is the tax system. A progressive tax system reduces the income of those at the top more than those at the bottom. Through evasion, complicated tax laws, and reliance on indirect taxes, the tax structure in many nations is much less progressive than is frequently believed. For example, despite the steeply rising tax rates for higher incomes, the distribution of incomes after taxes in the United States differs little from the distribution of income before taxes (Bishop, 1967, p. 27). If statistics on tax avoidance and evasion were taken into consideration, the picture of apparent progressive effects of taxation would look even bleaker. This situation is not unique to the United States (Titmuss, 1962). Our guess is that major reforms in tax systems will be an important item in many countries in the next decade.

Economic policy specifically designed to aid low-income groups is another instrument to be used to promote stratum mobility. In the United States, for example, a policy aimed at continuously high employment would significantly aid low-income groups by drawing them into the labor force and encouraging their upgrading. Wootton (1963) has contended that in post-Second World War Great Britain full employment improved the situation of the workers much more than the social welfare state improved it.[2]

2. Wootton (1963) notes, 'The origins of this progress [of the British working class since the Second World War] are not far to seek. Overwhelmingly, the most important factor is the immense reduction in the rate of unemployment.' In an analysis of the Michigan Employment Security Commission's 1962 data on 2114 of Detroit's hard-core unemployed ('hard-core unemployment' was defined as twenty-six weeks or more of joblessness at the time of the survey), Howard Wachtel (1970) found that 40 per cent of the hard-core unemployed had been employed in their last job for more than five years. Following his study, Wachtel recommended that

Selective economic programs rather than aggregative economic programs will be important for groups that are lagging behind the rest of society. This is particularly so for isolated regional groups that do not benefit from general economic expansion. One such selective policy is enactment of a minimum-wage law, which tends to push up the wages of those at the bottom. On the other hand, Marris and Rein (in press) contend on the basis of British experience that the pressure toward equity (fairness) rather than equality means that, over time, wage differentials and wage rates tend to be maintained even though there may be temporary compression or expansion. The conflict they detect between equity and equality deserves close attention.

Many countries are now pursuing – or attempting or contemplating pursuit of – an 'incomes policy'. Because of the pressures of inflation, such policies aim at restricting wages and prices. One tactic is for income policy boards to decide which occupations will be allowed to receive wage or salary increases. On a large scale, the question is a fundamental one (at least in market-oriented economies), for wages then are no longer regarded as an exclusively market-determined product. Incomes policy can be a way of increasing the stratum mobility of low-level groups without increasing the incomes of other groups. It also can be used to widen differentials between groups and improve the relative position of upper-income groups in society. The economic reform in Hungary, for example, has been criticized by Hegedus and Marcovitch (1969) because it widens differentials in order to increase, presumably, the motivation of managers to work more effectively. In the United States, Bluestone (1970) points out that there has never been explicit recognition of public manipulation of wage differentials, and yet, he notes, neither the federal corporate tax policy nor the government's expenditure policy has been neutral. Both policies have highly favored what are now core, high-wage industries.

The possibility of alternatives to individual occupational mobility as a way of improving one's situation does not mean that individual mobility has no significance. What may happen is that horizontal rather than vertical mobility becomes important. The desirable situation is certainly not zero mobility. Obviously, some jobs are more attractive to different people for various reasons at various points in their lives. Rather than concentrating

'rather than defining hard-core unemployment in terms of an individual's unemployment experiences as of a given point in time, an individual's unemployment experiences over the business cycle should be measured. In this way a more accurate focus on the size and character of hard-core unemployment would be obtained, permitting more meaningful research and policy concerning the problem of hard-core unemployment in the United States' (see also Reubens, 1970; Sinfie d 1970).

on a simple upward trajectory of occupations and careers, we might encourage individuals at different points in their lives to take on various kinds of jobs. This might mean more horizontal than vertical mobility. 'Higher' and 'lower' positions would be less important than having satisfying work at particular moments. (This is what happens to many women who discontinue working in a factory or office while their children are very young and then return; if their household and child-rearing roles were classified as 'work', they would be involved in horizontal mobility.) The diminution of inequalities does not necessarily mean the end of mobility. Rather, occupational mobility may be the means of job satisfaction rather than the route to economic improvement.

Mobility as target

In the perspective that has been developing over the last decade and longer, social mobility seems affected not only by structural developments but by economic and social policy forces that deliberately change its patterns. In this perspective, a structural pressure is not regarded as having only one possible kind of response. Increased skills may be achievable in ways other than through increased formal schooling; enlarging the supply of workers in a field may not require that income inequalities be expanded. When social mobility is an important objective of public policy, the structural requirements to achieve it may be blunted. Policy may address itself not only to structural goals, such as economic growth, but to the objective of expanding stratum or individual mobility.

An important example is the matter of wage differentials. Generally, increasing the relative gain of a group is seen as stimulating the incentive to work. As Goldthorpe (1969) and Halsey (1970) have stated in important articles on inequality, any argument for increasing inequalities in order to promote motivation must be concretely and carefully scrutinized rather than taken for granted. Goldthorpe then points out that there are social and economic costs in increasing inequalities; he attributes much of worker discontent and work disruption to an anomic response because the norms of society are not acceptable due to the maintenance or aggravation of inequality.[3]

Broad implications

We conclude by pushing toward some of the wider implications of this paper. If mobility is to be analysed as a policy question, that is, as a question of what a society wants, the study of it must drive toward the broader

3. As Wootton (1964) argues, moral considerations underlie the claims to higher wages even when these claims are couched in economic terms (see also Goldthorpe, 1969).

issues of economic and social policy and not rest with educationa policy alone.

Social mobility and social equality should not be kept as separate discussions. Just as policy, data and explanations need to be interwoven, social mobility and social equality need to be in part supplementary and interpenetrating perspectives and goals.

Mobility and equality concern more than income. They concern power, dignity and respect. As we have pointed out, it is misleading to focus solely on the income component of well-being (Miller and Roby, 1970, pp. 120–21). One reason is that income does not completely define economic well-being. The second and more important reason is that there are social, psychological and political characteristics of well-being that are not automatically produced by changes in income. In the United States among blacks, goals have become broader than economic security; they have become focused on political well-being around the slogan 'black power'. Sometimes, as Frances Piven (1970) contends, national policy fools people by substituting pseudo-power for economic gain. But a genuine concern for mobility and equality requires more than a narrow attention to economic events.

Finally, we believe that it is essential for sociologists to turn to (and to be equipped to deal with) questions of economic policy. Until recently, the limited interest of sociologists in economics has focused principally on organizations, structures and norms. But public economic policies are playing increasingly important roles in determining the operation of the economy and the effects of the economy upon social structure. Economists concentrate on a truncated but powerful theater of action; sociologists are largely unprepared to understand this theater and, therefore, do not understand its larger (social) import. This intellectual void harms both the development of effective and humane policy and the development and utilization of sociology.

References

BERG, I. (1970), *Education and Jobs*, Praeger; Penguin, 1973.

BISHOP, G. (1967), *Tax Burdens and Benefits of Government Expenditures by Income Class, 1961 and 1967*, Tax Foundation, New York.

BLUESTONE, B. (1970), 'The tripartite economy: labor markets and the working poor', *Poverty and Human Resources*, vol. 4, pp. 13–35.

CAMPBELL, A. (1966), 'The rich get richer and the poor get poorer . . .', *Carnegie Quarterly*, vol. 14, pp. 1–13.

COLEMAN, J. S., CAMPBELL, E. Q., and HOBSON, C. J. (1966), *Equality of Educational Opportunity*, US Government Printing Office, Washington.

DURBIN, E. (1969), *Welfare, Income and Employment*, Praeger.

FOX, T., and MILLER, S. M. (1966), 'Intra-country variations: occupational stratification and mobility', in R. Bendix and S. M. Lipset (eds.), *Class, Status and Power*, Free Press.

GLASS, D. V. (1954), *Social Mobility in Britain*, Routledge & Kegan Paul.

GOLDTHORPE, J. (1969), 'Social inequality and social integration in modern Britain', *Advancement of Science*, December, pp. 190–202.

GORZ, A. (1965), 'Work and consumption', in P. Anderson and R. Blackburn (eds.), *Towards Socialism*, Fontana, pp. 317–53.

HALSEY, A. H. (1970), 'Race relations: the lines to think on', *New Society*, vol. 16, pp. 412–14.

HEGEDUS, A., and MARCOVITCH, J. (1969), Paper delivered at the meetings on urbanization and industrialization of the Sociology Section, Hungarian Academy of Science, Balatonfured, September.

HOBSON, J. (1970), *The Damned Children*, Washington Institute for Quality Education.

ILLICH, I. D. (1970), *Celebration of Awareness: A Call for Industrial Revolution*, Doubleday; Penguin, 1973.

LIPSET, S. M. and BENDIX, R. (1959), *Social Mobility in Industrial Society*, University of California Press.

LIPSET, S. M., and ROGOFF, N. (1954), 'Class and opportunities in Europe and America', *Commentary*, vol. 19, pp. 562–8.

LIPSET, S. M., and ZETTERBERG, H. L. (1966), 'A theory of social mobility', in R. Bendix and S. M. Lipset (eds.), *Class, Status and Power*, Free Press, pp. 561–73.

MARRIS, P., and REIN, M. (in press), 'Stratification and social policy', *Poverty and Stratification*, American Academy of Arts and Sciences.

MILLER, S. M. (1968), 'Poverty', *Proceedings of the Sixth World Congress of Sociology*, International Sociological Association.

MILLER, S. M. (1970), 'Alternatives to schooling', *New York University Educ. Q.*, vol. 1, pp. 2–8.

MILLER, S. M., and KROLL, M. (1970), 'Strategies for reducing credentialism', *Good Government*, vol. 87, pp. 10–13.

MILLER, S. M., and REISSMAN, F. (1969), 'The credentials trap', in S. M. Miller and F. Reissman (eds.), *Social Class and Social Policy*, Basic Books, pp. 60–78.

MILLER, S. M., and ROBY, P. A. (1970), *The Future of Inequality*, Basic Books.

PIVEN, F. (1970), 'Whom does the advocate planner serve?', *Social Policy*, vol. 1, pp. 32–7.

RAINWATER, L. (1970), *Behind Ghetto Walls: Black Family Life in a Federal Slum*, Aldine.

REUBENS, B. (1970), *The Hard to Employ: European Programs*, Columbia University Press.

SCSPP (1969), *Is It Helping Poor Children?* (Title 4 of the Elementary and Secondary Education Act), Southern Center for Studies in Public Policy and the NAACP Legal Defense and Educational Fund, Washington.

SEXTON, P. C. (1961), *Education and Income: Inequalities in Our Public Schools*, Viking.

SINFIELD, A. (1970), 'Poor and out of work in Shields', in P. Townsend (ed.), *The Concept of Poverty*, Heinemann, pp. 220–35.

TITMUSS, R. (1962), *Income Distribution and Social Change*, Allen & Unwin.

UNITED KINGDOM COMMISSION ON HIGHER EDUCATION (1963), *Higher Education* (The Robbins Report), HMSO.

WACHTEL, H. M. (1970), 'The impact of labor market conditions on hardcore unemployment: a case study of Detroit', *Poverty and Human Resources*, vol. 5, p. 10.

WEDDERBURN, D. 1970), 'Work place inequality', *New Society*, vol. 16, pp. 593–5.

WEISBROD, B., and HANSEN, W. L. (1969), *Benefits, Costs and Finance of Public Higher Education*, Markham.

WOLFF, M., and STEIN, A. (1965a), 'Six months later: a comparison of children who had headstart summer, 1965, with their classmates in kindergarten', Firkauf Graduate School of Education, Yeshiva University OEO Project 141–61, study 1, New York.

WOLFF, M., and STEIN, A. (1965b), 'Long range effects of preschooling on reading achievement', Firkauf Graduate School of Education, Yeshiva University OEO Project 141–61, study 3, New York.

WOOTTON, B. (1963), 'Is there a welfare state? A review of social change in Britain', *Pol. Sci. Q.*, vol. 77, p. 181.

WOOTTON, B. (1964), *The Social Foundation of Wage Policy: A Study of Contemporary Wage and Salary Structure in Britain*, Fern-Hill.

18 T. W. Pullum

What Can Mathematical Models Tell Us about Occupational
Mobility?

Excerpts from T. W. Pullum, 'What can mathematical models tell us about
occupational mobility?' *Sociological Inquiry*, vol. 40, 1970, pp. 258–80.

Introduction

It is expected that most readers of this article will have a far better idea of
what is meant by 'social mobility' than of what is meant by 'mathematical
models'. A brief description at the outset of the modelling concept and a
broad classification of models which have been applied to social mobility
will thus be useful.

A mathematical model is a theoretical framework which can be expressed and elaborated through mathematical techniques. At root it is a
set of one or more assumptions. The utility of a model is dependent upon
the availability of (1) methods for generating hypotheses from the assumptions, (2) methods for testing these hypotheses, and (3) appropriate data. A
good model will also be derivative of a verbal analysis which is carefully
conceptualized and concerned with mechanisms of human social behavior.
A model is considerably more than an effort to 'fit' data (cf. the objectives
listed by Herbert Simon, 1957, p. 142).

It is essential to recognize that the structure which a model brings to a
sociological problem is more than a null hypothesis. Models also provide
bases for comparison, the residual differences from which often form patterns in themselves. The criticism that a model's assumptions are too general is not always in itself a constructive criticism, as detailed assumptions
can only evolve from a broader base. But we certainly do not mean to
defend the use of general assumptions which seem to originate solely in the
availability of mathematical methods for handling them, except insofar as
the assumptions are subsequently refined.

We may initially classify the modelling of mobility according to two
perspectives. Under the first perspective individuals are differentiated by an
interval level variable, usually prestige. Multivariate techniques permit
incorporation of additional qualitative attributes of the individual and a
fairly sophisticated analysis. Svalastoga (1959) and others have used a
continuous prestige scale, but the present state of the use of the general
linear model, particularly in this area, is demonstrated by Blau and
Duncan's *American Occupational Structure* (1967).

At the risk of seeming arbitrary, we shall exclude this perspective from the present paper, referring it to again only in the conclusion. The reason for this exclusion is simply that multivariate models for continuous variables are more accessible to sociologists than are the models to be discussed in this paper, but we believe the latter merit increased attention. The reader who wishes to pursue continuous models is referred to Blau and Duncan (1967) and their bibliography.

The second major perspective uses an ordinal or nominal level variable, usually occupational group membership. Again, men are the unit of observation. Within this perspective two foci dominate. The first deals with a single pattern of movement (e.g., father's to ego's category). The second deals with a sequence of patterns of movement (e.g., grandfather's to father's to ego's category) and the interdependencies between patterns more than the interdependencies within specific patterns. This perspective will form the major concern of this paper. [. . .]

Our objective is to describe briefly and to interrelate most of the models under the second perspective above. Virtually none of the authors cited have provided the non-mathematical arguments for their models which we feel they require, and we cannot develop these arguments in this short space. But we shall try to be explicit about the assumptions that are made and some of the inferences that are of greatest interest to a less mathematical reader.

Ordinal or nominal occupational variable single pattern

Once a number of states have been specified which can be accepted as sufficiently homogeneous internally, the presentation of movement by individuals between states is quite naturally given by a cross-classification table. This table is of a rather special type, however. On the one hand, its row and column categories refer to the same variable, with difference only in reference to time or generation. Consequently the table is square and if, for some reason, we wished to exchange positions of two rows, it would also be necessary to exchange the corresponding two columns. On the other hand, the mobility table does not describe a transaction flow, which also has the preceding properties, for immobility, as well as mobility, is recorded. When the number of categories is small, there may be some unambiguous ordering, e.g., according to prestige, so that ordinal level techniques will be available. With a dozen categories or more, however, there is usually reason to distrust a prestige ranking, and the researcher is limited to nominal level techniques; sometimes the occupational classification does not yield to a substantive ranking even with a small number of categories. It is thus useful to consider models at both the ordinal and nominal levels.

To make the discussion more specific, consider the data of Table 1, to which we shall refer repeatedly. These data were obtained by David Glass and associates (1954) for Great Britain; adult males were sampled and their own and their fathers' occupations were ascertained (our categories

Table 1 Intergenerational occupational
mobility in Great Britain,
adapted from Glass (1954)

| Category of father | Category of respondent | | | | |
	1	2	3	4	5
1	297	92	172	37	26
2	89	110	223	64	32
3	164	185	714	258	189
4	25	40	179	143	71
5	17	32	141	91	106

1, 2, 3, 4, 5 correspond to Glass's categories 1–3, 4, 5, 6, 7 respectively). The first step in an attempt to find a pattern in this table is to standardize (i.e., divide each entry) by the total frequency, 3497, since the pattern is presumably unaffected by the number of respondents in the sample. In this way we obtain Table 2. Denote the proportions in cell (i,j) of Table 2 by p_{ij}, the proportion in row i by $p_{i.}$ and the proportion in column j by $p_{.j}$.

Table 2 Table 1 standardized by total frequency, 3497

| Category of father | Category of respondent | | | | | |
	1	2	3	4	5	Total
1	0·0849	0·0263	0·0492	0·0106	0·0074	0·1784
2	0·0255	0·0315	0·0638	0·0183	0·0092	0·1483
3	0·0469	0·0529	0·2042	0·0738	0·0540	0·4318
4	0·0071	0·0114	0·0512	0·0409	0·0203	0·1309
5	0·0049	0·0092	0·0403	0·0260	0·0303	0·1107
total	0·1693	0·1313	0·4087	0·1696	0·1212	1·0001

The 'density' in cell (i,j) can be obtained by a graphical representation in which the proportion of persons in that cell is shown by a three-dimensional block erected on a base which is $p_{.j}$ wide and $p_{i.}$ deep. Let R_{ij} be the height of the block; then $p_{ij} = p_{i.} p_{.j} R_{ij}$ or $R_{ij} = p_{ij}/p_{i.} p_{.j}$. Figure 1 shows these blocks from 'above' and labels them with their heights, R_{ij}.

If Tables 1 and 2 were characterized by statistical independence then each of the R_{ij} would be unity and the collection of blocks in Figure 1 would comprise a unit cube. These heights are the ratios computed by Rogoff (1953), Glass (1954) and Carlsson (1958) in their cell-by-cell comparison of observed data with this model of 'perfect mobility'. Using this model as a standard, we observe from Figure 1 that (1) there is an excess of

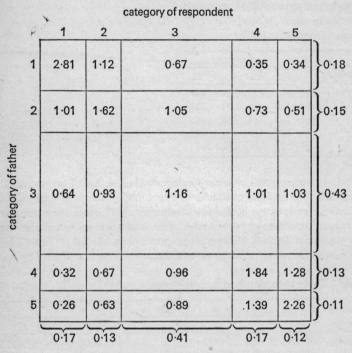

category of respondent

	1	2	3	4	5	
1	2·81	1·12	0·67	0·35	0·34	0·18
2	1·01	1·62	1·05	0·73	0·51	0·15
3	0·64	0·93	1·16	1·01	1·03	0·43
4	0·32	0·67	0·96	1·84	1·28	0·13
5	0·26	0·63	0·89	1·39	2·26	0·11
	0·17	0·13	0·41	0·17	0·12	

(category of father)

Figure 1 Ratios R_{ij} of observed frequencies to frequencies expected under statistical independence of origin and destination in Tables 1 and 2 expressed as heights of uniform-density blocks when viewed from 'above'

cases on the main diagonal, and if the classes are ordered along a prestige continuum, then (2) the excess is more pronounced at the upper and lower extremes (a 'ceiling' and 'floor' effect), and (3) there is a monotonic reduction in the values of R_{ij} as one moves from the diagonal toward the upper right and lower left corners of extreme movement; that is, there is a correspondence between the frequency of movement between two categories (relative to the standard) and their prestige ranking. Property (3) is a manifestation of the underlying order of the occupational categories along a continuum – in this case, clearly, a prestige continuum. Except for minor variation, these observations hold for mobility tables from all countries and inclusion of any number of categories. A useful summary measure is the average deviation, in a given table, of R_{ij} from unity. For our data that quantity is 0·43, indicating that the average cell departs in frequency by 43 per cent from the frequency implied by this first standard. Another indicator, the coefficient of dissimilarity (in which the terms in the preceding measure are now weighted by the base areas $p_{i.}\, p_{.j}$ and the resulting sum is multiplied by $\frac{1}{2}$) is 0·30. That is, if 30 per cent of the respondents in the table of perfect mobility were shifted then the observed table would be achieved; the model correctly locates 70 per cent of all individuals. Considering the simplicity of the assumption, however, we would not consider this a poor first step.

As Blau and Duncan (1967, p. 93) have shown, this approach does not have the desirable effect of standardizing for the marginals, since by inverting the matrix of the R_{ij} it is easy to reconstruct Table 2. (Strictly speaking, it is possible that the matrix of R_{ij} will not be invertible, but properties 1 to 3 above make this possibility slight.) The model reorganizes Table 2, but does not reduce it in any sense, nor does it remove any effects of non-uniform distributions over categories.

Following this initial grip on the pattern, one could proceed in various directions. Strictly in terms of mathematical logic, there are two ways to modify the model of independence without discarding the possibility that the number of persons in a given mobility route (i.e., cell of a table) is proportional to both the origin and destination frequencies. Supply and demand, as measured by the latter frequencies, should and do have major impact, and it is worth trying first only minor modifications of the model of perfect mobility. The first modification is limitation of the model to a subset of mobility routes. This modification, due to White (1963) and Goodman (1965), is referred to as quasi-perfect mobility. The second possibility would be incorporation of additional factors of proportionality.

First consider quasi-perfect mobility. As mentioned earlier, a table such as Table 1 contains cases of immobility as well as mobility. Blumen, Kogan and McCarthy (1955) were the first to suggest that these two phenomena be separated (in a different context). Table 1 can be expressed as the sum of two tables, one of which has the frequencies corresponding to immobility replaced by zeros (the 'mover' table), and the other of which has the frequencies corresponding to mobility replaced by zeros (the 'stayer' table). Immobility would first be conceived of as limited to the main diagonal, but could be generalized to include movement between categories which are 'near' one another according to an overall ordinal ranking by which the R_{ij} decrease monotonically with movement away from the diagonal (as described above). Under such a pattern of the R_{ij} and with this expanded view of immobility, it is in fact necessary to count as immobile nearly all persons in the upper left and lower right quadrants of the table; at most one occupational group can have non-zero entries in both the upward and downward mobility portions of the 'mover' table. (This is indeed a well-motivated implication and not a *post hoc* attempt to improve the fit; for a related discussion, see Goodman, 1965, and McFarland, 1968.) Thus as a number of categories increases, the proportion of cells on and near the diagonal which must be allocated to the 'stayer' table approaches 0·50.

An alternative decomposition of a mobility table would consider only persons on the main diagonal as stayers, but would subdivide the movers into 'upward movers' and 'downward movers'. Methods for such a tripartite decomposition have been described by Goodman (1968a) and are currently being applied in this context by the present author. By separating these two types of mobility one can use all cells except those on the main diagonal, and can formulate and answer new questions about differences between upward and downward patterns of movement.

If we follow the model of quasi-independence, which assumes that in the mover table frequencies in cells not constrained to zero are the simple product of an origin effect and a destination effect, then we obtain the ratios R_{ij}^* of the observed values to predicted values given in Table 3a. It

Table 3a The ratio R_{ij}^* of expected to observed frequency for the quasi-perfect model[a]

Category	Category of respondent				
of father	1	2	3	4	5
1	—	—	1·04	0·90	0·92
2	—	—	0·99	1·14	0·83
3	1·04	0·94	—	0·99	1·05
4	0·92	1·17	0·98	—	—
5	0·80	1·21	0·99	—	—

[a] Persons in cells marked with a dash were considered to be stayers

is clear that for these data, at least, the model fits the behavior of the movers quite well. Among the movers, the average departure of R_{ij}^* from unity is only 0·09, and 95 per cent of the movers are correctly classified by this model. When the χ^2 test is applied to the observed and expected frequencies of the movers, we obtain a value of 7·9, with 7 degrees of freedom, indicating that on statistical grounds we certainly cannot reject this model for the movers.

Although the original model of quasi-perfect mobility was applied to movers only, we can also check for quasi-independence in the 'stayer' table. Methods described by Goodman (1968a) yield the ratios R_{ij}^* for stayers given in Table 3b (one cell has an asterisk because no degrees of freedom were available for its estimation). For the stayers, the pattern of the R_{ij}^* is similar to the pattern of the R_{ij} in Figure 1, and it is clear that the model of quasi-independence does not adequately describe the movement of this sub-population.

Table 3b The ratio R_{ij}^* of expected to observed frequency when the concept of quasi-perfect mobility is applied to stayers rather than movers[a]

Category of father	Category of respondent				
	1	2	3	4	5
1	1·16	0·69	—	—	—
2	0·68	1·61	—	—	—
3	—	—	*	—	—
4	—	—	—	1·17	0·77
5	—	—	—	0·81	1·25

[a] Persons in cells marked with a dash were considered to be movers. The center cell (marked '*') has no degrees of freedom for a prediction

If the quasi-perfect model holds for movers, then there is an openness to the occupational class structure to the extent that all persons who have changed class enough to lie inside the 'mover' boundary have overcome any effect of 'distance' from their class of origin (at least any effect which can be detected in a crude classification with only five categories). The 'movers' are all in the same pool of individuals, their movement governed only by supply and demand, with no remaining impact by differential prestige, etc. Conditions of equal access to skills and positions over all origins would result in perfect mobility. If the bias in such access, which we know always exists, is limited only to class of origin or an adjacent class or two, then quasi-perfect mobility will result. The author has applied the model to a variety of tables and has found that it works best for industrialized societies, particularly when urban–farm movement is excluded. These findings are presumed to be due to the greater relevance of skills and lesser relevance of ascribed characteristics when the technology is advanced and education is widely available. The model does less well for a given country, however, when an increased number of occupational categories are employed. There appear to be special supply–demand relations between various pairs of categories under finer definitions of categories. At worst, however, the model draws our attention to these special relationships (Pullum, 1964).

Finally, note that the only sense in which the expected pattern for the movers is conditional upon, or is controlled for, the observed pattern of stayers, is in the adjustment for the marginal frequencies of the stayer sub-population.

A second modification of the model of independence would incorporate some indicators of distance between categories; for example, the frequency of cases in mobility route (i,j) could be hypothesized to be inversely proportional to the 'distance' from class i to class j. There seem to be at least three reasons why this direction has not received a place in the literature. The first is the conceptual difficulty associated with transference of distance from the physical world to the class structure. The second problem is that distance from class i to itself cannot be established, so treatment of diagonal entries is ambiguous. Thirdly, if estimates of cell frequencies under any model are required to add to observed frequencies for all origins and destinations, as they usually are, we would require different constants of proportionality for each cell. Evaluation of the model would then require evaluation of two arrays: the array of expected frequencies (to be compared with the observed) and the array of constants of proportionality ('gravitational' constants), which should be nearly equal if such a model were acceptable. Efforts by the writer, at least, to find a distance function in this categorical case which is plausible and corresponds well to observed data have not been fruitful. (Social distance is, of course, a concept which has received considerable theoretical and methodological attention. See, for example, Beshers and Laumann, 1967; and McFarland, 1969b).

If one considered the bivariate density of continuous occupational prestige over the unit square with uniform marginals (in effect, 'smoothing' Figure 1 to obtain a continuous surface), the result would be approximately a hyperbolic paraboloid (a 'saddle'). An adequate conceptualization of the metric and its functional elaboration would be crucial to the value of any mathematical analysis of this density, but the reduction of the pattern to a few parameters could permit useful comparisons of patterns from different countries, etc., and might also yield a continuous distance function.

Another mode of analysis which, like the above, makes no *a priori* assumption about the ordering of categories, depends on statistical interactions (Goodman, 1969a). Suppose we have a $K \times K$ array of numbers $\{a_{ij}\}$ which add to zero in each row and each column; if the mobility table is given by the array $\{n_{ij}\}$ then a quantity of the form

$$\sum_{i,j} a_{ij} \log n_{ij}$$

is defined to be an interaction. Subject to the constraints on the arrays $\{a_{ij}\}$ there will be exactly $(K-1)^2$ such arrays which are linearly independent; on the other hand, there is an infinite number of such collections of arrays, corresponding to different decompositions of the $(K-1)^2$ degrees of freedom of the original $K \times K$ table. Two useful properties, among others, are that (a) the sum of two interactions (or a linear combination of interactions) is an interaction and (b) if the model of independence holds, all interactions will be zero. The estimated variance of an interaction is

$$\sum_{i,j} (a_{ij}^2/n_{ij}),$$

and if an interaction is divided by its estimated standard deviation it is referred to as a standardized interaction. Interactions are useful in the analysis of any contingency table, since hypotheses about subtables or combinations of subtables can be evaluated. They are particularly applicable to mobility.

The converse of property (a) in the last paragraph is that any interaction, no matter how complex its associated array $\{a_{ij}\}$, can be expressed as a linear combination of interactions in 2×2 subtables of the main table. Thus if i and i' are two distinct rows, and j and j' are two distinct columns of the main table, then interactions of the form

$$(+1)\log n_{ij} + (-1)\log n_{ij'} + (-1)\log n_{i'j} + (+1)\log n_{i'j'}$$
$$= \log (n_{ij} n_{i'j'}/n_{ij'} n_{i'j})$$

are the 'fundamental' interactions by which it is possible to obtain *any* interaction through linear combinations.

The fundamental interactions with $i = j$ and $i' = j'$ can be used to relate pairs of categories. These have the form $d_{ij} = \log(n_{ii} n_{jj}/n_{ij} n_{ji})$, and the special properties (a) $d_{ij} = d_{ji}$ and (b) $d_{ij} = \infty$ if there is not some movement both from i to j and from j to i. As with all interactions, $d_{ij} = 0$ under independence; we know enough of the mobility pattern, however, to be

Table 4 Indices of immobility d_{ij} for Table 1

Category i	Category j			
	1	2	3	4
2	0·602			
3	0·876	0·280		
4	1·662	0·789	0·345	
5	1·852	1·056	0·453	0·370

sure that d_{ij} will always be positive. This index can be said to measure the immobility between categories i and j. The $\{d_{ij}\}$ for Table 1 are given in Table 4, and show a monotonic decrease with movement from the (undefined) cases $i = j$, so that the measure is a partial validation of the ranking of the categories and may at first appear to be a distance metric. However, for several cases it happens that d_{ij} is greater than the sum $d_{ik} + d_{kj}$ for a class k ranked between i and j. We thus wish to forestall any use of d_{ij} as a distance metric.

One can design arrays $\{a_{ij}\}$ to yield interactions which, rather than relating a pair of categories, instead measure an attribute of a single class, although in a context of several categories. One possible array with this use is built up as follows. Consider any fundamental interaction which has $i = j$, and thus has the form $\log(n_{ii}\, n_{i'j'}/n_{i'j}\, n_{i'i})$. Such an interaction gives positive weight to persons who inherit category i and negative weight to persons who are mobile out of category i (to category j') or are mobile into category i (from category i'). It gives positive weight to the number of persons who move directly from i' to j' in order to balance the role that origin i' has had in the magnitude of $n_{i'i}$ and the role that destination j' has had in the magnitude of $n_{ij'}$. Thus this interaction is a partial, positive indicator of the inheritance of category i. It will be zero if simple supply and demand operate within the 2×2 subtable.

A plausible index of the inheritance of i would be the arithmetic average of all distinct interactions of this form with specified i, an index which is itself an interaction. A preferable index, however, would limit the averaging of subtables which did not include any cells (other than $[i, i]$) inside an admissible 'stayer' blocking, discussed earlier. The index for category 1 of Table 1, under the blocking of Figure 1, would be defined by:

$$a_{11} = 1;\ a_{13} = a_{31} = -\tfrac{1}{2};\ a_{14} = a_{15} = a_{41} = a_{51} = -\tfrac{1}{4};$$
$$a_{34} = a_{35} = a_{43} = a_{53} = \tfrac{1}{4};$$

otherwise, $a_{ij} = 0$. In order both to obtain a measure which is invariant under multiples of the array $\{a_{ij}\}$ and which has unit normal sampling distribution when the standard of independence is used, we divide the preceding interaction by its standard deviation. The result is the intrinsic status inheritance of category i, as defined more generally by Goodman (1969a).

In column A of Table 5 we present these measures for all 5 categories of the British data. The results correspond in their horseshoe pattern with those given by Goodman for a collapsed version of Table 1 and are largely a second manifestation of the horseshoe pattern of the $\{R_{ii}\}$ of Table 2, with a pronounced 'ceiling' and 'floor' effect for the ranking used. The negative value for category 3 indicates a relative *dis*inheritance from this category. Any interpretation of this disinheritance must be tied to an understanding of the basis of the coefficient. For category 3, the total number of persons who have moved to (or from) categories 1 and 2 from (or to) categories 4 or 5 count just as heavily for inheritance as does the number of persons who actually inherit category 3. The fact that there are relatively few persons who make these fairly distant moves gives the measure its low – in fact, negative – value.

Goodman (1969a) has also proposed a new index of immobility for category i which is analogous to R_{ii} in that it is the ratio of an observed frequency to a predicted frequency. Specifically, it is the ratio of the observed diagonal frequency to the frequency predicted by the supply and

Table 5 Column A: intrinsic status inheritance.
Column B: index of immobility for mover-stayer
boundaries of Table 3 (from Goodman, 1969a).
Column C: conditional uncertainty about
destination, given origin

Category	A	B	C
1	17·32	12·00	0·57
2	4·85	2·62	0·62
3	−1·85	0·68	0·61
4	12·43	3·15	0·60
5	9·91	4·35	0·61

demand effects in the mover portion of Table 3 when extended to the stayer position. This measure is listed in column B of Table 5 and agrees substantially with the pattern of standardized interactions in column A. An index of 'persistence' of categories has also been suggested by Goodman (1969b).

Recently Mosteller (1968; see also Levine, 1967) has applied to mobility tables a longstanding technique associated with W. Edwards Deming and Frederick Stephan (Deming, 1943, ch. 7) for the adjustment of table entries to specified marginals in a manner which preserves all interactions (although not *standardized* interactions). Mosteller's motivation was indeed 'adjustment' to render tables from different countries, etc., more comparable by giving them the same marginals – typically, uniform marginals. Obviously, comparability of occupational categories is a major requirement if such comparisons are to be worthwhile. Mosteller has found remarkable similarities of patterns for Great Britain and Denmark.

The author has considered an alternative motivation for this technique. Kahl (1957) argued that mobility has four components: class differential, birth and death rates (actually, the role of death rates was overlooked by Kahl), immigration, and change in the occupational distribution – three structural components which 'force' an amount of movement – and circulatory mobility. If we conceptualize circulatory mobility not as a residual, as Kahl did, but as the pattern of relations between categories, the present object of investigation, which is modified by structural components, then the various models should be compared with a table of circulatory movement, rather than total movement. As a first approximation for recent decades in the United States and other industrial societies we can ignore structural factors other than change of occupational distribution since, as we shall see, this is the dominant factor. We shall also overlook for this presentation the difficulty of overlapping generations (see Duncan, 1966). The problem then is to relate the observed table to a 'stable' mobility table, representing the circulatory pattern, with the same origin marginals as are found in the observed table but with the same marginals for destinations as well.

To be specific, suppose that class j has increased in the observed table. We interpret this as an increase in the recruitment by that class from other classes, relative to the recruitment rates which would have maintained class j at the original level. The amount of increase is not immediately calculable, however, for simultaneously with this increase in recruitment, the out-flow rates from class j may have undergone adjustment. It is reasonable to assume that in order to effect the increase in class j, all frequencies of movement into j in the 'stable' table were multiplied by a constant c_j; that is, the relative sizes of the contributions from other classes into class j have been unchanged but all contributions have been altered by a single multiplier. An analogous argument can be made for the changes in outflow, with the effect that the circulatory frequencies differ from observed frequencies only by one multiplier effect for origin and another for destination. Given the restriction on the marginals of the circulatory table, and the observed entries, the circulatory table is uniquely determined by computational techniques identical to those used by Mosteller. The circulatory table for Table 1, presented as Table 6, necessarily shows as much total downward movement as total upward movement – that is, the upward or downward movements of average prestige, etc., for a society are eliminated. But there is remarkable similarity, as well, between corresponding frequencies of movement from class i to class j and from j to i. In fact, it is not possible to reject the hypothesis that the proportion moving from i to j is equal to the proportion moving from j to i, for any pair of i and j. We shall postpone further discussion of this concept for a later paper.

Kahl (1957) and Matras (1961) added information beyond that which has already been introduced to separate the effects of differential fertility and change in occupational distribution in the amount of mobility each effect 'forces', subject to the important assumption that the labor force is replaced by generations rather than continuously. We feel this kind of analysis is most useful in consideration of a single pattern, although Matras has projected the effects over several generations. Three distributions – that of the labor force at a point in time t_0 (assumed to be the distribution of fathers), that of the labor force at time t_1, and the origin distribution of those persons who are in the labor force at t_1 are compared. The index of dissimilarity computed for the first and third distributions gives the proportional shift from father's distribution to the origin distribution of their sons, due entirely to differential fertility. The index computed for the first and

Table 6 The 'stable' or circulatory table corresponding to Table 2 (with origin and destination marginals equal to the origin marginals of Table 2)

Category of father	Category of respondent				
	1	2	3	4	5
1	0·0871	0·0283	0·0491	0·0076	0·0063
2	0·0267	0·0347	0·0652	0·0135	0·0079
3	0·0509	0·0603	0·2158	0·0562	0·0486
4	0·0082	0·0138	0·0570	0·0328	0·0192
5	0·0055	0·0110	0·0448	0·0208	0·0286

second distributions gives the proportional shift from the distribution of the labor force at t_0 to that at t_1. The index computed for the second and third distributions (the destination and origin distributions of the usual mobility table) gives the net shift from origin to destination due to combined effects. Each of these indices gives the proportion of persons in each case who are 'forced' to move. Matras found that for a gross three-way classification in Western countries and Japan, the residual amount of movement is remarkably constant (Matras, 1961). For United States data from Kahl (1957) giving class-specific net reproduction rates for eight occupational groups and $t_0 = 1920$, $t_1 = 1950$, it was found that 23 per cent of the movement in the interval was 'forced'. In an extension of the analysis, the present author has found that 84 per cent of the forced movement is traceable to change in the occupational distribution, and only 16 per cent to differential fertility. Furthermore, 89 per cent of the forced movement occurred in categories in which the two effects 'reinforced' one another, i.e., in which both effects stimulated movements into the category or stimulated movements out of the category. For only 11 per cent of the sons did the effects partially 'compensate' one another. This is a manifestation of the well-known inverse relationship between relative growth of class and class-specific birth rates in the United States.

The analysis in the preceding paragraphs is seriously flawed by the concept of the 'generation' and the fact that the origin distribution of an intergenerational table does not comprise a distribution of the labor force at any point in time. But we believe this analysis is a good starting point for work which is yet to be done and, taken qualitatively, most of its conclusions are valid.

McFarland (1969a) has applied the uncertainty function for a set of categories,

$$H = -\sum_i p_i \log p_i,$$

to mobility tables, using a bivariate form for the function. The base of the logarithms is arbitrary, and since tables for base 10 are more easily found than tables for base 2, which is used in many applications, we shall (with McFarland) use base 10. Uncertainty is a non-negative function which is a maximum (log K, where K is the number of categories) when the probability is uniformly dispersed over all categories, and in this event one will gain the greatest amount of information when the actual outcome is learned. Thus H is also a measure of information. It makes no use of any ordinal property of the variable being considered. McFarland found that H can provide for categorical data an alternative to the product-moment correlation, which requires (as a minimum) continuity. In the context of occupational mobility, the level of uncertainty about destination, given origin, is an indicator of the 'permeability' of the occupational structure as it affects the movement of persons in each origin.

We have recomputed the conditional uncertainty for each category in the five-category British table (see column C of Table 5) to permit comparison with the quantities in columns A and B of Table 5. Although inheritance-immobility and permeability may complement one another as theoretical concepts, the measures which have been associated with the concepts are far from complementary. In particular, H does not distinguish between changing category (disinheritance) or being immobile (inheritance); it can only measure departures from a uniform distribution over destinations (given origin). It is thus not inconsistent that an inverse relation between column C and columns A and B is lacking. But we do find it surprising that the uncertainty levels should be so nearly constant over origins (the maximum uncertainty over five destinations would be 0·70).

Ordinal or nominal occupational variable: successive patterns

It is quite possible that the superficially most sophisticated models in sociology are found in this area, due to the wholesale application of powerful techniques of mathematical statistics in an inappropriate way. The review of these models will therefore have a critical tone, and will emphasize the recent awareness of the difficulties.

Suppose that we had data concerning occupational group membership for a cohort of men at time t who were, say, age 20 to 24 at last birthday. Of this group, we shall say $n_i(t)$ were in category i at time t. If we followed the movement of those who survived five years, to time $t+5$, we could readily compute transition rates $p_{ij}(t)$, the proportion of persons in category i at time t who are in category j at time $t+5$; if $\mu_i(20)$ is the proportion of persons of age 20–24 in category i who will die in five years then $\sum_j p_{ij}(t) = 1 - \mu_i(20)$ for each origin i. And, by definition of these rates,

$$n_j(t+5) = \sum_i n_i(t) p_{ij}(t)$$ for each destination j. If we have K categories

(including the employed and unemployed in each category) this activity can be represented by the matrix equation

$$\{n_1(t+5), \ldots, n_k(t+5), d(t+5)\}$$

$$= \{n_1(t), \ldots, n_k(t), 0\} \begin{bmatrix} p_{11}(t) & \ldots & p_{1K}(t) & \mu_1(20) \\ \vdots & & \vdots & \\ p_{K1}(t) & \ldots & p_{KK}(t) & \mu_K(20) \\ 0 & \ldots & 0 & \ldots & 1 \end{bmatrix}.$$

In abbreviated form, $N(t+5) = N(t) P(t, 20)$, where the $N(.)$ are row vectors. The far right entry in the row vector $N(t+5)$ is the number of persons in the original population who have died by time $t+5$. $P(t, 20)$ is a $(K+1) \times (K+1)$ stochastic matrix (each entry is non-negative and the sum over each of its rows is unity).

The preceding is nothing more than a method for naming some data; it is not in any sense a model, for we have made no assumptions. If we followed the cohort for another five years, with complete data, we could write $N(t+10) = N(t+5)P(t+5, 25) = N(t)P(t, 20)P(t+5, 25)$; we could, theoretically, describe the behavior of the cohort until it became extinct by the effect of a long sequence of transition matrices upon the original distribution vector. We would still not have a model.

We shall describe the assumptions concerning such a process that can be made to 'permit' application of the theory of Markov processes. We characteristically have data on only two points in time, say t and $t+5$, obtained from persons alive at time $t+5$. If we (1) ignore mortality, in particular age- and origin-specific mortality, then we can incompletely describe the cohort's activities by the equation $N(t+5) = N(t)P(t)$. Here $N(t+5)$ and $N(t)$ are row vectors missing the last entry of $N(t+5)$

and $N(t)$, the decedents, and the matrix $P(t)$ is stochastic but is based just upon the surviving population at time $t+5$. In order to project beyond time $t+5$ we might assume that (2) all persons in the population are subject to the same set of transition rates during the interval. That is, they are *homogeneous* with respect to characteristics other than occupation (equivalently, occupational movement is determined solely by previous occupation). We might assume that (3) the incomplete matrices $P(t)$, $P(t+5)$, etc., are all equal: the transition matrices are *stationary*. Finally, we might assume that (4) only one's occupation 5 years previous is relevant to present occupation; there is no carry-over effect from earlier categories; this is the *Markovian* (first-order Markovian) property. Then the projection to time $t+5s$ for integral positive s will be $N(t+5s) = N(t)P(t)^s$.

Perhaps the two greatest shortcomings of such an intragenerational projection are the concealment of the well-known reduction in mobility as a cohort ages and of the even better known extinction of the cohort for large s. When applied to *inter*generational movement, the model (5) ignores differential fertility and (6) assumes instantaneous replacement of one generation by another, rather than a fluid overlap of cohorts. More subtly, perhaps, stationarity ignores the impact of changes in the technology, etc., on the occupational distribution, and (1) and (5) ignore the effect (though slight, in the short run) of a changing age structure on occupational supply and demand. For further discussion, the reader is again referred to Duncan (1966).

Prais (1955) and Blumen, Kogan and McCarthy (1955; partly reprinted in Lazarsfeld and Henry, 1966) were the first to apply the model of a first-order regular Markov process to mobility – the former to intergenerational movement, the latter to intragenerational movement. The motivation has largely been the convergence of the alleged process to a stable distribution which does not depend on the origin distribution (see Kemeny and Snell, 1960, ch. 4). As in stable population theory, this distribution should be viewed as a characterization or summary of the present rates rather than as a prediction; even so, the assumptions are of a much greater magnitude than in mathematical demography. Matras (1960) computed eventual distributions for several countries. Other authors, including Bartholomew (1967) have used the eventual occupational distribution to compute indices of mobility.

Attempts have been made to weaken the assumptions singly or in combinations. Since it has not thus far been possible to test each assumption separately, it may happen that some assumptions will prove justifiable in the absence of others, when more complete data are available. For instance, Hodge (1966) has shown that the Markovian property (4) does not hold for certain inter- and intragenerational data. But McFarland (1970) has pointed out that if the data could be recognized to overcome a possible lumpability effect (Kemeny and Snell, 1960, ch. 6) the process might still come out Markovian. McFarland goes on, however, to argue that the above type of model must be rejected on other grounds.

Matras (1961) incorporated differential fertility in the paper discussed above, and he has more recently (1967) proposed a way to overcome assumptions (1), (5) and (6) by using the growth matrix of the discrete-age demographic model (see, for example, Keyfitz, 1968, ch. 2) to incorporate occupational category with age. Pullum (1968) has made the further bifurcation of the population into persons who have not yet assumed a first job and those who have (although the latter may at some time experience unemployment), which is essential to the evaluation of such a model and, building on Goodman (1968b) has given the form of the variance–covariance matrix of the age-occupational distribution, the eventual distribution, and the reproductive values of any category for any other category.

Another major improvement is a weakening of the homogeneity assumption, described in the 'mover-stayer' model of Blumen, Kogan and McCarthy (1955). We can suppose that there are *two* kinds of persons for each origin: movers, who may change their category over time (but are not required to), and stayers, who are committed to that given category and will never move. If there are K categories, then the diagonal matrix S has, as diagonal entries, the proportion of stayers in each category; I-S will have as diagonal entries the proportion of movers in each category. If M is the stochastic matrix of transition probabilities for the movers, then the transition matrix P for the whole population will be given by $P = S+(I$-$S)M$. P will be known, but S and M will not be. However, reasonable estimates of these quantities can be obtained (Goodman, 1961). Projection over s intervals of time will then be estimated by the transition matrix $S+(I$-$S)M^s$. Blumen, Kogan and McCarthy were able to improve their predictions remarkably through this change.

The mover-stayer model for one mobility pattern uses very different means of estimation of parameters, but is conceptually equivalent, with the difference that immobility for origin i does not require remaining in category i – it means staying within a region of i, as described earlier. The more restricted definition of immobility by Blumen, Kogan and McCarthy does not require an ordering of categories. If the categories could be ordered, and if they could be constructed such that the boundaries were nearly equally permeable, then one could generalize to one kind of stayer and K-1 kind of movers. The diagonal matrix S_0 would give the proportions of stayres in each category and the diagonal matrix S_i would give the proportions of persons in each category who *may* move, but by at most

i categories; $\sum_i S_i = I$. If M_i were the transition matrix for i-movers then

$$P = S_0 + \sum_1^{K-1} S_i M_i.$$

Projection over s intervals of time would be estimated by the transition matrix

$$S_0 + \sum_1^{K-1} S_i M_i^s.$$

Estimation of parameters would not be easy but would, I believe, be possible. The matrix M_i would have zero entries in all cells more than i rows or columns off the main diagonal.

Blumen, Kogan, and McCarthy suggested a different kind of generalization, which is described more completely by Bartholomew (1967). For a given interval of time (say one year) the population may be heterogeneous according to the number of 'decision points' at which the possibility of movement arises. Persons will be stayers except at these points, when they may or may not move. There are good reasons for supposing that the distribution of persons over numbers of decision points in a fixed time interval would be a Poisson distribution. Estimation methods and application of this generalization also have yet to be made.

It would also be possible to subdivide the act of changing category into stages, similar to stages in the adoption of an innovation, a change of attitude, etc. Only actual behavior would be recorded, of course, but the introduction of intermediate stages is attractive for sociological reasons and, mathematically, will yield better predictions (although more parameters are required, so improvement must be balanced against a loss in degrees of freedom). Mayer (1968), Conner (1969) and Goodman (1969b) have made some first steps in this direction.

Another distinct line of alteration of the basic model is elimination of the stationarity assumption. The most distinctive characteristic of a sequence of patterns for an age cohort is the decrease in movement with increased age. The most significant contribution to the incorporation into a model of this well-known trend is due to Mayer (1968). The modification is best made in conjunction with a continuous-time Markov chain (for mathematical background see, for example, Karlin, 1968, chs. 7 and 8). The discrete-time chain imposes upon movement an artificially static implication; movement can of course occur at any time during an interval, and any time or (concomitant) aging effect is continuous (just as under a constant Malthusian rate populations will grow by a continuous exponential, rather than by a discrete geometric function). Let $P(t)$ be a stochastic transition matrix with continuous entries defined for positive t, which describes how the distribution at time t can be obtained from that at time 0. Associated with such a matrix is an instantaneous generating matrix $A(t)$ (whose rows sum to zero) which is related to $P(t)$ by

$$P(t) = \exp \int_0^t A(s)\ ds,$$

$$\text{or} \quad P(t) = I + \sum_{k=0}^\infty \{ \int_0^t A(s)\ ds \}^k / k!.$$

Methods exist for using an observed $P(t_0)$ to obtain $A(s)$ and thereby obtaining $P(t)$ for t other than t_0. It is easily shown that for a stationary process $A(s)$ must be a constant matrix, independent of time. Mayer has considered the case of $A(t) = Ag(t)$, in which all entries of the generator are modified by the same scalar function of time. If $g(t)$ is, in particular, a negative exponential, then the model is markedly improved, even though Mayer was handicapped in having to use a synthetic cohort for data. Further work with generators which depend upon time, in more complex ways, should be most fruitful.

McGinnis (1968) has suggested use of an enlarged transition matrix which records the number of intervals in which a person has resided in a category. This 'Cornell Mobility Model' or 'retention model of social mobility' includes the hypothesis that tendency to move declines with increased tenure. Simulation and geographical migration investigations, reported by McGinnis, support this hypothesis. Levine (1969) has used the Blumen, Kogan and McCarthy occupational mobility data to show that a measure of immobility between pairs of categories decays inversely according to a power of the elapsed time over a two-year period (for each of three five-year age groups). Morrison (1967), using data on residential movement, found evidence that tenure and age interact in predicting movement. Fairly neat analytical forms may be obtained by thus considering higher-order Markov chains for several age groups. Investigations of this sort clearly face severe challenges in terms of technique and availability of data.

Social reality should be further approached by a combination of the weakening of the stationarity and homogeneity assumptions. For example, the parameter of the Poisson distribution over decision frequencies, discussed above, could be made a decreasing function of time (the age of the cohort). It should be clear that any intragenerational model which does not stratify by age, at least, permits a great amount of confounding of the nonhomogeneity and nonstationarity implicit in actual mobility.

Conclusions

Although the models and methods described in this paper are fairly sophisticated, most readers will have observed that they are strictly demographic in nature. Without exception, they could have been rephrased for regional or residential mobility or for movement through any set of categories. In other words, there is no distinctive use of nonascriptive variables, such as educational aspiration, self-esteem, etc. The overriding view has been of occupational categories as entities which persist over time, the movement through and between them governed by each individual's history within the set of categories, and selected demographic characteristics. It is surprising that with such a skeletal view of social mobility we are able to detect patterns and regularities.

There are many questions about social mobility, however, to which this structural, demographic approach can never yield answers. Many answers probably lie in an extension of the Blau and Duncan (1967) use of a continuous prestige scale. In particular, we could take as the components of an analysis (a) a bivariate or trivariate status vector, in which the aspects of status are kept separate, to allow for the possibility of status inconsistency; (b) evaluation of this vector over a long period of time for each individual, tracing out his career, beginning with first job; (c) parallel to this time series, another vector function of time recording theoretically relevant variables which change over time; and (d) for each individual a vector of background characteristics, such as parental statuses and education, standing prior to the two time series. The choice of variables and postulated links could be evaluated with methods of econometrics, going beyond the linear model. It is not clear how most of the specific methods we have encountered in this paper, however, could be extended to incorporate continuous characteristics of individuals without becoming hopelessly complex.

But there is a desirable complementarity between use of the nominal–ordinal variable of occupational category and use of a continuous (perhaps multivariate) variable of prestige or status. The former is far better able to integrate movement with changes in demographic supply and in technological demand, by the use of persistent categories. On the other hand, the latter, by restandardizing the individual's statuses at each time interval against the distribution of these statuses over the whole population, can describe how it may happen that a person who has held the same occupation through his whole career may actually have declined in prestige and been downwardly mobile, for example. There are other complementarities.

Finally, there is a great need in future work with models of the type discussed in this paper, as in all mathematical models in social science, for more careful interpretation of the substance of the findings. If, for instance, it is discovered that a cohort's instantaneous transition matrix is modified by a simple function of the cohort's age, then it remains to be found why all the opposing factors involved blend into this particular regularity, rather than another, and how the parameters of this pattern distinguish one cohort from another. It is only by this kind of careful conjunction of a mathematical framework with a social substance that useful future models can, in fact, be generated.

References

BARTHOLOMEW, D. J. (1967), *Stochastic Models for Social Processes*, Wiley.

BESHERS, J. M., and LAUMANN, E. O. (1967), 'Social distance: a network approach', *Amer. Sociol. Rev.*, vol. 32, pp. 225–36.

BLAU, P. M., and DUNCAN, O. D. (1967), *The American Occupational Structure*, Wiley.

BLUMEN, L., KOGAN, M., and McCARTHY, P. J. (1955), *The Industrial Mobility of Labor as a Probability Process. Studies of Industrial and Labor Relations*, vol. 6, Cornell.

CARLSSON, G. (1958), *Social Mobility and Class Structure*, Gleerup, Lund, Sweden.

CONNER, T. L. (1969), 'A stochastic model for change of occupation', unpublished, Michigan State University.

DUNCAN, O. D. (1966), 'Methodological issues in the analysis of social mobility', in N. J. Smelser and S. M. Lipset (eds.), *Social Structure and Mobility in Economic Development*, Aldine.

GLASS, D. V. (ed.) (1954), *Social Mobility in Britain*, Free Press.

GOODMAN, L. A. (1961), 'Statistical methods for the mover-stayer model', *J. Amer. Stat. Assn*, vol. 56, pp. 841–68.

GOODMAN, L. A. (1965), 'On the statistical analysis of mobility tables', *Amer. J. Sociol.*, vol. 70, pp. 564–85.

GOODMAN, L. A. (1968a), 'The analysis of cross classified data: independence, quasi-independence and interactions in contingency tables with or without missing entries', *J. Amer. Stat. Assn*, vol. 63, pp. 1091–1131.

GOODMAN, L. A. (1968b), 'Stochastic models for the population growth of the sexes', *Biometrika*, vol. 55, pp. 469–87.

GOODMAN, L. A. (1969a), 'How to ransack social mobility tables and other kinds of cross-classification tables', *Amer. J. Sociol.*, vol. 75, pp. 1–40.

GOODMAN, L. A. (1969b), 'On the measurement of social mobility: an index of status persistence', *Amer. Sociol. Rev.*, vol. 34, pp. 831–50.

HODGE, R. W. (1966), 'Occupational mobility as a probability process', *Demography*, vol. 3, pp. 19–34.

KAHL, J. A. (1957), *The American Class Structure*, Holt, Rinehart & Winston.

KARLIN, S. (1968), *A First Course in Stochastic Processes*, Academic Press.

KEMENY, J. G., and SNELL, J. L. (1960), *Finite Markov Chains*, Van Nostrand.

KEYFITZ, N. (1968), *Introduction to the Mathematics of Population*, Addison-Wesley.

LAZARSFELD, P. F., and HENRY, N. W. (1966), *Readings in Mathematical Social Science*, Science Research Associates.

LEVINE, J. H. (1967), *Measurement in the Study of Inter-Generational Status Mobility*, Ph.D. thesis, Department of Social Relations, Harvard University.

LEVINE, J. H. (1969), 'Decay analysis of a coefficient of labor immobility', unpublished, University of Michigan.

MCFARLAND, D. D. (1968), 'An extension of conjoint measurement to test the theory of quasi-perfect mobility', *Michigan Studies in Mathematical Sociology*, University of Michigan.

MCFARLAND, D. D. (1969a), 'Measuring the permeability of occupational structures', *Amer. J. Sociol.*, vol. 75, pp. 41–61.

MCFARLAND, D. D. (1969b), 'Social distance as a metric', unpublished, University of Michigan.

MCFARLAND, D. D. (1970), 'Intragenerational social mobility as a Markov process: including a time-stationary Markovian model that explains observed declines in mobility rates over time', *Amer. Sociol. Rev.*, vol. 35, pp. 463–76.

MCGINNIS, R. (1968), 'A stochastic model of social mobility', *Amer. Sociol. Rev.*, vol. 33, pp. 712–22.

MATRAS, J. (1960), 'Comparison of intergenerational occupational mobility patterns', *Pop. Stud.*, vol. 14, pp. 163–9.

MATRAS, J. (1961), 'Differential fertility, intergenerational mobility, and change in the occupational structure', *Pop. Stud.*, vol. 15, pp. 187–97.

MATRAS, J. (1967), 'Social mobility and social structure: some insights from the linear model', *Amer. Sociol. Rev.*, vol. 32, pp. 608–14.

MAYER, T. F. (1967), 'Birth and death process models of social mobility', *Michigan Studies in Mathematical Sociology*, no. 2, University of Michigan.

MAYER, T. F. (1968), 'Age and mobility: two approaches to the problem of non-stationarity', *Michigan Studies in Mathematical Sociology*, no. 6, University of Michigan.

MORRISON, P. A. (1967), 'Duration of residence and prospective migration: the evaluation of a stochastic model', *Demography*, vol. 4, pp. 559–60.

MOSTELLER, F. (1968), 'Association and estimation in contingency tables', *J. Amer. Stat. Assn*, vol. 63, pp. 1–28.

PRAIS, S. J. (1955), 'The formal theory of social mobility', *Pop. Stud.*, vol. 9, pp. 72–81.

PULLUM, T. W. (1964), 'The theoretical implications of quasi-perfect mobility', unpublished, University of Chicago.

PULLUM, T. W. (1968), 'Occupational mobility as a branching process', unpublished, University of Chicago.

ROGOFF, N. (1953), *Recent Trends in Occupational Mobility*, Free Press.

SIMON, H. A. (1957), *Models of Man*, Wiley.

SVALASTOGA, K. (1959), *Prestige, Class and Mobility*, Gyldendal, Copenhagen.

WHITE, H. C. (1963), 'Cause and effect in social mobility tables', *Behav. Sci.*, vol. 8, pp. 14–27.

WHITE, H. C. (1970), *Chains of Opportunity*, Harvard University Press.

19 H. C. White

Chains of Opportunity

Excerpts from H. C. White, *Chains of Opportunity*, Harvard University Press, 1970, pp. 1–20.

Many jobs are social entities as stable and independent as men. This fact about social systems requires a new view of the nature of mobility. Marriage provides a convenient paradigm. A job no more than a woman can safely be considered a passive, pliant partner in initial choice of a union or in decision to terminate a union. A society in which frequent divorce and remarriage is institutionalized would have a pattern of mobility parallel in form to that in a system of stable jobs. The duality between men and jobs is the distinctive feature of such mobility, and it helps explain why mobility has been so hard to analyse systematically.

'Job' is often used loosely to refer to a general occupational status; it then becomes a mere description of class membership, usually by some major skill criterion, as in the 'job of welder'. Many men, mainly at lower levels of prestige, hold jobs which have little further structure; their position is specified by simultaneous categorization by function, say laborer, and employing organization. The minimal requirement for a job to be a stable and independent entity is that it have a recognized individual identity, if not an explicit title. Such a job will normally have a stable number of occupants, and if it does it is called a fixed job.

Mobility among fixed jobs is highly constrained; movements must dovetail in order to maintain the fixed numbers of occupants. Mobility is enmeshed in a network of contingencies. When an incumbent leaves the job, one speaks of the creation of a 'vacancy' and then the filling of the vacancy when a replacement enters the job. A tenure is the concept parallel to marriage. Each tenure is preceded by a vacancy and followed by another vacancy, but these two are too far apart in time to be part of the same pattern of contingencies. Instead, tenures just ending must alternate with tenures just beginning.

The discussion thus far could be applied to many kinds of positions – offices in voluntary organizations, committee memberships, perhaps even certain role-types in face-to-face groups and property ownership of some kinds. In Western societies, jobs are very distinctive types of positions. Occupations are defined with respect to an economic system which is a relatively separable and paramount aspect of the social system. Essentially all men try to have jobs during the full period of adulthood, and the cost of men is such that redundant jobs are eliminated. There are two crucial points: (1) jobs are so defined that a man has but one at a given time (or if there are more, one is usually primary in terms of effort and identification); (2) men are so defined that a job tends to have a minimal and fixed number of incumbents. Mobility by a well-defined population of eligible men among a system of fixed jobs independently demarcated is the general theme of the present work.

Strategy

The strategy is to deal primarily with the overall structure of events in a mobility process rather than with the individual's motives. There is some long-range order in mobility, as influences pass along complex networks of interrelations. A given event is usually caused in some sense by events remote from both it and the participants. These indirect structural effects are the target. Official records of the organizations studied are the source of data.

The causal sequence of moves cannot be analysed without examining mobility into and out of specific individual jobs. A descriptive study may observe and trace moves only when they cross the boundaries of large strata or categories, measuring the corresponding rates and correlating changes in them with other variables. Such an approach, however, ignores all moves within strata and is unable to trace sequential dependencies. Few studies, even traditional economic studies of mobility in labor markets, reach the level of the individual jobs; even then, the moves are studied as isolated events and not in connected sequences (see, for example, Palmer, *et al.*, 1962).

Sociologists since the Second World War have put a great deal of effort into the study of a particular kind of social mobility; namely, mobility between occupational strata in successive generations. As Duncan (1966) has shown recently in an incisive critique, such studies do not really deal directly with successive generations. In mobility studies generations are a myth, a construct with only the vaguest connection with replacement of observable cohorts of men in actual jobs. Such studies in fact deal with change in status of one population of men over a long period of time, say from the year of entering the labor market to the present. This study is such a different kind of process from the study of mobility from one job to the next that a different term would reduce confusion.

It is hard to measure movement directly in any science. It is usually inferred from a change in state between successive times. Most studies of mobility, including this one, have to work with such inferences, instead of with reliable reports for entire populations of moves as such. The spacing of successive observations in time becomes a crucial choice because moves within the spacing are missed. This is the central problem in the major monograph on mathematical sociology by James S. Coleman (1964, ch. 5), and he suggests that one should try to find the underlying structure of instantaneous rates which could generate the more complex structure of rates actually observed with discrete spacing. This problem is of little importance in the present study. The tenures of men in fixed jobs are long enough to find all moves, including those which actually take place between successive observation times, by a combination of observation and detailed logical inference. Since individual tenures are examined, moves confined within a large stratum are included – moves which are omitted in the usual mobility study even when they do not fall between observation times.

When a mobility investigation attempts to fit individual moves into larger sequences the focus is usually the career (see, for example, Svalastoga, 1959, sec. 5.3; Clements, 1958). The career, though important as a concept, tends to obscure causal analysis. Men have long work-lives as measured on a time scale appropriate to social structures. Most organizations have shorter lives than men. Even when a bureaucracy continues as a whole over long periods its constituent departments are not likely to remain unchanged for even a decade. Some men may shape their own careers and some organizations may try to do the job for them; but at best, the shaping is vague and unreliable. Not only do causes precede effects, but also efficient causes are those close in time to their effects.

Concomitants of mobility

An understanding of mobility should help clarify basic conceptual difficulties in theories of social structure. Current theories of social structure have an abstract, ideological quality. Actors in roles abound, but concrete persons and positions seem to belong to another, divorced, level of discourse. Balanced structures of roles are filled by actors subject to the abstract harmonies of generalized value orientations. The harmonies are so strong that most of the conceptual problems of a system of men in positions defined relative to one another disappear; at most a few actors with a few very general attributes suffice logically to people the system.[1]

Sociology seems to have had less trouble in dealing with people. Demography is a well-established field, as are methods for the study of

1. A basic analysis of types of theories, emphasizing general issues, can be found in Davis (1948, especially pp. 167–9). One of the four main approaches he distinguishes, 'views a society as a system of social positions'; but the view ends with some simple categories of people (classes, strata, and so on) and a few principles of recruitment of individuals to categories (ascriptions versus achievement, and so on).

attitudes. Both censuses and sample surveys of persons have elaborate methodologies. But the study of persons is not effectively joined to the analysis of social structure. Positions in social structure, as are physical attributes, are treated as if they were solely a matter of class membership. Ingenious forms of contextual analysis give some structural depth to survey analysis – the attitudes or other attributes of persons are shown to depend on the composition of the collectivities to which they belong (see, for example, Davis, 1961). Simultaneous cross-classification of persons on many attributes increases the 'dimensionality' of the social 'space' in which they are required to dwell; all kinds of social 'distances' and measures of association can thus be created and analysed.[2]

The view of social reality implicit in these approaches seems incomplete. Individual identity is always in the end defined by position in an interlocking structure. A fixed job cannot be defined merely by a title or set of skills, however specific. It must be referred to a set of counterpart jobs with which it has regular, prescribed relations; each of them is defined similarly so that a fixed job is defined relative to a whole structure of cumulated, interlocking relations. Names of men have an almost magical power in Western societies; the implicit assumption is that the name defines the man. The effective definition of a man, however, rests primarily on locating him by his position in a network of regular, prescribed relations among persons, often largely in terms of kinship. Consider how an imposter is exposed. The interlocking structures defining fixed jobs and those defining men cannot be kept entirely apart. Fixed jobs are a later social invention than are independent persons, but there is some duality.[3] The tendency is for fixed jobs to exist in systems with well-defined populations of eligible men. Churches and their priesthoods are surely the oldest example, and they are the main empirical basis for the work reported here. The 'persona' of a priest can only be defined relative to his church – and is relatively independent of his membership in networks of kin and non-church friends – and a priestly office must be defined with respect to the sacerdotal validity of the men who can fill it (Tillich, 1963, especially pp. 12–13).

Mobility, including recruitment and retirement as special cases, is a

2. See Lazarsfeld and Rosenberg (1955), especially the article by A. Barton; see also Coombs (1964). A recent survey of measures of association is Goodman and Kruskal (1954, 1959, 1963). Some effects of marginal constraints on how association should be measured have been discussed in several articles published in the 1940s; see Barnard (1947).
3. Chrimes (1959) shows the slow and complex generation of a stable structure of offices in a society. No one office or title was meaningful except in the context of the interlocking set of positions at that time. The process of formation of organizations is greatly speeded once prototypes exist to be copied, and the real nature of positions in an interlocking structure is then obscured.

process wherein the interconnection of persons and positions in social structure should be especially evident. Nadel (1956), in his brilliant analysis of the meaning of social structure, suggests that mobility is one of the three processes whose study can give reality to the concept of social structure. Mobility studies usually have more concrete motives, but there are surprisingly few explicit statements of their purpose and value. Sorokin's (1959) book is a landmark in the area, both in summarizing previous scattered work and in stimulating subsequent large-scale surveys. He emphasizes the study of mobility essentially for its intrinsic interest, and draws analogies between mobility in society and the circulation of vital fluids in living organisms. Sorokin's actual analysis emphasizes a geometrical view of movements among locations in social space, with horizontal geographical dimensions and vertical prestige dimensions.

Mobility may have impact on an individual's feelings and perceptions and in turn the latter presumably affect his chances and choices in mobility. Large sample surveys of mobility are necessary to establish the actual numbers of moves as well as to permit assessment of their consequences and antecedents in attitudes. Duncan (1966) has argued that there is no convincing evidence of the impact of moving, as such, on individuals. He therefore suggests that changes in attitudes and behavior may be accounted for as a simple additive mixture of habits in the initial and in the terminal statuses, with no role left to the experience of moving itself. However, perhaps the main impact of mobility experiences on the individual may evade current techniques of measurement. Almost invariably the latter are formulated in terms of categories, usually gross strata in prestige or classes of similar jobs. The implicit assumption is that gross changes in status constitute the major share of the impact of mobility experience on the individual. This may not make sense in terms of the frame of reference of most persons. Introspection will suggest that great amounts of thought and emotion are devoted to changes in status which seem minuscule in terms of overall social structure. Large jumps in standing or type of job may be rare. They may have the all-or-nothing quality suggested by Duncan: once in a new stratum, a man may rapidly adapt to it, with some retention of old habits, and may thereafter think in a framework conditioned almost exclusively by the microscopic changes of job and pay normal there. The overall impact of the small successive changes and the amount of conscious thought and planning devoted to them may well be the bulk of the total effects of mobility. Only study of individual job changes within systems of related jobs and eligible men can deal with this impact.

More important to the study of social structure may be the changes in sociometric patterns caused by mobility. A set of positions is little more than an ideological program until filled by persons; persons in turn have social identities largely defined by their simultaneous position in several networks and structures of positions filled by other persons. To study mobility is to get at the nature of these structures and interrelations, especially the closeness of coupling of different institutional areas and the extent of the empirical duality between man and position.

Mobility necessarily suggests questions about attractiveness of jobs for men and appropriateness of men for jobs. It is plausible that study of mobility in terms of gross categories may identify the coupling of most importance in overall social structure. It is hard to see how attractiveness of jobs for men can be separated from mobility in terms of individual jobs. Men mainly think in terms of moves to particular jobs. The circulation of elites is the classic mobility topic related to appropriateness of man to job (attractiveness of elite jobs to any man being taken for granted). The impact of mobility on men's emotions is being assessed in some sense, but the main interest runs the other way and is more social than psychological. If 'ability' is needed in positions of great authority, and ability is either distributed randomly or at least is not easy to inculcate deliberately, then for the system to function effectively there must be mobility of men from all strata to the elite (Pareto, 1963, paras 2025–58). Studies of the whole pattern of moves among individual jobs in a system are more relevant than they may seem at first sight. Whether a man moves to a higher stratum by achievement or ascription, he rarely moves directly into a specific position of high authority, rather, he enters a system of particular high-level jobs where movement thereafter is subject to the same kind of logic and constraint as in wider systems of jobs. In many societies and organizations, recruitment to elite strata cannot be completely open and visible.[4] The man marked for highest success must appear to be part of the same system of mobility as others. Thus he must to some extent be implicated in the dynamics of the larger system, and often he may slip out of the implicit elite route and some other man step in.

Delays between mobility events in a system of fixed jobs

Two types of decisions are being made in the mobility process: one on the termination and the other on the formation of incumbencies of men in fixed jobs. At least two sides are involved in each type of decision, the job controllers and the man who leaves (is to enter) the job. In the entry to a job, the choice of man is as important as the timing, whereas timing is the substance of the choice to terminate. An analysis is to be made of the inter-

4. Kelsall (1955) has carried through one of the few intensive studies of career mobility within a well-defined organization of men and jobs. Explicit selection of young men for elite positions has been maintained there so far but only after two adjustments: extensive superficial changes in the direction of impartiality of selection and more explicit allowance for promotion to elite positions at later ages.

connections of moves in a large system of fixed jobs and eligible men. Detailed inquiry into the putative motives and perceptions of all parties to each change is impractical and possibly misleading. Instead, primary reliance is placed on the observed sequences of events and the lengths of delays as clues to the causal structure of the mobility process. These sequences and lengths can, in general, form extremely complex patterns which reflect the multiplicity and complexity of the constituent decisions and their interlocking. My main practical goal is to show how in some kinds of systems the number of independent events is reduced and the pattern of mobility brought within the reach of rather simple models.

Consider a set of fixed jobs and a set of men qualified to fill them who normally hold posts. The two taken together are the system in which mobility is to be examined. Changes of men by jobs and jobs by men must be intercalated together in the mobility process. Time intervals between successive events are an obvious criterion of classification. Natural labels are shown in the following chart:

Type of interval	Successive incumbencies	
	Men in a job	Jobs for a man
delay	vacancy	limbo
anticipation	split	merge

Four major types of system operation are differentiated by examining the lengths of delays:

1 *Tight* systems – limbos are shorter than vacancies; men move with little or no interval from one incumbency to the next whereas some time is required to fill vacancies.

2 *Loose* systems – vacancies are shorter than limbos; vacancies are usually filled at once whereas men spend some time floating in a limbo status between successive jobs.

3 *Coordinated* systems – vacancies and limbos are both negligible in length.

4 *Matchmaking* systems – limbos and vacancies are (on the average) comparable and substantial in length (*note:* some part of the defined system of jobs, if examined separately, might fall within this type although the whole system is tight or loose).

When delays are not negligible it follows that at any given instant either some appreciable fraction of the population of fixed jobs must be temporarily vacant or many men are unsettled. Such frictional effects must be common in even the most rigid social structures. The volume, accuracy and timing of the information needed to keep assignments of men to jobs completely matched would alone stagger any control system. Yet much can be done through legal fictions to obscure the mismatches. Appointments can be predated and departures postdated. Reported delays are a useful but fallible guide.

Tight systems are those that are tight in men but have jobs to spare. There is a prima facie case for incumbents being in a favorable bargaining position and jobs in an unfavorable one. The converse applies to loose systems. The close timing in coordinated systems may be explained by some kind of central planning and control, but it may also reflect a convention as to the announcement of changes. The full duality between jobs and men possible in mobility is most likely to be manifest in matchmaking systems, where, as in marriage, both sides are usually circulating freely before matches are made. In matchmaking systems it seems likely that complex interdependencies between different sets of bargains arise during sequences of offers and moves. Carried to the limit of long vacancies and limbos, the matchmaking case will differ in basic structure from the others. Men will no longer be moving *from* one job *to* another, nor will jobs be moving *from* one man *to* another. The explanation of mobility would be broken into disjunct parts: first, the movement of a man and his job from status in a tenure to generalized status in a pool of free agents and, second, movement of jobs and men from the pool to create tenures.

Only during tenure in a job does a man draw pay, which he uses in all other aspects of his life; thus he tries to maintain an unbroken occupational tenure. Partly for this reason a man without a job is usually in a weaker bargaining position. Job controllers often reason that he is not as prudent a man as a candidate who is incumbent in a job. A fixed job, however, can remain effective for short periods even without an incumbent; the services rendered are not usually so clearcut that cessation has immediate effects. The controllers of the job often need time for the sheer mechanics of search. If they neither control other jobs to which an incumbent may move nor have the effective option of dismissing an incumbent, the controllers will have little advance notice of vacancies. In any case, vacancies can be to the advantage of the job controllers: their authority is more effective during the vacancy, for example in redefining the nature of the jobs.

These arguments are neither proposed for social positions in general nor for jobs in general but rather for systems of fixed jobs, which normally are jobs of substantial status. By these arguments both very short limbos and appreciable vacancies, that is, a tight system, will be the norm. A critical question is: when is a vacancy substantial but still not too long to be a normal part of the mobility pattern? An obvious rule of thumb is that it should not be comparable in length to an average tenure. Beyond that, boundaries must be established for each concrete system. The temporary vacancy normal in the given mobility process must be differentiated from the chronic empty state in a job. The latter often signals an eventual abolition of the job. Similarly, chronic unemployment must be divided from temporary limbo.

Chains of moves among 1–1 jobs

For simplicity, consider a system in which at most one person enters and one person leaves each fixed job in the period under consideration. The simplest way to guarantee this is to consider only the job which is defined as being for a single incumbent. Call it a 1–1 (one-to-one) job. Then, the replacement of one person by another in a job can be uniquely identified in the mobility process. Only 1–1 jobs will be considered here.

Bumper chains

Suppose the system is a loose one; that is, there is a surplus of men, vacancies are filled almost instantly, men spend some time in limbo between one incumbency and the next. Look at a man F, in such an interim limbo. He will, after some months, move into a new incumbency. The previous incumbent, E, will at that point enter limbo; a few months later, E can be expected to enter another job, leading to still another man, C, departing to temporary limbo and so on.

The chain traced from F must end somehow. C may retire or otherwise leave the system or he may move into a new job or one that had been empty until C's arrival so that no one leaves on his arrival. The chain also must have begun somewhere. Suppose that F had been pushed out of his former job by the arrival of the incumbent, L. L began the chain, considered as events within the defined system of jobs and men, if he were a new recruit. The chain could also have been begun by the abolition of a job that L had heretofore held so that no entry by some antecedent man, A, need be assumed. Figure 1 is a diagrammatic representation of the chain.

Examine the time structure of the chain in this loose system. Vacancies are of negligible duration, so the time span of the chain consists of a series of periods spent in temporary limbo by men, each starting at the end of the preceding period. The earliest event is the arrival of the man, L, from outside or from a job that had been abolished. If, in some sense, one event causes the chain, it should be the arrival of L, given the accepted ideas about the direction in which cause flows in time and if the possibility of prior understandings between men in the chain is neglected. F is unlikely to have left his job for limbo voluntarily. The job controllers are able to choose among a variety of candidates at a time of their own choice.

There are prestige differentials in jobs and men, and these affect the dynamics of mobility. A bump of one man by another seems plausible when the bumper is of much higher status than the bumpee and than the normal level of men expected in the particular type of job. A bump is also plausible, and often seen in unionized factories, when one man has a

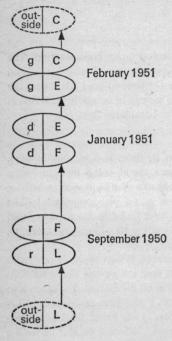

Figure 1 Bumper chain. The chain begins at the bottom and ends at the top because all delays in filling vacant jobs are assumed to be zero. Tenures are represented by ovals with the man in the right half and the job in the left. Delays – the length of time in limbo for each man – are represented by arrows of varying lengths. The direction of each arrow is from an earlier to a later time. (The same conventions are used in Figures 2 and 3)

prescriptive right to move to another job if his current tenure is terminated. Such prescriptive rights are often determined by seniority in a well-defined system of jobs and men. Given an average of promotion to higher status jobs over time, prescriptive bumping also would be by higher status men bumping into lower status jobs. The bumping will be defined and arranged by controllers of the whole system of jobs.

It is hard to see how a system of men and jobs could persistently function as a loose system. The loose system implies bump chains. Bump chains imply mobility downward on seniority or prestige grounds, and men enter the system in high jobs and leave the system from low jobs. This picture is logically consistent, but it does not conform to the usual pattern in most societies in which social standing increases with seniority. A system is likely to be loose only temporarily, say, during a depression or if the job is in a special auxiliary relation to a larger system.

Simultaneous chains

In a coordinated system there will be no delays, by definition. If the jobs are fixed, however, which man replaces another man in a given job can be seen and a chain can be traced out. The order of moves can be inferred logically to an extent: of any three moves in a chain it can be said which one is in the middle. There must either be a pair of boundary events or else the moves must form a loop, that is, a circle, as in the 'musical chairs' chain with no one left out. If there are end events one must be like the beginning of a vacancy chain – death of man or birth of job – and the other must be like the beginning of a bump chain – abolition of a job or recruitment of a man. It cannot be said which boundary event is the cause (the earliest) and which the effect. The presumption is that some central authority arranged the whole chain, since the problem of coordinating the negotiations of all incumbents and job controllers to arrive at a simultaneous chain would be a formidable one to be solved by local initiative.

Musical chairs: chains of matchmaking

The matchmaking system is completely different from the coordinated system. Consider a job, d, from which a man, E, leaves; and a job, r, left by a man, F, who will eventually replace E in job d. The departure of F may well precede the departure of E, or it can coincide or follow. Both the vacancy period in a job and the period a man spends in limbo between incumbencies are substantial and of the same size on the average. It is therefore implausible to speak of a flow of causation. The successive departure and entry events in a chain zig forward and then backward in time. Figure 2 illustrates such a chain; the game of musical chairs is a natural analogy.[5] When the music starts everyone gets up and circulates; all 'men' are in limbo and all 'jobs' vacant. Everyone scrambles when the music stops, no central person directs the flow. Some men are left over, as in the marriage market.

Mobility in the matchmaking system is intrinsically a complex process. The acts of entry and departure are independent and must normally be

5. Chains of matchmaking were used in earlier work by the author: White (1963). Many abstract formulations of matchmaking problems, such as the committee chairman problem, can be found in Ore (1962).

treated separately. Yet the same kind of status considerations can enter as in the other systems; for example, a man's attractiveness may be defined in large part by the kind of job he has held. In each act it is possible that both the job controllers and the man have some bargaining power. The

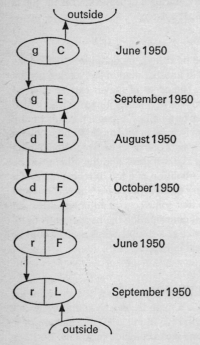

Figure 2 Time structure of events and delays in a musical chairs chain

important point is that the numbers of jobs vacant and the numbers of men in limbo are comparable. Mobility negotiations are carried on between two sides with roughly equal numbers. Each man's chances will interact with those of several other men directly and with much of the group in limbo indirectly, because several jobs will consider the same man and several men will canvas the same job. Game theory would seem an appropriate tool for such a structure of interdependent bargaining.[6] [. . .]

Vacancy chains

Suppose now that the system is tight: there is a slight surplus of vacant jobs, men move almost instantaneously from the old to the new job, but

6. A recent survey of game theory is Luce and Raiffa (1957).

jobs remain vacant for some time between the departure of one incumbent and the arrival of the next. Look at a job, g, in such an interim vacancy. After, say, a few months the controllers of job g will recruit a new incumbent from a job, d; the move of the man is instantaneous so there is a corresponding instantaneous transfer of the vacancy status from a job, c, to job d, and so on. Figure 3 illustrates this: time now flows consecutively

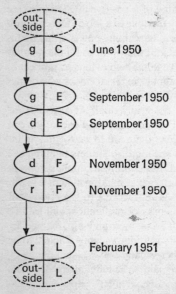

Figure 3 Vacancy chain. All delays between successive jobs for men are zero, and the tenures occur in pairs in which the upper one is just beginning and the lower one just ending. L's entry from and C's departure to the 'outside' end and begin the chain

in the chain from a beginning – here a retirement – at the top to an end – in recruitment of man L to job r – at the bottom. Cause and effect is assumed to operate in the series of steps in this same order. The vacancy created by C's retirement becomes the vacancy in job d, and so on. It is convenient to say that an identifiable vacancy is created at the top and moves through a series of jobs before being absorbed by the 'outside' at the bottom. The lengths of time spent by the vacancy in the various jobs differ.

Mobility takes place as if a vacancy jumped from job to job in a system of jobs that were usually filled. The creation of a vacancy, whose subsequent movements define a chain, can be either the disappearance of a man or the appearance of a new job. The disappearance of a vacancy, which ends the chain, can be either recruitment of a man from outside or the abolition of a job. The time structure of the chain is simple. The earliest event is the creation of a vacancy. The periods men spend in limbo are negligible, so the chain length in time is the sum of the successive vacancies, each beginning when the previous one ends.

It is plausible that the incumbent in a job effectively controls his time of departure, and this is coincident with his entry to a new job previously vacant. It follows that he will move because of a positive attraction to the vacant job offered him; that is, he is likely to move to a job of higher standing. There will be no clear preponderance in bargaining power either on his side or that of the controllers of the vacant job; they want to fill the vacancy and he wishes to move to a more attractive job. The previous incumbent in the vacant job is likely to have little say about the replacement who comes in some months later.

Again, the structure of bargaining is not really dual. At a given time there are only a fraction of jobs vacant. The controllers of a vacant job can canvas any of the incumbents of other jobs; there are so many that an incumbent is unlikely to receive more than one inquiry. Success in filling one vacancy may not be interlinked with, and thus contingent upon, success in filling other vacancies. The contrast with the matchmaking system is great. There the numbers of active job hunters is comparable to the number of available vacancies, and overlapping networks of preferences will lead to strong coupling between choices by different men and also choice by different jobs. In a vacancy chain, mobility into one vacancy is likely to be decoupled from mobility chances for other vacancies.

A system of jobs and men can well remain tight indefinitely. Recruits normally fill vacancies in jobs of low standing, whereas deaths and retirements tend to occur in jobs of higher standing, conforming to the normal pattern of career mobility. The chain of movements of men is a series of pulls of a man out of one job into a more attractive one. It is natural to call this pull chain a vacancy chain; the vacancy is moving from the job appearing earliest in the chain to the one appearing last, whereas the dual series of men change jobs in the direction opposite to the flow of cause and effect. The beginning event – creation of a vacancy as through death of an incumbent – causes the chain; it generates the opportunity to move seized by the new incumbent, whose departure in turn generates a new opportunity, and so on.

It is an idealization to say mobility is moves by vacancies. If it is just the vacancy that moves, some degrees of freedom have been lost somewhere. Specifically, the decision to leave a job is considered not an independent one but rather an integral part of the decision to move into a specific vacant job. Various detailed interpretations of who decides what are logically consistent with the vacancy chain. One concept is that controllers of a vacant job have the initiative on hiring, a candidate is in a passive position and says 'yes or no', and the controllers of his job have little say about his departure.

The vacancy chain is an abstraction, a theoretical construct. The models to be proposed to explain the vacancy chains add further layers of abstraction and idealization.[7] Nevertheless, the remarkable feature of opportunity chain models in general and vacancy chain models in particular is that they are able to show the interrelations of a wide range of social phenomena at both structure and process levels.

The coupling and decoupling of events in mobility is the central issue. It has arisen at three different levels of aggregation. In the perspective of the whole system of jobs and men, mobility acts are seen as necessarily coupled together in a set of sequences, in some kind of chains of mobility acts. Yet, in the usual operation of mobility processes in a system of fixed jobs, the various chains are decoupled from one another, each running its course independently. At the level of individual acts, leaving one job and entering the next are treated as a coupled, integral unit in vacancy chains; in bump chains, it is the arrival of one individual in a job and the departure of his predecessor that are coupled as an integral unit. The middle level, of coupling between different moves in the same vacancy chain, is treated as problematic, to be assessed for each observed system in terms of the basic model.

Vacancy chains and organizations

A system of fixed jobs and eligible men will not normally coincide with a formal organization. System boundaries should be chosen so that transactions with the environment – the outside – have a once-and-for-all quality; that is, a recruit to the system normally can be expected to remain for periods of the same order as careers. System boundaries should also be chosen such that all parts of the system have some interconnection through mobility with one another.

In a given organization there often are several broad categories of men whose careers intersect little if at all – say blue collar versus white collar versus administrative-professional. The lower categories may move to and from wholly different kinds of organizations, since the nature of their work may have little connection with what is special about a particular organization. It is men and jobs of the upper category, administrative and professional, whose mobility can best be cast in chains of movements in a system

7. Some discussions of the philosophy of science which bear on these arguments are Weyl (1949, part II, chs. 2 and 3) and Kuhn (1964).

of fixed jobs. Even here mobility is not usually confined within a particular organization but rather within an institutional system of organizations.[8]

There are four broad types of connection between vacancy chains and organizational structure. *Degree of centralization* is a major concern of organization theory. So far there is not even an accepted measure or criterion for centralization (Whisler, 1964, ch. 18). The structure and length of vacancy chains could be material for such a measure. The single most important question about a mobility chain is whether it has a beginning point and an end point. If it does not, the chain is really a loop, a closed cycle of events. The alternation of time flow in successive limbos and vacancies in the cycle must be such as to make closure possible. It is hard to see how this could often happen without centralized planning and coordination. If the number of loops is not consistently negligible, then the percentage of mobility which occurs in loops could in itself be a measure of centralization.

Recruitment is recognized as a central problem in all organizations. Usually it is thought of as a special, separate process, the continuing renewal of a pool of newly eligible men. In the perspective of vacancy models, recruitment is not a separate process (except when vacancy chains are loops) but an integral aspect of the whole process of reassignment and mobility within the organization. A recruit comes in to fill a vacancy that has been generated as a byproduct of reassignments within the organization and transfers between the several organizations in the system. Conversely, retirements have more causal impact on the dynamics of matching men to jobs in an organization than is usually noticed. Even if personnel is controlled in a highly centralized way, the planners will be constrained by the sequential logic of vacancy chains. The planning of careers, either by the individual or the company, will not be a realistic endeavor except as it is keyed to the vacancy chains which are the operational constraint on mobility. The same remarks will apply in a dual sense to jobs. Each act for creation or expulsion of either a man or a job from the system will tend to create a chain of effects, possibly for jobs and men remote from the initial act.

Merger and fission are fairly common occurrences in most types of organizations.[9] It is often difficult to know how real and effective an announced fusion or split-off is. Turnover of personnel – percentage of movers who cross new or former boundaries – can say a lot about the extent

8. Terms such as 'institutional system' are common in sociological writing. See the definition of 'institutional complex' in MacIver (1937). An explication of what is intended here by institutional system can be found in White and White (1963, pp. 2–4).
9. A recent review of this area is by Starbuck (1965, ch. 11).

of integration of different segments of an organization. In themselves, such percentages are an incomplete representation of causes of mobility. The rate of crossing between two organizations recently split may be low, but these movers may all be in vacancy chains that reach across the boundary so that all the moves in one are contingent upon boundary events in the other organization. New jobs and retirements may appear mainly in one organization, so that the pattern and amount of mobility in the other organization is dependent on policies of the former.

Prestige and authority differentials are the most difficult aspect of organization structure to measure and assess (see Evans, 1963). Salary scales are common[10] and so are elaborate tables of organization;[11] each, however, may be violated so often in concrete cases as to be meaningless except as a convenient ideology and language for discussion. Attitudes can be surveyed and opinions of the insiders probed. It is never clear that either guides concrete individual acts, nor is it obvious that either will get at the overall interconnections of acts in a system. There is no reason to think that any individuals perceive, much less control, the chains of events in large organizations and systems. Undoubtedly there are lawful, subtle connections between what happens and what is perceived, but it is too much to hope that these connections are a perfect match.

The main question is how the overall structure of prestige and authority affects and is affected by the patterns of mobility.[12] Individuals surely do respond to opportunities for what is viewed as promotion. Individuals do try to shape careers. However, when all the individual acts and perceptions are pieced together, what is the overall result? Does the degree of inequality in the distribution of prestige among jobs control the amount of mobility? Perhaps, but it is not clear that the correlation is positive. A very steep gradient of prestige may inhibit mobility. A vacancy implies the departure of an incumbent, and an incumbent faced with a steep step to the next job may not be able or inclined to move at all. Sharp differentials in a prestige structure could imply short vacancy chains and low mobility. As always, the question is only meaningful in terms of a comparison with another possible state of affairs. Consider the extreme case of equality in jobs. Mobility could well be very high. A job is always a complex entity with many attributes and many interconnections with other jobs. Even if jobs

10. See Whisler (1964) and Roberts (1959). Salary schedules for civil servants are not rigid in practice either; see, for example, Subcommittee on Manpower Utilization (1958).
11. The National Industrial Conference Board in *Studies in Personnel Policy* has sponsored a number of useful surveys of practices that are partly normative but partly reportorial; see nos. 157, 168 and 183.
12. One work which directly attacks the problem of the generation of prestige structures is Tuck (1954).

are equal in some kind of generalized status, they will always differ in an enormous number of ways. Just because there is no difference in prestige, men may be more ready to respond to other kinds of differences or to move in sheer restlessness. It is conceivable that the main effect of prestige differentials is to reduce mobility when the structure is viewed as a whole. The natural restlessness of most men may be controlled by training them to respond only to differences in a limited kind of social assessment known as prestige. Vacancy chains might be longest in an egalitarian system.

References

BARNARD, G. A. (1947), 'Significance tests for 2×2 tables', *Biometrika*, vol. 34, pp. 123–32.

CHRIMES, S. B. (1959), *An Introduction to the Administrative History of Medieval England*, 2nd edn, Blackwell.

CLEMENTS, R. V. (1958), *Managers: A Study of their Careers in Industry*, Allen & Unwin.

COLEMAN, J. S. (1964), *Introduction to Mathematical Sociology*, Free Press.

COOMBS, C. (1964), *A Theory of Data*, Wiley.

DAVIS, J. A. (1961), *Great Books and Small Groups*, Free Press.

DAVIS, K. (1948), *Human Society*, Macmillan.

DUNCAN, O. D. (1966), 'Methodological issues in the analysis of social mobility', in N. J. Smelser and S. M. Lipset (eds.), *Social Structure and Mobility in Economic Development*, Aldine; Routledge & Kegan Paul.

EVANS, W. (1963), 'Indices of the hierarchical structure of organizations', *Man. Sci.*, vol. 9, pp. 468–77.

GOODMAN, L., and KRUSKAL, W. H. (1954), 'Measures of association for cross classifications, I', *J. Amer. stat. Assn*, vol. 49, pp. 732–64.

GOODMAN, L., and KRUSKAL, W. H. (1959), 'Measures of association for cross classifications, II', *J. Amer. stat. Assn*, vol. 54, pp. 123–63.

GOODMAN, L., and KRUSKAL, W. H. (1963), 'Measures of association for cross classifications, III', *J. Amer. stat. Assn*, vol. 58, pp. 310–64.

KELSALL, R. K. (1955), *Higher Civil Servants in Britain*, Routledge & Kegan Paul.

KUHN, T. (1964), *The Structure of Scientific Revolutions*, University of Chicago Press.

LAZARSFELD, P. F., and ROSENBERG, M. (eds.) (1955), *The Language of Social Research*, Free Press.

LUCE, R. D., and RAIFFA, H. (1957), *Games and Decisions*, Wiley.

MACIVER, R. M. (1937), *Society*, Holt, Rinehart & Winston.

NADEL, S. F. (1956), *The Theory of Social Structure*, Cohen & West.

ORE, O. (1962), *The Theory of Graphs*, American Mathematical Society, Providence.

PALMER, G. L., et al (1962), *The Reluctant Job Changer*, University of Pennsylvania Press.

PARETO, V. (1963), *Treatise on General Sociology* (ed. A. Livingston), Dover.

ROBERTS, D. (1959), *Executive Compensation*, Free Press.

SOROKIN, P. M. (1959), *Social and Cultural Mobility*, Free Press.

STARBUCK, R. (1965), 'Organizational growth and development', in J. G. March ed.), *Handbook of Organizations*, Rand McNally.

SUBCOMMITTEE ON MANPOWER UTILIZATION (1958), 'Legislative control of federal positions and salaries', Report to the Committee on Post Office and Civil Service, US House of Representatives, 85th Congress, 2nd Session, November.

SVALASTOGA, K. (1959), *Prestige, Class and Mobility*, Heinemann.

TILLICH, P. (1963), *Systematic Theology*, vol. 3, University of Chicago Press.

TUCK, R. (1954), *An Economic Theory of Rank*, Oxford University Press.

WEYL, H. (1949), *Philosophy of Mathematics and Natural Science*, Princeton University Press.

WHISLER, T. (1964), 'Measuring centralization of control in business organizations', in W. W. Cooper *et al.* (eds.), *New Perspectives in Organizational Research*, Wiley.

WHITE, H. C. (1963), 'Cause and effect in social mobility tables', *Behav. Sci.*, vol. 8, pp. 14–27.

WHITE, H. C., and WHITE, C. (1963), *Canvases and Careers*, Wiley.

20 M. S. Granovetter

The Strength of Weak Ties

Excerpts from M. S. Granovetter, 'The strength of weak ties', *American Journal of Sociology*, vol. 78, 1973, pp. 1360–80.

A fundamental weakness of current sociological theory is that it does not relate micro-level interactions to macro-level patterns in any convincing way. Large-scale statistical, as well as qualitative, studies offer a good deal of insight into such macro phenomena as social mobility, community organization and political structure. At the micro level, a large and increasing body of data and theory offers useful and illuminating ideas about what transpires within the confines of the small group. But how interaction in small groups aggregates to form large-scale patterns eludes us in most cases.

I will argue, in this paper, that the analysis of processes in interpersonal networks provides the most fruitful micro–macro bridge. In one way or another, it is through these networks that small-scale interaction becomes translated into large-scale patterns, and that these, in turn, feed back into small groups. [. . .]

The strategy of the present paper is to choose a rather limited aspect of small-scale interaction – the strength of interpersonal ties – and to show, in some detail, how the use of network analysis can relate this aspect to such varied macro phenomena as diffusion, social mobility, political organization and social cohesion in general. While the analysis is essentially qualitative, a mathematically inclined reader will recognize the potential for models; mathematical arguments, leads and references are suggested mostly in footnotes.

The strength of ties

Most intuitive notions of the 'strength' of an interpersonal tie should be satisfied by the following definition: the strength of a tie is a (probably linear) combination of the amount of time, the emotional intensity, the intimacy (mutual confiding) and the reciprocal services which characterize the tie.[1] Each of these is somewhat independent of the other, though the set

1. Ties discussed in this paper are assumed to be positive and symmetric; a comprehensive theory might require discussion of negative and/or asymmetric ties, but this would add unnecessary complexity to the present, exploratory comments.

is obviously highly intracorrelated. Discussion of operational measures of and weights attaching to each of the four elements is postponed to future empirical studies.[2] It is sufficient for the present purpose if most of us can agree, on a rough intuitive basis, whether a given tie is strong, weak or absent.[3]

Consider, now, any two arbitrarily selected individuals – call them A and B – and the set, S = C, D, E,..., of all persons with ties to either *or* both of them.[4] The hypothesis which enables us to relate dyadic ties to larger structures is: the stronger the tie between A and B, the larger the proportion of individuals in S to whom they will *both* be tied, that is, connected by a weak or strong tie. This overlap in their friendship circles is predicted to be least when their tie is absent, most when it is strong, and intermediate when it is weak.

The proposed relationship results, first, from the tendency (by definition) of stronger ties to involve larger time commitments. If A–B and A–C ties exist, then the amount of time C spends with B depends (in part) on the amount A spends with B and C, respectively. (If the events 'A is with B' and 'A is with C' were independent, then the event 'C is with A and B' would have probability equal to the product of their probabilities. For example, if A and B are together 60 per cent of the time, and A and C 40 per cent, then C, A and B would be together 24 per cent of the time. Such independence would be less likely after than before B and C became acquainted.) If C and B have no relationship, common strong ties to A will probably bring them into interaction and generate one. Implicit here is Homans's idea that 'the more frequently persons interact with one another, the stronger their sentiments of friendship for one another are apt to be' (1950, p. 133).

The hypothesis is made plausible also by empirical evidence that the stronger the tie connecting two individuals, the more similar they are, in

2. Some anthropologists suggest 'multiplexity', that is, multiple contents in a relationship, as indicating a strong tie (Kapferer, 1969, p. 213). While this may be accurate in some circumstances, ties with only one content or with diffuse content may be strong as well (Simmel, 1950, pp. 317–29). The present definition would show most multiplex ties to be strong but also allow for other possibilities.
3. Included in 'absent' are both the lack of any relationship and ties without substantial significance, such as a 'nodding' relationship between people living on the same street, or the 'tie' to the vendor from whom one customarily buys a morning newspaper. That two people 'know' each other by name need not move their relation out of this category if their interaction is negligible. In some contexts, however (disasters, for example), such 'negligible' ties might usefully be distinguished from the absence of one. This is an ambiguity caused by substitution, for convenience of exposition, of discrete values for an underlying continuous variable.
4. In Barnes's terminology, the union of their respective primary stars (1969, p. 58).

various ways (Berscheid and Walster, 1969, pp. 69–91; Bramel, 1969, pp. 9–16; Brown, 1965, pp. 71–90; Laumann, 1968; Newcomb, 1961, ch. 5; Precker, 1952). Thus, if strong ties connect A to B and A to C, both C and B, being similar to A, are probably similar to one another, increasing the likelihood of a friendship once they have met. Applied in reverse, these two factors – time and similarity – indicate why weaker A–B and A–C ties make a C–B tie less likely than strong ones: C and B are less likely to interact and less likely to be compatible if they do.

The theory of cognitive balance, as formulated by Heider (1958) and especially by Newcomb (1961, pp. 4–23), also predicts this result. If strong ties A–B and A–C exist, and if B and C are aware of one another, anything short of a positive tie would introduce a 'psychological strain' into the situation since C will want his own feelings to be congruent with those of his good friend, A, and similarly, for B and *his* friend, A. Where the ties are weak, however, such consistency is psychologically less crucial. (On this point see also Homans, 1950, p. 255; and Davis, 1963, p. 448.)

Some direct evidence for the basic hypothesis exists (Kapferer, 1969, p. 299n.; Laumann and Schuman, 1967; Rapoport and Horvath, 1961; Rapoport, 1963).[5] This evidence is less comprehensive than one might hope. In addition, however, certain inferences from the hypothesis have received empirical support. Description of these inferences will suggest some of the substantive implications of the above argument.

Weak ties in diffusion processes

To derive implications for large networks of relations, it is necessary to frame the basic hypothesis more precisely. This can be done by investigating the possible triads consisting of strong, weak or absent ties among A, B and any arbitrarily chosen friend of either or both (i.e., some member of the set S, described above). A thorough mathematical model would do this in some detail, suggesting probabilities for various types. This analysis becomes rather involved, however, and it is sufficient for my purpose in this paper to say that the triad which is most *unlikely* to occur, under the hypothesis stated above, is that in which A and B are strongly linked, A

5. The models and experiments of Rapoport and his associates have been a major stimulus to this paper. In 1954 he commented on the 'well-known fact that the likely contacts of two individuals who are closely acquainted tend to be more overlapping than those of two arbitrarily selected individuals' (p. 75). His and Horvath's 1961 hypothesis is even closer to mine: 'one would expect the friendship relations, and therefore the overlap bias of the acquaintance circles, to become less tight with increasing numerical rank-order' (p. 290) (i.e., best friend, second-best friend, third-best, etc.). Their development of this hypothesis, however, is quite different, substantively and mathematically, from mine (Rapoport, 1953a, 1953b, 1954, 1963; Rapoport and Horvath, 1961).

has a strong tie to some friend C, but the tie between C and B is absent. This triad is shown in Figure 1. To see the consequences of this assertion, I will exaggerate it in what follows by supposing that the triad shown *never* occurs – that is, that the B–C tie is always present (whether weak or strong), given the other two strong ties. Whatever results are inferred from this supposition should tend to occur in the degree that the triad in question tends to be absent.

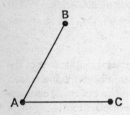

Figure 1 Forbidden triad

Some evidence exists for this absence. Analysing 651 sociograms, Davis (1970, p. 845) found that in 90 per cent of them triads consisting of two mutual choices and one nonchoice occurred less than the expected random number of times. If we assume that mutual choice indicates a strong tie, this is strong evidence in the direction of my argument.[6] Newcomb (1961, pp. 160–65) reports that in triads consisting of dyads expressing mutual 'high attraction', the configuration of three strong ties became increasingly frequent as people knew one another longer and better; the frequency of the triad pictured in Figure 1 is not analysed, but it is implied that processes of cognitive balance tended to eliminate it.

The significance of this triad's absence can be shown by using the concept of a 'bridge'; this is a line in a network which provides the *only* path between two points (Harary, Norman and Cartwright, 1965, p. 198). Since, in general, each person has a great many contacts, a bridge between A and B provides the only route along which information or influence can flow from any contact of A to any contact of B, and, consequently, from anyone connected *indirectly* to A to anyone connected indirectly to B. Thus, in the study of diffusion, we can expect bridges to assume an important role.

6. This assumption is suggested by one of Davis's models (1970, p. 846) and made explicitly by Mazur (1971). It is not obvious, however. In a free-choice sociometric test or a fixed-choice one with a large number of choices, most strong ties would probably result in mutual choice, but some weak ones might as well. With a small, fixed number of choices, most mutual choices should be strong ties, but some strong ties might show up as asymmetric. For a general discussion of the biases introduced by sociometric procedures, see Holland and Leinhardt (1971).

Now, if the stipulated triad is absent, it follows that, except under unlikely conditions, *no strong tie is a bridge*. Consider the strong tie A–B: if A has another strong tie to C, then forbidding the triad of Figure 1 implies that a tie exists between C and B, so that the path A–C–B exists between A and B; hence, A–B is not a bridge. A strong tie can be a bridge, therefore, *only if* neither party to it has any *other* strong ties, unlikely in a social network of any size (though possible in a small group). Weak ties suffer no such restriction, though they are certainly not automatically bridges. What is important, rather, is that all bridges are weak ties. [. . .]

Weak ties in egocentric networks

In this section and the next, I want to discuss the general significance of the above findings and arguments at two levels: first that of individuals, then that of communities. These discussions make no pretense of being comprehensive; they are meant only to illustrate possible applications.

In recent years, a great deal of literature has appeared analysing the impact on the behavior of individuals of the social networks in which they are embedded. Some of the studies have emphasized the ways in which behavior is shaped and constrained by one's network (Bott, 1957; Mayer, 1961; Frankenberg, 1965), others the ways in which individuals can manipulate these networks to achieve specific goals (Mayer, 1966; Boissevain, 1968; Kapferer, 1969). Both facets are generally supposed to be affected by the structure of one's network. Bott argued that the crucial variable is that of whether one's friends tend to know one another ('close-knit' network) or not ('loose-knit' network). Barnes makes this dichotomy into a continuous variable by counting the number of ties observed in the network formed by ego and his friends and dividing it by the ratio of possible ones; this then corresponds to what is often called network 'density' (Barnes, 1969; Tilly, 1969).[7]

Epstein (1969) points out, however, that different *parts* of ego's network may have different density. He calls those with whom one 'interacts most intensely and most regularly, and who are therefore also likely to come to know one another,' the 'effective network'; the 'remainder constitute the *extended* network' (pp. 110–11). This is close to saying, in my terms, that one's strong ties form a dense network, one's weak ties a less dense one.

7. But if the crucial question is really whether ego's *friends* know each other, this measure should probably be computed after ego and his ties have been subtracted from the network; distortions caused by failure to do so will be especially great in small networks. It is important to note, also, that in *non*egocentric networks, there is no simple correspondence between density and any 'average' measure of the extent to which the various egos have friends who know one another. 'Density', as used here, should not be confused with the 'axone density' of Rapoport's models – the number of choices issuing from each node of a network.

I would add that one's weak ties which are not local bridges might as well be counted with the strong ties, to maximize separation of the dense from the less dense network sectors.

One point on which there is no general agreement is whether ego's network should be treated as composed only of those to whom he is tied directly, or should include the contacts of his contacts, and/or others. Analyses stressing encapsulation of an individual by his network tend to take the former position, those stressing manipulation of networks, the latter, since information or favors available through direct contacts may depend on who *their* contacts are. I would argue that by dividing ego's network into that part made up of strong and nonbridging weak ties on the one hand, and that of bridging weak ties on the other, both orientations can be dealt with. Ties in the former part should tend to be to people who not only know one another, but who also have few contacts not tied to ego as well. In the 'weak' sector, however, not only will ego's contacts not be tied to one another, but they *will* be tied to individuals not tied to ego. Indirect contacts are thus typically reached through ties in this sector; such ties are then of importance not only in ego's manipulation of networks, but also in that they are the channels through which ideas, influences, or information socially distant from ego may reach him. The fewer indirect contacts one has the more encapsulated he will be in terms of knowledge of the world beyond his own friendship circle; thus, bridging weak ties (and the consequent indirect contacts) are important in both ways.

I will develop this point empirically by citing some results from a labor-market study I have recently completed Labor economists have long been aware that American blue-collar workers find out about new jobs more through personal contacts than by any other method. (Many studies are reviewed by Parnes, 1954, ch. 5.) Recent studies suggest that this is also true for those in professional, technical and managerial positions (Shapero, Howell and Tombaugh, 1965; Brown, 1967; Granovetter, 1970). My study of this question laid special emphasis on the nature of the *tie* between the job changer and the contact person who provided the necessary information.

In a random sample of recent professional, technical and managerial job changers living in a Boston suburb, I asked those who found a new job through contacts how often they *saw* the contact around the time that he passed on job information to them. I will use this as a measure of tie strength.[8] A natural *a priori* idea is that those with whom one has strong

8. Although this corresponds only to the first of the four dimensions in my definition, supplementary anecdotal evidence from interviews makes it likely that, in this case, the entire definition is satisfied by this measure. At the time of research, it had not occurred to me that tie strength would be a useful variable.

ties are more motivated to help with job information. Opposed to this greater motivation are the structural arguments I have been making: those to whom we are weakly tied are more likely to move in circles different from our own and will thus have access to information different from that which we receive.

I have used the following categories for frequency of contact: often = at least twice a week; occasionally = more than once a year but less than twice a week; rarely = once a year or less. Of those finding a job through contacts, 16·7 per cent reported that they saw their contact often at the time, 55·6 per cent said occasionally, and 27·8 per cent rarely ($N = 54$).[9] The skew is clearly to the weak end of the continuum, suggesting the primacy of structure over motivation.

In many cases, the contact was someone only marginally included in the current network of contacts, such as an old college friend or a former workmate or employer, with whom sporadic contact had been maintained (Granovetter, 1970, pp. 76–80). Usually such ties had not even been very strong when first forged. For work-related ties, respondents almost invariably said that they never saw the person in a nonwork context.[10] Chance meetings or mutual friends operated to reactivate such ties. It is remarkable that people receive crucial information from individuals whose very existence they have forgotten.[11]

I also asked respondents where their contacts *got* the information they transmitted. In most cases, I traced the information to its initial source. I had expected that, as in the diffusion of rumors or diseases, long paths

9. The numbers reported are small because they represent a random subsample of 100, who were interviewed personally, of the total sample of 282. The personal interview allowed more detailed questioning. Comparisons between the mail sample and the interview sample on the large number of items which were put to both show almost no significant differences; this suggests that results observed in the smaller sample on those items put to it alone would not be much different in the mail sample.
10. Often when I asked respondents whether a friend had told them about their current job, they said, 'Not a friend, an acquaintance.' It was the frequency of this comment which suggested this section of the paper to me.
11. Donald Light has suggested to me an alternative reason to expect predominance of weak ties in transfer of job information. He reasons that most of any given person's ties are weak, so that we should expect, on a 'random' model, that most ties through which job information flows should be weak. Since baseline data on acquaintance networks are lacking, this objection remains inconclusive. Even if the premise were correct, however, one might still expect that greater motivation of close friends would overcome their being outnumbered. Different assumptions yield different 'random' models; it is not clear which one should be accepted as a starting point. One plausible such model would expect information to flow through ties in proportion to the time expended in interaction; this model would predict much more information via strong ties than one which merely counted all ties equally.

would be involved. But in 39·1 per cent of the cases information came directly from the prospective employer, whom the respondent already knew; 45·3 per cent said that there was one intermediary between himself and the employer; 12·5 per cent reported two; and 3·1 per cent more than two ($N = 64$). This suggests that for some important purposes it may be sufficient to discuss, as I have, the egocentric network made up of ego, his contacts, and *their* contacts. Had long information paths been involved, large numbers might have found out about any given job, and no particular tie would have been crucial. Such a model of job-information flow actually does correspond to the economists' model of a 'perfect' labor market. But those few who did acquire information through paths with more than one intermediary tended to be young and under the threat of unemployment; influence was much less likely to have been exerted by their contact on their behalf. These respondents were, in fact, more similar to those using *formal* intermediaries (agencies, advertisements) than to those hearing through short paths: both of the former are badly placed and dissatisfied in the labor market, and both receive information without influence. Just as reading about a job in the newspaper affords one no recommendation in applying for it, neither does it to have heard about it fifth-hand.

The usual dichotomy between 'formal' or mass procedures and diffusion through personal contacts may thus be invalid in some cases where, instead, the former may be seen as a limiting case of long diffusion chains. This is especially likely where information of instrumental significance is involved. Such information is most valuable when earmarked for one person.

From the individual's point of view, then, weak ties are an important resource in making possible mobility opportunity. Seen from a more macroscopic vantage, weak ties play a role in effecting social cohesion. When a man changes jobs, he is not only moving from one network of ties to another, but also establishing a link between these. Such a link is often of the same kind which facilitated his own movement. Especially within professional and technical specialties which are well defined and limited in size, this mobility sets up elaborate structures of bridging weak ties between the more coherent clusters that constitute operative networks in particular locations. Information and ideas thus flow more easily through the specialty, giving it some 'sense of community', activated at meetings and conventions. Maintenance of weak ties may well be the most important consequence of such meetings. [. . .]

Conclusion

The major implication intended by this paper is that the personal experience of individuals is closely bound up with larger-scale aspects of social structure, well beyond the purview or control of particular individuals. Linkage of micro and macro levels is thus no luxury but of central importance to the development of sociological theory. Such linkage generates paradoxes: weak ties, often denounced as generative of alienation (Wirth, 1938) are here seen as indispensable to individuals' opportunities and to their integration into communities; strong ties, breeding local cohesion, lead to overall fragmentation. Paradoxes are a welcome antidote to theories which explain everything all too neatly.

The model offered here is a very limited step in the linking of levels; it is a fragment of a theory. Treating only the *strength* of ties ignores, for instance, all the important issues involving their content. What is the relation between strength and degree of specialization of ties, or between strength and hierarchical structure? How can 'negative' ties be handled? Should tie strength be developed as a continuous variable? What is the developmental sequence of network structure over time?

As such questions are resolved, others will arise. Demography, coalition structure, and mobility are just a few of the variables which would be of special importance in developing micro–macro linkage with the help of network analysis; how these are related to the present discussion needs specification. My contribution here is mainly, then, exploratory and programmatic, its primary purpose being to generate interest in the proposed program of theory and research.

References

BARNES, J. A. (1969), 'Networks and political process', in J. C. Mitchell (ed.), *Social Networks in Urban Situations*, Manchester University Press.

BERSCHEID, E., and WALSTER, E. (1969), *Interpersonal Attraction*, Addison-Wesley.

BOISSEVAIN, J. (1968), 'The place of non-groups in the social sciences', *Man*, vol. 3, pp. 542–56.

BOTT, E. (1957), *Family and Social Network*, Tavistock.

BRAMEL, D. (1969), 'Interpersonal attraction, hostility and perception', in J. Mills (ed.), *Experimental Social Psychology*, Macmillan.

BROWN, D. (1967), *The Mobile Professors*, American Council on Education, Washington.

BROWN, R. (1965), *Social Psychology*, Free Press.

DAVIS, J. A. (1963), 'Structural balance, mechanical solidarity and interpersonal relations', *Amer. J. Sociol.*, vol. 68, pp. 444–62.

DAVIS, J. A. (1970), 'Clustering and hierarchy in interpersonal relations', *Amer. Sociol. Rev.*, vol. 35, pp. 843–52.

EPSTEIN, A. (1969), 'The network and urban social organization', in J. C. Mitchell (ed.), *Social Networks in Urban Situations*, Manchester University Press.

FRANKENBERG, R. (1965), *Communities in Britain*, Penguin.

GRANOVETTER, M. S. (1970), 'Changing jobs: channels of mobility information in a suburban community', unpublished phD. thesis, Harvard University.

HARARY, F., NORMAN, R., and CARTWRIGHT, D. (1965), *Structural Models*, Wiley.

HEIDER, F. (1958), *The Psychology of Interpersonal Relations*, Wiley.

HOLLAND, P., and LEINHARDT, S. (1970), 'Detecting structure in sociometric data', *Amer. J. Sociol.*, vol. 76, pp. 492–513.

HOLLAND, P., and LEINHARDT, S. (1971), 'Masking: the structural implications of measurement error in sociometry', unpublished, Carnegie-Mellon University.

HOMANS, G. (1950), *The Human Group*, Harcourt Brace & World.

KAPFERER, B. (1969), 'Norms and the manipulation of relationships in a work context', in J. C. Mitchell (ed.), *Social Networks in Urban Situations*, Manchester University Press.

LAUMANN, E. (1968), 'Interlocking and radial friendship networks: a cross-sectional analysis', unpublished, University of Michigan.

LAUMANN, E., and SCHUMAN, H. (1967), 'Open and closed structures', Paper prepared for the 1967 ASA meeting, unpublished.

MAYER, A. (1966), 'The significance of quasi-groups in the study of complex societies', in M. Banton (ed.), *The Social Anthropology of Complex Societies*, Praeger.

MAYER, P. (1961), *Townsmen or Tribesmen?* Oxford University Press.

MAZUR, B. (1971), 'Comment', *Amer. Sociol. Rev.*, vol. 36, pp. 308–9.

NEWCOMB, T. M. (1961), *The Acquaintance Process*, Holt, Rinehart & Winston.

PARNES, H. (1954), *Research on Labor Mobility*, Social Science Research Council.

PRECKER, J. (1952), 'Similarity of valuings as a factor in selection of peers and near-authority figures', *J. abnorm. soc. Psychol.*, vol. 47, (supplement), pp. 406–14.

RAPOPORT, A. (1953a), 'Spread of information through a population with socio-structural bias. I. Assumption of transitivity', *Bull. math. Biophys.*, vol. 15, pp. 523–33.

RAPOPORT, A. (1953b), 'Spread of information through a population with socio-structural bias. II. Various models with partial transitivity', *Bull. math. Biophys.*, vol. 15, pp. 535–46.

RAPOPORT, A. (1954), 'Spread of information through a population with socio-structural bias. III. Suggested experimental procedures', *Bull. math. Biophys.*, vol. 16, pp. 75–81.

RAPOPORT, A. (1963), 'Mathematical models of social interaction', in R. Luce, R. Bush and E. Galanter (eds.), *Handbook of Mathematical Psychology*, vol. 2, Wiley.

RAPOPORT, A., and HORVATH, W. (1961), 'A study of a large sociogram', *Behav. Sci.*, vol. 6, pp. 279–91.

SHAPERO, A., HOWELL, R., and TOMBAUGH, J. (1965), *The Structure and Dynamics of the Defense R & D Industry*, J. Stanford Research Institute.

SIMMEL, G. (1950), *The Sociology of Georg Simmel*, Free Press.

TILLY, C. (1969), 'Community: city: urbanization', unpublished, University of Michigan.

WIRTH, L. (1938), 'Urbanism as a way of life', *Amer. J. Sociol.*, vol. 44, pp. 1–24.

Further Reading

An appreciable number of the Readings in this volume have been excerpted from books or from longer articles, and of course the serious student should follow up our selection by consulting the original sources. This applies especially to *Chains of Opportunity* by White, *The American Occupational Structure* by Blau and Duncan, *Social Mobility in Britain* by Glass, and *Theories of Poverty and Underemployment* by Gordon. In addition, we have provided a general guide to further reading. Those books and papers that we consider especially important are marked with an asterisk.

Part One Conceptual Organization

B. Barber, *Social Stratification: A Comparative Analysis of Structure and Process*, Harcourt, Brace & World, 1957.

*R. Boudon, *The Mathematical Structures of Social Mobility*, Elsevier, 1973.

G. Carlsson, *Social Mobility and Class Structure*, Gleerup, Lund, Sweden, 1958.

*O. D. Duncan, 'Social stratification and mobility: problems in the measurement of trend', in E. B. Sheldon and W. E. Moore (eds.), *Indicators of Social Change*, Russell Sage, 1968.

H. Goldhamer, 'Social mobility', in D. L. Sills (ed.), *The International Encyclopaedia of the Social Sciences*, Macmillan, 1968.

J. H. Goldthorpe, 'Social stratification in industrial society', in P. Halmos (ed.), *Sociological Review, Monograph no. 8*, 1964, pp. 97–112.

S. M. Lipset and R. Bendix, *Social Mobility in Industrial Society*, University of California Press, 1959.

S. M. Lipset and H. L. Zetterberg, 'A theory of social mobility', *Transactions of the Third World Congress of Sociology*, vol. 3, International Sociological Association, 1956, part 2, pp. 155–77; reprinted in R. Bendix and S. Lipset (1967), *Class, Status and Power* (2nd edn.) Free Press.

K. U. Mayer, 'Social mobility and the perception of social inequality', *Zeitschrift für Soziologie*, vol. 1, 1972, pp. 156–76.

A. J. Reiss *et al.*, *Occupations and Social Status*, Free Press, 1961.

*N. J. Smelser and S. M. Lipset (eds.), *Social Structure and Mobility in Economic Development*, Aldine Atherton; Routledge & Kegan Paul, 1966.

J. A. Smyth, 'Utility and the social order: the axiological problem in sociology', *British Journal of Sociology*, vol. 22, 1971, pp. 381–94.

P. A. Sorokin, *Social and Cultural Mobility*, Macmillan, 1959.

K. Svalastoga, *Social Differentiation*, McKay, 1965.

*S. Thernstrom, *Poverty and Progress: Social Mobility in a Nineteenth-Century City*, Harvard University Press, 1964.

*D. J. Treiman, 'Industrialization and social stratification', *Sociological Inquiry*, vol. 40, 19 , pp. 207–34.

J. Westergaard, 'The withering away of class: a contemporary myth', in P. Anderson and R. Blackburn (eds.), *Towards Socialism*, Fontana, 1965, pp. 77–113.

Part Two Analysing Intergenerational Occupational Mobility

The first two volumes contain a large number of theoretical and empirical studies of social stratification and social mobility.

Transactions of the Second World Congress of Sociology, vol. 2, International Sociological Association, 1954.

Transactions of the Third World Congress of Sociology, vol. 2, International Sociological Association, 1956.

Z. Bauman, 'Economic growth, social structure, elite formation', *International Social Science Journal*, vol. 5, 1964, pp. 203–16.

*B. Benjamin, 'Intergeneration differences in occupation', *Population Studies*, vol. 11, 1957, pp. 262–8.

D. Bertaux, 'Nouvelles perspectives sur la mobilité sociale en France', *Quality and Quantity*, vol. 5, 1971, pp. 87–130.

V. Capecchi, 'Problèmes méthodologiques dans la mesure de la mobilité sociale', *Archives Européennes de Sociologie*, vol. 8, 1967, pp. 285–318.

P. Cutright, 'Studying cross-national mobility rates', *Acta Sociologica*, vol. 11, 1968, pp. 170–76.

T. G. Fox and S. M. Miller, 'Economic, political and social determinants of mobility: an international cross-sectional analysis', *Acta Sociologica*, vol. 9, 1966, pp. 76–93.

*J. Lopreato and L. E. Hazelrigg, *Class, Conflict and Mobility: Theories and Studies of Class Structure*, Chandler, 1973.

K. U. Mayer and W. Müller, 'Trendanalyse in der Mobilitätsforschung', *Kölner Zeitschrift für Soziologie und Sozial-Psychologie*, vol. 23, 1971, pp. 761–88.

*N. Rogoff, *Recent Trends in Occupational Mobility*, Free Press, 1953.

Part Three Conditions and Mechanisms of Mobility

P. R. Abramson, 'Educational certification and life chances among British schoolboys', *Research in Education*, vol. 5, 1971, pp. 52–9.

*C. A. Anderson, 'A sceptical note on the relation of vertical mobility to education', *American Journal of Sociology*, vol. 66, 1961, pp. 560–70.

H. S. Becker and A. L. Strauss, 'Careers, personality and adult socialization', *American Journal of Sociology*, vol. 62, 1956, pp. 253–63.

R. Boudon, *Education, Opportunity and Social Inequality: Changing Prospects in Western Society*, Wiley, 1974.

*B. Bluestone, 'The tripartite economy: labor markets and the working poor', *Poverty and Human Resources*, vol. 5, 1970, pp. 15–35.

L. Broom and F. L. Jones, 'Career mobility in three societies: Australia, Italy and the United States', *American Sociological Review*, vol. 34, 1969, pp. 650–58.

J. S. Coleman, 'The concept of equality of educational opportunity', *Harvard Educational Review*, vol. 38, 1968, pp. 7–22.

*P. B. Doeringer and M. J. Piore, *Internal Labour Markets and Manpower Analysis*, Lexington, 1971.

B. G. Glaser (ed.), *Organizational Careers*, Aldine Atherton, 1968.

D. M. Gordon (ed.), *Problems in Political Economy*, Lexington, 1971.

A. I. Harris and R. Clausen, *Labour Mobility in Great Britain 1953–63*, HMSO Government Social Survey Report S333, 1966.

E. Hopper (ed.), *Readings in the Theory of Educational Systems*, Hutchinson, 1971.

*C. Jencks, *Inequality: A Reassessment of the Effect of Family and Schooling in America*, Basic Books, 1972.

R. K. Kelsall, *Higher Civil Servants in Britain from 1870 to the Present Day*, Routledge & Kegan Paul, 1955.

D. I. MacKay, *Geographical Mobility and the Brain Drain*, Allen & Unwin, 1969.

D. C. Miller and W. H. Form, *Industrial Sociology*, 2nd edn, Harper & Row, 1964.

N. Rogoff Ramsy, 'On the flow of talent in society', *Acta Sociologica*, vol. 9, 1966, pp. 152–74.

H. A. Sheppard and A. H. Belitsky, *The Job Hunt: Job Seeking Behavior of Unemployed Workers in a Local Economy*, Johns Hopkins University Press, 1966.

A. L. Strauss, *The Contexts of Social Mobility: Ideology and Theory*, Aldine Atherton, 1971.

*W. G. Spady, 'Educational mobility and access: growth and paradoxes', *American Journal of Sociology*, vol. 73, 1967, pp. 273–87.

S. Thernstrom, 'Urbanization, migration and social mobility in the late nineteenth-century America', in B. J. Bernstein (ed.), *Towards a New Past*, Random House, 1970, pp. 61–81.

C. Tilly, *The Vendee*, Edward Arnold, 1964.

*R. H. Turner, 'Sponsored and contest mobility and the school system', *American Sociological Review*, vol. 25, 1960, pp. 855–67.

W. Watson, 'Social mobility and social class in industrial communities', in M. Gluckman (ed.), *Closed Systems and Open Minds*, Oliver & Boyd, 1964, pp. 129–57.

*J. Westergaard and A. Little, 'Educational policy and social selection in England and Wales: trends and policy implications', in *Social Objectives in Educational Planning*, OECD, 1967, pp. 215–32.

*H. L. Wilensky, 'Measures and effect of social mobility', in N. J. Smelser and S. M. Lipset (eds.) (1966), *Social Structure and Mobility in Economic Development*, Routledge & Kegan Paul, pp. 94–140.

*M. Young, *The Rise of the Meritocracy*, Penguin, 1961.

Part Four **Recent Developments in Analysing Social Mobility**

J. Balan, H. L. Browning, E. Jalin and L. Litzler, 'A computerized approach to the processing and analysis of life histories', *Behavioral Science*, vol. 14, 1969, pp. 105–20.

D. J. Bartholomew, *Stochastic Models for Social Processes*, 2nd edn, Wiley, 1973.

I. Blumen, M. Kogan and P. J. McCarthy, *The Industrial Mobility of Labour as a Probability Process*, Cornell University Press, 1955.

R. Boudon, 'Eléments pour une théorie formelle de la mobilité sociale', *Quality and Quantity*, vol. 5, 1971, pp. 39–86.

*O. D. Duncan, 'Inheritance of poverty or inheritance of race?', in D. P. Moynihan (ed.), *On Understanding Poverty: Perspectives from the Social Sciences*, Basic Books, 1969.

O. D. Duncan, A. O. Halles and A. Porter, 'Peer influence on aspirations: a reinterpretation', *American Journal of Sociology*, vol. 74, 1968, pp. 119–37.

O. D. Duncan, D. L. Featherman and B. Duncan, *Socioeconomic Background and Achievement*, Seminar Press, 1972.

*M. S. Granovetter, *Getting a Job: a Study of Contacts and Careers*, Harvard University Press, 1974.

*R. M. Hauser, 'Disaggregating a social-psychological model of educational attainment', *Social Science Research*, vol. 1, 1972, pp. 159–88.

N. W. Henry, R. McGinnis and H. W. Tegtmeyer, 'A finite model of mobility', *Journal of Mathematical Sociology*, vol. 1, 1971, pp. 107–18.

K. Hope (ed.), *The Analysis of Social Mobility: Methods and Approaches*, Clarendon Press, 1972.

S. Levitan, G. L. Mangum and R. Marshall, *Human Resources and Labor Markets*, Harper & Row, 1972.

T. McGinnis, 'A stochastic model of social mobility', *American Sociological Review*, vol. 33, 1968, pp. 712–22.

*S. M. Miller, 'The future of social mobility studies', *American Journal of Sociology*, vol. 77, 1971, pp. 62–65.

*W. Müller and K. U. Mayer (eds.), 'Papers and discussion from the Konstanz workshop on social mobility', *Social Science Information*, vol. 11, 1972, pp. 7–390.

J. Ridge (ed.), *Social Mobility Reconsidered*, Clarendon Press, 1974.

*P. H. Rossi and M. D. Ornstein, 'The impact of labor market entry factors: illustrations from the Hopkins Social Accounts Project', *Social Science Information*, part 5, 1972, pp. 269–311.

*A. B. Sørensen, *The Occupational Mobility Process: An Analysis of Occupational Careers*, Report 125, Centre for Social Organization of Schools, Johns Hopkins University Press, 1972.

H. Theil, 'Social mobility and social distance: a Markov chain approach', in *Statistical Decomposition Analysis*, North-Holland Press, 1972.

Acknowledgements

For Readings reproduced in this volume Acknowledgement is made to the following sources:

Reading 1   International Sociological Association
Reading 2   John Wiley & Sons, Inc.
Reading 3   Holt, Rinehart & Winston, Inc.
Reading 4   Routledge & Kegan Paul Ltd.
Reading 5   Basil Blackwell Ltd.
Reading 6   University of North Carolina Press
Reading 7   American Sociological Association
Reading 8   Routledge & Kegan Paul Ltd.
Reading 9   *Societa editrice il Mulino*, Bologna
Reading 10   John Wiley & Sons, Inc.
Reading 11   *Societa editrice il Mulino*, Bologna
Reading 12   Lexington Books, D.C. Heath & Company
Reading 13   University of North Carolina Press
Reading 14   University of Michigan Press
Reading 15   David McKay Company Inc.
Reading 16   *Societa editrice il Mulino*, Bologna
Reading 17   American Sociological Association
Reading 18   Bobbs-Merrill Co. Inc.
Reading 19   Harvard University Press
Reading 20   University of Chicago Press

Author Index

Centers, R., 50n., 103n., 284, 294, 295, 296
Charles, E., 33
Chavetz, J. S., 173n.
Chessa, F., 73, 104n.
Chinoy, E., 21, 24, 25, 104n., 132n.
Chrimes, S. B., 338n.
Chow, Y-T, 242n.
Cipolla, C., 259n.
Clark, C., 24
Clark, K., 225n.
Clausen, R., 367n.
Clements, R. V., 337
Cohen, D., 263n., 268n.
Coleman, J. S., 242n., 269n., 304, 367n.
Conner, T. L., 330
Constas, H., 104n.
Conti, G., 104n.
Coombs, C. H., 338n.
Cooper, T., 261n.
Cooley, W. W., 270
Coser, L. A., 104n.
Costa Pinto, L. A., 104n.
Cremin, L., 263n.
Crockett, H. J., 115, 123n.
Crozier, M., 229
Curtis, R. E., 115, 116, 170n., 241
Cutright, P., 172n., 366n.

Dahrendorf, R., 170n., 172, 173n., 174n., 241, 242, 244, 245, 246
Davidson, P. E., 50n., 102n.
Davis, K., 23n., 104n., 283, 337
Davis, J. A., 338, 356, 357
DeJocas, Y., 104n.
Deming, W. E., 126n., 323
Desabie, J., 104n.
Desannois, M., 104n.
Deutsch, K. W., 175
Dobb, M., 218, 221, 229
Doeringer, P. B., 183, 208n., 209n., 210, 211, 212, 213n., 228n., 229n., 230n., 367n.
Dolger, L., 274n.
Dreeben, R., 275n.
Dumenil, M., 104n.
Duncan, B., 368n.
Duncan, O. D., 9, 18, 19, 32n., 34, 35, 39, 40, 41, 61, 114, 115, 116, 117, 119, 121, 123n., 124, 126n., 129, 134n., 152, 169, 171, 173n., 175, 183, 184,

189n., 193, 204, 206, 232n., 242n., 243, 270n., 302, 313. 314, 317, 324, 328, 332, 336, 339, 365, 365n., 368n
Duncan-Jones, P., 171
Durbin, E., 307
Durbin J., 28n.
Durkheim, E., 184, 241, 252, 253, 254

Eckland, B. K., 190
Edwards, A. M., 33, 46, 217n., 221, 222, 223, 241, 244, 245, 246
Eggar, F., 105n.
Eisenstadt, S. N., 105n.
Engleborghs-Bertels, M., 105n.
Epstein, A., 358
Ellis, R. A., 241
Elson, W. H., 263n.
Engels, F., 218, 260, 261n.
Erickson, C., 105n.
Etzioni, A., 175

Featherman, D. L., 368n.
Feldman, P., 208n.
Feldmann, A. S., 91, 105n., 111n., 142
Feldmesser, R. A., 105n.
Ferman, L., 184
Fisher, S. N., 105n.
Florquin, M., 104n.
Field, A., 262n.
Flannagan, J. C., 270
Floud, J. E., 242n., 283
Foote, N. N., 105n.
Form, N. H., 367n.
Form, W. H., 50n.
Foster, P., 242n.
Fox, T., 172n., 303n., 366n.
Frankenberg, R., 358
Freeman, L., 101, 108n., 132n.
Friedenberg, E. Z., 268
Friedmann, G., 236n.
Friedrich, C. L., 105n.
Froomkin, J., 106n.

Gabor, A., 28n.
Galtung, J., 174n., 179n.
Geiger, T., 176n., 178n.
Germani, G., 102n.
Gibbs, M., 243, 274n.
Ginandes, J., 274n.
Ginger, R., 106n.
Gini, G., 173

Lane, W. C., 241
Lang, O., 108n.
Lasswell, H. D., 108n.
Laumann, C. O., 320, 356
Lazarsfeld, P. F., 108n., 328, 338n.
Lazerson, M., 263n., 268n.
Leggett, J., 232n., 233
Lehner, A., 108n.
Leinhardt, S., 357
Lenski, G. E., 132, 138, 139, 140n.,
    179
Levine, J. H., 323, 331
Levitan, S., 368n.
Levy, M. J., 108n.
Lewis, H., 274n.
Lieberson, S., 134n.
Linz, J., 108n.
Lipset, S. M., 21n., 25n., 26, 27, 29,
    50n., 55, 79, 85, 101, 104n., 105n.,
    108n., 139, 140, 146, 160, 161, 170n.,
    172n., 174, 175, 220, 242n., 252, 254,
    274, 290n., 303, 365n.
Little, A., 301, 368n.
Livi, L., 73, 78, 108n.
Lockwood, D., 229n., 230n., 234n.,
    236n.
Lopreato, J., 173n., 184, 366n.
Lorimer, F., 48n.
Luce, R. D., 346n.
Lunt, P. S., 269

McCarthy, K. M., 317, 328, 329, 330,
    331, 368n.
Maccoby, E. E., 274n.
MacDonald, K. I., 14
MacEwan, A., 217n., 221, 222, 223
MacFarland, D. D., 318, 320, 326, 328,
    329
McGinnis, R., 331, 368n., 369n.
McGuire, C., 48n.
MacIver, R. M., 350
Mack, R. W., 101, 108n., 132n.
MacKay, D. I., 367n.
McRae, D. G., 109, 283
McTavish, D. G., 119n.
Malm, T., 50n., 60
Mandel, E., 219, 221, 224, 225,
    227
Mangum, G. L., 368n.
Marcovitch, J., 308
Marris, P., 308

Marshall, R., 368n.
Martin, F. M., 242n.
Marx, K., 218, 219, 220, 221, 222, 223,
    224, 225, 231, 236n., 260, 261n.
Matras, J., 115n., 123n., 156, 324, 325,
    328, 329
Mayer, A., 358
Mayer, K. M., 26n., 109n.
Mayer, K. U., 18, 62, 169n., 365n.,
    366n., 369n.
Mayer, T. F., 330, 331
Mazur, B., 357
Miller, H. P., 50n.
Milliband, R., 222n.
Miller, S. M., 17, 18, 23, 61, 62, 91,
    109n., 119n., 115, 171, 172n., 173n.,
    174n., 176n., 183, 274n., 301, 303n.,
    305, 306, 310, 366n., 367n., 369n.
Minkes, A. L., 24n.
Mishler, E. G., 109n.
Mitras, J., 109n.
Moore, W. E., 109n., 283
Morgan, E. S., 258n., 259n.
Morgenstern, O., 109n.
Morrison, P. A., 331
Mosteller, F. W., 323
Mukherjee, R., 139
Müller, W., 62, 366n., 369n.
Myers, P. F., 109n.

Nadel, S. F., 339
Namenwirth, J. Z., 129
Neugarten, N., 107n.
Newcomb, T. M., 356, 357
Nishira, S., 109n.
Norman, R., 357
North, C. C., 26, 27, 109n.

Odaka, K., 109n.
Oeser, O. A., 109n.
Olexa, C., 269
Olsen, M. E., 116n.
Ore, O., 345n.
Ornstein, M. D., 369n.
Orshansky, M., 188, 195
Osborn, F., 48n.
Ossowski, S., 218, 219, 220
Owen, J. D., 267, 277

Pagani, A., 110n.
Palmer, G. L., 336

National Reference Index

Because so much attention has been focused upon the nation-state as the system within which social mobility is studied, we provide a brief index to the main national references.

(See also entries under the heading of National Comparisons in the Subject Index) (*Eds.*)

Subject Index

hierarchy fetishism, 236
status distinctions, 179, 238
wage differentials, 308
Discipline, 211, 275
Discrimination, 210, 251
positive, 184
by race, sex and age, 58, 237, 256
Displacement from jobs, 248, 251
Dissociation, index of (Glass), 73, 76
see also Association
Distance, social, 32, 86, 101, 170, 172, 320, 338
distance traversed, 68
Distribution, age, 118
age-occupational, 329
Distributions, occupational, 147–8, 324–5
index of dissimilarity, 156–8
Distribution, origin, 158
stable, 328
Division of labour, 218, 223, 259, 261, 264, 269, 273
Dropout, as officially sanctioned concept, 188
Dual labour market
see Labour market, dual
Duality, between men and jobs, 340

Economic development, 110, 175
Economic theory
radical, 217
see also Labour market, dual
Economy, 10, 17, 25, 95, 101, 359
Education, 64, 126, 129, 184, 191, 200, 205, 242, 261–2, 332
and ability, 275, 340
access to, 10, 286
academic curriculum, 263
and constraints on mobility, 243
effects of, 130
enrichment, 11
equality of opportunity, 279
see also Opportunity
and income, 304, 306
mass, 260
mobility through, 279
principle of maximum efficacy of (Boudon), 289
public expenditure on, 266
recurrent, 305
as a screening device, 214

secondary and high school, 43, 263
Educational
provision, 301
reform, 304
resources, 304
systems, 88, 129, 171, 207, 269
see also Schools
Elites, 80–81
circulation, 94–5, 340
downward mobility, 92–3, 291
fluctuation, 172
Miller's elite I and elite II, 81
mobility, into, 21–2, 95, 340
recruitment, 70, 93
Embourgeoisement, 18
Equality, 101
and equity, 308
and social mobility, 310
and rewarding excellence, 277
Exploitation rate, 227

Family, 111, 142
family size, 150
self-employed families, 142
Farmers, 46–7, 56, 115–19, 134, 142, 152, 172
Fertility, 19, 28, 57, 64–5, 72, 116, 184, 286
differential, 58, 74, 114, 123, 161, 288, 297, 324–5, 329
Flows of job information, 361
Friendship networks, 355, 360
see also Networks
Fringe benefits, perks, 307
'Frontier', farm and technological, 45

Generation, 288, 326, 336
procession of generations, 151
Grandfathers, 64
Groups,
minority, 232
occupational, 35
primary and secondary, 253–4
professional, 56

Hawthorne experiment, 236
Head start, 304
Hierarchies,
occupational, 275
prestige, 68
status, 78, 179